# EDMUND BLUNDEN

## A Biography

Barry Webb

---

*To have known Blunden is to have known a divine poet. Whether he is a great and sublime poet, or whether he is of secondary importance as a writer, he is indeed a living emblem of all that is finest in this hazardous world of dust and dreams.*
Siegfried Sassoon, Diary, 2 June 1922

---

Yale University Press
New Haven and London
1990

Designed by Tim Higgins

Set in 11/12 ½ pt Bembo by Pure Tech Corporation, India, and printed and bound in Great Britain at The Bath Press, Avon.

**Library of Congress Cataloging-in-Publication Data**

Webb, Barry.
    Edmund Blunden: a biography / Barry Webb.
       p.      cm.
    Includes bibliographical references (p.    ) and index.
    ISBN 0-300-04634-0
    1. Blunden, Edmund, 1896-1974—Biography.  2. Poets, English—20th century—Biography.  3. Critics—Great Britain—Biography.
    4. Scholars—Great Britain—Biography.  I. Title.
    PR6003.L8Z98  1990
    821'.912—DC20                          90-12501
    [B]                                                 CIP

In Memoriam

E. B.

---

*The book represents the warm affection which I feel to this day for one of the kindest and brightest of men, one who received the youngest of us without the faintest shade of distance or inequality, and whose memory, even from days all too few of walks and talks, shines steadily through all decline and change.*
E. B.'s Preface to *Thomas Hardy*, 1942

*Forgive what I, adventuring highest themes,*
*Have spoiled and darkened.*
'The Author's Last Words to his Students', 1927

*What a clumsy affair any biography truly must be, even the best — how all the fine clues and unique experiences dodge one!*
Letter from E. B. to Philip Tomlinson, 22 May 1940

---

# Contents

# List of Illustrations

# Acknowledgements

One morning in early 1966, as an Oxford undergraduate, I presented myself for my weekly tutorial and discovered a visitor in the room. He sat in the arm-chair next to mine and I was instantly aware of his penetrating eyes, sensitive fingers and an aura of dreamy perceptiveness which enveloped him. It transpired that my tutor was double-booked for lunch and he asked me if I could entertain Professor Edmund Blunden – for such the visitor turned out to be. Rather nervously I agreed, relieved at the suggestion of beer and sandwiches at the local pub. I was nineteen; he was sixty-nine. The lunch lasted three hours – three hours which changed my life. This book springs from the desire to record the life of the shy and modest personality who yet changed many lives, and my first thanks must be to the man who instigated that original lunchtime meeting and thus unwittingly inspired what follows: Francis Warner. His many acts of kindness to ensure completion of this book are most gratefully acknowledged.

Ten years later I spent a weekend in Marske-in-Swaledale as the guest of Sir Rupert Hart-Davis. I left with his approval to write this biography. Since then I have been privileged to benefit from Sir Rupert's constant encouragement, endless generosity and unparalleled knowledge of the subject. He painstakingly read the whole book in two drafts, offering numerous suggestions and pointing out several errors and infelicities. For the rare occasions where I have stubbornly stuck to my original text I take full responsibility. Visits to Yorkshire have provided a literary education far beyond the confines of this work, for which I can not adequately express my gratitude.

For information about Edmund's schooldays I was fortunate to have access to the incomparable memory of his friend of sixty years, Hector Buck. All who knew 'Buckie' will know that a few minutes spent in his company was a memorable experience; I was privileged to spend many hours. His powers of concentration, his eye for detail and his insistence on accuracy, made him the perfect proof-reader – and the early chapters were subject to his scrutiny. I discussed them with him on the last afternoon of his life; on the following morning the text was found fully corrected on his table, his pencil lying across the final page of the chapter on Christ's Hospital. He had spent his last

# Acknowledgements

hours thinking of the school to which he had given a lifetime's dedication. Nobody was more devoted to Edmund.

To Charles Mussett I owe a special debt. His generous provision of accommodation – and many other kindnesses – while the book was in its last stages enabled the work to be completed within thirteen years rather than thirty. He also provided two sketch maps for Part Two. I owe nobody more.

Edmund's literary archive is considerable: in addition to his extensive published material (for which Brownlee Kirkpatrick's superb bibliography has been my daily reference), more than ten thousand letters exist, together with several diaries and many personal notes and memoranda. Visits to America, Japan and Hong Kong – for which I acknowledge the generous travel award of the Goldsmiths' Company – enabled me to work through this material and meet many of Edmund's friends and contacts. The biggest single collection (nearly a hundred box files) is in the Humanities Research Center at Texas. The courtesy and efficiency of the staff there – particularly Ellen Dunlap and her successor Cathy Henderson – are faultless and no visitor can leave without a feeling of envy and gratitude. In Japan I was most generously supported by the Blunden Society of Japan and the Japan Literary Society, and was privileged to enjoy the hospitality and conversation of Edmund's lifelong friend, the late Professor Takeshi Saito. I am also grateful for the interpreting skills and travelling companionship of Professor Yuichi Midzunoe.

I owe thanks to many institutions, but in particular to the Master and Fellows of Sidney Sussex College, Cambridge, for a term as a Fellow-Commoner in 1983, to Cranleigh School for two terms as Visiting Fellow, and to Radley College for many years of support. The Warden of Radley, Dennis Silk, first encouraged the idea of my attempting this work and came to the rescue when I had to provide accommodation for Edmund's library of ten thousand volumes. I also record my gratitude to Donald Paine for many hours of help in the formidable task of sorting the books into catalogue order.

In a later list I include the names of those who gave me typing and secretarial assistance but I must make separate mention of the help given by Deborah and Michael Spens. They worked uncomplainingly far beyond the call of duty and at many unsociable hours, and saved me from having to cope with the mysteries of word-processing and computing.

My grateful thanks go also to my expert editors at Yale University Press, Robert Baldock and Peter James. I am indebted too to Simon Beaufoy who compiled the index.

I am aware of many debts to many people, all of whom can not be mentioned here, but for assistance in a variety of ways I thank the following:

# Acknowledgements

Hamish Aird; Major J. F. Ainsworth (Royal Sussex Regimental Association);
The Ashmolean Museum, Oxford; The late Adrian Bell; The late Sir John
Betjeman; Lance Blunden; Margi Blunden; The Bodleian Library, Oxford;
Caroline Brown; The late Dr John Buxton; The late Phoebe Carter; The
late Chau Wah Ching; Christ's Hospital; Arthur Crook; Professor Thomas
Dilworth; Lucy Edgeley; Professor Paul Engle; Catherine Ferron; Joy Finzi;
The late Sir Hugh Greene; Harnam Grewal; The late Keiko Hani; Alec
Hardie; Edward Herrmann; Dr Roger Highfield; Professor Masao Hirai;
Professor Mikio Hiramatsu; The University of Hong Kong; Derek Hudson;
The Imperial War Museum; The University of Iowa; The late Sir Geoffrey
Keynes; Daphne Levens; David Machin; Professor Michio Masue; Dr Ber-
nard Mellor; Merton College, Oxford; Michael Meyer; Father Peter Mil-
ward S.J.; Professor Jack Morpurgo; Francis Marquand; St Peter's College,
Oxford; The New York Public Library (Berg Collection); Phyllis Pritchard;
The Queen's College, Oxford; Gunnel Rosengard; Clare Ross; Sheila
Rowley; The late Professor Yoshitaka Sakai; Richard Smail; The late Dr
John Treherne; Guy and Hilary Waller; Peter Way; Sir Edgar Williams;
Winchester College; Laurence Whistler; Jim White; Robert Wyke; Yeung
Nghai Hin; Yung Kai Kin.

My final record of gratitude is to Edmund's widow, Claire Blunden. She
has patiently watched the progress of the book, given me complete co-
operation, read the manuscript with great sensitivity, and – even at moments
which can not have been easy – never asked me to change a word. The task
would have been immeasurably more difficult without this, and her confidence and friendship have been most valued supports throughout the years
of preparation and writing. I can only ask, in Edmund's words, that she will
'forgive that eyeless lethargy' which has 'I fear dimmed much fine gold'.

St Peter's College                                                  March
Oxford                                                               1990

# Copyright Acknowledgements

Acknowledgement is made to the following - and apologies offered for any oversights.

To Mrs Claire Blunden and A.D. Peters Ltd. for all published Blunden material; to Mrs Claire Blunden for all unpublished Blunden material; to Sir Rupert Hart-Davis and Faber and Faber Ltd. for all published Sassoon material; to Sir Rupert Hart-Davis for unpublished Sassoon material; to Sir Rupert Hart-Davis and John Murray Ltd. for quotation from *The Lyttelton Hart-Davis Letters*; to A.P. Watt Ltd. on behalf of the Trustees of the Robert Graves Copyright Trust and Paul O'Prey for quotations from the letters of Robert Graves; to the Bodleian Library and the estate of A.H. Buck for quotations from the letters of Blunden to Hector Buck; to the Royal Literary Fund, and to the Society of Authors as the literary representatives of the Estate of A.E. Housman for quotations from a letter of A.E. Housman; to the Society of Authors as the literary representative of the Estate of John Middleton Murry for quotation of letters from John Middleton Murry to Katherine Mansfield; to Robson Books and Vernon Scannell for quotations from *A Proper Gentleman* and to Vernon Scannell for reproducing his poem 'Meeting in Manchester'; to Professor Quentin Bell and The Hogarth Press for quotation from the *Diaries of Virginia Woolf*; to Merton College, Oxford, for quotations from the diary of Sylva Norman; to A.D. Peters Ltd. and Mrs Jill Day-Lewis for quotation from a poem of Cecil Day-Lewis; to the Humanities Research Center, University of Texas at Austin, for quotations from their Blunden archive and for quotations from letters of H.W. Garrod, Sir Edmund Gosse and Robert Lowell; to the estate of Takeshi Saito for quotations from letters of Blunden to Takeshi Saito; to Kenkyusha Ltd. for quotations from *Edmund Blunden: A Tribute from Japan*.

# PART ONE
## 1896 – 1915

# 1

# Ancestors

*Perhaps one's ancestors are much the same whether they have biographies or not, they are gone and it's unnecessary to argue with their funeral certificates. However, I am always meddling with some small detail or other about the dear departed.*
Letter to Rupert Hart-Davis, 1941[1]

'He's a very remarkable child,' declared the midwife who had been summoned to the home of Charles Edmund and Georgina Margaret Blunden at 54a Tottenham Court Road to deliver their first child, Edmund. 'He has a particularly deep forehead.'[2] It was All Saints' Day, 1 November, 1896, and the Blundens had now started the family which they had hoped for since their marriage in the previous year. A busy London thoroughfare was thus the unlikely cradle for the man who was to become one of the century's foremost pastoral poets. It was to be the first of many unexpected homes and many surprising contrasts between his private life and public image; for Edmund, contradictions started early.

He was soon to develop the rather aquiline physical appearance of the Blunden family, which was to be accentuated by his thin, short body, quick eyes, darting movements and prominent nose. Bird comparisons were to stay with him for life. Sometimes referred to at school as 'the beaky bard', he was described by Robert Graves as 'a cross between Julius Caesar and a bird.'[3] Virginia Woolf remembered him both as 'a London house sparrow, that pecks and cheeps' and as 'crow-like',[4] while Siegfried Sassoon referred to him as 'perching' or 'hopping about the house'.[5] These avian physical characteristics

3

mirrored a private inner restlessness, though to the world at large he was to become the embodiment of quiet, gentle calm. Henry Williamson saw these contrasts as further facets of Edmund's bird-like qualities, extending the image to describe Edmund's handwriting and literary style: 'I didn't realise before what you are: a night-jar! Your writing has exactly the flight and appearance of that gentle bird, soft-plumaged – the curves and strokes of a twilight flyer, his wing-clapping; sudden, queer, tilted glidings and almost perchings; his serenity.'[6]

This quickness of movement was also responsible for the nickname 'Rabbit', given to him in France and Flanders. Asthma, inherited from his father, racked his frail body for most of his life – not assisted by the effects of poison-gas in the war and years of cigarette-smoking. Yet even in later years, when steroids had swollen his features, the darting Blunden eyes and prominent nose were unmistakable.

Even as a child, he was to show a marked pleasure in biographical detail and genealogical research. As each new literary hero emerged (and from the age of ten he was rarely without one) he set to work to explore his history – and that of anyone connected with him. His greatest pleasure was finding ancestral associations within his own family, though he could never prove descent from Humphrey Blunden, the seventeenth-century publisher of Donne, Herbert and Vaughan, or from Alice Blunden, the rather indifferent illustrator of Thomas Hood. He was delighted to find charges for drink against a Blunden – who had left Oxford without a degree – in a Merton College account-book of Queen Anne's time, but any evidence of a family association proved elusive. More certain (much to Edmund's delight) was a connection with Mrs Blunden of Basingstoke, who was mistakenly buried alive at the end of the seventeenth century, was disinterred when noises were heard from within the coffin, but was reburied when judged to be beyond hope of revival.[7] In Ireland there was a definite relationship with the Blundens who had lived for three centuries at Castle Blunden: indeed, Sir William Blunden was to visit Edmund in Hong Kong in the early 1950s, and the facial resemblances (not least the tell-tale nose) were strikingly clear.

Whatever the significance of the distant past may have been, the immediate background of Edmund's parents, Charles and Georgina, certainly represented a marriage of traditional rural simplicity and literary and social sophistication which were to be interwoven throughout his life.

The Blundens had been a country family for several generations and Edmund was proud of the tradition of rural craft in his ancestry. He often felt that he had a writer's vocation to preserve the best elements of a fast-fading pastoral tradition and he explored all possible family ties with such a past. His great-grandfather, Charles, had been a market-gardener and his grandfather, Edmund, had been apprenticed in 1864 as a harness-maker in Brighton. After marrying Charlotte Trapnell, the daughter of a Taunton cattle-dealer, in 1870, grandfather Edmund became the out-of-door bailiff at the Kent County Asylum at Barming, Maidstone. It was from here that he wrote to his son at the time of Charles's and Georgina's marriage in December 1895 – a letter which Edmund always treasured for its rural references, good humour, unsophisticated spelling and punctuation, and simple evocation of country life:

Dear Charles,

Rec'd yours this afternoon glad to hear your Mother arrived safely you had better give her plenty of room. . . .

Mr John Brown brought a pair of Salts made of polished wood with metal hoops, resembles a beer barrel cut in halves, with the usual wishes, shall not send them up you can take them with you when you go up after the holidays.

Mr Duncan Smith is going to give you a Coal (something). I quite forget what he called it but in Plain English it would be called a scuttle.

I think that is all I have got to write about at present except to be kindly remembered to all concerned.

I remain with best wishes for your welfare,

    E. Blunden.

P.S. Don't forget to get two Bears to keep in your house, *Bear and Forbear*, (advice for both).[8]

Country sport was also a prominent factor in Blunden life and a love of cricket and angling were two strong influences which Edmund felt he inherited from his paternal grandfather, although he was never to meet him. A characteristic combination of Edmund's pleasure in tracking down family history and his pleasure in exploring churchyards is evident in a description in 1933 of a visit he made with his brother Gilbert to look for their grandfather's grave at Allington:

I expect it has not been moved far since he occupied it. It is very difficult to get him to give us a practical opinion about it. I am told he could not, himself, get any expressions in favour or otherwise from those who had some experience of the neighbouring vaults. It was not like him to make moves of this magnitude without proper advice, and indeed as Gilbert and I called lately at the Barming Bull we wondered how the old boy had consented to leave the public bar for the very private bar. His liking for social manifestations was considerable, and maybe he misunderstood the term 'the spiritual life'. He was a great reader of [William] Paley, Adam Smith, and Lillywhite (*Cricketer's Annual*). He kept wicket, and I fancy he will have turned out for St Peter's Wanderers versus Lucifer's All Saints.[9]

Edmund's father, Charles Edmund, an only child, was born on 5 May 1871. He decided to take up teaching as a profession and became a pupil teacher in Maidstone in 1886 before moving to St Mark's College, Chelsea, where Coleridge's son Derwent had been principal. In 1891 he was appointed headmaster of the Church of England primary school of St John's, Fitzroy Square, London.

Edmund's mother, Georgina Margaret Tyler, was born on 5 July 1868, the daughter of Henry Tyler and Georgina Margaret Rogers. The Tyler family liked to claim descent from Wat Tyler, though Edmund was more anxious to find a connection with the Tyler brothers who kept a shop at Marlow and befriended Shelley,[10] and he also tried to find a family link, on his mother's side, with the early-nineteenth-century poet Samuel Rogers. Henry Tyler spent most of his early life at sea, and in 1866 was aboard HMS *Oberon* off the west coast of Africa. His commander was Sir Edmund Verney. A rapport appears to have been established between the two men which was to prove most significant, for on their return to England Tyler became valet and personal secretary to Sir Edmund at the Verneys' family home, Claydon House, Buckinghamshire. Claydon had been the seat of the Verneys since 1620, though the family had been in Buckinghamshire since the thirteenth century. One of the most distinguished Verney ancestors had been Sir Edmund, Knight-Marshal and Standard Bearer to Charles I, and the history of the Verney family is recorded in *The Memoirs, Letters and Papers* of the Verneys, the first two volumes of which were edited by Frances Parthenope, wife of Sir Harry Verney and sister of Florence Nightingale. A further three volumes of *Verney Papers*[11] were to be edited by Sir Edmund's wife, Margaret Maria Williams, whom he married in 1868 and who was to play an important part in Blunden history. Henry Tyler quickly gained the confidence of the Verneys and Margaret was delighted to accept an invitation to become godmother to the Tylers' daughter, Georgina Margaret. In 1869 Sir Edmund had a serious gun accident in which he lost a foot, and Lady Verney recalled in a letter to her god-daughter in 1919:

How kindly Mr Tyler shared the anxious nursing with me. We were not fortunate in the professional nurse, who was rather rough and ready. Your father often spent part of the night in the outer room, with a book and a reading-lamp, and I used to look in, in my dressing-gown, to see how they were getting on. One of the long books your father read was d'Aubigné's *History of the Reformation*.[12]

Until her death in 1930 Lady Verney wrote regularly to her god-daughter and took a particular interest in her eldest son Edmund, proving to be a perceptive and sympathetic critic of his early writing, as well as noting a family resemblance in his 'beautiful and sensitive face',[13] together with 'a keen look in his eyes which reminds me of your father'.[14]

After the birth of his daughter, Tyler joined HMS *Growler* for a tour of the Mediterranean, from where he wrote romantic poems to his wife and urged her to remember to thank Miss Nightingale (a regular visitor to Claydon) for 'the christening present'[15] – thus supplying further interesting historical associations in Edmund's immediate ancestry.

Like her husband, Lady Verney was a Liberal in politics. She also took a keen interest in higher education in Wales, particularly the education of women, and became a Junior Deputy Chancellor of the University of Wales. The young Georgina Tyler (more often called by her second name, Margaret – or Maggie) was thus brought up in the surroundings of politics and learning, encouraged all the time by her godmother. Edmund never met his grandfather Tyler, but he was a forceful influence as well as something of a mystery-figure in Blunden family history. He involved himself in fringe political movements, becoming Assistant Secretary to the Liberty and Property Defence League[16] and editor of a journal called *Jus*. He also had connections with the Leigh Hunt family,[17] and Edmund was always eager to question Tyler's sister (known as Aunt Robinson) about these associations. Tyler's name, however, was rarely mentioned in the family and it was always assumed that he took his own life – that was certainly Edmund's belief. The smell of scandal may have drifted to the Tyler family from Sir Edmund Verney's later problems. He had become Liberal MP for North Buckinghamshire in 1885, but in May 1891 was expelled from the House of Commons after being convicted at the Central Criminal Court of 'conspiring to procure a girl under twenty-one years of age for an immoral purpose'.[18] But Tyler died, aged forty-one on 28 June 1883, in the presence of his wife, having been in a diabetic coma for two days. It remains a mystery why he was buried in West Brompton Cemetery in an unmarked common grave, the location of which Edmund unsuccessfully attempted to discover on several visits to the cemetery.[19]

Not long after Tyler's death, Georgina was admitted to a mental hospital – by strange coincidence to Barming asylum, where Edmund's paternal grandfather was the outdoor bailiff – and she remained there until her death in 1911. Edmund recalled visiting Barming, and being held in the arms of some of the calmer patients; it was a memory which made a very firm impression on his young imagination. He was always to show particular sympathy for writers who were mentally troubled ('it seems', he observed, 'to be my destiny to edit the writings of those who lost their minds: Smart, Lamb,[20] Clare[21] and Ivor Gurney'),[22] and he was to visit Ivor Gurney at the asylum in Dartford. This – together with his Barming memories – provides a personal background for Edmund's poem 'Mental Hospital':

> He sinks away as a dead leaf cast
> Into some slack gray pool; the light
> Was brief, how long the night![23]

Reflecting on his grandmother's problems, on what he believed to be his grandfather's distress, and later on the history of his first father-in-law, he had recurring fears that he might himself suffer a similar fate.

By 1888 Margaret Tyler had shown an inclination to become a school-teacher, and Lady Verney paid for her to undergo training at Whitelands College in London. Here she met the college's founder, Ruskin, and was introduced to Oscar Wilde and his wife – occasions which were proudly described to the young Edmund. On leaving college, she acquired a position at the primary school of St John's, Fitzroy Square, where the newly appointed headmaster was Charles Edmund Blunden. She soon discovered that the violets which appeared on her desk every Monday morning were not from doting pupils but from a doting headmaster. On 19 December 1895 Charles and Margaret were married in St John's Church, Fitzroy Square.

When it came to choosing a name for their son a year later, there was little room for manoeuvre – for at least four generations the eldest Blunden sons had been alternately Charles and Edmund. The added association with Sir Edmund Verney through Margaret made the choice obvious and the child was duly christened Edmund Charles.

Their stay in London was to be short-lived, for the pull of the country was too strong for Edmund's father. He had a couple of short contracts as a supply-teacher in two villages on the Kent – Sussex border, Sandgate and Framfield, but when a permanent position became available as headmaster of a Church of England primary school in Kent, between Maidstone and Tonbridge, in a village which had attracted him when he had been taken on a fishing expedition by his father, he applied and was appointed. The seeds of Edmund's long association with and love of London had now been sown; but it was to be a highly significant event when, in 1900, the family moved to the place that was to become the focal point of Edmund's pastoral imagination – the village of Yalding.

# 2

# Yalding

*Ever before me is the picture of the High Street,*
*Yalding. I smell the hop wagons rucking down from*
*the farms whose least Bramling weighed ten times as*
*much as was ever raised at impious Pembury or baleful*
*Paddock Wood. I see my cricket bat, newly bound,*
*gleaming on a nail outside the saddlers. Avast, ye*
*heart-breaking memories!*
Letter to Siegfried Sassoon, 1927[1]

Edmund's affection for villages was deep-rooted. They represented a way of life – simple, communal, related to the cycle of the seasons - which he felt reflected the best elements in English society and which had been the source of some of finest writing in the language. His enthusiasm for preserving such a tradition was thus both a literary and a patriotic crusade. The searcher after the perfect village, he declared in 1941, 'will probably come to regard one favourite village as having more virtues than the others, and he will be right; for it is only by deep and sweet intimacy that these will be revealed, by a single love-affair.'[2] For Edmund this love-affair was with Yalding – the inspiration for over fifty poems, and a regular retreat from the pressures of academic life or the bruises of domestic unhappiness. Like Wordsworth's passion for the Lake District, Edmund's love of Yalding never faded:

> *O happiest village! How I turned to you*
> *Beyond estranging years that cloaked my view*
> *With all their wintriness of fear and strain;*
> *I turned to you, I never turned in vain . . . .*

*My day still breaks beyond your poplared East*
*And in your pastoral still my life has rest.* [3]

And his love-affair started from his earliest impressions.

The village of Yalding in 1900 was as typical an Edwardian English village as could be found. A pedestrian would leave the branch-line station, and walk for about a mile to the village itself, passing by hop-gardens and orchards, then skirting the edge of a small canal before crossing the River Medway over Twyford Bridge by the Anchor Inn (home of the genial landlord Mr Freeman, whose wife, with a Mrs Mitchener, was a colleague of Edmund's mother at the infant school). Further on, past chestnut, elm, acacia and cedar, and having crossed a second stone bridge, he would see the long village street, lined by a mixture of eighteenth-century brick houses and simple weatherboard cottages, leading to the gabled and red-tiled Cleave's Grammar School, set behind a line of chestnut trees opposite the Walnut Tree Inn. By the bridge stood the twelfth-century church of St Peter and St Paul, its tall tower – surmounted by a strange eighteenth-century cupola like a large green onion – looking out over a rambling graveyard, dominated by a huge yew tree.

Almost adjacent to the church was the schoolmaster's house, which was to become the Blundens' home for the next four years. By this time a daughter, Charlotte (always known as Lottie), had been born – closely followed in 1900 by another son, Gilbert, in the following year by Phyllis, and then by Lancelot in 1902. The family were fond of nicknames: Mother and Father were invariably called Mugg and Pugg; Lottie became Loggin and Phyllis became Figg. Edmund was usually referred to as Eddie.

Edmund's father dominated family life. He was a tall man, and a mixture of authoritarian firmness and sensitive generosity. He felt the awkwardness of being in something of a social vacuum within the rigid feudalism of village life – he was schoolmaster, church organist and choir-master; he was also manager in the hop-gardens during early autumn hop-picking, and secretary of the working men's club. Thus he 'was awkwardly placed between the class in the big houses and the farm labourers and small tradesmen',[4] and he felt that he was kept at arm's length from the vicarage. He carried authority with the choristers from his musical talents – in London he had sung bass in the voluntary choir at St Paul's Cathedral and his organ-playing had been praised by Sir John Stainer, organist at the cathedral and Professor of Music at Oxford – but he resented being considered a servant of the landowners who came to morning service, and made a point himself of wearing a silk hat and morning-coat to church. Cricket did not escape class distinction either, for the two village teams were chosen on social grounds rather than on merit; and if the managers of the school summoned the schoolmaster to play for the first team, he could not refuse – though he felt uncomfortable in an atmosphere of superiority. He was not efficient in financial matters, regularly finding himself in debt, which resulted in bouts of nervous depression; when he had money, he spent it quickly – often at the local inn (a pleasure which Edmund inherited). As Edmund was to recall in later years, 'He did not content himself with borrowing money: he lent it with much greater ease, and gave at the door and at the bar beyond all reason'.[5] He had great hopes for his eldest son and set high standards which Edmund was sharply conscious of not always satisfying; and Edmund was to sense his father's critical but encouraging eye throughout his adult life. The aura which surrounded Pugg – of quiet but anxious authority mixed with rural wisdom – was painted by Edmund in the closing lines of 'An Empty Chair' (which was his reserved seat at the village inn):

> *A Sussex man but domiciled in Kent,*
> *And loving those earth-skills (thought little of)*
> *By which the whole's sustained. – O it was great*
> *To watch him talking with the binman, fine*
> *To have him ask the roadman to bowl straight,*
> *And lend the harness-maker his best line,*
> *And still, the chief thing in this country touch; –*
> *How did he say so little, rule so much?* [6]

Margaret was a warmer and more stable personality. Short and motherly, with 'rounded cheeks of rose and primrose',[7] she quickly won Edmund's devotion: 'My mother! so well known to me and so mysterious. . . . One day I was made to wait in her room with her. . . . and then it was that a picture of woman's grace was first impressed on me. How lovely she was as she took off her bodice and washed her white shoulders, and stood (not long, poor busy darling) at her mirror!'[8] She was intelligent and well read ('Her mind was a pantheon of wonderful men and women, from Florence Nightingale to Blondin and Captain Webb, and earls and bishops')[9] and she became Edmund's confidante for life.

Fifty years later a correspondent recalled these early Yalding days in a letter to Edmund:

The dear and handsome Mr Blunden, who I always thought ought to have had ruffles and a duelling sword! I don't know why, but he reminded me of the days of Louis XVIII and Daddy said he must have had Huguenot blood. A most remarkable man and so *elegant*. He was so utterly 'refined' (not in the modern sense) and should never have been situated so as to cope with the tougher side of life. It was a good thing your mother was practical, as I suppose poets and dreamers need food and clothing![10]

The complementary personalities of Mugg and Pugg provided a happy combination of adult company for Edmund's early years – supplemented by regular visits from Margaret's much travelled sister Maude.

All the family shared a love for Yalding and this was particularly true of Pugg. At the outbreak of war in 1914 he was posted to Plymouth where he became schoolmaster of a training-ship,[11] moving after the war to Salcombe until retirement in 1935 brought him back to Yalding – living first in the old school-house, Cleave's, and then in Vicarage Road. Edmund inherited his pleasure in simple country pastimes, his passion for cricket and fishing, his love of church music and something of his private, inner tension. All these facets were to be combined in a poem which Edmund wrote 'without planning it'[12] on board ship sailing for Hong Kong in 1953, two years after his father's death:

> Are all your eighty years defined at last
> In so few terms? The chair and bookshelves by,
> The latest pipe, the cared-for shoes, the stick
> (Long since presented with some public thanks)
> As good as new, but latterly less astir;
> The post and railway times penned as of old
> Beautifully for the fireside wall?
> Not even your cricket-bag attending now,
> Not the bream-ledger, nor the hopground picture,
> Nor one school register, nor book of chants
> Though these will come to hand as days press on,
> When your monastic face that seemed to pass
> In a high procession from our local world,
> Set on some boyhood vision, never uttered
> To any but one, will be but village clay. [13]

It was the self-contained quality of Yalding life which made an early impression on Edmund, typified by the busy main street with its variety of stores and trades – butcher, grocer, ironmonger, cobbler and saddler. His love of detail is clear in the titles of the essays and poems in *The Face of England* (1932) in which he evokes country life: 'The Starling's Nest', 'The Hop Leaf', 'A Corner of the Meadow', 'The Village Chimneys'. As a young boy he enjoyed watching the simple adaptation of a predominantly agricultural community to the demands of the changing seasons, and had great affection for the implements of farming – the scythes and waggons, ploughs and harnesses – which were to appear so frequently in his poems: 'Golden-age beckonings, lost pastoral things',[14] and 'the old hedger with his half-moon hook'.[15]

The colourful characters of Yalding were both childhood companions and poetic inspirations: Mr Longley, the rosy-cheeked sexton, who let Edmund climb the tower with him to wind the clock; Albert Cheeseman, 'the very picture of a yeoman' and 'one of the unofficial rulers of the village',[16] commemorated in the poem 'Farm Bailiff'[17]; Sid Mercer, the driver of the baker's van, and Mr Brooker, the leader of the bell-ringers; Mr Baldock who supervised the floodgates and penstocks, and Zachariah Cozens, the gardener. Edmund, who always had a sweet tooth, soon became something of an authority on the culinary expertise of the village ladies. He found Mrs Cheeseman's cakes and cocoa 'beyond all praise', and Mrs Cozens's cakes such as 'modern dreams cannot guess at' – these he preferred to his mother's, which 'were certainly good, but had a moral tendency'.[18] Music and entertainment were also commonplace pleasures, ranging from evenings at home when Mugg and her friend Miss Kett would sing and play, to village concerts with conjurers and attempts at comic turns from the fish-and-chip proprietor Mr Thredgold.

At the centre of village life was the church, where Edmund sang in the choir under the direction of his father, who sat at the new organ built to his own specifications. Everything connected with the church fed Edmund's imagination, from the inscriptions on the gravestones to the entries in the Visitors' Books and the smell of the pews. The sound of the church bells held a particular fascination for him: 'Come all who hear our song, say Yalding bells,'[19] and special services, when personalities, music and community seemed to harmonise, were high spots of local life: 'it was a Hardy poem in real life.'[20] From the mud of Ypres in 1917 in a letter to his mother, he recalled the humorous splendour of harvest festivals:

Casting my nebulous eye back over a period of years, I seem to see the Yalding choir once more assembled in gorgeous conclave to celebrate the Harvest-Home. There they go up the aisle, little shy-eyed boys (one apparently George Baldock and the other E.B.) leading their haughty elders following with varying degrees of pride as their stature entitles, gradually tapering up to A. Cheeseman and W. Longley who have donned cassock and surplice for this auspicious occasion. The Vicar intones a hymn number and text and repeats same backwards to make quite sure – a flutter of leaves, a brilliant fantasia from the organ, and the procession moves on with chirping and croaking and deep booming voices balanced in one request to the audience – 'Come, you thankful people, come!'

They stalk between the enormous melons and cottage twists with that air of indifference which proves them above the cares of the flesh. At length, momentum and music cease awhile, ladies rustle, and the biscuity accents begin. By this time the smaller members of the choir are already quarrelling as to the number present. A eucalyptus smell begins to dominate that of the pink potatoes arranged with rustic art: but it is noted in louder tones than necessary that Mr Cozens is munching acid drops. You can hear him so he must be. Someone coughs and is offered a blackcurrant lozenge.

In this way does the thanksgiving for rural felicity begin.[21]

From a very early age, Edmund was to show himself to be acutely sensitive to atmosphere, and to have a poet's eye for detail and a sense of excitement at the life of natural things:

Playing with my ball on the stairs of our small house, I could often see the ray of light stream through the keyhole of the front door, and in it such populous throngs of tiny atoms tingling and dancing, bright to the eye but ever free of the catching hand. Icicles, fallen feathers, shed snake-skins, young birds, earwigs hiding in droves under the coil of rope at the end of the clothes-line, robins tapping the pane, and many other things were hailed as wonders.[22]

This sense of wonder and mystery sometimes became visionary. He discovered that significant moments in his later life had their origins in dream-like experiences of childhood. In the midst of a wild storm he heard the sound of what seemed like dreadful drumming coming from the churchyard and beyond. His father found him lying on his bed in tears of fear, but told him indignantly that there was no such sound. It was only on the battlefields of Flanders that he identified the sound as the thumps of mortar-fire pounding in the distance. The pull of Japan also had early origins, for he was fascinated by the effect of the sunset on an avenue of slender trees, which seemed to him to be a Japanese scene. The first picture which he remembered being attracted to was a brightly tinted Japanese print of finches on a bough; and a young girl who lived in one of the houses by the school seemed, with her dark hair, rounded cheeks and small curved figure, to be Japanese. The most lasting vivid childhood vision came one summer evening when, unable to sleep, he looked out of his bedroom window at the brilliant sky and saw there a range of architecture which he had never seen before – a mixture of red brick and white stone, with tall towers. It was a vision which was not to fade.

These reflective moods were often shared with his sisters: Lottie, round, clear-complexioned, thoughtful and sensitive, and Phyllis, 'a pretty little girl, rather podgy and very, very good'.[23] Expeditions were more often shared with his brother, Gilbert, the daring and impulsive explorer, and later with Lance. These outings were invariably connected with the rivers, streams and water meadows of the village; and Yalding was uncommonly rich in water. The River Medway divides at the village into two tributaries, the Teise and the Beult:

> Here winds
> The chiding chiming brook caught in two minds, [24]

but these were supplemented by dykes and ponds on every farm, and numerous deep ditches, standing pools, streams running through orchards, solitary swampy thickets and rushy groves. Nothing delighted Edmund more than the sight and sound of water:

> Some worship mountains, some the sea;
> But a river god is the god for me,
> And to live in a house by the din of a weir,
> Or a mill with a mill-head huge and deep,
> And yellow lilies and white in the mere,
> Or a farm that looks on rambling brooks
> Is a thing I hold as dear as sleep. [25]

By the side of the Beult was a sloping meadow known as the Kintons, regularly visited by Edmund, often in the company of Alfred and Alice Cheeseman. A little further along the stream was a small shallow with a steep headland, hidden by sorrel, called the Sands. This became Edmund's 'secret place'. Here, from the age of about eight, he would escape to watch the water, collect minnows, observe the dragonfly and learn the names of the flowers, quickly becoming familiar with the wood-anemones, kingcups, bluebells, celandine, marsh marigolds, yellow flag-flowers, horse mushrooms and dewberries, which grew in abundance.

On the edge of the village at Cheveney was the old water-mill – the home of his friends Will and George Baldock. As the Beult approached the mill, it flowed slowly through willows on one bank and many bushes on the other, towards a mill-dam where it forked, one stream going through the mill-wheel, and the other through a floodgate, over a weir, to a deep pool screened by a copse and oak trees, where there were local memories of drownings – and where kingfishers were not uncommon. It was mostly in this pool that Edmund pursued his passion for fishing, enthusiastically coached by his father:

> Happily through my years this small stream ran;
> It charmed the boy, and purified the man. [26]

Edmund always distrusted too much sophisticated equipment, preferring a willow-rod cut from a tree to which he attached cord, corks and hooks. He was remarkably successful and began to record his triumphs in a notebook. The river was clear and clean, and provided a rich variety of fish – bream, roach, gudgeon, dace, rudd, tench, perch, chub and salmon-trout – but the fish which caught Edmund's imagination most was the pike. Twice he had one on his line, but he never achieved a landing – once the fish quietly swam away after ejecting the hook from its mouth; on the other occasion, the flimsy line proved no match for the strength of the pike which raced away to be greeted by another angler, with the cry: 'So help me God he is a bloody fine fish!' It was, declared Edmund, 'like a bit of the Benedicite.'[27]

In many ways, Edmund's feelings for water and for fishing reflect the attitude to nature in his poetry. At least fifty of his poems involve description of water –

> I wonder not the Poets love the brooks
> And throughout life seek their society, [28]

– and record the changing moods of rivers and streams, from the gentle ripple of a pool mirroring the peace of nature –

> Tranquilly beats the country's heart today . . .
> The feather-footed moments tiptoe past, [29]

– to the wildness of storms and the lurking viciousness of the pike beneath the calm surface, 'a gross giant with murder in his eye and jaw'.[30] He was always conscious of these changes of mood and the ambiguities which they reveal:

> Here joy shall muse what melancholy tells,
> And melancholy smile because of joy, [31]

and the ambivalent world of fish, where the harmless gudgeon and the destructive pike share one river, taught him this at an early age. It is a vision of a 'rural admixture of shrill and sweet;'[32] he remembered with pleasure the sounds of the hens and the cows which he heard from his bedroom window, but he also heard the screeching of the doomed pig. Animals of prey are ironically celebrated in 'The Malefactors',[33] and in 'The Pike'[34] the 'murderous patriarch' has nobility as well as cruelty. Another poem set in Yalding, 'Sheet Lightning', moves to a climax in which a young jack rabbit is blinded by the lamps of the brake. It ends baldly: 'Joe beat its brain out on the wheel.'[35] Strangely, in peace the emphasis is often on the harsher side of nature; in war he was more often to celebrate natural beauty.

When the winter ice came, and fishing became impossible, another enthusiasm of the Blunden family brought them to the river – skating. Edmund's much anthologised poem 'The Midnight Skaters', is a kaleidoscope of Yalding impressions: skaters against a background of hop-gardens, with death itself lurking beneath the surface in place of the pike:

> The hop-poles stand in cones,
>    The icy pond lurks under,
> The pole-tops steeple to the thrones
>    Of stars, sound gulfs of wonder;
> But not the tallest there, 'tis said,
> Could fathom to this pond's black bed,
>
> Then is not death at watch
>    Within those secret waters?
> What wants he but to catch
>    Earth's heedless sons and daughters?
> With but a crystal parapet
> Between, he has his engines set.
>
> Then on, blood shouts, on, on,
>    Twirl, wheel and whip above him,
> Dance on this ball-floor thin and wan,
>    Use him as though you love him;
> Court him, elude him, reel and pass,
> And let him hate you through the glass.[36]

With the arrival of another child, Geoffrey, in 1904, the school-house was becoming too small and the family became tenants of a large old farmhouse just outside the village, called Congelow. It was a rambling, timber house with spacious rooms, a dairy and a brewery, an attic reached by a ladder, a garden full of yew trees, and outhouses and kilns, granaries, apple-lofts and a working pump. It was generally believed to be haunted (a characteristic much to Edmund's taste), and he described the atmosphere of ghostliness in 'The Sighing Time':

*The sighing time, the sighing time! . . .*
*The old house mourns and shudders so;*
*And the bleak garrets' crevices*
*Like whirring distaffs utter dread;*
*Streams of shadow people go*
*By hollow stairs and passages.*[37]

He loved exploring the corners of the house – finding a cupboard full of books: encyclopaedias, Bibles with copper engravings, and old sets of the eighteenth-century journals the *Tatler* and the *Spectator*, which supplemented his reading of Captain Marryat, R. M. Ballantyne and – his great favourite – Jules Verne. Congelow was the ideal home for a large young family, particularly since the full complement of children was to be nine with the arrivals of Anne in 1906, Frances three years later and finally Hubert in 1910. But they were not all able to enjoy the house together, for Pugg's life remained unsettled, his financial position was precarious, and several more moves were forced upon him. To add to the financial worries, irregularities were discovered in the accounts of the cricket club, of which he was treasurer. He was certainly not guilty himself but he felt that he must take responsibility. On two occasions he had to 'sell up', and when the bailiffs arrived at the house in 1908 he suffered something close to a collapse at the sight of the furniture piled up outside the family home. He left the village school – though Margaret continued to teach – and became a supply-teacher in London, moving the family into two simple adjoining cottages by the Anchor Inn at Twyford Bridge, which Edmund remembered as 'flimsy, desolate and damp'[38]. Pugg sold a complete set of Charles Dickens to raise money (and Edmund felt that his father, with his financial worries, had similarities with Dickens's father), though he managed to retain the family piano. He was not by nature a man to cope with such troubles, being happiest 'fishing for bream all Summer evenings that were free, than which there is no greater proof of tranquillity. . . . he painted bright migrations and brighter destinations, and his children ridiculed him; with that, the sense of being much discussed and dissected hurt him. . . . In Yalding he had spent twelve years, and he left it while still in debt and now and then in despair'.[39]

Relief came in 1913 when Pugg was reappointed to the school in Framfield, where the vicarage welcomed him as a respected member of the community. In early days, however, in contrast with the unhappy periods of financial worry, Congelow was a haven of security and Edmund was still celebrating it – in poems such as 'The Farm-house Family'[40]– as late as 1950.

There was another reason for happy memories of this time, for in the next hamlet, Benover, a young girl – Lavinia Pattenden – was living with her grandmother. Every day this pretty girl would pass Congelow, and share a love of flowers and poetry with Edmund. He would give her primroses, gathered from the fields. It was his first romance:

> *A love I had, as childhood ever will,*
> *And our first meeting I'll remember still . . .*
> *I got a flower, she put it in her book*
> *And after, many eves, we walked for hours*
> *Like loving flowers among the other flowers,*
> *And blushed for pride when other girls and boys*
> *Laughed at us sweethearts in the playhour's noise.*[41]

As he grew older, Edmund began to explore the neighbouring parishes, borrowing Gilbert's 'Threepenny Bicycle' with solid tyres. Again, his poetic eye delighted in the unique quality of country scenes: 'these rides were delightful, for every crooked lane and smithy and timber-yard and country-box came before me in its individuality. Even in the battlefields of Flanders, I generally saw and felt every communication trench and every sandbagged ruin as a personal, separate figure, quite distinct from every other one.'[42]

This sense of the individuality of things extended to rivers too, and in 1944, in 'To Teise, a Stream in Kent', he claimed that he could no more confuse the Teise with the Beult:

> *Than take our smith or carrier for*
> *Our saddler.*[43]

A sharp eye for detail and a fresh delight in natural things – these were to become the hallmarks of Edmund's pastoral poetry: and they stemmed from his Yalding childhood. J. C. Squire noted this in his introduction to *The Face of England*: 'There never was snow like the snow of infancy, nor cider like the first cider taken with the mowers under the hedge: it is Mr Blunden's great gift to have lost none of the intensity of early sensation. Having found beauty in common things, he never lost it again.'[44]

From the age of about eight he was able to indulge in what was to become a great obsession – cricket. It was certainly an obsession of his father's, and Edmund claimed surprise when a paternal homily began:

'But cricket's not everything.'[45] Pugg upheld the traditions of sportsmanship and after Edmund had queried an umpire's decision he refused to speak to his son for some time. In an obituary for the Yalding parish magazine, Edmund wrote of his father, 'I sometimes thought that the achievement of a name in first-class cricket was his idea of human greatness',[46] and it had not seemed beyond the bounds of possibility that he might achieve this, for he was an athletic fielder and his long musician's fingers enabled him to produce cunning legbreaks, which once bowled K. S. Ranjitsinhjhi in the nets at Brighton, a feat which was sometimes claimed to have been achieved with three successive balls. Pugg belonged to a nineteenth-century world of cricket and described his memories of 1912 in a letter to Edmund:

Sussex at that time had a most dismal record. The Hove ground provided a single ring of rough planks (rarely full); the lunch hour was unlimited: four balls made an over; players came almost direct from the village green; amateurs paraded grandly; captains like W. G. Grace sat grimly in the pavilion for hours after rain had stopped; bowlers threw without penalty; even W.G. was wont to aid his side by bantering the opposing batsmen; a wicket-keeper without long-stop caused head-shaking; and your county player might repair your shoes in the evening. Tall hats did not appear on the field, but stiff white shirts, stiff collars and cuffs and silk ties were worn by amateurs. Professionals had shirts of various hues – pink, blue and striped, and suspension was maintained by belts with metal clasps. Bowling was underhand, round-armed or over-arm; beards were usual.[47]

Edmund enjoyed visits to first-class matches at Tonbridge and Chichester, but was more concerned with the fortunes of the village teams – which, for the most part, consisted of the members of the church choir. Edmund became the regular scorer for the first eleven, earned some extra pocket-money carrying the bags of visitors of the 'many-coloured blazer class',[48] and was allowed to bat at number eleven for the second eleven when occasion demanded. There were few things that gave him greater pleasure. On one memorable occasion he went in at number eleven when a local hero, Fred Latter, was on sixty; Edmund managed to stay until his partner completed his century. Fred Latter is commemorated, as Tom, in the poem 'Pride of the Village':

> Cricket to us, like you, was more than play,
> It was a worship in the summer sun.[49]

Edmund was also able to play on the delightful old ground, the Ring, surrounded by trees on the bank of the River Teise – for this was the ground of Cleave's Grammar School. In the spring of 1907 he left the elementary school run by the Misses Lewis and came under the instruction of Mr Samuel Williams at Cleave's, founded in 1665. It was a school of sixty pupils and two teachers. Mr Williams, though a firm disciplinarian, was devoted to his pupils, and was a particularly fine teacher of French. He shared with Edmund's father a desire to push his new pupil as hard as possible, and Edmund was responsive. He was outclassed only by one older pupil, Tom Singyard, whom Edmund revered despite being humiliated by him:

He lived some way beyond Congelow in a house near a disused brickworks, which had become a chain of ponds hidden in thickets and sagbeds, full of carp and tench and water lilies and moorhens. He kept me in state of misery all the road home by pulling my hair and swinging me round and using me as a butt for his wit; but I was devoted to him. One day I appeared at school wearing some knickers of a certain breadth hurriedly made by my mother. Tom Singyard raised his eyebrows, and, to the boys round, he uttered the sufficient description 'Bells'. Thereafter, when he would torment me, he merely uttered this word in a lovely tunable voice, 'Bells',[50] and it became my nickname.[51]

Edmund was always grateful for the academic grounding which he received from Yalding, and he humorously characterised Mr Williams in the poem 'No Continuing City' (1920)[52] – and more seriously in 'Sententiae' (as late as 1958)[53].

After eighteen months it became clear that, intellectually, he had outgrown Cleave's. His talents needed greater challenges and encouragement, and Mr Williams suggested that Edmund should try for a place at Christ's Hospital, the famous school founded by the boy-king Edward VI in 1552. Moved by a sermon from Bishop Ridley, Edward gave his blessing for the old monastery of the Grey Friars, dissolved under his father's reign, to become a school for the poor of London. For nearly 400 years it had continued to educate those who were considered academically able but whose parents could not afford the fees of a traditional public school. The only grounds for acceptance were talent; the only bar was wealth. In 1902 the school moved from its premises near St Paul's Cathedral to occupy part of the Shelley estates just west of Horsham in Sussex. Arrangements were accordingly made for Edmund to take an entrance examination in Rochester. He was only dimly aware of the significance of the event;

he was more excited at the thought of spending a night with his kindly Uncle Hubert in the sophistication of the big town where, for sixpence, he could proudly order 'lunch' rather than 'dinner' at mid-day.

Some days later his father summoned him to tell him that he had been given a place at Christ's Hospital. He received the news with mixed feelings. The sense of adventure at the prospect of going to a great school and moving in the grand world beyond Twyford Bridge was appealing. Less attractive was the thought of leaving the homely security of Yalding, the old stove at Cleave's and the fishing raids on the Teise and the Beult. His position in the cricket team would be in jeopardy, and the bells of St Peter and St Paul would not sound in Horsham. Most important was the inevitable separation from Mugg and Pugg and the warm simplicity of Congelow. Was he not in danger of putting himself at a distance from his family?

This was a question which was never to be fully resolved. His love of the simple life was to make him suspicious of sophistication, and he was never to relax completely in a purely academic or official atmosphere – though he spent a good deal of his working life in both. That he would become somewhat set apart from his family was inevitable. From the family's point of view, he was in a rather privileged position. Being away at school, he did not have to suffer the indignities of the bailiff's visit in such a personal way as the others; returning from boarding school for the holidays, he had his own room in an already crowded house. A revealing anecdote is told by his brother Lance after a visit to Edmund in London in the late 1920s. As Lance boarded the train to return to Yalding, Edmund handed him a cheque to cover the travelling expenses. It was never cashed, for Lance (in common with the rest of his family) had no bank-account, which was seen as a symbol of city life rather than village custom.[54] Nonetheless, regardless of all the strains which Edmund's changed circumstances would impose, the ties of Yalding made any breach impossible. In 1928, in the poem 'The Complaint', he personifies Yalding:

> The village spoke: 'You come again,
> You left me for a world of men,
> Tell
> How you feel now my former spell?'

The answer comes in the final line: 'I answered, all my ways led here'[55]

Edmund's most vivid evocation of village life, incorporating rural pastimes, the church, cottages and farm buildings, the cricket pitch and the sense of historical continuity, is his poem 'Forefathers', first published in 1920 and constantly reprinted over the next fifty years:

> Here they went with smock and crook,
>     Toiled in the sun, lolled in the shade,
> Here they mudded out the brook
>     And here their hatchet cleared the glade:
> Harvest-supper woke their wit,
> Huntsman's moon their wooings lit.
>
> From this church they led their brides,
>     From this church themselves were led
> Shoulder-high; on these waysides
>     Sat to take their beer and bread.
> Names are gone – what men they were
> These their cottages declare.
>
> Names are vanished, save the few
>     In the old brown Bible scrawled;
> These were men of pith and thew,
>     Whom the city never called;
> Scarce could read or hold a quill,
> Built the barn, the forge, the mill.
>
> On the green they watched their sons
>     Playing till too dark to see,
> As their fathers watched them once,
>     As my father once watched me;
> While the bat and beetle flew
> On the warm air webbed with dew.
>
> Unrecorded, unrenowned,
>     Men from whom my ways begin,
> Here I know you by your ground
>     But I know you not within –
> There is silence, there survives
> Not a moment of your lives.
>
> Like the bee that now is blown
>     Honey-heavy on my hand,
> From his toppling tansy-throne
>     In the green tempestuous land –
> I'm in clover now, nor know
> Who made honey long ago.[55]

His father, however, had his eye on more practical matters in the summer of 1909. A medical examination in London was required, and an interview with the headmaster of Christ's Hospital, Dr Upcott – a Tennysonian figure, bearded and broad-shouldered – when the important academic decision was taken that Edmund should follow the 'classical' rather than the 'modern' side. After the interview there was time for a brief visit to see some cricket at the Oval. 'Perhaps we shall see you playing for Oxford yet,' said his father. It was, wrote Edmund, 'as though I had been transferred into a Jules Verne story'.[57] For the next few weeks he was to enjoy his last childhood moments as a 'full' resident of Yalding. His claim that his relationship with his home village was a 'love-affair' was to be repeated in the poem 'The Deeper Friendship' (1929). Here, perhaps more that anywhere else, he describes his feelings of a spiritual bond with Yalding – which becomes identified with the spirit of nature itself:

> *Were all eyes changed, were even poetry cold . . .*
>
> *still I should keep one final hold,*
> *Since clearer and clearer returns my first-found joy.*

And that 'hold' would be a return to:

> *. . . the gate and deserted siding,*
> *The inn with the tattered arbour, the choking weir;*

to 'one hearth' and 'one love' which 'shine beyond fear' and where he would be at peace: 'And well content that Nature should bury me.'[58]

In September 1909 the twelve-year-old Edmund, carrying in his pocket a volume of selections from Charles Lamb, the gift of the curate's wife, arrived at Christ's Hospital station with all the excitement and foreboding of a young boy's first day at a new school. As he left the station, he was led round the edge of the playing fields and there ahead of him were the school buildings – a mixture of red brick and white stone with tall towers. He recognised them immediately. They were the buildings he had seen from his bedroom window, some six years previously, in the glowing Yalding sky.

# 3

# Christ's Hospital

*He is so immaculate that man, and so ashamed of*
*Christ's Hospital – which I think is a hanging offence.*
Letter to Hector Buck, 1920[1]

'Christ's Hospital is a thing without parallel in the country, and *sui generis*.' So said the report of the School's Inquiry Commissioners in 1867–8, and Old Blues are proud to quote it. The unique nature of its entrance system understandably tends to generate three qualities: a desire to succeed, a sense of gratitude to the foundation ('Housie' – or 'Housey' – as it is affectionately called) and a feeling of brotherhood and equality among its pupils. Edmund was to show these traits to a marked degree. Several old boys had achieved literary distinction, from George Peele and Edmund Campion in the sixteenth century to the extraordinary trio of Coleridge,[2] Lamb and Leigh Hunt in the late eighteenth century – all of whom acknowledged the strong influence of the school on their lives. Coleridge wrote in the *Courier* of 1811, in response to an attack on the method of entry to the school: 'We are confident that the Lord Chancellor will hesitate long before he attempts to remove a blessing of which there is no parallel in Europe.' Although the requirement for admission – to be of 'honest origin and poverty' – could be reasonably elastic, the sense of social anonymity was treasured. Leigh Hunt described the school as a 'medium between the patrician pretension of such schools as Eton and Westminster, and the plebeian submission of the charity schools', and had:

. . . a strong recollection that in my time there were two boys, one of whom went up to the drawing-room to his father, the master of the house; and the other down in to the kitchen to *his* father, the coachman. One thing I know to be certain, and it is the noblest of all, namely that the boys themselves (at least it was so in my time) had no sort of feeling of the difference of one another's ranks out of doors. The cleverest boy was the noblest, let his father be who he might.[3]

This sense of corporate identity was further stressed by the traditional costume, little changed since Edward VI's time, consisting of clerical bands, long blue coat and yellow stockings.

Many of the school's traditions travelled with the uniform to Sussex, and Edmund was particularly sensitive to the feeling of historical continuity which was evident in many of the idiosyncratic aspects of Christ's Hospital life. The hierarchy of the school remained as before, with boys passing through the junior classes – on the classical side, Little Erasmus and Great Erasmus – and staying on after the age of sixteen for promotion to become Deputy Grecians and then Grecians only if they appeared capable of winning a scholarship to Oxford or Cambridge. Grecians were marked out with a more magnificent coat, of finer cloth, with fourteen large buttons, velvet cuffs turned up and no epaulettes. At the top of the pyramid was the Senior Grecian, or head boy – a position Edmund was eventually to hold. Since an Oxford or Cambridge scholarship usually meant an exhibition from the school as well, a successful pupil could look forward to free education until he left university.

School slang also survived the move (and delighted Edmund), from the colourful 'spadge' ('to walk with dignity', apparently from Virgil's description of the crow: '*et solus secum sicca spatiatur harena*') to 'gag' ('the fat of fresh beef boiled', as quoted by Charles Lamb), and such ingenious coinings as 'flab' (butter), 'kiff' (tea or coffee) and 'taffs' (potatoes). Two unique punishments were also retained: the 'fotch' (a blow on the face with the open hand) and the 'owl' (a hit on the head with clenched knuckles). The formidable wide-hipped 'Dame' Annie Wass, Edmund's much respected house matron, was held in great awe not least for the fact that she was known to have fotched a Grecian.

There were visible reminders, too, of the past – in particular the huge painting by Antonio Verrio which hung in the dining hall, depicting of the founding of the Mathematical School. Charles II had founded this school for navigation and incorporated it within Christ's Hospital, where it had been promoted and shaped by Samuel Pepys to prepare boys for the Navy and Merchant Service. Also from London came the beadle, 'Daddy' Horn, who rang the bells and walked around the school in his traditional costume of top hat and tails, in blue and gold.

The traffic was not all one way. Edmund was greatly impressed by an early experience of the annual celebration of St Matthew's Day, when the whole school marched in uniform from London Bridge station to Christ Church, Newgate Street, and sat in the galleries for a service attended by the Lord Mayor. Many of the boys' parents lined the streets and cheered the procession. Yalding suddenly seemed far away and Edmund felt momentarily like Lamb's Elia, 'a poor friendless boy'.[4] Afterwards tea was served in the Mansion House, a new shilling was given to the younger boys and buns for the return journey; some of the boys used the buns as missiles to pelt the railway platelayers – who signalled what was interpreted as appreciation.

Another strong tradition of the school was its calligraphy. Christ's Hospital had always had a Writing School and along the corridors were framed examples of past achievements in the art. Edmund was to be a most distinguished exponent of it, and his handwriting was to show a striking resemblance to that of Charles Lamb. The legendary writing-master H. J. Stalley had moved to Sussex with the school and cut a grave and impressive figure, with a beard reaching almost to his waist. He invariably wore a black frock-coat to match his sombre looks, and the only colour in his costume was the teetotaller's blue ribbon that hung from his lapel. He was assisted by J. S. Armstrong, 'Kidger' Cole, and 'Cabby' Barrett – who insisted that his pupils write with a triangular-shaped penholder. Throughout his life Edmund favoured the use of a steel-nibbed dip-pen and most of his books were written with the aid of such simple implements, following his own advice in *Cricket Country*, 'dip your pen and say what you have to say.'[5]

Edmund was not unique in his passionate feelings about his school-days, for it was characteristic of many contemporary public schoolboys to exhibit a loyalty and warm affection towards their schools; in Edmund's case, however, his response was something close to religious awe. It was in part an extension of his acute sensitivity to atmosphere and his readiness to see experiences as symbolic – at times almost as signs of destiny. As Yalding represented an ideal of rural simplicity, so Christ's Hospital became a symbol of sophisticated culture. These two contrasting elements were often in tension within Edmund, finding a partial resolution in the composition of poetry evoking simple pastoral scenes in rhetorical literary vocabulary and form.

In some aspects, certainly, his view was sentimentalised for there is a brutal side to school life everywhere and Christ's Hospital could certainly boast one of the more outrageous pedagogues of the eighteenth century in the headmaster James Boyer – described by Coleridge as a

ABCDEFGHIJKL
MNOPQRSTUVWX
YZ

abcdefghijklmnopqrstuvw
xyz

That's to give my vanity a run. But
would it have appeased the old Christ's
Hospital writing—masters? Not it. I'd
have been set on

Take great Care
and you'll Write fair.

I think you would, by the natural slant of
y^r handwriting, have escaped with fewer
stripes.
The recognition you gave Hood as it was
delighted

yours sincerely
Edmund Blunden

observe
dirty mark

12 Dec^r 1923

An example of EB's calligraphy: a 'letter' to Walter de la Mare,
12 December 1923 (*Bodleian Library*)

'*plagose Orbilius*',[6] by Leigh Hunt as 'a proper tyrant, passionate and capricious', [7] and by Lamb as a 'rabid pedant'.[8] On discovering the young Coleridge in tears, Boyer bellowed to him: 'Boy, the school is your father! Boy, the school is your mother! Boy, the school is your brother! The school is your sister! The school is your first cousin and your second cousin and all the rest of your relations. Let's have no more crying!'[9]

But the school made an indelible mark on the three Romantic writers and Edmund felt an almost mystical affinity with them through the shared association. He understood the constant references to their schooldays, exemplified in Lamb's letter to George Dyer, another Old Blue and wonderful eccentric:

You ever wrote what I call a Grecian's hand; mine is a sort of deputy Grecian's hand. I don't know how it is, but I keep my rank in fancy still since school-days. I can never forget I was a deputy Grecian! And writing to you or Coleridge, besides affection, I feel a reverential deference as to Grecians still. I keep my soaring away above the Great Erasmians, yet far beneath the other.[10]

There were of course moments of homesickness, especially when Edmund received letters from Lavinia with primroses and violets enclosed, and loneliness awoke an 'intense longing for home, and the cricket pitch and the river, and all that domestic intimacy which can't so easily be recorded, being anything from bath-night to the smell of breakfast as cooked by one's own mother'.[11] Edmund could easily adapt Lamb's exclamation from school: 'How I would wake weeping, and in the anguish of my heart exclaim upon sweet Calne in Wiltshire',[12] but they were isolated moments. For him Christ's Hospital represented a world of possibilities which he had never imagined existed. He was surrounded by ability and found that he could shine in talented company. He was introduced to a new world of literature and learning which he embraced enthusiastically, and he was able to make friends with like-minded contemporaries. In the miseries of the war, 'Housie' became a life-line with sanity, constantly referred to in his letters, and it remained an image of civilisation throughout his life. It became a spur and an inspiration to be worthy of his privilege, and it gave him a deep respect for traditional values and the achievements of the past; it also emphasised his tendency to hero-worship, which could sometimes blur his critical edge.

Not that he was totally blind to the school's shortcomings. In 1952, when Edmund became a joint editor of *The Christ's Hospital Book* in celebration of the school's quatercentenary, Barnes Wallis (inventor of the 'dam-buster' bomb) contributed an article which was critical of the school's science and questioned the validity of the entry system in the age of the welfare state. The editorial body decided that it should be published, despite the stir which it would inevitably cause in some circles, but they wanted to be unanimous and Edmund was in Hong Kong. They cabled him and he immediately agreed that they should go ahead, writing: 'We all love Housey too much to love her idly'.

Edmund was certainly quick to see the best in people, and held his headmaster in high esteem. A younger contemporary, E. F. Watling, composed facetious alcaics celebrating the more commonly held opinion of Upcott's dreary teaching:

> O Doctor Upcott, is it essential
> That you should sit here every Saturday
>   Grunting your incoherent babblings
>   Making a fool of yourself completely?

> Why don't you go and talk to your gardener?
> He'd like to hear of Plato's Apology.
>   Why torture us poor luckless Grecians?
>   What have we done to deserve this hardship?[13]

But Edmund preferred to remember the man who had brought the school from London to Horsham and safeguarded its traditions 'with devoted energy and memorable success' (as his memorial tablet in the Western Cloister reads) and who presided over the school when every day brought fresh news of Old Blues killed in action. Others were certainly less enthusiastic. Upcott was known as 'the Butch', and abbreviation of 'the Butcher', for when headmaster of St Edmund's School, Canterbury, he used to refer to his pupils as 'my Canterbury Lambs'. The artist Philip Youngman Carter, who drew a fine portrait of Edmund, remembers Upcott as 'a sanctimonious sadist',[14] but Edmund liked to recall being entertained at venison lunches as Senior Grecian. Loyalty for the man who had promoted him certainly played a part, for Edmund was someone for whom loyalty was natural; and there were those who were surprised at the choice, expecting athletic rather than academic success to be reflected in the appointment. In *The Dede of Pittie*, Edmund's dramatic masque for the quatercentenary celebrations in 1953, he describes the reign of Upcott as 'serene'. In contrast to most boys' recollections of schooldays, Edmund was always recalling the feeling of peace which prevailed, and it was this sense of security and tranquillity which was to haunt him at Ypres and

Passchendaele. He saw Upcott as the author of this, and was to pay his homage in 1928 in the poem 'Recollections of Christ's Hospital':

> And beauty was the ordinance
> Of that dear school. [15]

Edmund's house was Coleridge A, named after the poet, and presided over by H. S. Goodwin, who was to remain a lifelong friend and influence. Goodwin was a rare schoolmaster, having a talent for mixing incisive discipline with warm human understanding. He was athletic and vigorous, with strong artistic sympathies to match. He loved cricket, theatre, the music-hall baritone Harry Lauder, chocolate and self-discipline in equal proportion, and some saw him as the *Laughing Cavalier* in Frans Hals's portrait, a copy of which hung in his study. Goodwin had played cricket for Gloucestershire, but a greater distinction in Edmund's eyes was that he had played under the captaincy of W. G. Grace. He could tell stories of G. L. Jessop who dared to use improper language to W.G. when, having criticised most of the players for missed catches, Grace directed his complaints even at Jessop who had just managed by a supreme effort, to get his finger-tips to a skimming first-bounce-to-the-boundary hit. He also recalled being reprimanded himself by the great man for holding a catch off Grace's bowling, from a fierce stroke, close to the wicket – a man had been specially placed further out for this precise shot. A favourite trick of Goodwin's was to place a shilling on the middle stump of the wicket in the cricket nets and offer it as a prize to whoever bowled him out; he rarely lost his bet. Edmund was quick to respond to the challenges of physical exercise: to the love of cricket which his father had fostered in Yalding was to be added the distinctive public school reverence for all athletic pursuits, with an emphasis on good sportsmanship and respect for the authority of umpires and referees. Certainly Goodwin encouraged sporting activities and by the time Edmund left school he was captain of his house cricket team and, though he occasionally played for the school's first eleven, usually played in the second eleven, keeping wicket, sometimes scoring impressively – his highest score being ninety not-out against St John's Leatherhead. He was stand-off half in the house rugby team and also played fives. Remarkably, he always batted and played fives without wearing gloves.

Goodwin had a quick perception of what the boys in his care needed. One example of his sensitivity remained in Edmund's memory for life. Before his first month was out, homesickness had set in and he was delighted to received a telegram informing him that his parents were to make an unexpected visit. It was raining as they walked across the school fields and they were overtaken by Goodwin, who offered his umbrella to Mrs Blunden. Edmund was too embarrassed to introduce him, but when his father realised who it was he rushed after him to thank him for all that he was doing for his son – and to shake the hand of a first-class cricketer. It was only much later that Edmund discovered that it was Goodwin who had suggested the visit and contrived the accidental meeting. Goodwin was always fond of doing the unexpected. One winter's night he took a group of boys, including Edmund, to slide on a frozen pond at Broadbridge Heath. Memories of skating at Yalding came flooding back.

Edmund had received no Latin instruction from Mr Williams in Yalding, but having opted for the Classical Side, he worked most enthusiastically to fill the gap. Goodwin was in charge of *Little Erasmus Special*, where Edmund soon found himself, and noticing Edmund's industry and promise he gave him extra coaching. Edmund enjoyed his teaching, which was enlivened by moments of theatrical eccentricity when Latin would be interrupted by bouts of physical jerks and the window would be flung open for breathing exercises. He drew engaging pictures of dog-kennels against particular howlers in exercises and was fond of composing rhymes to assist the remembering of grammar:

> *You'll feel a pain, but not in front,*
> *If you forget* iens, eunt:
> *In* eo's *compounds too you'll find*
> Eunt *will save you pain behind.*[16]

Goodwin was also able to give Edmund some literary encouragement, although at times he was a little suspicious of his 'mania' for poetry. Perhaps he felt the impact of the anonymous nineteenth-century Commissioners of Christ's Hospital who wrote: 'Of the 150 exhibitioners examined, some have died and some have gone into literature'. Goodwin subscribed to the *English Review* and passed on his copies to Edmund. It was in these pages that Edmund discovered the narrative poems of John Masefield, seeming then 'so daring, so impassioned, so un-Victorian'.[17]

Goodwin's perceptive understanding of Edmund is clear in his end-of-term reports, some of which could equally well apply to Edmund in later stages of life:

Quite good, but somehow not spruce and tidy.

I hear the best accounts of his work. I hope he will go far. He must read some good English now, and try to develop his character, which is at present somewhat nebulous.

Very good. A clever boy who must now choose good friends of his own intelligence and establish himself.

Good, but still wants a good bit of stiffening. He must learn to say 'No' and begin to give his friends a proper lead.

Good, but getting a bit slack in observing rules, and inclined to be a law to himself.[18]

Goodwin left Coleridge A in 1914 to join the Public Schools and Universities Battalion as a private. He clearly falsified his age, for he was forty-four and the maximum age for enlisting was thirty-seven. He was soon captain and adjutant in the 22nd Royal Fusiliers, and was wounded in action. His replacement as housemaster for Edmund's final year was A. E. Johnson, who continued the tradition of perceptive end-of-term reports:

Still enthusiastic, but seems to me too apt to fear the opinions of those he should command.[19]

Goodwin returned to Christ's Hospital and Coleridge A in 1919. Until his death in 1955 he remained Edmund's friend and adviser and when Edmund published *Christ's Hospital, A Retrospect* in 1923 he dedicated it to 'H. S. Goodwin, My House Master: With Grateful Respect'.

Edmund was fortunate in having several masters who took an interest in his writing. One was his young history master, A. C. W. Edwards, who had a sensitive eye for art and a keen appreciation of literature. 'Teddy' was a lively character with liberal ideas – even allowing his house captain of 1924–5 to abolish punishments. His strong personality did not charm everyone, and when some years later the future poet and writer Keith Douglas was in his house, the equally strong-minded Douglas was transferred to another by mutual agreement. Edmund, however, found Edwards's company stimulating and encouraging and a lasting friendship was established, with Edmund dedicating his *Poems of Many Years* to him in 1957. Edwards recalled Edmund at school: 'Apparently here was the really perfect boy, keen as mustard in class and in games, who was eccentric in one respect only – he wrote poems. Good ones too. I made haste to get to know him. I found him a nervous-speaking, weakly-built boy, bulging with brains and bursting with enthusiasms.'[20] After retirement Edwards remained at the school as librarian until his death in 1964.

Also influential as a literary encourager was G. W. Palmer, mathematician and inspirer of Grecians. He succeeded another of Edmund's mentors, W. de H. Robinson, as president of the Grecians' Reading Society, and at his home he encouraged the reading of modern authors: Shaw, Stevenson and Conrad. Edmund was to read a paper on Masefield's poetry to this society in December 1913. It was a long and closely written essay showing some of the naivety one might expect from a seventeen-year-old, but he enthusiastically recited the recently published *Sea Fever* claiming it 'to be worth fifty *Widows in Bye Streets* and *Daffodil Fields*', declaring *Dauber* to be 'the absolute epic of the sea' and concluding that '*Ballads* and *Lyrics*, *Dauber* and *The River* seem destined to go far and to last'.[21] Palmer died in 1919, and Edmund described him as a friend 'whom most I should have sought to please with poem or any work whatsoever'.[22]

Another out-of-class activity which occupied a good deal of Edmund's time was the Natural History Society, presided over by the Reverend L. H. ('Buggy') White, a descendant of White of Selborne.[23] Edmund soon knew the course of the rivers, the rarer flowers, the butterflies, the birds and the meadows in the surrounding area. As he was to write in 'The Country Round Christ's Hospital':

> *Sylvan and human, still it blows and calls . . .*
> *And asks the closest conscience of observant love.*[24]

In the classroom he was quick to show distinction and the strongest influences were French and Classics. H. Szumowski, a tall elegant Pole, was senior French master and a stimulating and generous man who rewarded good translations with a French novel or classic. Edmund's ability in translation is manifest in his first publication, *Poems Translated from the French*, printed at his own expense in 1914 at the same time as *Poems*. The eight translations are mostly from *The Oxford Book of French Verse*, and show a remarkable control of rhythm and rhyme, though the vocabulary is often mannered. Some of the best are translations of Verlaine – such as the sonnet 'After Three Years', which shows a linguistic and poetic competence considerably beyond what one might expect from a young sixth-former:

> *Opening the narrow tottering door, alone*
> *I passed within the garden, which the throng*
> *Of morning sunbeams softly strayed along,*
> *So that the dewy flowers glistened and shone.*

> *No change is there. The arbour overgrown*
> *With tangling vines, its chairs within, stands strong.*
> *Ever the fountain sings its silver song:*
> *Ever the aspen makes its ancient moan.*
> *And still the roses tremble there, and still*
> *Upon the wind the great proud lilies sway.*
> *I know each lark that drops there singing shrill,*
> *I found the very Velleda still set*
> *Beyond the elms, its plaster peeled away –*
> *Slender, among the odorous mignonette.*

Two men dominated the Classics side of the sixth form, and there could not have been a greater contrast between the two – F. H. Merk, senior Classics master, and his assistant S. E. Winbolt.

With 'Pimmy' Winbolt Edmund found an instant rapport. He was an Old Blue, youthful in manner and a brisk and lively talker. His range of interests was wide, covering literature, archaeology, drama and music. He wrote several archaeological handbooks and school texts, and edited an anthology of Coleridge, Lamb and Leigh Hunt – though surprisingly he omitted the lively autobiographical description of Leigh Hunt's schooldays. His enthusiasm sometimes led him into embarrassments. Commissioned to write a series of guide-books to English towns, he extolled the virtues of a particular town's museum, urging his readers not to omit a visit. Unfortunately the museum had been destroyed by fire some years earlier. On another occasion he wrote eagerly to *The Times* about archaeological discoveries in Folkestone, only to discover that he had been the victim of a practical joke. Despite these unscholarly lapses, or perhaps because of them, he endeared himself to his pupils. Edmund recalls him 'listening to one's tales and prejudices with utter gentleness'.[25] His love of Shelley was quickly passed on to his listeners and he was to supply much local information for Edmund's life of the poet thirty years later. Indeed, Edmund felt that there were some Shelley-like characteristics in Winbolt himself – something 'tameless, swift and proud'.[26] Edmund rarely left a debt unpaid, and his volume of poems, *Pastorals*, published in 1916, is dedicated to 'S. E. Winbolt, who has done more for my poetry than anyone beside'. Winbolt died in 1944 and Edmund described him as 'exhilarating, radiant, freedom-loving'.[27]

These would not have been the adjectives he would have used of his other no less influential teacher, 'Pill' Merk. Also an Old Blue, and a double-first from Balliol, Merk was a small, dark-complexioned, pedantic, somewhat humourless man, standing five foot three and largely bald. Where Winbolt was expansive, Merk shrank from the flamboyant. He was a greater scholar but a less accessible personality. Where Winbolt would sit behind his desk, surrounding himself with commentaries and never giving his own translation, Merk would stand in front of the class, listen to his pupils' efforts and then give his own original version. He was scornful of Winbolt's output of school texts, dismissing his efforts with the observation: 'Give Sammy some scissors and a pot of paste and he's happy.'[28] A revealing anecdote is told of a young colleague who witnessed Merk opening a window in Common Room, complaining of stuffiness. The younger man observed in an aside that it was extraordinary for a man of Merk's personality and sartorial habits to object to stuffiness; Merk overheard the remark and refused to speak to the man for years. It was this element of arid stuffiness which Edmund found so uncongenial, and it was a characteristic which was evident in Merk's manner of setting passages of English verse to be translated into alcaics or sapphics. Extracts from Shelley were his favourites, which he would read to the class in a grey monotone with his characteristic stifled vowels and curious hissings. Rarely can the spirit of delight have been more elusive. But Edmund owed a great deal to Merk, and his influence remained with him. In letters from the front to his schoolfriend Hector Buck, he is constantly recalling him – albeit not always favourably. Certainly he was an influential teacher. Middleton Murry, who was at Christ's Hospital just before Edmund, also came under the Merk spell. Murry discovered that Merk was highly regarded in Oxford classical circles and considered to be one of the great teachers of his time, and he was struck by Merk's reverence for his subject: 'in his heart was the religious humility of the priest before the sacrament'.[29] He also admired his insistence on 'precise and definite terms' in translation. Certainly Edmund benefited from this and he appeared some half-dozen times in the copy-book containing particularly noteworthy pieces of written work, a considerable achievement for a boy who had been learning Latin for barely five years. Some lines of Tennyson's *Enoch Arden* are represented, and a section of Coleridge's *Kubla Khan*:

> But oh! that deep romantic chasm which slanted
> Down the green hill athwart a cedarn cover!
> A savage place! as holy and enchanted
> As e'er beneath a waning moon was haunted
> By woman wailing for her demon-lover!

which became:

# PART ONE 1896 – 1915

*Rupibus et celsis o quam venerabilis illa*
*Vallis, ubi umbra tegit viridantem gramine collem*
*Cedrorum; quam saeva, et verbis dira malignis*
*In tali, perhibent, pronae sub lumine lunae*
*Infernum mulier deflens ululabat amantem.*[30]

An interesting insight into Merk is shown in his review for the school magazine of March 1924 of Edmund's *Christ's Hospital, A Retrospect*. It shows the usual loyalty of an Old Blue ('Christ's Hospital is fortunate beyond others in the devotion of her sons'), and it perceptively pinpoints Edmund's informal prose style, his attention to detail and his obsession with the opinions of the Romantic writers. It also shows how little Merk saw beneath the shy exterior of the schoolboy to the lively passions below:

Many of us remember Blunden here well enough and notice with pleasure that the literary promise he showed as a boy has been realised in the man. What comes as more of a surprise, though it need not be a surprise, is the ardent love the author shows for his old school. He reveals feelings which, perhaps, with a boy's shyness or reticence, were kept hidden before. He pays now, in this excellent work, his full debt of gratitude to this classic house.

Edmund had begun to read voraciously and the school library became the centre of his enthusiasm. It was part library, part museum, with fossils and Leigh Hunt's flowered silk waistcoat sharing the company of the books. The headmaster's secretary, 'Ratty' Rathbone, reluctantly opened the library for half an hour a day. This meagre ration was not enough for Edmund, eager to explore beyond the copies of the *Captain* and *Chums* (popular periodicals for boys) or the editions of G.A. Henty and Conan Doyle, to the enticing volumes beyond. One afternoon he was struck by the possibility of breaking into the library alone. The windows were only a little above the grass outside and, when he tried one, it yielded. Unfortunately he was inside for only a few moments before he was detected by the Housie bobby and handed over to his housemaster. The civilised Mr Goodwin did not mete out the expected thrashing, but merely enquired whether Edmund had a wheelbarrow waiting outside the window. Edmund recalled in an unpublished memorandum his fascination with the library, showing an early passion for the look, feel, illustrations and associations of books as well as the contents, which was to develop into expert book-hunting in the barrows of the Farringdon Road:

I was enchanted with the Library not so much on account of all the friendly fiction as because of the untold regions of books which it opened to my fancy. Never had I seen such wealth. I found poets who had never been names to me yet, and I had strange prepossessions about them – I felt they must all be good or they would not be here. The very bindings, the beautifully tinted and polished leathers – the usual old typographies – the grand sizes even of such volumes fascinated me. I believed it my destiny, if not duty, to read as many of them as I could – but time was against me, and all too soon Mr Rathbone was bawling out the order to put books away. James Thomson's *Seasons* or his *Castle of Indolence*, Leigh Hunt's *Imagination and Fancy*, Lytton's[31] translations from the German – how could I let you go? It presently occurred to me that I could have much greater freedom in the Library if I were to make myself better known, and even useful, to Mr Rathbone. There might be some point in his letting *me* serve out books to the Houses on occasions when he was otherwise employed. He was clearly pleased with the scheme, and I was entrusted with a key very often for the purpose. When I would then, I would go alone, and explore at will. Now there was a magnificent old bookcase, containing the John Thackeray Library, the bequest of a contemporary of Lamb and Coleridge – a delightful collection of fine books, eighteenth-century for the most part. That became my special prowling-ground; but I specially remember out of all its variety of prose and verse one handsome work. It was Samuel Ireland's *Picturesque Medway*, wherein were sepia pictures of Brandtbridges and Twyford Bridge, my chief haunts at home. There they were, yet not quite as I knew them; their earlier life, so to speak, was closed to me, and I dwelt on every similarity, every difference, as one in a dream.[32]

Edmund published his first poem in the school magazine, *The Blue*, in February 1913. It was a sonnet entitled 'The First Winter'. It was not a particularly distinguished piece ('When first dark winter, wrapt in scudding clouds') and it was never to be republished, but together with eleven further poems written for *The Blue* during his schooldays it reflects several characteristics of his later writing: a careful control of form, detailed description, close observation, love of dialect, a consciously literary tone and an eye cast backwards to traditional structures and themes rather than any modern experimentation. The self-conscious literary pose is emphasised by his sometimes signing with Greek pseudonyms. By October 1914 Edmund considered that he had forty-four poems worth preserving and he approached a printer, Mr Price of West Street in Horsham, with a view to publishing them – a bold step, revealing some of the toughness that lay behind the shy and modest exterior. The generous Mr Price agreed, was reluctant to accept payment, and a hundred copies were printed for sale at sixpence each, together with the same number of *Poems Translated from the French*. The subject-matter was predictably English pastoral – rivers, fishing, farmland and thunderstorms mixed with personal reminiscence ('Twyford Bridge'), and literary allusions ('On J. Blanco White'). None of the poems was to be reprinted but the voice of an acute observer of nature and a lyrical facility beyond the ordinary are abundantly clear. Perhaps the most successful is 'Joy and Grief'. It is a simple but delicate lyric, expressing in its opening lines the bittersweet mixture in nature which is also reflected in human experience:

> There is a joy in Spring,
> There is a grief in Spring.

Edmund's mother sent a copy of *Poems* to her godmother Lady Verney, who replied in a letter of 1915, from Claydon House, including some shrewd observations:

I think your son has a remarkable command of language and probably translating from the French is excellent practice. In his own poems it strikes me that sometimes the thought is rather slender to carry the words – but that is not the case in 'Joy and Grief' and 'Christmas Eve' and others that I like. I hope he will persevere and read a great deal, and hammer out his thoughts as well as polish his words.[33]

The 'good bit of stiffening' that Goodwin wanted to see in his character needed to be reflected in his writing. To some of Edmund's later critics it was too often to remain elusive, his poetry being seen as concentrating too much on exact description and avoiding human analysis. A very early critic suggested the same – a schoolboy companion, David Timothy, who composed a sonnet on Edmund in July 1914. It was flattering indeed to be already acknowledged at the age of seventeen as 'Blunden, the poet of the earth and sky', but Timothy urged Edmund to surrender his celebrations of nature and turn instead to 'sing of man':

> So shalt thou be as those great poets then,
> That did both please and teach their fellow-men.[34]

With his romantic good looks, generous personality and sharp mind, combined with a quiet authority which belied the initial aura of shyness, Edmund made friends easily and – as was to be the case in later life – across the age-range. Two of his contemporaries were to be commemorated in the poem 'Recollections of Christ's Hospital'. One was his first house captain, Geoffrey Woodhams, an early schoolboy hero who won the school steeplechase in 1910 ('burst through the gusts and sleet to finish first') and who was to be killed in action; the other was P. W. J. Stevenson, who had won the Latin Hexameter Prize ('the lofty Rhyme'). Edmund was never to forget Dr Upcott in chapel – where he had seen him alone, at prayer – announcing Stevenson's death at Festubert, the first Old Blue casualty of the war. More intimate friends were Colquhoun Fox, later to become a major-general, and the handsome sportsman and musician Dick Creese. When the news reached Edmund that Creese had died of pneumonia in November 1918 after returning from R A F service in Italy, it was a blow as heavy as any he had encountered. He immediately wrote a tribute for *The Blue*, a remarkable piece of writing for a young man of twenty-two:

He was my fellow ranger through all the pleasant land from Horsham to Pulborough. We tired the sun with talking . . . .

I see him yet by the study fire, giving and taking tea and comfortable advice: quoting Ovid in defence of nut butter, preparing Demosthenes and now and then remembering some small sin of omission, and as quickly forgetting it again. Those few friends of this evening freemasonry will hardly see life in such roseate hues again. He was the antidote to the day's worries and bade dull care begone with his slightest smile and twinkle. Some of us should have sat under his easy spell and fireside jollity at Oxford, but we reckoned without the blind Fury. Italy, which almost spelt his death in his crumpled plane, more quietly murdered him; I saw him a week before the end, tired and pale and – disguise it as he would – heavy-hearted. But the tragedy of death, subtly approaching even then, would have seemed a grotesque spectre. He stood with us on the bourne of new worlds for old. . . . But the edict had gone forth. . . .

The forenoon was so bright that the sudden dark is hoarse with an evil wind. Other friends remain; he was one in a thousand. We shall close our eyes in many a revery; remembering him – his happy, handsome looks; *sans souci* comradeship; inborn beauty of mind and manner. No one ever looked or stepped so true a gentleman.[35]

Another intimate friend was George Rheam, to whom Edmund was occasionally to send poems from France in 1917. An example of Edmund's generosity is the letter which he put in a sealed envelope, addressed to the Governors of Christ's Hospital, just before leaving for France in 1916, to be sent in the event of his death:

Sirs,

By the time that this letter is put before you, my death in action will have been noticed. I ask you, therefore, Sirs, particularly to consider what is the foremost of my dying wishes.

In July 1915 you were so generous as to award me (the Senior Grecian of Christ's Hospital) an exhibition for classics to the value of £70 p.a. This will now pass from me; but I wonder whether you would do me the great last honour of giving the exhibition, or part of it, to my friend George Turner Tatham Rheam of Coleridge A, Christ's Hospital. He is hoping to become an electrical engineer, and first of all to enter the City and Guilds Technical College, Finsbury; this ideal he cannot realise without help, and I long to see him doing well. This is why, Sirs, I ask that you be so good as to let my exhibition go to him: if he can by any means win through, I shall rest content.

That is my dying wish.[36]

Edmund also made arrangements for specific volumes from his own library to go to Rheam, Creese and Fox.

A slightly younger contemporary was Hector Buck, who was to remain a close friend for sixty years. He remembers being 'trades monitor to Edmund's house captaincy, classical Deputy Grecian to his Grecianship, scrum-half to his stand-off', and recalls that as Senior Grecian Edmund:

was a shy performer in public, and one of his first duties was to read an honorific address to A. L. Smith, a distinguished Old Blue, soon to become Master of Balliol, lunching with Dr Upcott in Dining Hall. Edmund mounted the dais in something near stage-fright; the blood drained from his face; his whole body could be seen to tremble; the scroll in his hands shook intolerably. In later life he was to conquer this nervousness and attain a platform manner; but his apprehension at the prospect of speaking or lecturing in public never quite left him.[37]

In 1922 Edmund admitted: 'Poetry is one thing; lecturing another; the very nature which drives a man into poetry is likely to make him shrink from the platform, and I do not feel equal to the nervous strain'.[38]

'Buckie' was to be main recipient, apart from Edmund's family, of letters from the trenches – filled with enquiries about life at school. Later Buckie was to return to Christ's Hospital as a Classics teacher and housemaster and regularly act as host for Edmund, often joining him on the cricket field. He wrote in 1974: 'C.H. was never out of Edmund's mind, or if it was, the slightest reminder, a name, an allusion, would bring it back.'[39] Edmund followed its fortunes throughout his life, compiling what he hoped would be a comprehensive bibliography of Old Blue writers and taking a special interest in the literary and academic careers of such Old Blues as Keith Douglas and Jack Morpurgo[40] and in the sporting success of such old boys as

Billy Cullen, Tom Pearce and Dennis Silk.[41] He also had a particular respect and affection for Upcott's successor, Sir William Hamilton Fyfe, and approved of his declaration that it was his 'mature and unshakeable conviction that Christ's Hospital is the best school in the world'.[42]

One other friendship was to have unusual repercussions later. The son of Rudyard Kipling's schoolmaster, Cornell Price, was Kipling's ward and Edmund recalls him as a 'quiet, gracious, rather lonely boy, whose sweet serious looks I see as I write, and altogether he answers to Lamb's description of a Blue as stealing along with the self-concentration of a young monk. I do not know how it came about, but Price and I became romantic friends.'[43] Price invited Edmund to stay with him in the holidays and meet Mr Kipling. Edmund was longing for Yalding and declined the invitation, which was never repeated. 'The mystery is that our friendship ever ended or when it did. Perhaps my gloomy resistance to Mr Kipling's compositions was the reason!'[44] And the resistance was intense, despite his father's admiration and that of his friend C. L. Fox. Years later he was to record: 'In 1915 my antipathy to Kipling took its lasting form when I became a voluntary member of the New Armies and bought a pamphlet in which he described people like me. It was so hideous a dismissal of such creatures into the bottomless pit of war that I never could forgive. To him they were the merest cannon-fodder.'[45]

In the *Nation and Athenaeum* in 1923 Edmund wrote one of his rare hostile notices when reviewing Kipling's *The Irish Guards in the Great War*. After four paragraphs of evocative prose describing his own war experiences he complains that Kipling ignores the 'pandemonium and nerve-strain of war' and the 'appalling misery which brought seasoned men down.'[46]

Kipling died in 1936. For seventeen years he had been literary adviser to the Imperial War Graves Commission, and Sir Fabian Ware asked Edmund to replace him. Edmund had no desire to accept: 'for I can think of nothing I resent more than the extinction of young men in battle; and I had no desire to play a Kipling part when it comes to incising three or four words of respect on the tombstones of those who, but for the Kipling mind, would be quietly increasing the fruits of the earth, material and immaterial.'[47] He suggested that Kipling would not have approved of him as a successor, but Sir Fabian replied that Kipling had been very much Edmund's admirer and would have applauded the appointment. Edmund was later to feel that war cemeteries commemorated those who had 'died for their friends' and that they were 'in a sense the poetry of that action'.[48] Reluctantly he accepted the appointment, partly because Sir Fabian was so 'amiable and graceful', partly out of a feeling of guilt for his antipathy to Kipling and also out of respect for his school friend Price. Once again he failed to take Goodwin's advice and learn to say no; indeed, it was advice he was never to follow.

By July 1914 the shadow of war was growing darker, though Edmund had no great awareness of its imminence. He had though already begun to wear military uniform, for membership of the school Officers' Training Corps was compulsory. This marked the beginning of Edmund's ambivalent relationship with soldiering – an activity which both stimulated and appalled him. His respect for tradition, his enjoyment of physical activity, and his pleasure in communal life, all found release in military training. An inspection by Field Marshal Sir John French was a memorable, impressive occasion: 'He looked at me with a deep gentleness, asked my age, and slowly passed by'[49]. When the horrors of fighting revealed themselves, he came to see the OTC as a dehumanising force – propagating 'the old lie' of patriotic sacrifice. He was, though, too much of a conventional schoolboy in 1914 to feel the contradictions more than obliquely. Not for him the flamboyant assertivenss of Robert Graves who resigned from his school OTC at Charterhouse.

Some isolated incidents unnerved him. In a geography lesson of 'Cabbie' Barrett's he had been reprimanded for inattention: 'Blunden. A blunderer by name and nature. Now, in a time of national crisis, all the Blundens will be knocked on the head.'[50] The phrase 'a time of national crisis' was disturbing as was Goodwin's quiet prophecy one lunchtime that 'it looks as though within a month the whole of Europe will be at war.'[51] It was school policy, however, that those boys working for university places should complete their courses, so Edmund did not discard his blue coat until the summer of 1915. He had arrived in 1909, an unsophisticated country boy; he left as Senior Grecian, with an Oxford scholarship and with two small volumes of published verse. He had learned to 'love the Brotherhood'[52] and was a widely read and well-educated young man. A far grimmer education was waiting for him, however, just across the Channel.

# PART TWO
## 1915 – 1919

As to my return to panting war, war crying for water
from a myriad blackening lips, war lying in seeping
blood with the sweat still on the cheeks, war looking up
with flat, squat, livid face from the churned mudflat —
three weeks dead and only good as a stepping stone — no
news as yet.

I don't say war is all like that — those are his most
terrible masks. Sometimes war means painted ladies
hovering over the bar with drinks and effusive smiles; or
sometimes it means a deck-chair outside a Watteauesque
maisonette, where the vine is just empurpling and the
aspen lisps and glistens, and the housedog dozes in the
sun. . . .

War's classical name should have been Proteus.
Picture this scene. The Division is on the move: the
roads are alive with tramping men and mules, cars,
chargers, ambulances, limbers, lorries and crunching
tractors hauling the heavier guns; and the dreamy spires
of Béthune catch the splinter-like sun-ray that first
pierces the mist; and the miners troop along to the pits
with clumsy clogs and crimson cravats — slightly soiled;
and hares prick up their ears and watch in wonder; and
windmill sails perk over the gentle downs just like the
listening ears of these shy hares.

Letter to his mother, 1918[1]

# 4

# Training
## August 1915 – May 1916

*Blunden, always known to me as 'The Rabbit', with his gentle ways and his unassuming manner, was not born to be a soldier but he became one in spite of himself. His acute brain was tuned for instant action and he performed arduous duties with conspicuous success and courage. He ruled by 'love' and earned the respect and real affection of all with whom he came in contact.*
Colonel G. H. Harrison, 11th Royal Sussex Regiment [1]

*I was not anxious to go.*
Undertones of War, 1928

On a fine sunny day in August 1915 Edmund took a bicycle-ride across country from Framfield to Chichester to the headquarters of the Royal Sussex Regiment, carrying with him letters of recommendation for a commission. A fortnight later, having spent his £50 clothing allowance on uniform and a sword, he reported as a second lieutenant to a training camp at Weymouth, before moving to a larger one at Shoreham. It was a strangely peaceful introduction to the art of war. There were far more officers than 'other ranks', so there was time between lectures and bouts of physical exercise to browse in Brighton bookshops (discovering some cheap eighteenth-century volumes) or even to walk the forty miles home – and although some officers in the camp had seen active service, they were curiously silent about their experiences and more likely to compose bawdy limericks. Life became still less warlike at the end of the year when Edmund was moved to a camp in Ireland, in a large ruined mansion a few miles outside Cork. Even at the age of eighteen he took every opportunity to explore literary avenues – buying an edition of Tom Moore's *Irish Songs* in Fermoy for a penny, discovering that the occupant of the next bed was a descendant of Keats's[2] friend Richards, and finding an eager literary conversationalist in the Adjutant, Gordon Reah.

Every spare moment was dedicated to writing poetry in celebration of the countryside around him and he began to experiment with longer narrative poems. By the spring of 1916 he was able to publish three slim volumes with the help of his brother Gilbert and J. Brooker of Uckfield, the dedications clearly showing Edmund's sense of personal association with the Romantic writers – even as a young school-leaver. The first – consisting of four poems including 'The Barn'[3] (a long piece celebrating the 'simple wane and change' of rural life) – was dedicated to Leigh Hunt: 'one of the most lovely-hearted men that have ever been'. On the front page was printed the facetious inscription:

'I hate your loathesome Poems.' (One Critic)

'Surprisingly mature and original.' (Another Critic)

The second volume was *Three Poems*, this time dedicated to John Clare: 'Truly he caught the soul of the village and farm in the fine-meshed net of poetry surprisingly beautiful.' The three poems were 'Stane Street',[4] 'The Gods of the World Beneath'[5] and (much more significant) 'The Silver Bird of Herndyke Mill'[6] – a poem showing a control of narrative combined with close observation, and telling a moral similar to Wordsworth's 'Goody Blake and Harry Gill'. The third volume was a combination of the other two and was published as *The Harbingers*. This caught the perceptive eye of Lady Verney, who wrote to Edmund's mother: 'I think *The Harbingers* shows a very distinct advance on the poems you sent me before, in thought and technical execution and in observation of Nature. I feel there is a great deal of movement and animation in all the descriptions of running water.'[7] As well as developing his narrative skill, Edmund was still writing shorter poems and he sent off some twenty lyrics and sonnets to Gertrude Ford for her series of *Little Books of Georgian Verse*. He declared his intention in his introductory poem:

> *I sing of the rivers and hamlets and woodlands*
> *of Sussex and Kent,*[8]

and the collection was published as *Pastorals* in June 1916.

But this represented a brief poetic interlude. In the early spring of 1916 he found himself back at Shoreham, taking a company of convalescent soldiers on a daily march. They would not talk of war, so the young Edmund was still basically in ignorance of what lay in store for him when he saw his name posted on the Mess notice-board among those who would proceed to the British Expeditionary Force in France in two or three days.

There was just time for a brief visit to Framfield to say farewell to the family, and to see the young girl who had succeeded Lavinia in his affections – Nora Morley. She lived at Heaver's Mill, and their youthful, brief but tender relationship is the inspiration of the poem 'The Watermill'.[9] After a walk through the glebe-lands and attendance at Sunday-morning service at Yalding, it was time to take the train to Victoria and thence to Folkestone and Boulogne. On the platform at Victoria there were several soldiers returning to France after leave. One was a sturdy Scotsman who asked Edmund his age. On discovering that he was nineteen, his eyes filled with tears and he murmured to himself, 'Only a boy – only a boy!'[10]

From Boulogne he was sent to Etaples for a day's military instruction – a final session in the 'Bull-Ring, that thirsty savage, interminable training-ground'[11] – where he was taught to use a Hales rifle-grenade. It was a dramatic moment of instruction for there was a loud explosion, and the sergeant-major who was demonstrating its use, and boasting about his safety record, suddenly fell to the ground with half his head blown off.

On the next afternoon they moved south-east to Béthune and then a little north, first to Locon and then to Le Touret, where they found themselves billeted in a pleasant farm. The teenaged Edmund was about to experience his first day of war.

# 5

# Festubert, Cuinchy, Richebourg
## May – July 1916

*I see myself at many a spot from Neuve Chapelle to*
*Cuinchy Brickstacks, a humble Don Quixote facing war*
*with beautiful idiocy.*
De Bello Germanico, 1918[1]

Edmund thus arrived in France as a young pastoral poet unexpectedly transformed into an inexperienced soldier. Unlike many of his contemporary writers he did not develop a markedly new wartime poetic voice, but remained a predominantly pastoral poet within a war setting – still describing himself in 1919 as 'a harmless young shepherd in a soldier's coat'.[2] While Wilfred Owen and Isaac Rosenberg were depicting the grim realities of war, while Siegfried Sassoon was sharpening his ironic voice to expose the arrogant isolation of the High Command, Edmund was more often celebrating the variety of the changing seasons and refining the focus of his poetic eye. With a few striking exceptions his war poems concentrate on the courage of his comrades, the nature of the landscape or life away from the Front Line; the horrors and ironies are muted, the tone still often deliberately literary, as if he were striving to keep the role of observing poet separate from that of active soldier. His prose too reflects this detachment in descriptions as vivid in their poetic richness as the starkly realistic language of Frederic Manning's *The Middle Parts of Fortune*.[3]

It was not that Edmund was to have little Front Line experience for it is likely that he spent more time in the trenches than any other recognised war writer. Wilfred Owen was to see about eight months at the Front, Charles Sorley less than a year, Robert Graves almost exactly a year, Ivor Gurney approximately fifteen months, Siegfried Sassoon sixteen and Isaac Rosenberg nineteen months. It is probable that only David Jones's[4] twenty-two months could compete with Edmund's two years in the firing-line. It was perhaps not just good fortune which saved him from being wounded or shell-shocked, for although he was not a natural soldier he was athletic, fit and quick in movement as well as mind. Photographs from this period show a sensitive young man looking uncomfortable in untidy uniform; they also reveal penetrating eyes and a set of the face which suggest a strong will and a firm determination.

In mid-1916 the British held the Front Line from Ypres in the north to the Somme in the south. The 11th Sussex were almost halfway between the two, around the canal which ran between Béthune to the west and La Bassée to the east. Though still subject to daily firing, it was relatively quiet at the time of Edmund's arrival, but was horribly scarred from the heavy fighting in the previous year, just five miles south at Loos and Hill 70. The battalion's main activity was holding a series of 'keeps' (old sandbagged ruins) and 'islands' (isolated one-man posts) around Givenchy, just north of the canal. There were a few duckboards between these islands but the usual route was through mud and, as there were no communication trenches, all movement had to be by night.

On his first evening Edmund's job was to take provisions towards the Front Line and he joined the transport convoy of wagons and mules, taking rations to the islands around Canadian Orchard. The realities of war were not slow to reveal themselves; in the afternoon, in the quiet of Le Touret, he had enjoyed the peace of the French landscape: 'I had seen nothing but green fields and plumy grey-green trees and intervening tall roofs; it was as though in this part the line could only be a trifling interruption of a happy landscape. I thought the Vicarage must lie among those sheltering boughs';[5] by the evening, he was hearing the 'zip' of shells passing his ear and 'Knew that the fear of my infancy, to be among flying bullets, was now realised'.[6] He then prepared for his first night in a trench – surroundings which were to become only too horribly familiar as his 'home' over the next three years.

Edmund was attached to C Company, who were occupying reserve trenches, and his first evening was undramatic. He was introduced to the trench slang of 'Minnies' and 'ack-ack'[7] and to the ubiquitous rats, but having drunk his first trench 'lemonade' – 'a powerful ration of lime-juice, trench sugar (duly blended with tea) and chlorinated water' – he slept soundly until mid-morning on a bed of sandbags and blankets. Each day following was to be a painful education as he tried to marry conflicting sensations and come to terms with the ever-changing face of war. He remembered the beautiful tranquillity of the first morning at Festubert:

The hot gold sun was already drowsy in the blue, and the war seemed to have slunk into a corner and fallen asleep. Old friends seemed to be all round; a skylark was floating and climbing steep above us, like his cousins over Sussex lands, with his fine melody let fall in prodigal enchantments. There was the growing drone of summer in the grassfields and orchards behind, and on the broken hawthorn tree the blackbird was asking what war was; and did not see the sparrowhawk hanging blood-thirstily over the stubbles. A tabby cat came sleekly round a traverse and purred peace and goodwill.[8]

Within a few hours he was being taken on a tour of the immediate area and returned with visions of bones sticking through trench-walls, skulls, wooden crosses marking graves and unburied bodies in rotted uniforms. A sense of the country itself being made to suffer was brought home even more clearly when he was taken to the Front Line by the 'overland route', crossing the Old German Line of the Aubers Ridge battle of the previous year. He was soon scrambling across the ground by moonlight, with whizzing bullets overhead and festoons of wire at his feet. On his return, he recorded his feeling of the earth itself suffering, in 'Festubert: The Old German Line':

> Sparse mists of moonlight hurt our eyes
> With gouged and scourged uncertainties
> Of soul and soil in agonies. [9]

He was seeing and recording everything with a poet's eye and became acutely sensitive to the changing light, both natural and artificial. In the 'cover trench' at Canadian Orchard he had been instructed in the use of flares and also learned the unnerving truth that the British Very lights were so inferior to the enemy's that the Germans used to throw up lighted matches from their trenches in mock retaliation.

Within a few days he was back in 'stand-to' billets in Festubert, where life was quieter. His main duties were to go round the company at evening and daybreak, and organise nightly pick-and-shovel parties to dig communication trenches – when casualties were frequent. Two things made a particular impression: the natural beauty of Festubert and the honest good-humour of the soldiers. With his fellow Sussex men he found it easy to relax (with those senior to him he was generally nervous and ill at ease) and there was for him, at this stage, still an element of the shared adventure of war: 'The sound sense of what I had seen in this short time, the chances of excitement, the return to nature feeling, and the goodwill of everyone, made a great appeal to me.'[10]

As to Festubert itself, there was plenty to be enchanted with. There was the pretty little chapelle to the Virgin Mary, which he portrayed in 'The Festubert Shrine'.[11] He enclosed this poem in a letter to his mother, and described an eerie experience: 'The church of this village is spattered and shattered but the crucifix stands: I passed it unsuspectingly at two a.m. one morning and I could hardly believe my eyes to see the crucifixion before me. But then I realised this was only an effigy and no vision. The machine-gun began to put bullets across, and I moved on.'[12] He began to be haunted, in virtually every town or village which he visited, by the ghosts of the pre-war life – typically recording in 'A House in Festubert':

> It held, one time, such happy hours;
> The tables shone with smiles and filled
> The hungry – Home! 'twas theirs,' tis ours;
> We house it here and laugh unkilled.
> Hoarse gun, now, pray you – .[13]

In *De Bello Germanico*, written in 1918, he was also to recall Festubert, significantly remembering the beauty of the place more than the cries of the wounded:

. . . the heavy dew and ricochets and blackbird-flutes of early morning; the incredible tom-tom croaking of innumerable frogs in the dikes and culverts; the indolent mid-day under runaway flowering boughs; the evening tramp up communication trenches full of the 'dead-man smell' of that marshland, suggesting a ferment of Church lilies; and starry midnight dreaming a majesty on those lath-and-plaster ruins, the whooping owls by the Church corner, the groaning stretcher-cases borne along the street, past my fairy rosebush blossomed silverly beyond belief, all these things and many more still make Festubert for me what it was then, 'a tale, a dream', the village beyond the world. There I truly enjoyed the war, and touched new mentality.

But this mood was not to last for long. For one thing, there was the constant reminder that things were 'hotting up' just south of the canal; for another, he was soon back in the Front Line. The trenches had been flooded in the previous winter and some of the troops had even drowned in them. The warmer weather was now drying them to a

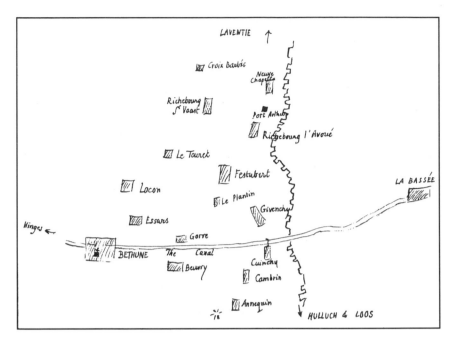

EB's own sketch of the area around Festubert in 1916, drawn in
Aki Hayashi's copy of *Undertones of War*

sticky clay. The daytime routine was mostly tedious inactivity; the
night-time consisted of excursions into No Man's Land to 'mend the
wire'. On one of these expeditions Edmund came under what seemed
like uncannily accurate fire on the part of the Germans – only to
discover that an electric torch in his pocket had turned itself on,
making him a sitting target; it was to be the first of many miraculous
escapes. Enemy activity was beginning to increase in volume, and
particularly sinister was the effectiveness of two German machine-
guns, Blighty Albert and Quinque Jimmy, whose firing caused havoc
in the food supply, so that the rations of bread and bacon often arrived
impregnated with sugar and wet sandbag. Added to these discomforts
were the effects of sleeplessness and a growing irritation with
'Authority' and what he saw as an obsession with red-tape – an attitude brought sharply into focus after a patrol, sent out to investigate a
suspected sniper's post, had returned with a wounded man who later
died from the injuries sustained in the exercise. The leader of the

54

patrol sent in a full and detailed report. Edmund recorded the reaction of the General: 'The Olympian comment was, "Too flowery for a military report". Our chieftain could not encourage anything that bore the semblance of the mental method of a world before the war. That temperaments vary was a conception which he doggedly cancelled.'[14] If Edmund's baptism into war had had its gentler moments and feelings of 'adventure', the mood was certainly changing in the late spring of 1916, and two extra spectres began to haunt him as the battalion moved into rest billets at Hinges, west of Béthune: 'the Possible Intrusion of catechizing Generals, and the Probable Duration of the War'.[15]

The area around Hinges was attractive enough with well-cultivated fields, pleasant barns and orchards. It was a time for letter-writing and relaxation, despite the embarrassment caused by Edmund's reading about himself while censoring the mail: 'judging by the latest specimen of an officer we have had sent to our Company, I shan't have any trouble getting my commission.'[16] He was billeted in a comfortable farmhouse where the genial farmer recited a couple of La Fontaine's fables over dinner, and where there was a welcome opportunity for some sustained reading.

Edmund's wartime library – whatever was small enough to cram into his pockets – was a varied collection and, as he explained to his mother, 'all are amused and amazed by my book habits.'[17] The collection consisted in part of books like the rarely consulted New Testament, which had been given him on leaving England, and in part of books which he requested from Sussex booksellers, such as Shelley, Masefield, Cobbett and Leigh Hunt (which arrived just in time to provide his reading during the opening days of Passchendaele). He also asked to be sent books and magazines from home, discovering Siegfried Sassoon's poems in the *Cambridge Magazine* at Ypres, and he brought some favourite volumes with him – *John Clare*, which he had chosen as a prize at Christ's Hospital, and, surprisingly, Edward Young's *Night Thoughts*. He often found Young's moods and thoughts appropriate:

> *Today is so like yesterday, it cheats;*
> *We take the lying sister for the same.*
> *Life glides away, Lorenzo! like a brook,*
> *For ever changing, unperceived the change.*
> *In the same brook none ever bathed him twice;*
> *To the same life none ever twice awoke.*

'I felt', he wrote,

the benefit of this grave and intellectual voice, speaking out of a profound eighteenth-century calm, often in metaphor which came home to one even in a pillbox. The mere amusement of discovering lines applicable to our crisis kept me from despair:

> *Dreadful post*
> *of observation! darker every hour.*[18]

Such reading was supplemented by chance discoveries in ruined and derelict houses where he picked up volumes of Tennyson and H. G. Wells as well as Caesar's *De Bello Gallico* and an edition of Horace. One find late in 1918 caused him particular pleasure. Billeted in a ruined house in Arras, he found a hole in the wall by the side of his bed. Feeling inside, his hand rested on a copy of Edward Thomas's study of John Keats. Thomas had been killed at the battle of Arras, and Edmund never gave up hope that it was the author's own copy: 'I fancied that I could see the tall, Shelley-like figure of the poet gathering together his equipment for the last time, hastening out of this ruined building to join his men and march into battle, and forgetting his copy of John Keats.'[19]

The respite at Hinges was short-lived. Late one afternoon, all officers were ordered to report to battalion headquarters. There was 'something in the air', and the dreaded orders to move into trenches south of the canal were received. Edmund, however, was sent to Essars on a brief gas course. His asthma was giving him trouble, and he was allowed exemption from wearing the flannel mask over his head – a temporary relief, but an ominous warning of what could happen if he was to be exposed to any quantity of gas in the future. Three days later he joined his company in trenches at Cuinchy.

The area south of the canal was far bleaker than that to the north and showed signs of recent heavy warfare. The ground was pocked with shell-holes and littered with tangled telegraph wires. The canal itself was green, glutinous, stagnant and stinking. Edmund's immediate destination, 'Whizzbang Keep', had received 600 shells in the morning of his arrival and he was not sorry to be called back to company headquarters at homely-sounding Kingsclere, a large dugout that had once been a cellar, where he was required to update maps of the surrounding trenches. Firing was heavy at times, particularly on Esperanto Terrace – a deep trench lined with dugouts, where he first experienced the hot blasts of air from exploding shells. Another new experience occurred at midnight some days later, when a mine was blown under the front trenches, causing sixty casualties, and Edmund's dugout was blown to and fro like a see-saw. He went out with a volunteer stretcher-party, through whizzing cross-fire and 'the death dance of flares and rockets'.[20] As he described it, simply: 'It was my first wild night.'[21] In the midst of all these discomforts he never lost his eye for moments of natural beauty in an otherwise bleak landscape. In his diary entry for 19 May 1916 he recorded his pleasure at seeing the 'deep red poppies, white and blue cornflowers, darnel and moondaisies' which adorn the 'back of our communication trench'.[22]

The company was very soon moved into the Front Line to defend the 'brickstacks', twenty or so of which stuck out of the wild landscape at erratic intervals. Their stifling · interiors held secret machine-gun posts or look-outs, and underneath them were tunnels, stores and telephone positions. From these nerve centres ran a series of steps towards the ditch which was the Front Line, and then there was No Man's Land, gouged into mine-craters. Right in front of Edmund's trench was Jerusalem Crater, a deep ditch with muddy water at the bottom. It could be entered under a sandbag parapet, where a sentry was positioned with a periscope trained on the opposite lip. Edmund went, one night, to investigate the other side but saw no signs of any Germans, though *Minenwerfers* (small black trench-mortars which hovered menacingly in the air) fell into the crater daily, with monotonous regularity, and firing increased the next day in retaliation for a British plane flying over and dropping half-a-dozen bombs into the German trenches – an action bitterly resented by the British soldiers. Tiredness to the point of exhaustion was becoming an increasing burden and, having crawled out of the trenches after a gruelling dawn 'stand-to' duty, he collapsed on a pile of sandbags and instantly fell asleep, miraculously escaping injury or detection. A couple of nights' relief in the little village of Annequin, with lobster salad and evening walks by the marshes, provided brief refreshment before the Cuinchy trenches called again; and then the welcome orders came to retire to the rest-billets at Hinges. It was a body of staggering men who set out on that long nine-mile march westward. The 'rest' consisted of an inevitably rigorous training programme, and Edmund was pleased to escape to take charge of a bombing-school store in the outbuildings of a château in Paradis, where the owner and his two daughters entertained him in the evenings to singing and conversation in the drawing room. It seemed like Paradise indeed. All too soon, however, he was back at Hinges, before the battalion moved north to the Richebourgs – two villages just south of Neuve Chapelle.

## PART TWO   1915 – 1919

For a while there was the comfort of lodgings with wire-netting bunks and the relaxation of a concert party, before holding the Front Line again in very wet and muddy conditions. Mounds of trench-mortar bombs, known as plum puddings and footballs, were a threatening sign; and the Germans bombarded them with howitzer shells, 'black crumps', which were shot a hundred feet into the air before bursting in sooty smoke. Edmund began to have a nervous phobia about the gunfire of his own men, which disturbed him, at times, more than that of the Germans. He had good reason to be concerned, for after exploring a sap which snaked out into No Man's Land and coming within twenty paces of a German soldier he returned the next night to explore a hidden dyke and – having over-extended his absence – was fired on by his own sentry on his return. He described the incident in a letter to his father, who was now installed as a schoolmaster on the training ship *Mount Edgcumbe* at Plymouth:

My nightly steps have been, on two occasions lately, out towards Fritz's wire. By a misunderstanding we were almost done-in by our own riflemen, as we were coming into our own wire. Small splinters hit me in the face, off the wire. There is a rose tree flowering near some pollards which mark an old sap of the shock-headed Hun; and I hope to bring back one of its roseate blooms as a souvenir tonight. One takes a Colt [revolver] and two or three Mills [grenades] on these occasions, some also take knobkerries. Of course I have the wind up about twenty knots per hour![23]

The battalion's main function was to act as a decoy to keep the German troops away from the Somme in the south, and an unsuccessful but costly attack was made on a section of the German line known as the Boar's Head, on 30 June. On the next day, 20,000 British troops were to die on the opening day of the battle of the Somme, which was to rage fiercely for the next five months. On the same day Edmund wrote a letter home which, like so many letters from the Front, is a moving moment of domesticity in contrast to the horrors around him. He enclosed £2 7s 6d to cover the cost of some more books to be sent out to him and also to supplement the pocket-money of his young sisters. He reminisces about the Yalding Church choir and ends simply: 'A nightingale sang on our barbed wire a few nights ago but was greeted only with bullets from Fritz. He stuck to it well!'[24]

In early July his company was south of the canal again in the Cambrin sector occupying a position at the head of a mineshaft. Gas was becoming a more common hazard, and Edmund's asthma was particularly irritated by the effects of a tear-gas known as pineapple gas. But this was small discomfort in comparison with the macabre sights of the trenches: a *Minenwerfer* exploded at the entrance of a mineshaft and a soldier was carried past Edmund, 'collapsing like a sack of potatoes, spouting blood at twenty places';[25] a young lance-corporal, making tea one afternoon, was hit by a shell and Edmund recalled 'the gobbets of blackening flesh, the earth-wall sotted with blood, with flesh, the eye under the duckboard, the pulpy bone';[26] It was a relief to be taken back to Béthune in the bizarre comfort of a camouflaged London bus, but he was soon in the trenches at Richebourg, where he found in a rubbish pit a pair of boots still containing someone's feet. After a further brief spell in Cuinchy, he was back at Givenchy, where he received a summons from the Colonel. Nervously he reported to him, only to discover that the first reason for the meeting was to congratulate him on a favourable review of *Pastorals* which the civilised Colonel had read in the *Times Literary Supplement*, and secondly to inform him that he was to remain at battalion headquarters as Field Works Officer. It was to be a brief interlude, however, for the Somme was ominously beckoning. Of an evening in mid-July Edmund wrote:

And now, as I lie in bed in my billet, after a conversation on infant schools with the lady teacher whose house it is, with trees softly swaying almost to the window, and only the odd night voices of an ancient town about me, I conjecture briefly, yet with a heaving breast, of that march southward which begins tomorrow morning. It will be a new world again.[27]

# 6

# The Somme
## July – December 1916

*But still 'There's something in the air', I hear
And still 'We're going south, man, deadly near'.*
'Two Voices'[1]

*We go to the holocaust of the Somme, but kindly
heaven has blessed us with ignorance – when ignorance
is bliss!*
Letter to his mother, 1916[2]

The Somme was to offer a vivid contrast to the previous months, both
in landscape and warfare. Hills, valleys and woods replaced the flat
countryside around the Béthune – La Bassée canal, and it was easy to
see why the area had been a favoured holiday spot before 1914. Just
east of Amiens the River Somme is joined by the River Ancre, which
flows down from north-west of Bapaume – the final goal of the British
advance. Between its source and the town of Albert, the Ancre runs
through a wooded valley, and a hundred feet above the village of
Thiepval and its wood stands the plateau of Thiepval Ridge – commanding an unrivalled view of the surrounding countryside, looking
across the river to Mesnil Ridge and Aveluy Wood. The Germans had
held Thiepval and its side of the river since September 1914; the
British had occupied the opposite bank only since relieving the French
army some ten months previously. The Germans had cut their lines
out of the chalk with precision, they had ingeniously hidden their
command posts and gun emplacements around the wooded landscape,
and they could view most of the British activity with ease; the British
were in trenches which, apart from exceptions like the long Jacob's
Ladder which ran from Mesnil to Hamel, were often rough and ready,

confused and horribly vulnerable and exposed. No Man's Land was not a defined stretch of wasteland which needed the attention of stealthy wiring-parties: it was an ill-defined nightmare world, where one could easily lose direction and which was under constant fire. No longer would the battalion be moved from place to place. It was to be a few months of static war, based in uninhabited ghost villages, making constant raids on the enemy in order to drive him back – all part of the Big Push which was intended to drive the Germans off French soil by the end of the year.

This was the theatre of war which Edmund entered in late August. The battalion had paused for several days on the journey south, at Monchy-Breton, whose terrain resembled that of the Somme valley. Here they became more familiar with the use of gas, and were initiated into the violent secrets of the bayonet. Apart from some light-hearted moments – including an hour's catching practice with apples in an orchard at Le Souich – the journey south was a solemn one through hot, sultry weather and with little co-operation from the French. Edmund complained in a letter of 26 August:

I regret to say that the French villagers show a nasty spirit in many cases, to the Tommies – they dismantle wells and pumps to prevent them from getting water, they swindle outrageously in their everyday deals, and they are constantly probing them for information. Another war will see some remarkable differences, for the men are not encouraged by these things from the people they are defending.[3]

As they approached the Ancre valley the weather turned to rain, and remained wet for much of the next few months. The battalion was based first in Warnimont Wood, six miles west of Beaumont Hamel, and then in a wood just outside Mailly-Maillet, three miles from the German lines. Edmund was kept busy organising the movement of supplies of bombs and ammunition to suitable positions forward of Hamel, in preparation for projected attacks. The British were liable to be fired on at any point – the Germans were constantly on the look-out, both from their superior position on Thiepval Ridge and from observation balloons – and Mesnil, in particular, was a vulnerable area in Edmund's daily routine of fetching and carrying: it was 'a vile, unnerving and desperate place'.[4] The immediate target was an attack on Beaumont Ridge on 3 September. Edmund was fortunate to be behind the main attack as the massive bombardment begun, but then had to run with buckets of bombs to the forward trenches as required. His carrying party was not enthusiastic and he was forced to shout and swear as he led them through the thick, green smoke which screened the presence of flying white-hot chunks of iron shrapnel. The situation quickly became chaotic. The confusion of No Man's Land, and the unexpectedly efficient and elaborate communication system in the German trenches, quickly forced a British retreat with heavy casualties. The 49th Division had managed an advance of scarcely twenty yards. Immediately afterwards, Edmund recorded his feelings in a poem ironically entitled 'Preparations for Victory', which ended:

> Days or eternities like swelling waves
> Surge on, and still we drudge in this dark maze,
> The bombs and coils and cans by strings of slaves
> Are borne to serve the coming day of days;
> Pale sleep in slimy cellars scarce allays
> With its brief blank the burden. Look, we lose;
> The sky is gone, the lightless drenching haze
> Of rainstorm chills the bone; earth, air are foes,
> The black fiend leaps brick-red as life's last picture goes. [5]

After the failure of the attack of 3 September the battalion withdrew to the village of Englebelmer to reorganise and was then sent to Auchonvillers, 'a good example of the miscellaneous picturesque, pitiable, pleasing, appalling, woundingly intimate village ruin close to the line'.[6] Edmund was reappointed Field Works Officer and spent the next few weeks repairing and reorganising the trenches, an occupation which gave him curious satisfaction. It was a relatively quiet period, and there was time for letter-writing. Edmund managed to maintain a regular correspondence, often in lengthy letters, throughout the war and longed for letters in return. He complained to his mother that his brothers and sisters did not write more regularly:

I often wonder why some of them don't find time to write me a letter – surely they can do so more easily than I can? For very often with us it's a case of: 'Write that letter or get that hour's sleep?' A nasty dilemma.

They don't realise how much we depend on the mail from England to keep our spirits up. The war may look comfortable and amusing through the curious glasses of the newspapers but to those actually in it, it shows a very different face.[7]

As well as writing letters he also managed to sustain an intensity of reading which would have done justice to a peacetime undergraduate – but he felt the lack of books particularly deeply: 'I miss the companionship of books ever so and after the blessed war I shall be still more buried in the dust of old libraries and compassed about with leather quartos.'[8] In his lists of requests for items to be sent from home, books figure significantly. He wrote to his mother:

I send a cheque for £5, yours except for the following things:
1. Pocket-money for Figg.
2. Six razor-blades for me.
3. A small notebook and copying pencil.
4. One pair of socks.
5. A toothbrush.
6. Envelopes.
7. One or two bookstall books of poetry.

'Bookstall books of poetry' means – an old *Clare* or *Leigh Hunt* or *Coleridge* or any book of verse that you could pick up for a few pence amongst the old urns. At least, I suppose there are some old bookshops at Plymouth. At all events please send me out some verses and, if you can, some that I haven't read already, but no trash by 'a lady of England' or 'a Gentlewoman', or 'a scriptorial person'.

Can you be good and get these? And make sure you go to the theatre or somewhere good with the rest of the cheque. I am buying some new clothes this month but with all expenses cleared I hope to have a balance of well over £30 at the end of the month and this is creditable to me, I think, as I had next to nothing when I came out.[9]

All was not quiet, however, for there was constant activity around Thiepval and its ominous wood. On one night, a particularly heavy bombardment of *Minenwerfers* pounded the Front Line and on the following morning, on entering the store dug-out to look for duckboards, Edmund found instead the mangled, half-naked and bloody remains of the corpses awaiting burial.

Thiepval eventually fell to the British at the end of September, but the Germans still held some hopes of recapturing it and trained all their efforts on its northern tip, Thiepval Wood. By this time the Royal Sussex were camped in a wood at Martinsart, and Edmund found himself assigned to a reconnaissance party setting off for Thiepval Wood. It was an eerie, wild and confusing place and while looking for company headquarters the party managed to go too far forward. Suddenly a violent salvo opened up and shells whistled over their heads as they scrambled back to safety – miraculously without casualties. The wood had always held particular horror for Edmund, and the thought of having to spend time in it was an alarming prospect – even the miseries of Cuinchy now seemed mild by comparison. But new orders came through, and for the next ten days he was to be back in the line at Hamel, facing the same German trenches which had so stubbornly refused to be taken on 3 September.

The spectre of Thiepval, however, was not to be removed entirely. The Germans had been forced to retreat from the edge of Thiepval Ridge, but they still held positions just behind, with particularly strong defensive positions at Schwaben, Stuff and Zollern Redoubts. The Stuff Redoubt was taken on 14 October, but Edmund's company was ordered to capture and consolidate the fearful Stuff Trench – the memory of which was to cause Edmund sleepless nights for the rest of his life. After crossing grisly terrain, gouged by incessant fire and littered with shell-cases, rifles and dead bodies (and with the unnerving presence of a German observation plane) the company prepared for an attack just after midday on 21 October. Edmund was acting as right-hand man to the Colonel situated in Zollern Trench – a foul position, where the shell-hole used as a latrine was guarded by two German corpses, one with his fingers still clasping the handle of a bomb. All they could do was wait, listening to the heavy firing ahead. Eventually news arrived that the trench was taken and some German prisoners captured, one of whom had his jaw badly damaged. With typical gentleness Edmund bandaged the wound as best he could and was rewarded with a look of smiling gratitude which he was never to forget. As it was impossible to reach those who were in possession of Stuff Trench during the next day, Edmund led a party of relief at nightfall through the grim Schwaben Trench, through heavy shell-fire, to reach their destination: 'three feet deep, corpses under foot, corpses on the parapet'.[10] Incongruously, a stray dog accompanied them for a while but there was little other comfort for the small group of struggling, exhausted men whom Edmund led back to the safety of Aveluy Wood. It was the first time that the battalion had actually wrested land from the Germans, but their pride was sadly muted by the enormous cost. Edmund recalled the men who only a few days earlier had been efficiently restoring the trenches at Hamel: 'What men were they? Willing, shy, mostly rather like invalids, thinking of their families. . . . they were all doomed. Almost all finished their peaceful lives in the fury of Stuff Trench.'[11]

For a brief spell the company recovered at Aveluy as the autumn turned colder, and they listened to the gun-fire along the ridges and watched the novel sight of tanks moving at dusk, before Thiepval called again – but it was a much gentler wood around which they found themselves entrenched than it had been in the previous months. Rain and fog were the worst irritations for a week or so before they moved to relief at Senlis, a village about six miles behind the line, which Edmund recalled with enthusiasm – 'O how comely it was and how reviving'[12] – and where a divisional concert party evoked sharp pangs of home-sickness with the singing of 'Take me back to dear old Blighty' and 'When you're a long, long way from home'.

It was now approaching November and they had been in the Somme region for nearly four months. It seemed as though the campaign was coming to an end as they marched from Senlis back to the dreaded Schwaben Redoubt, via the forbidding St Martin's Lane Trench, which was still shelled at irregular intervals. The area around the Redoubt was covered in bodies – one, with an arm swinging uselessly, was being used to prop up a precarious doorway. There were unnerving sights all around, as he described to his mother:

Cold and wet and lack of sleep are enemies to the finest soldiers. There is also the added enemy of the presence of so many dead men. And after a while the dead become more than frightful to the mind. Some of the dugouts where some Germans were killed with bombs are indescribable – and, in any case, must not be described.[13]

Any idea that things had quietened down, however, was quickly dispelled on the morning of 11 November, when the Adjutant declared that in two days' time there was 'to be the biggest attack of the lot'.[14] In the meantime an unsuccessful raid was made on a German stronghold just ahead of the Schwaben, but some prisoners were brought back to headquarters – including a milkman and an elementary schoolmaster whom Edmund considered most welcome guests. The attack of the 13th took the Germans by surprise and was remarkably successful – St Pierre Divion, just north of Thiepval Wood, was taken, as well as Beaucourt and Beaumont to the west. Edmund was beginning to feel left behind in Thiepval when he was ordered to go on a reconnaissance mission to prepare for the movement of men and to positions in advance of those newly captured. It was to be his most dangerous mission yet.

Together with a young runner, he set off in the dusk. Passing the Schwaben, they crossed the wrecks of redoubts and communication trenches, always pressing forward in search of their new Front Line. Suddenly they found themselves in darkness and in the centre of a vicious barrage: 'Never had shells seemed so torrentially swift, so murderous; each seemed to swoop over one's shoulder. We ran, we tore ourselves out of the clay to run, and lived. The shells at last skidded and spattered behind us, and now where were we? We went

on.'[15] They came across heavy wooden shelters which they took to be
German howitzer positions. These appeared to be only recently
evacuated – and the dead bodies suggested the same story. Climbing
another ridge, they found themselves under rifle-fire, horrifically
close. They turned and scrambled back down the slope. Seeming to
recognise a position in the Ancre valley they ran, crouching, waiting
to be caught at any moment, and burst through the cross-fire of British
and German bullets until they heard themselves challenged in English.
They fell into the trenches occupied by men of their own division,
and, after resting, returned to headquarters. They were greeted with
unbelieving silence – the blaze of shelling over the Schwaben had
been accepted as their certain death-warrant.

The Colonel was able to inform the General that the proposed
advance would be disastrous, and Edmund was summoned to the
General's presence for a debriefing. It became clear that he had crossed
into enemy territory in the area of Grandcourt and had come right up
against the German line. The unexpected but welcome news was that
Edmund's bravery in the action had won him the award of the
Military Cross. The award was gazetted, with the official citation:

For conspicuous gallantry in action. He displayed great courage and determination when in charge of a carrying party under heavy fire. He has
previously done fine work.

Equally welcome news was orders for the division's withdrawal
from the Somme region. Salvage parties quickly filled in the gaps in
equipment by taking packs from the dead bodies, and they were ready
to leave the world of sudden raids for a while. As Edmund wrote to
his mother in early December:

In the present war, even a small trench can be held strongly (after two years
of preparation) with machine guns, and take a battalion or so to capture.
With the ground eaten up with shell-holes and about three-feet deep in
sludge of the octopus type, it has been impossible to advance quickly enough
to break through.[16]

There had been some successes to record, though, as the men
marched away, singing, through Albert to Doullens before travelling
north by train. Had they known they were destined for Ypres and
Passchendaele, perhaps they would have marched with a little less
enthusiasm.

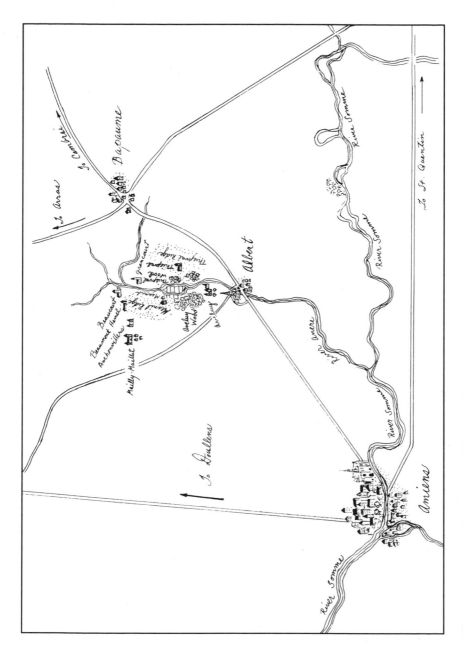

The area around the Somme, 1916 (drawn by Charles Mussett)

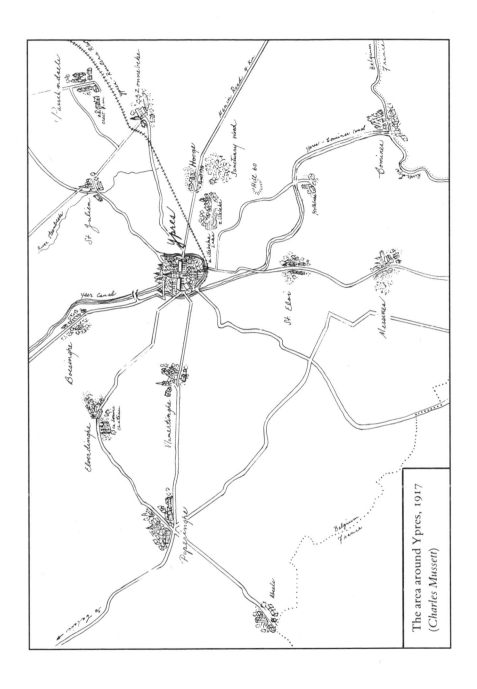

The area around Ypres, 1917
(Charles Mussett)

# 7

# Ypres and Passchendaele
## December 1916 – December 1917

*Walking one day on a duckboard,*
*I was weary and ill at ease,*
*And my hands grasped vainly at nothing,*
*And the mud came up to my knees,*
*The duckboard began oscillating,*
*I knew that I had to go,*
*So I gave one wild and final plunge,*
*And fell in the mud below.*

From the *B.E.F. Times*, 1 November 1917: Edmund's
twenty-first birthday

*Our minds receded with actual joy to the 1916 war, and*
*particularly that season when we were within the kindly*
*influence of Béthune. When had we heard the words*
*'bon time' since? How few there were left even to*
*understand what hopes had then borne the battalion on*
*singing towards the Somme! When we left this camp of*
*disastered 1917, to be merged again in the slow*
*amputation of Passchendaele, there was no singing.*
*I think there were tears on some cheeks.*

'Undertones of War'

Ypres, and in particular the Ypres salient – that small semi-circle of land just east of the city which jutted into enemy territory – had become a tiny area of land of great military significance. To the British and German High Command it had to be attacked or defended as a symbol of national pride; to the soldiers who fought there it was a symbol of slaughter. The battle of Ypres had begun in 1914 and was to rage on, with intermittent pauses for breath, through the 'second battle' of 1915, and 'Third Ypres' in the early summer of 1917. After three years of fighting, and 250,000 casualties, the battle expired in the nightmare of Passchendaele – the name commonly given to the whole of the third and final phase of the campaign

The ancient city of Ypres, with its medieval towers and gabled houses, stands between the two canals which reach out to Boesinghe, towards the River Yser in the north, and Comines on the River Lys in the south. Behind Ypres, to the west, runs the road to Poperinghe – passing through the flat rural countryside around Vlamertinghe; on the eastern front are a series of small hills and woods, with the village of Passchendaele on the northern tip and the Messines Ridge to the south. Between the two runs the Menin Road. The salient itself, in naturally boggy Flemish terrain, lay just in front of these hill-slopes enfolding Ypres in a half-embrace, whose right arm was Boesinghe, whose left arm was the Messines Ridge, and whose centre was Zillebeke. The salient was particularly vulnerable because the Germans occupied the higher ground and could attack from any angle and either send fire across the bulge or slip in from the sides and attack from the rear. They also had direct railway links from Roulers, just north-east of Passchendaele, to the armament factories in the Ruhr. The only solution for the British, it seemed, was to sink deep mineshafts and blow the Germans off the Messines Ridge.

Edmund's entry into this arena was to be delayed for a while. The train which brought the battalion north from the Somme discharged them at a training camp by a farm a mile or so from the road to Poperinghe – a pleasant town, full of narrow streets, and well stocked with food and drink. Unlike the deserted land around the Ancre, the villages here were still inhabited, and windmills and ploughs were both at work. After a brief and largely unsuccessful attempt to learn to ride a horse, Edmund was moved even further away from the firing-line, to attend a gas course, behind St Omer on the road to Calais. And then he found himself clutching the prized yellow leave-warrant, on his way to ten days in Blighty. During his leave he spent a few days in Yalding and also visited a theatre in London, where he made the chance acquaintance of a young girl called Alison. They were never to see each other again, but their meeting reminded Edmund only too sharply of the bleak loneliness which he felt without regular female company.

On his return he joined the battalion in dugouts north of Ypres, on the Yser Canal. It was probably the quietest period which that part of Flanders had known for two years, and they were able to retire to the woods of Elverdinghe to celebrate Christmas – complete with Christmas dinner, carols and heavy snow. On Boxing Day, he wrote home: 'We had Church on Christmas morning and dealt with the usual hymns in the best style. The Swains' Vigil, or While Shepherds Watched, was favourably received – especially at the back part of the room. After prayers we had supper for the rest of the day – truly Gargantuan scenes were witnessed.'[1]

The area around Beosinghe, on the edge of the Yser Canal, was bleak – and its defences crude. The château was a hollow shell, the main street a heap of rubble, the communication trenches fragile pieces of wickerwork. Across the canal, at Steam Hill, the Germans pounded fire from their *Minenwerfer*. Such was the company's home in the New Year of 1917, before a more permanent base was established in trenches at Potijze, in the centre – but not the worst – sector of the salient. It was here, however, that a German offensive was expected and Edmund – now an intelligence officer – was constantly moving between the battalion headquarters in the shell-shocked château at Potijze and the Front Line – via the communication trenches, Haymarket and Piccadilly, and the suffocating support trench, St James's Street. He made frequent sorties into No Man's Land, where stick-bombs lay hidden in the snow and the journey home was often accompanied by sniper-fire. It was a strangely eerie world: the ghostly medieval ramparts of Ypres behind, and the snowy uncertainties of No Man's Land ahead. The snow had a strange effect on the sound of the shelling, creating a kind of flat concussive thud, but it also gave rise to an incident of comedy. White suits had been ordered for the patrols as camouflage; when the package supposedly containing these arrived, it was found to be full of ladies' flimsy nightdresses.

The monotonous sequence of raiding or being raided, taking prisoners or losing one's own men, continued throughout January 1917 as the British waited nervously for the expected major attack on the salient. Reconnaissance was the key activity, and every inch of the area had to be plotted – Edmund being responsible for discovering the details of all the houses and buildings along the Potijze Road, many of which he came to regard with considerable affection.

By February the battalion had been relieved from the breastworks at Potijze and moved into billets in Ypres, whose many crumbling and waterlogged cellars offered some precarious protection. Headquarters was situated in a shelled convent, with more secure and rambling cellars which offered greater shelter from the increasing action in the air over Ypres. Over the past few months Edmund had been receiving letters from his ten-year-old sister Anne, with poems enclosed. He replied praising the poems, and described the Ypres scene:

Things don't change much. Only the ruined houses get a little more ruinous. . . . You could never find such a forbidding place. And by day, the sight of so many fine old churches, convents and high houses turned into rubble is a most depressing one. Of course the cellars are very useful to us and there are some cosy corners underground even here. Once when we were here before, a shell broke open a cellar which turned out to be full of wine, but the town mayor got there before we did and we (like Mother Hubbard's notorious dog) had none. . . . I bought a sack of coal and had my room as warm as summer weather every night – in spite of the wind which shook the cracked window-panes and hollered down the flues in a sort of sleepy displeasure with me.   But today is a sudden change. The snow has almost gone and a warm foggy weather has come to take over. Serve out my love all round and say I am well and plump.[2]

As the thaw gradually set in, more activity was possible in the open fields. Edmund devised a new method of speeding up the erection of barbed-wire and was practising this one day, resplendent in a pair of new but vastly oversize wellington boots, when the divisional General passed by. He was impressed by the ingenuity, but asked the Colonel in amazement, 'Who was that subaltern in the extraordinary boots?'[3] Edmund was rarely, as his housemaster at school had complained, 'spruce and tidy'. As he admitted to his mother, 'I don't think I shall ever be a smart and tidy soldier for parade purposes, but I hope and trust that I do prove myself of some use in over the top displays.'[4]

The change of weather also brought about a change in activity.  The battalion was ordered to return to trenches near Hill 60, in Sanctuary Wood – looking horribly similar to Thiepval Wood, whose 'gunpits hardly looked strong enough to store potatoes'.[5] Edmund, however, learned that he was to be the Brigade Intelligence Officer, working from a brick vault under the ramparts close to the Lille Gate, compiling daily reports giving full details of all defences and activities at the Front. He felt ill at ease as a bureaucrat and missed the trusted company of his fellow infantrymen. Of the trenches themselves he saw plenty, sometimes spending lonely nights in isolated areas, and the names and details of every sap and dugout became more than familiar. The names were mostly humorously anglicised versions of the Flemish (Hallebast Corner becoming Hellblast Corner), or homely evocations such as Bond Street, Moated Grange or Lover's Lane. They were often to occur in Edmund's poetry, and became the basis of such poems as 'Trench Nomenclature':

> *Genius named them, as I live! What but genius could compress*
> *In a title what man's humour said to man's supreme distress?* [6]

The journey from the Lille Gate to the Front Line was certainly a complicated and hazardous one. After crossing a moat and then open fields, where sniper bullets were a constant danger, he would reach the dam of Zillebeke Lake. Along the sides of this he passed a row of small and exposed ditches which ran to the entrance of the communication trench, and the mud of Hellblast Corner, leading to Zillebeke Church. From here he could choose one of two approaches to the Front Line. One route, Vince Street, went north; the other, Zillebeke Street, went south via Valley Cottages, where one had to leave the trench and walk in the open, under threat of fire, to a copse. It was on one such expedition that, in the midst of a salvo, Edmund looked down and saw a helmet holding fresh blood, hair and brains.

From the copse two positions could be gained: Observatory Ridge (leading to little cuttings known as Krab Krawl), and the mouth of an old well (named Rudkin House) – both directly under the eye of German telescopes on Hill 60. The living conditions in the trenches of this area were cramped and inhospitable with increased shelling from the air and the added hazards of suffocation from smoke in the airless tunnels. Edmund's efficiency as an observer and report-writer had its drawbacks, for he was under constant pressure to provide even more detail and found himself making tours of inspection twice a day. It was obvious that something was in the air and that detailed preparations were afoot. This seemed confirmed when, after a brief rest in Poperinghe, the battalion was back in positions north of Ypres at the beginning of May. All along the Yser Canal the firing was becoming daily more intensive (Edmund began to expect to be ferried across by Charon in 'greasy cardigan and indigo pantaloons'),[7] and a training course in the area around St Omer was an obvious herald of increasing activity in store for the infantrymen. The awful shadow of Third Ypres was becoming more defined, but an unexpected respite came to Edmund in the form of a few days' rest by the coast, during which he recalled a chance romantic moment:

After a visit to an estaminet, I sauntered by the canal, and then settled myself with my book in an empty cattle-truck. There came along a girl of fourteen or so, with a small brother, and looked in. we talked, and – we fell in love.

71

# PART TWO    1915 – 1919

That 'I' may be still in love with her, Marie-Louise of course, so black-eyed and serious, and early-old with the inheritance of peasant experience – I have seen her alone since in many a moment of escape and fantasy. Still she looks in on this life's sultry cattle-truck, halted a while in some drab siding, and once again we kiss, innocent as petals in the breeze. With what sad resignation to the tyrannical moment, which she hardly credits to be true, lifting her slow hand doubtfully to wave farewell, does that child-love of only one day's courting watch me pass into the voluminous, angry, darkening distance: ah, Marie-Louise![8]

If the expectation of a big attack was well founded, the confidence that it would result in a British success was less so, but Edmund's letter home on 28 May was typical of the feeling of many:

For the last week I have been at the Second Army Rest Camp on the sandhills north of Boulogne, but I shall be glad to go up to the Front on Sunday next and do something towards finishing the war. It is not pleasing (after one has done rather more than a year at the business) to read some lantern-jawed man's whim in the press that the war is only just beginning and everyone must prepare for greater sacrifices etc. But I strongly believe that this Autumn finishes it, and finishes it on Boche territory too – if Russia only keeps up a certain amount of hostility.[9]

The regularity of Edmund's correspondence was remarkable. The nervous activity which was to characterise his later years was already evident. In the midst of the exhausting horrors of warfare, he still found time for extensive reading and for writing poetry, and he began to keep a diary. Apart from letters home, he started – in January 1917 – to correspond regularly, and at length, with his schoolfriend Hector Buck, now a Grecian at Christ's Hospital. This correspondence offered some respite from trench life, and showed his affection for his old school: 'You don't know how heartily I wish I were able to live my six years at Housey over again';[10] 'I often long for a game of Fives, or the School Library, fuggy and full of learning, or the shop; but most of all for the study and a quiet life'.[11] All connections with Christ's Hospital were treasured. He told his mother of an unexpected association with his old teacher, W. de H. Robinson: 'I saw a notice against Looting the other day, in a now deserted village, and underneath the old familiar signature, W. de H.R. This was somehow a comfort.'[12]

There are constant enquiries in the letters about the health of the school's cricket or rugby, and much reference to books he is reading – from Demosthenes to H. G. Wells – and inevitable laughter at the expense of such Housey characters as 'Pill' Merk. Mixed with this are more sombre moments: 'I need not stress . . . the depth of despondency to which I am permanently lowered.'[13] His letter of 22 June 1917 is typical:

The war is a sort of slow poison to me that keeps on drugging and deadening my mind. And I can tell you that the shelling just lately is far worse that anything we have been through before except in actual attacks. The Boche is so windy that he puts on a barrage every few hours in case we are just assembling to attack him. . . . Anyway I loathe war and the army too. Why shouldn't coves like Merk who go on in their petty self-inflations have some of the discomforts? There was more shriek in England over several hundred casualties in a bombing raid than there has been over several hundred thousand out here. . . . So off poise I am that I read 'The Princess' by Tennyson the other day. Tennyson trying to be humorous, or realistic, is like a hippopotamus in violet tights attempting to cross Niagara Falls on a tightrope, so I laughed long and loud. But afterwards I read some of 'In Memoriam' and repented myself.

But literature languishes as a whole in the battalion except for two books (*Flossie* and *Aphrodite*) which the Archbishop of Canterbury has probably not read. I have got my John Clare's *Poems* and often tub-thump over them, claiming him as one of the best. But no one wants to agree with me. Please get the war stopped pretty soon. Some of us are mummies, only we still carry on the motion of breathing, swathed round with red-tape and monotony. I wish you all jolly good luck.

Edmund also continued to follow the fortunes of his friend George Rheam, now a monitor at Christ's Hospital, enclosing £1 in a letter home with a request that his mother use it partly on a postal order and partly on a food parcel – both to be sent to George at school – because he had just received a letter from George suggested that his spirits were particularly low. No wartime preoccupations were to diminish Edmund's constant generosity, or his feeling that he should act in a paternal way to his contemporaries, and even to those slightly older.

It was also at this time that his letters to his mother became more frequent and lengthy. Apart from domestic moments, complaints about painful teeth and requests for luxuries such as honey, they often dwell on literary matters – he sketches out his plan for an edition of Leigh Hunt, records his pleasure in reading Sydney Dobell's[14] poems, noticing that the minor Victorians can sometimes reach peaks of expression that the great ones rarely attain. His familiarity with lesser-known poets as well as major writers was remarkable for a young man of twenty, and it is difficult to remember that Edmund had left school only two years before, and gone straight to war. He was particularly enjoying the minor paths of the eighteenth century, having been reading Samuel Rogers and Allan Ramsay. In an elaborate fantasy he describes a great Flemish barn being transformed into an eighteenth-century room, where William Shenstone, James Thomson and Henry Kirke White meet and then melt into the landscape.[15] Earlier he had observed:

What a placid and affectionate century that much maligned eighteenth century was! Their careful lawns and landscaped gardens, solemn with figured groves and diversified with alleys green and fountains tinkling, beckoning Cupids in stone, and painted alcoves.

I also wish I could have picked up my knowledge of farming from William Ellis[16] of Little Gaddesden or from Gilbert White or his amiable Thomas Markwit[17] – or even from Cowper, with his pet hares and his little dog which divined his desire for a water-lily and dashed fearlessly in and brought back the flower to lay at the gentle old dreamer's feet. Where's our Morland? Our Reynolds? Our Crabbe?[18] Our nature nowadays seems something prim, or effete, or respectable compared with the rough heaths and sandy warrens, the rude palings and tumbledown cottages, the hurly-burly of strong character, faces, and unattempted beauty that seemed to belong to that time. And some of our Tennyson-fomented enthusiasts talk of the eighteenth century as 'arid wastes' and 'the most unproductive century of all.'[19]

But escape by means of books was only partial:

The other day I saw a French girl I like, but I haven't seen her again. I am so tired of being with people I don't love that I shall be pleased to find someone I can love out here. I am like the rest of mortality, I must have some flesh-and-blood person near who loves me – not that I love the others I can't see any less on that account, but somehow I feel I would like to see smiles and happiness in reality with me.

Several poems of the usual quiet melancholy type have made their appearance, and two or three I have left broken off through lack of heart to go on. I had half a mind to turn Roman Catholic whilst walking round Omer Cathedral the other day, but I can't convince myself. I don't know what to do. Aunt Maude writes saying that I haven't written lately – but I have. Still, tomorrow evening I will cudgel my brains for flippancies about this most damnable war 'such as her soul loveth'. For she seems to think that the war is merely an opportunity for us poor devils to show our courage and cheerfulness: I see in it an opportunity for battle-murder and sudden death, and 'Good Lord, deliver us!' But I think things have got beyond *him*.

I am ashamed I do not keep my promise to write to all the young ones – I must pull my socks up soon, only I find very little to say but that I am alive and shall shortly be otherwise, if lucky. Forgive this writing which is obviously that of a pale wretch gibbering through the iron bars of his cage at the bright unthinking people passing by. 'Why I am shut up, I don't know,' said

John Clare: and I seem as unreasonably walled in as he. I don't believe they let the dead rest either. I shocked a well-brought-up Padre the other day who said: 'Do you believe that there is a resurrection?' Answer: 'Well I'm very much afraid there is'. But if death is troubled with dreams like sleep, and finally fades out into the same staring day and brutal light, I think I shall have to think out some antidote or anodyne powerful to stop life and death as well. So extremely downcast I am, and have been for a long time, getting worse and worse.

In spite of all which, like Tom Campbell's[20] sailor who argued the toss with Bonaparte, 'great was the longing I had to see my mother'. Well, let me try to twinkle a little with, anyway, the outward glimmer of hope – perhaps things will square up and mysteries fade off the landscape leaving things clear and recognisable. And if the gods who play counters with us have any pity at all, they will burn us when done with – but I am not sure that I am going to kow-tow to chance, the wheel and the drift of things.

So good night, with lullaby, my dear old Mugg – and though so taciturn, or rather heavy-hearted, I love you still, and all of you.[21]

His continual reading of John Clare, and his nostalgia for Congelow, combined to produce a haunting poem written at this time, 'Clare's Ghost', which is remarkable for its evocation of Framfield as well as the spirit of Clare, yet was written in the surroundings of war-shocked Ypres:

> Pitch-dark night shuts in, and the rising gale
>   Is full of the presage of rain,
>   And there comes a withered wail
>   From the wainscot and jarring pane,
>   And a long funeral surge
>   Like a wood-god's dirge,
> Like the wash of the shoreward tides, from the firs on the crest . . .
>
>   And a stranger stands with me here in the glow
>   Chinked through the door, and marks
>     The sparks
>   Perish in whirlpool wind, and if I go
> To the delta of cypress, where the glebe gate cries,
>   I see him there, with his streaming hair
>     And his eyes
>   Piercing beyond our human firmament
>   Lit with a burning deathless discontent.[22]

By early June he was back in the woods just west of Vlamertinghe, where the activity of the past months had changed both landscape and atmosphere, and where confidence was less assured. There were new wooden tracks in the wood, new bridges over the canal, new railway tracks alongside. Reinforcements in the form of men, stores, guns, tanks, transport and animals had been packed into the area and Edmund felt the shadow of death on the bread and cheese rations and in the discoloured tepid liquid in his water bottle.

Night patrols became more frequent, and it grew clear that the Germans were equally prepared for fierce fighting. After two officers had failed to return from patrols on two successive nights, Edmund was sent out on the third to try his luck. It was reminiscent of the raids in the Somme – within minutes of leaving the British Front Line, he was dodging non-stop shelling, forced by erratic advance to go deep into No Man's Land and then found himself within a few yards of a German sap. The return journey was no less tortuous, but he eventually reached the canal bank and safety, after running through mists of foul gas. He could only report that the Germans, too, seemed just waiting to move. The scene was set for Passchendaele.

The days leading up to the attack were tense and nervous. Edmund walked past the château at Vlamertinghe surrounded by flowers and was struck by its aura of peacefulness in contrast to the sense of foreboding felt by the battalion, and wrote an ironic Keatsian sonnet beginning:

'And all her silken flanks with garlands drest' –
But we are coming to the sacrifice. [23]

During the four days before the opening shots of Passchendaele were fired, the battalion was situated around the canal bank in the area of La Brique – a group of battered houses where many dead bodies lay – moving towards battle headquarters, below Bilge Street trench, on 28 July.

The following day brought a heavy thunderstorm, which was a herald of rain for most of the following week, transforming the thick mud into slimy clay. His diary records 'much debating on peace terms – is this Armageddon?'[24] but also records the safe arrival in the mail of Leigh Hunt's *Poems* and his novel, *Sir Ralph Esher*:

I got out at three-fifteen to look at the light. A Boche plane came over and we were shrapnelled for half an hour, don't know why. Heavy rain again for part of the day. . . . Since we have been in, we have been quite unlucky and have had between forty and fifty casualties. The weather looks none too promising – but perhaps 'everything will come out in the wash'. . . . So far all quiet. But how these tunnels reek! I finish the page on the stroke of twelve, which brings on tomorrow.[25]

And the 'tomorrow' was Tuesday 31 July – a date which was to haunt him for the rest of his life. In the eerie darkness of breaking dawn, with the ghostly figures of tree-stumps guarding the slippery entrances to the trenches, the British guns opened fire at 3.50 a.m., with a deafening roar which almost stunned the British soldiers and which brought identical retaliation from the Germans – 'we now began to sweat blood and my tongue seemed to cleave to the roof of my mouth'.[26] Edmund leaped into No Man's Land, and ran past empty concrete emplacements towards the German lines. There were instant casualties and injuries, but there was little opportunity to take in details as the manic rush through the fire and morning mist continued. Immediately it seemed as though some success had been achieved as German lines were captured – but they were only deserted, flimsy, shallow ditches protected by brushwood. It soon became clear that the attack further on – along what was called the Black Line – had failed, 'and one more brilliant hope, expressed a few hours before in shouts of joy, sank into the mud.'[27] That evening the battalion headquarters consisted of wet, cold, tired men, feasting on tinned sausages, surrounded by many wounded colleagues and the aura of silent uncertainty. Edmund's diary states simply: 'I was never so hideously apprehensive.'[28]

The next day followed a similar pattern. The heavy rain persisted, the shelling was uninterrupted, the ground became littered with men and mules, and the mud was eighteen inches deep. News arrived that the 13th Royal Sussex had suffered heavy casualties, as had all divisions – and death or injury could strike with dramatic suddenness. One young runner was struck by a bullet, just as he set out on his mission, and fell dead on one knee with his message still clutched in his outstretched hand; an Irish doctor, generously waving a bottle of whisky in his hand, fell suddenly down on the floor of a concrete shelter, the bottle still in his grasp. The diary described the day as 'the most wicked twenty-four hours I have ever been through, Somme included. . . . Another retreat from Moscow.'[29]

Friday 3 August saw Edmund back at the Canal Bank, where he spent most of the day sleeping after the exhausting walk on feet whose soles had become corrugated. By good fortune, the rain being so persistent, orders to relieve in the Black Line were cancelled. Instead, orders came to retire to Poperinghe, where a Charlie Chaplin film was shown at the end of a day in which the town had been shelled without interruption. Edmund was now thirsty for mail and his impatience was evident by 5 August:

## PART TWO  1915 – 1919

A fairly idle day. I did paper raid and read Leigh Hunt. . . . There was a big bombardment again this evening. Some of our party went over I suppose – God help them in the mud. Just as we were settling down for the night, Boche came over. Our knees knocked and teeth chattered, but nothing fell on us – 'but not on us the oysters cried'. Still no letter.

The desire for news from home was granted, in just a few days, with three weeks' leave. He was able to visit Yalding and once more take strength from the waters of the Teise and the Beult, celebrating them in his poem 'The Unchangeable':

> *Though I within these two last years of grace*
> *Have seen bright Ancre scourged to brackish mire,*
> *And meagre Belgian becks by dale and chace*
> *Stamped into sloughs of death with battering fire –*
> *Spite of all this, I sing you high and low,*
> *My old loves, Waters, be you shoal or deep,*
> *Waters whose lazy and continual flow*
> *Learns at the drizzling weir the tongue of sleep.*[30]

It was not, however, a totally happy period of leave and the foremost impressions were of:

. . . the large decay of lively bright love of country, the crystallization of dull civilian hatred on the basis of 'the last drop of blood'; the fact that the German air raids had almost persuaded my London friends that London was the sole battle front; the illusion that the British Army beyond Ypres was going from success to success; the ration system. Perhaps the ration system weighed most upon us. This was not the ancient reward of the warrior![31]

By 26 August he was back in Flanders. The battalion had been moved westward to the outskirts of Meteren, but Edmund was immediately diverted to a signalling school at Zuytpeene. This was not welcome news, 'for experience proved that to be with one's battalion, or part of it, alone nourished the infantryman's spirit. Now amid a thousand tables I should pine and want food.'[32] He eventually made contact with his battalion close to Vierstraat before being sent to a transport camp some five or six miles from the battlefield. The journey to the Front Line was a dangerous one, crossing the endless mud by means of a plank road. To deviate from this was to fall into slime; to remain on it was to lay oneself open to ruthlessly accurate firing:

> *And so they go, night after night, and chance the shrapnel fire,*
> *The sappers' wagons stowed with frames and concertina wire,*
> *The ration-limbers for the line, the lorries for the guns:*
> *While overhead with fleeting light stare down those withered suns.*[33]

Before long he was summoned to join the main battalion in attacks on buildings close to Gheluvelt on the main sector, in an area known as Tower Hamlets, from where he directed the signallers. The Germans were determined not to allow the British to advance any further along the Menin road and pounded the British positions unmercifully, while the September climate made the pillboxes cold at night but insufferably hot by day. The trenches just around them were full of bodies, and their number was increased when a shell came into the door of the adjacent pillbox and blasted the inhabitants to death. Relief was almost as dangerous as being in the line, for all movement had to be in broad daylight under enemy observation, and there were more casualties to add to the 300 incurred in the action, as the battalion withdrew to Bodmin Copse and thence west to St Eloi and the rest camp in the fields near Mont Kokereele, behind Kemmel. He described the scene in a letter to Hector Buck:

After the most vigorous display by the Boche artillery that I have yet had to cast my eye upon and a narrow escape from being pulled under in a swamp on the way out (I was in such a hurry to get out that my foot missed the dead man I was going to use as a duckboard), we came back to this Corydonian spot for a B.E.F. rest. We feed in a barn which smells most pleasantly of hops, and a keen imagination might picture a cask of IIII ale[34] every time the door opens.[35]

This pastoral relaxation was soon interrupted, for Edmund was sent, as Tunnel Major of Hedge Street Tunnels, back in the salient. His job was to control the very limited accommodation and he once again visited Zillebeke and the terrible valley cottages, spending a week patrolling the cramped, dirty but much coveted underground quarters. Unexpected literary moments could suddenly occur and on one memorable occasion an artillery major, arriving with port and cheroots, proceeded to spend the evening in dramatic recitations from *The Ingoldsby Legends*, Browning, Shelley and Kipling.

At Mont Kokereele his Colonel had recommended him for promotion to captain, but the General considered him too young. Nevertheless, he was put in command of B Company when they moved towards Bass Wood, and took a position three or four hundred yards behind the Menin Road, in a pillbox which was nearly a foot deep in water, and aptly named Hunwater Dugout. He gave Hector Buck a vivid picture of it:

This place is . . . an old Boche pillbox with the typical Boche smell and a large doorway facing right towards the Boche gunners, machine-gunners, minnymen, snipers, and whatso else there be that crump, zonk, bump, plonk, or in any other way soever, worry, annoy, or badger the nonchalant Englishman. But mark you, there is no means of getting into the dugout except this doorway, screened though it be with two or three groundsheets and some German equipment and once inside, the unguarded foot suddenly falls lovingly into about eighteen inches of Hunwater, with noisome bubbles winking at the brim. In this black cistern float a few coops and boxes a few thousand bottles and meat canisters – attached to the less waterlogged of this jetsam are a number of officers and their Seneschals, thicketed with unshavennes; this air is quite devoid of oxygen and the candle's light is not of this world. At times the snores of the sleeper drown the glutinous gurglings of the Hunwater – or the arrival of a muster of 5.9's just outside the door causes the last drain of whisky to jolt off the pro-table and vanish for ever in the seething depths.[36]

They were under constant German surveillance, and at times the enemy fired so many illuminants that 'the ground with its pools was like a jeweller's shop.'[37] After a night spent in patrol of No Man's Land, the battalion retired to a bivouac camp at Voormezeele and two days later the company – having been returned to its ordinary commander – was billeted in a hutted camp called Chippewa. Edmund's letters at this period begin to show a more tense element – a mixture of nervous humour and macabre imagination and an increasing impatience with High Command. On 7 October he wrote to his sister Phyllis:

I cannot say what caused it, but I had a terrible dream last night. I was paying out, the orderly sergeant was shouting out the names and the men were rolling up for the swag. Suddenly a clap of thunder sounded above, the clouds parted, and a fat angel dressed in a striped football jersey and a bombazine loincloth gazed down with an eye all bloodshot; in his right hand a trumpet, in his left hand a roll-call divided into two columns: Sheap and Gotes. Surrounding him were a horde of gorgeous cherubims in pea-green lingerie and holding similar roll-calls and a Venus pencil. The corpulent angel now uplifted his trumpet and puffed his cheeks out like the frog in the fable, blew a tremendous blast. Immediately the stars began darting hither and thither, the pay-table vanished into space, the company and myself were whirled aloft and immediately placed in the Gotes class. A seraphim with two warts on his left ear now asked us whether we had our emergency rations and identity discs. I had not. I was immediately hailed before God. He asked me how long I had been in the army. I said about forty-five years, man and boy. He said 'and you come on parade without your iron rations and identity disc? I never heard such a thing. You probably think it's a small offence. Report to the Angel Gabriel's office immediately'. I reported, and found the obese party described waiting with a movement order. It read: 'Menin Road; Front

Line; For All Eternity'. I yelled with terror and awoke to find my batman cleaning my Sunday jacket and the wind howling dreamily between my toes.[38]

A few days later he was ordered to the Larch Wood area, near Hill 60, to prepare for some trench-digging. Just behind the intended site was the ruin of a British aeroplane. Edmund approached it and instantly came under furious shelling – it was again obvious that all activity was observed by the enemy. The trench was successfully dug, but not without casualties. On one evening the Germans fired a mixture of gas and high explosive, and for a third time the gas worked its insidious power, causing Edmund to cough almost to choking point for several nights. As the firing died down, the clock passed midnight and it was 1 November 1917 – Festubert, Cuinchy, the Somme and now Passchendaele: and Edmund was celebrating his twenty-first birthday.

The immediate news was that he was to be sent on a two months' signalling course, midway between Poperinghe and Bailleul. As always, Edmund received the information with mixed feelings. 'It was wonderful to be promised an exeat from war for weeks' but he also 'felt as usual the injustice of my own temporary escape while others who had seen and suffered more went on in the mud and the muck'.[39] The course was irksome and the instructions less than perfect, but it afforded a useful period of reflection as the year drew to a close. At midnight on 31 December he recorded:

I stood with some acquaintances in a camp finely overlooking the whole Ypres battlefield. . . . Midnight; successions of coloured lights from one point, of white pendants from another, bullying salutes of guns in brief bombardment, echoes racing into space, crackling of machine-guns small on the tingling air; but the sole answer to unspoken but importunate questions was the line of lights in the same relation to Flanders and our lives as at midnight a year before. All agreed that 1917 had been a sad offender. All observed that 1918 did not look promising at its birth, or commissioned to solve this dark enigma scrawled in blood.[40]

# 8

# The Somme and Demobilisation
## January 1918 – February 1919

*How can the man at the front speak his mind? He has
no chance, but must await his turn of being disparted by
a shell, or swallowing some gas, or stopping a few
rounds from a machine-gun or being drawn down into
grey, reeking mud.*
Letter to his mother, 1918[1]

> *How unpurposed, how inconsequential*
> *Seemed those southern lines when in pallor*
> *Of the dying winter*
> *First we went there!*
> 'Gouzeaucourt: The Deceitful Calm'[2]

As the thaw set in, Edmund joined the battalion north-east of Ypres at
Westroosebeke – where the situation was bleak, the weather vicious
and all shelter flooded – for a brief tour of duty before his turn for
leave came round again.

When he returned, the battalion had moved south – back to the
Somme area, south-east of Albert at Mont St Quentin. For most of
frosty February he was in trenches south of Gouzeaucourt. It was a
horribly desolate area with all the depression of the aftermath of
fighting – and it mirrored a personal feeling of depression and desola-
tion after two years of war. There was considerable distance between
the German and British lines in the district, and the dispersal of troops
was somewhat erratic and economical. The British were consolidating
and extending southwards, and the Germans seemed equally half-

hearted. It was an unnerving kind of lull before the next storm of 21 March, which Edmund was to be spared.

His position was beneath a ridge, in the cutting of a railway, with a valley on one side and a pattern of criss-crossing trenches on the other. All round were relics of the Cambrin fighting in the previous November: burned-out tanks, guns with crumpled barrels, cavalry lances, machine-gun belts, as well as corpses preserved by the wintry weather. Edmund was responsible for supervising the signallers and observers, and in an attempt to provide some alternative communications he climbed a tall tree to flash a message to battalion headquarters by means of a lamp. His sense of direction untypically failed him and the signal was detected by Germans entrenched opposite. A barrage of machine-gun fire was immediately directed towards the tree. As Edmund recorded in characteristic understatement: 'I made a lucky jump.'[3]

Within a few weeks he received the news which many would have thought most welcome – he was to be taken out of the theatre of war and posted to six months' duty at a training centre in England. For Edmund it proved as usual to be a double-edged blessing. He was physically tired, felt uneasy in his job and found his relations with his seniors becoming increasingly strained. Added to this, the battalion was dispersed and disordered and had lost its sense of corporate familiarity. For release from these irritations and the discomforts of war, he was clearly thankful: but he felt guilty about leaving others behind. Although he was to return to France by the end of the year it was to be after the armistice, so his departure from Gouzeaucourt was to mark the end of authentic active service – and he could sense that the quiet of the past month was indeed a 'deceitful calm'. He was to recall ten years later:

> *There it was, my dears, that I departed,*
> *Scarce a greater traitor ever! There too*
> *Many of you soon paid for*
> *That false mildness.*[4]

The training camp was in Suffolk, at Stowlangtoft, by Stowmarket. It was in a pleasant rural setting, surrounded by trees and overlooked by windmills recalled in his poem 'Wild Cherry Tree'.[5] But life within the camp was anything but placid. There was hostility between those who had not seen action and those who had returned – who were often regarded with suspicion – which resulted in at least one suicide. It was 'merely a mill for the purpose of crushing the soul out of eighteen-year-old boys and sending them wholesale into the world's fiercest furnaces'.[6] Within a week of arrival Edmund filed a request to be returned to his battalion; it was met with tolerant amusement. A week later he repeated the request; he was ordered to take a medical and was pronounced 'unfit'. In desperation he decided to indulge in forgery, erasing the pencilled cancellation of the blank half of the warrant which had brought him back from France. But while planning his escape, an event of great significance occurred.

One morning he was summoned to give evidence in a military court of inquiry at Bury St Edmunds. In the evening he went for a drink at the White Hart Hotel in Newmarket with some fellow officers, and they were served by a young, attractive local girl, Mary Daines. Edmund was immediately attracted to her simple grace, striking beauty and clear, sparkling eyes. He quickly discovered that her background read like a Hardy novel.  She lived at Cheveley, just outside Newmarket, and was the third youngest of thirteen children of the village blacksmith and his wife. She had received the minimum of formal education and was entirely unbookish. Edmund took every opportunity of seeing her while the court of inquiry was in progress. Mary had no shortage of admirers – not all of them to Edmund's taste. He felt protective towards her, convincing himself that he was rescuing her from unsavoury liaisons and on 1 June 1918 they were married in the Congregational Chapel in Newmarket. Edmund was twenty-one; Mary was just eighteen.

In hindsight it was probably clear that it was something of an impulsive fantasy on both sides – she being attracted by the figure of the sensitive soldier-poet and the fact that he was an officer, he by the natural epitome of rural England that he saw in her. At the time it was an intense and loving relationship.

For Edmund the whole atmosphere of the Daines's home-life was a release from war time nightmares: 'Anything more remote from the army life in which I had been submerged for some years could not be imagined than that almost silent snowy road, the park wall, the dull inn, the rows of brick cottages without a shellhole in their roofs or in their gardens, the church and the clockface on the tower.'[7]

Edmund never met his father-in-law, who began to be fired by intense religious fervour in later life and who one night, aged fifty-six, left home and admitted himself to Fulbourn asylum. He and his wife were devoted parents and the atmosphere of their cottage was one of rural warmth and goodness. Edmund soon became friendly with Mary's brother Jack, with whom he shared sporting interests – he was once Edmund's guest at Lord's – and who is the figure behind the poem 'Winter, East Anglia.'[8] A more poetic influence, however, was Mary's brother Bert:

He seemed like an apple from the wildest, crabbiest tree in the orchard, dried or drying, coloured, bittersweet, bright among the nettles. Not only was he a figure begotten and shaped by the country community of East Anglia, the region of George Borrow, John Crome, Robert Bloomfield[9] – he was also a connoisseur of that community as it presented itself to observant eyes in 1900 and onwards. He was a part of it, a reporter of it, a repository of Anglian anecdote, fable, dialect and wickedness.

He would tell me with perfect contentment whatever he knew of country life and occupation, and one day he found me very ready to hear about the Shepherd whose tall figure I had watched with fascination as he gravely passed on the road. The account he gave was long, and went through the four seasons, often lightened with an affectionate word of praise for the knowledge and the skill of such shepherds and with a straightforward thankfulness for the nature-pictures which life had given to the speaker. When I had heard all, I felt better able to write a poem on the Shepherd,[10] blending my old recollection of Congelow Farm with the talk, and indeed the vision of Bert.[11]

The poem 'Mole Catcher'[12] also originated from such a conversation. On Bert's death Edmund recalled his eccentricities in dress, his fund of rustic knowledge and his sensitivity:

Bert took almost as much care with his dress as a West End Clubman, although the effect was rather different: but he was attentive to every detail. He had the fancy of ordering a weird suit with a battery of pearl buttons upon it, much in the costermonger's style, but cut to his own special order. Sometimes he put on a white hat. In that attire he blazed into view among the street crowds, yet not, from what I could tell, for notoriety; he was simply wearing what he liked. Perhaps it was the old-fashioned conjurer's costume.

He is gone, and with him the oddest collection of conundrums, proverbs, dialect phrases, out-of-the-way knowledge, superstition and stories of village life which perhaps any man between Norwich and Bury St Edmunds had in his time. His mystery was that with all his command of hard, rough and bold experience he so often fell into sadness, which brought tears down those weather-beaten cheeks with no word said.[13]

He was to be further commemorated as B.D. in the poem 'Autolycus Again'[14] in 1962.

Edmund's courtship of Mary, and his marriage, clearly deadened the desire to cross the Channel again, but the call could not be ignored for ever. A chronic bout of asthma delayed his departure until a few days after the Armistice on 11 November 1918, but then he found himself detraining at Douai before joining his new battalion at Hornaing. It was exciting to be moving in areas where the Germans had been recently billeted, but there was also a sterile atmosphere. For the old soldiers, the quiet evenings of peace within the setting of war were strange and made them restless and irritable while the routine of drill, marching, inspections, games, concert-parties and educational lectures created a false sense of activity. A brief release came to Edmund when he was sent off to the Arras district to arrange the battalion's Christmas dinner, but it was a muted pleasure and he sought solace in the works of Charles Lamb and Verlaine.

Added to all other pressures was the separation from Mary – who was now pregnant. He wrote short love verses to her constantly:

> You'll always be my little love,
> Your clear eyes told me true,
> And never now a moment flies,
> But my heart dreams of you,
> You with your twilight, odorous hair,
> You with your rose-leaf cheeks,
> And soft sweet sighing voice
> Like shadows where cool water speaks . . .
> And all the music and merriment and beauty of time gone by
> Shall live for me in every look of your love-charming eye. [15]

For Christmas 1918 he wrote to her:

Dearest of all, little one, this letter cannot be but in rhyme, for that represents best the lackadaisical state of mind I have slid into:

> My dreams have been so many, dear
> Since I was robbed of you;
> They come so bright and glad and clear,
> That I rejoice when night is here
> And mourn at night's adieu. [16]

A letter to his mother revealed both the wide gap in intellectual interests which existed between Edmund and Mary as well as Edmund's concern for Mary's condition. He asked that she be allowed to live with Mugg after Christmas:

as a companion, beautiful and young. In January and afterwards I shall send you a pound or two monthly with the idea that you will go with her to any good music, or concerts, or art galleries – indeed anything at all which will give her babe a stimulus to become an artist of whatever sort. And also anything which will keep her from making moan because I have been sent out here away from her – she quite went to pieces over it and cries far too much to do her any good. You won't let her do that will you? Show her the good books, too – (poems, essays, Dickens, Brontë) – and see that she reads something. Indeed, I have made sure of her improving her education and enriching her powers of talking by setting her to catalogue my books . . . but the great thing is to keep her smiling and bright-eyed. She really grows prettier than ever, but paler, and goes all in black.[17]

But there were more problems on the horizon. Edmund's claims as a 'student' gave him preferential status in terms of demobilisation and he was considering his financial position. He was intending to use his gratuity on leaving the army (£180) to support Mary for eighteen months while he 'set the wheels of learning on fire in Oxford'[18] and lived off his Oxford scholarship and Christ's Hospital exhibition. He was warned, however, that his exhibition might not be honoured because of his marriage. This alarmed him, for it meant either staying in the army (which with the war over seemed both depressing and futile) or setting up as a printer and publisher. The real bombshell came when Oxford declared that his marriage prevented confirmation of his scholarship. It was a blow that sent him into an angry depression and he drafted a response to 'the withered Pooh-Bahs' at Oxford 'who have docked me of my beautiful dreams'.[19] The letter was a lively one:

I had expected juggling and niggling from what is by comparison a private authority (The Christ's Hospital Education Committee). From such an enlightened and plutocratic body, however, as the University of Oxford, such a curt and casual act of spoliation comes as an utter surprise. . . .

With the probability of demise in the war and to rescue the woman I loved from dangerous people advantaged by the war, I had the temerity to marry. Now sir, I submit that the duty of the college authorities to the fighting man who has played his part in saving them from certain disastrous chances, is not to inform him that an ancient technical point destroys his career, but in some sense of gratitude to fight for the forgoing of his pound of flesh with the Convocation or Reichstag or whatever high authority it is that makes and breaks degrees. Your phrase: 'We can do nothing' is a sentiment which to a platoon commander faced with terror and murder in a welter of bodies and slime would usually have brought death (impromptu) or death (firing-party). But it is this statuesque, bloodless tyranny which drives the free-thinker into Bolshevism. . . .

I have not ventured this *fiat justitia* from the point view of the pauper wailing his huge baksheesh, for fortunately the army of occupation is open even to married men, but in despair at the survival of primitive ritual, more ridiculous than the immolation of shrew-mice in ash trees to cure warts, at our greatest English university.[20]

## PART TWO    1915 – 1919

There seemed no alternative but to offer to stay in the army and go to the Rhine, where promotion seemed certain and a child allowance was assured. But the pull to Mary was too strong and, when demobilisation was offered in mid-February, he accepted it and returned to England to face the financial uncertainties of marriage and Oxford. It was a bitterly cold journey home, and two of his fellow passengers were suffering from a new and virulent strain of flu. They died soon after being detrained in Kent – war's final twist of the knife. As for many young war veterans it was a time of confusion for Edmund, and adjustment was to be a lengthy process. In 1934 he wrote of these days:

Looking back over 1918 and this opening quarter of 1919, I became desperately confused over war and peace. Clearly, no man who knew and felt could wish for a second that the war should have lasted for a second longer. But, where it was not, and where the traditions and government which it had called into being had ceased to be, we who had been brought up to it were lost men. Strangers surrounded me. No tried values existed now.[21]

Or as he complained in 'Behind the Line':

> *About you spreads the world anew . . .*
> *And still you wander muttering on*
> *Over the shades of shadows gone.*[22]

# 9

# *Undertones of War*

---

*I believe nobody else who wrote about the war of 1914
to 1918 remained so aware of the procession of the
seasons and the birds and wild flowers which somehow
managed to survive even on the edges of the battle-field.*
George Orwell, BBC broadcast, 1943[1]

*When this poet talks of the men who soldiered with
him, he talks simply and beautifully of his friends.*
J. B. Priestley[2]

*It was a beautiful world even then.*
'Undertones of War'

---

Edmund's prose account of his war experiences, *Undertones of War*,
went into numerous editions and reissues in England, as well as in
America, Germany, Japan, Denmark and Sweden. Yet it was not
published until 1928, and was written – with the help of a few maps,
but otherwise entirely from memory – while Edmund was in Tokyo.
This was not a matter of chance, but a calculated attempt on Edmund's
part to distance himself from events, and to allow the undertones of
time to add perspective to the narrative. He stresses in the preface that
there will be 'uncertainties of time and situation' and some 'confusions
and telescopings', but sees these as advantages. In his description of the
area around Ypres, he claims that 'a peculiar difficulty would exist for
the artist to select the sights, faces, words, incidents which characterised the time. The art is rather to collect them, in their original
form of incoherence.'

## PART TWO  1915 – 1919

He recorded plenty of contemporary impressions in letters, diaries and poems. It is difficult to be precise about the dating of all the poems, but some twenty[3] can almost certainly be attributed to the war itself, and he also referred in the preface to *Poems 1914–30* to numerous pieces having 'vanished in the mud of 1917'.[4] Edmund was, however, to continue to write 'war' poems throughout his life and did not seem particularly concerned to separate those composed in the trenches from those composed in the study – indeed the latter may have collected some undertones from the passage of time and have acquired the 'strange perspective'[5] which he sought. The choice of titles for his collections of poetry emphasises his sense of continued war experience – *The Shepherd* (1922) is subtitled 'Poems of peace and war', *After the Bombing* is the title of his 1949 collection and *Shells by a Stream* (1944) includes an obvious pun.

An intentional distancing from the personal is another reason for the contemporary poems' concentration on the landscape behind the Front Line and on the characters of the battalion, more often than on the horrors of action. At first Edmund intended to record his experiences in an extended poem, 'recollected in tranquillity', with Wordsworth's *Prelude* as his model, feeling that the elusive suggestions of verse would be more suitable than the starker statements of prose, and 'Third Ypres' is a kind of first draft.[6] Significantly, the thirty-two poems which he published as an appendix to *Undertones of War* are entitled 'poetical interpretations and variations' and are mostly undated. They are usually lyrical, rarely bitter, but there is a gentle, telling irony – sometimes in the title ('Rural Economy'),[7] often in an apparently throw-away last line. His description of a 47th Division revue at Ypres, entitled 'Concert Party: Busseboom', is cruelly understated:

> The stage was set, the house was packed,
>   The famous troop began;
> Our laughter thundered, act by act;
>   Time light as sunbeams ran . . .
>
> And standing on the sandy way,
>   With the cracked church peering past,
> We heard another matinée
>   We heard the maniac blast
>
> Of barrage south by Saint Eloi,
>   And the red lights flaming there
> Called madness: Come, my bonny boy
>   And dance to the latest air.

> *To this new concert, white we stood;*
> *Cold certainty held our breath;*
> *While men in the tunnels below Larch Wood*
> *Were kicking men to death.* [8]

Several of the poems attempt to see the war from the distance of ten years, such as 'Flanders Now'[9] and 'Another Journey from Béthune to Cuinchy'.[10] This was to become a familiar theme in later poems. A typical title, included in a section of *Poems 1914–30* called 'War: Impacts and Delayed Actions,' is '1916 Seen from 1921':

> *Tired with dull grief, grown old before my day,*
> *I sit in solitude and only hear*
> *Long silent laughters, murmurings of dismay,*
> *The lost intensities of hope and fear;*

*Undertones of War* is an attempt to see 1916 – 18 from 1928. Edmund's attitude to the prose work which he did write in the heat of battle confirms his view of the danger of being too close to one's subject. In 1918 he wrote a full account of his experiences from landing in France to his leaving Richebourg for the Somme in 1916, entitled *De Bello Germanico*. It was not published until 1930, and then only because Edmund gave it to his brother Gilbert, who was looking for material to set up as a printer. Had it not been for this generous gesture, it would probably not have seen the light of day. To some readers its freshness makes it superior to the more studied mannerisms of *Undertones of War* – and it is difficult to believe that it was written by a young man of twenty-two. Edmund was somewhat embarrassed by it. He found it 'noisy with a depressing forced gaity' because it had not been 'affected by the perplexities of distancing memory'.[11] He felt the same many years later when he wrote to Siegfried Sassoon about Keith Douglas's narrative of the Second World War, *Alamein to Zem Zem*. While acknowledging it as a 'brilliant account', he felt it lacked 'reflective intervals' and was a 'hammering sort of book'.[12]

A comparison between Edmund's two descriptions of the cherry orchard at Festubert shows his changed perspective. In *De Bello Germanico* it reads:

Presently I found the other officers of the billeting party, and meekly followed them through an orchard complete with cemetery, barricades of broken tumbrils and barrels, and dud shells piously enclosed in barbed wire, on to a trolley line through fields of untilled luxuriance. We passed some of the early attempts at digging in, which once more suggested how long the war could be expected to last considering how long it had lasted already, and the present monotony. Nature at least seemed to approve of it in this district; small lizards slid from their sunbath into their dugouts as we passed; the self-sown wheat was swarming with small birds, hares and wild-flowers; and not a ditch but was in a flurry with tiny fish such as Walton called skipjacks.

In *Undertones of War* some ten years later this becomes expanded and generalised:

The joyful path away from the line, on that glittering summer morning, was full of pictures from my infant war-mind. History and nature were beginning to harmonize in the quiet of that sector. In the orchard through which we passed immediately, waggons had been dragged together once with casks and farm gear to form barricades; I felt that they should never be disturbed again, and the memorial raised near them to the dead of 1915 implied a closed chapter. The empty farm houses behind were not yet effigies of agony or mounds of punished, atomized materials, they could still shelter, and they did. Their hearths could still boil the pot. Acres of self-sown wheat glistened and sighed as we wound our way between, where rough scattered pits recorded a hurried firing-line of long ago. Life, life abundant sang here and smiled; the lizard ran warless in the warm dust; and the ditches were trembling quick with odd tiny fish, in worlds as remote as Saturn.

The warless lizard is joined throughout the narrative by wagtail, yellowhammer and robin, by perch and roach, by poplar and rose. Away from the trenches, he records how 'musically sounded the summer wind in the trees of Festubert'.[13] His darting eye was always looking for the natural beauty of a countryside which he felt was 'incapable of dreaming a field-gun',[14] or for the details of architecture in the farm houses and the serenity of the village churches:

> The glance, the pause, the guess
> Must be my amulets of resurrection.[15]

He had even been able to admire the falling of a shell, which he described to his sister, Lottie: 'I had never seen shells falling into a pond until yesterday when . . . about eight dropped "whish", into a huge plash behind. Though at death's door with cowardly fears, I yet recovered consciousness enough to admire the sudden fountain of water among all the stunted willows and rushy pools',[16] even at Passchendaele he enjoyed the 'marvellous pale-green and brimstone lightnings' and the 'deep-red blast-furnace glare'[17] of the incendiaries. In *Undertones of War* his affectionate descriptions of Festubert, Ypres and Acuin are as memorable as the horrors of the Schwaben, and just as his nature poetry so often revealed a sombre and violent undercurrent, so his war writing revealed a natural 'grace that war never overcast'.[18]

It is this grace which tempers the strains of bitterness. The mildness of temper so often associated with Edmund is belied in passages in his letters, particularly when referring to academics who found war exemption, and have their 'bed every night, the comfort wanted and safety corner. One gets astonishingly fed up with such persons.'[19] These outbursts in *Undertones of War* are reserved for those in authority who encouraged 'petty militarism'. He scorns 'the irrelevant air of G.H.Q., far beyond the stars', and suggests that the Boar's Head offensive was ordered so that the 'small sharp cape in the German line' could be 'bitten off – no doubt to render the maps in the Châteaux of the mighty more symmetrical'.

He certainly felt no bitterness towards the German soldier. He always showed understanding and courtesy to German prisoners and tended their wounds as best he could. His refusal to hate the enemy did not endear him to authority, and was to have wider repercussions in 1939. At Ypres; 'I began to air my convictions that the war was useless and inhuman, even inflicting these on a highly conservative general (an unnaturally fearless man) who dined with us one evening, and who asked me why I wasn't fighting for the Germans? to which I answered with all too triumphant a simplicity that it was only due to my having been born in England not Germany.' Among many letters of enthusiasm from readers of *Undertones of War* (from generals, privates and writers), Edmund was particularly pleased to receive one in 1932 from Germany, from General Haushofer, praising him for capturing the spirit of the fighting man. In a drafted reply Edmund recalled the:

Faith and fortitude and good sense which even as we stood behind our parapets we perceived to be the spirit which reigned behind the opposite sandbags. At every stage of my front-line experience, I honoured that spirit and felt as many did a pathetic desire to be able to go over and have a quiet talk with people whom I supposed to be much like my own companions – as indeed they were. We still lack in England, I believe, one plain volume on Germany's war (and even that of France) – but the survivors from our army do not need one in order to feel that wonderful unselfishness which existed over No Man's Land.[20]

When editing the poems of Wilfred Owen in 1931 he was similarly moved by an extract from a letter Owen wrote from the Somme: 'Christ is literally in No Man's Land. There men often hear His voice.'[21]

# PART TWO   1915 – 1919

Above all, *Undertones of War* is an account of the infantryman's war and the characters of the men who fought beside Edmund, for he wanted the book to describe 'not so much myself and my opinions as what happened to my generation'.[22] Of all the many letters which he received after publication one of the most treasured was from a man who had been a private in the Northumberland Fusiliers:

I am so glad you have written *Undertones of War*. The feeling it gave me when reading it, nobody could ever understand. . . . To really understand your book one must have gone through the mill as an infantryman. . . . I must tell you how much I enjoyed your book, and the very odd feeling that came over me. I cannot properly express it here. I am just an ordinary working man.[23]

H. M. Tomlinson described the book as 'a tribute to the unknown soldier more lasting than the pomps about a cenotaph'.[24] The 'unnamed' are celebrated:

Man, ruddy-cheeked under your squat chin-strapped iron helmet, sturdy under your leather jerkin, clapping your burden of burning-cold steel, grinning and flinging old-home repartee at your pal passing by, you endured that winter of winters, as it seems to me, in the best way of manliness. I forget your name. . . . It is time to hint to a new age what your value, what your love was; your Ypres is gone, and you are gone; we were lucky to see you 'in the pink' against white-ribbed and socket-eyed despair.

The named men are unforgettable: the stammering Limbery-Buse (the lumbering bus); 'the plump ironical, unscarable Irishman' Doogan – killed at Stuff Trench; 'the rosy-faced, slender, argumentative Penruddock' – killed at Beaumont Hamel; 'the witty, kind and fearless Daniels', 'the philosophic, artistic Naylor', 'the modest, invaluable Clifford' – all three killed at Ypres; 'the plain, brave, affectionate Swain' – killed in the March offensive of 1918; 'the satirical artist Edmond Kapp', Neville Lytton 'outspoken in his loathing of war', Lindsay Clarke 'the most resolute of our officers' and Johnson 'the red-cheeked, silent runner'. These and many others join the 'practically minded' James Cassells (who became the model for the poem 'An Infantryman'), the cricketing Millward, N. C. Olive his companion through most of the Ypres offensive, the colourful Maycock shaking his fist at 'the bloody old witch' the moon, 'the tall blasphemous and brave' C. S. M. Lee, the ever-faithful batman Shearing, and 'our wisest, heartiest, safest guide' Jake Lintot, as the real heroes of the book: 'Davey, Ashford, Roberts . . . Seall, Unsted, do you remember me yet? I should know you among ten thousand. Your voices are heard, and each man longed for, beyond the maze of mutability.'

In particular, Edmund took pleasure in the company of four Old Blues in the regiment who found themselves together by the Yser Canal – Horace Amon, W. J. Collyer, Ernest Tice and Arnold Vidler. Tice had lost a lover, and is remembered in the poem 'E.W.T.: On the Death of His Betty'. This loss 'made him seem a little sombre to strangers; to those who knew him better he was a perfect friend'.[25] Collyer 'was cheerful at all times, and gifted with an odd humour which made him a most agreeable companion'.[26] Vidler was a carefree mimic, and Edmund's regular companion in night patrols. In the spring of 1917 at St Omer they all met for a reunion, 'The Feast of Five', and enjoyed a 'colloquy of Sussex in her days of peace'.[27] On 31 July during the first minutes of Passchendaele, Collyer was killed in No Man's Land; a few hours later Tice met some Germans coming out of a dugout. Using his revolver butt he knobkerried the first but was shot and fatally wounded by the second. A week later Edmund wrote:

Through the gloomy smoke of war, and dull obliterations of all our old guiding marks, it is not within the fighting man's power to see the Delectable Mountains and the Happy Valleys to which we trust to come: yet your nobility and your excellent sacrifice, dear Tice and dear Collyer, now seem to me like the kindly light which leads us through the dark to inevitable good. Where you are, I am sure you know all is well.[28]

Vidler survived the war but suffered extreme mental depression and, in a fit of despair, shot himself in 1924. Edmund's verse tributes are the poems entitled 'A.G.A.V.' – 'If one cause I have for pride, it is to have been your friend'[29] – and 'Company Commander, 1917', when he recalls Vidler singing in the trenches, 'How lovely are the messengers that preach us the gospel of peace' and 'O for the peace that floweth like a river.' He concludes:

> Dead lies my friend, the fighter, from whom I have rarely heard,
> Against a human enemy one unhumorous word.[30]

Of others who survived, two became life-long friends – Sergeant Frank Worley and Colonel G. H. Harrison.

From a butcher's shop in Sussex Frank Worley was sent to Festubert in 1916, and became the NCO whom Edmund most respected. His good humour was limitless, his courage taken for granted. His cheerful cry of 'Come on, my lucky lads,' was matched by his comforting words to young soldiers under fire, to whom he would whisper, 'Don't fret, lay still.'[31] He was an expert in the intricacies of erecting

95

barbed wire, and spent many hours engaged in this occupation with
Edmund. They became close companions, and their friendship continued after the war when Worley ran a fish shop in Worthing. As the
years passed, the memories of war increasingly played on his nerves,
and he died in 1954. Edmund had tried to have him honoured with a
VC, but his award remained a DCM. On Worley's death, Edmund
wrote a commemorative poem whose opening lines recall the courage
which Edmund never forgot:

> There was no death but you would face it
> Even in your youth;
> No riddle of life but you would grace it
> With your brave truth.[32]

And as he stated in *Undertones of War* : 'A kinder heart there never was:
a gentler spirit never.'

If Edmund did not always relate easily to those in authority, there
was one outstanding exception in the figure of his commanding officer, Colonel George Hyde Harrison, for whom he felt nothing but
admiration and affection – 'his likeness cannot come again in this life,
nor can man be more beloved'.[33] Harrison began his army career in
the Border Regiment, serving in South Africa, before commanding
the 11th Royal Sussex at Festubert, the Somme and their early days at
Ypres. He was a talented soldier, an outstanding leader and a man of
culture – he it was who noticed the review of *Pastorals* in the *Times
Literary Supplement*. He was particularly adept at raising the morale of
his men at moments of despair, and Edmund felt his absence acutely
when Harrison was summoned back to England just before Passchendaele. One of his ancestors, John Butler Harrison, was a close friend –
and fellow soldier in the Hampshire Militia – of Edward Gibbon.
Edmund liked to see connections between G. H. and J. B. Harrison –
of whom Gibbon wrote: 'His feelings were tender and noble and he
was always guided by them. His principles were just and generous and
he acted up to them'.[34] For his part, Harrison liked to compare
Edmund with Gibbon, who wrote of his military career: 'What I value
most is the knowledge it has given me of mankind in general, and of
my own Country in particular,' but 'I sighed for my proper station in
society and letters.'[35]

Harrison became a brigadier-general and retired to Guildford until
his death in 1965. Edmund's friendship deepened over the years, and
his poetic salute to him is 'On the Portrait of a Colonel', in which he
acknowledges Harrison's continuing influence:

*Where through the inhuman tempestings of night*
*This man's commanding trust will be my sight.* [36]

The friendship and the heroism of trenches, linked with the natural beauty of France and Flanders, supply the tone of 'simple joy'[37] which Edmund felt as he left the Ancre in 1918. But time was needed to supply another tone – 'I might have known the war by this time, but I was still too young to know its depth of ironic cruelty.'[38] *Undertones of War* attempts to fuse the simple joys with the ironic cruelty, for this admixture was Edmund's unique vision of war.

# 10

# Aftertones of War

*Yea, how they set themselves in battle-array I shall remember to my dying day.*
John Bunyan[1]

*My experiences in the First World War have haunted me all my life and for many days I have, it seemed, lived in that world rather than this.*
from 'Let the Poet Choose', 1973[2]

Edmund never finally exorcised the spectres of the war. Unlike Robert Graves, he was unable to say 'Goodbye to all that', and memories and allusions to warfare were cruelly faithful companions. A row of trees, the quality of light on a landscape, the sound of the wind – any of these could transport him to the trenches. With friends like Siegfried Sassoon, war became a constant topic of conversation – indeed he described his relationship with Sassoon in war imagery: 'I am as a neighbouring platoon commander, who often visits Siegfried's G.H.Q. and shows and is shown the sentry groups and gaps in the wire.'[3] *Poems 1914–30* includes the poem 'In Wiltshire', which is subtitled, 'Suggested by points of similarity with the Somme country'. Edmund's collection of *Poems 1930–40* includes over twenty 'new' war poems and a section entitled 'Echoes from the Great War', while two of the *Eleven Poems* of 1965 are also on war themes. Some memories were a matter of pride ('I knew that I did better one or two nights on the River Ancre than I ever can with my ink bottle')[4] but nightmares were more common. In 1964 he wrote to Laurence Whistler and referred to 'that Somme battle which I revisited last night to the last coil of barbed wire, but before I slept'.[5]

From the evidence of occasional diary entries - factual rather than descriptive – the nightmares were vivid memories of details of violence and bloodshed which are so restrained in his written accounts. They were a private world which he shared with surviving fellow soldiers, but most intimately with those who had not survived. The preservation of the memory of his dead colleagues became a life-long trust; it meant, of course, that attempts to forget the past were a betrayal – and he thus fed his dreams with the poison of trench memories. He felt a compulsion to revisit the sites of war – in addition to official inspections on behalf of the Imperial War Grave Commission – where he had left some part of himself:

> *. . . I*
> *Am in the soil and sap, and in the becks and conduits*
> *My blood is flowing, and my sigh of consummation*
> *Is the wind in the rampart trees,*[6]

and he was as regular an attender as possible at the annual South Downs' Battalion's Reunion. His essay about one such occasion, tellingly entitled 'Fall in, Ghosts' (1932),[7] honours the memory of his fellow soldiers, past and present, and he described the evening of the January 1928 gathering in a letter to Sassoon:

The old hands were glorious and we would have gone over the top from there, had our Colonel required it. I hadn't seen them for ten or twelve years, but they were waiting for me and threw their arms round my neck and stroked my head. I had to write poem after poem for our 'lucky lads' and showed my skill by composing some on the spot to suit particular wits and admirers. I am still absolutely happy in the glow of those men's unselfishness and faith, and so grateful to see most of them well and full of character, still unaware that they had reached the outward limits of human idealism, and still such masters of themselves as to treat their old officers as officers, and with courtesy like Philip Sidney's.[8]

Significant dates made sure that he would annually experience what he called 'a sympathetic day or two'.[9] The guilt he felt about not being part of the action in the Somme in 1918 is often repeated. In a letter to Rupert Hart-Davis on 21 March 1948 he refers to 'thirty years ago, and the Spring offensive which was one I escaped'. On the same date, in 1925, he began a letter to Kathleen Lion: 'Seven years ago the Germans indicated a desire to thrust my old battalion, alas minus me, into the Channel' – but his subconcious had caused him to date the letter 21 March 1918.[10] On 29 December 1932 he wrote to Philip Tomlinson, 'I should now send you a New Year poem but the only imagery at the moment is the Ypres Salient in snow and gun flashes, at the last gasp of 1917. Horrible shadow.' Guilt at having survived when so many fellow soldiers were killed was a familiar sensation. In the poem 'War Autobiography', he captured his feelings in 1919:

> *Then down and down I sank from joy*
> *To shrivelled age, though scarce a boy,*
> *And knew for all my fear to die*
> *That I with those lost friends should lie.* [11]

It was an emotion to be repeated in 'Reunion in War':

> *Why slept not I in Flanders clay*
> *With all the murdered men?* [12]

Memories could occur at the most unexpected times. On a cargo boat around South America in 1922 he had a haircut on the bridge – a canvas sheet reminded him of the trenches at Richebourg, a glass of lime-juice suggested trench lemonade: 'and there goes the foolish ghost back to Flanders. Even here, in the Atlantic's healthy blue, I am at the mercy of a coincidence in lime juice.' [13] Not even the cricket field was immune. He admitted to the cricketer, C. S. Marriott, in 1931: 'I have sometimes been able to excuse myself from missing a catch or a long-hop, by the revelation that my mind had floated off to Flanders. My body I sometimes transfer there.' [14] He felt a kind of schizophrenia, as though one identity was left in the war, and a second peacetime identity had to be discovered. He described the sensation in 'The Watchers':

> *I heard the challenge 'Who goes there?'*
> *Close-kept but mine through midnight air;*
> *I answered and was recognised*
> *And passed, and kindly thus advised:*
> *'There's someone crawlin' through the grass*
> *By the red ruin, or there was,*
> *And them machine guns been a firin'*
> *All the time the chaps was wirin',*
> *So sir if you're goin' out*
> *You'll keep your 'ead well down no doubt.'*
>
> *When will the stern fine 'Who goes there?'*
> *Meet me again in midnight air?*
> *And the gruff sentry's kindness, when*
> *Will kindness have such power again?*
> *It seems, as now I wake and brood,*
> *And know my hour's decrepitude,*
> *That on some dewy parapet*

*The sentry's spirit gazes yet,*
*Who will not speak with altered tone*
*When I at last am seen and known.* [15]

There was a time when he thought that he had overcome the past. In November 1968 he wrote for the *Daily Express*:

I have of course wondered when the effect of the Old War would lose its imprisoning power. Since 1918 hardly a day or night passed without my losing the present and living in a ghost story. Even when the detail of dreams is fantasy, the setting of that strange world insists on torturing.

Once I thought I had lost it. About a year ago, at the time of the death of my old friend and masterly fellow soldier, Siegfried Sassoon, I was with several old soldiers and their friends who were re-visiting the celebrated battlefields. It was requested of me one mournful day to give a little historical talk on the region of the Ypres Salient visible from Mt Kemmel, which commands so many frightening battlefields. As I stood pointing out a few places in the drifting mist, I had the sensation that suddenly, after so long, the obstinate scenes were at last vanishing. It was as though I was looking at a countryside where there had never been any war. Even the enormous Messines minecrater, which is just one of the effects of Ypres, no longer demanded my notice. Now, perhaps, escape from memory was to be granted. And yet, even as I think of that incredible war work, it stops any question of forgetting. I know, now I am an old man, that I take with me something that will never yield to the restoratives of time. [16]

Edmund knew that the ghosts would not 'fall in' in this life. As he proclaimed in the 'Preliminary' to *Undertones of War*.

I must go over the ground again.
A voice, perhaps not my own, answers within me. You will be going over the ground again, it says, until that hour when agony's clawed face softens into the smilingness of a young spring day; when you, like Hamlet, your prince of peaceful war-makers, give the ghost a *'Hic et Ubique?* then we'll change our ground', [17] and not that time in vain; when it shall be the simplest thing to take in your hands the hands of companions like E.W.T. and W.J.C. and A.G.V., [18] in whose recaptured gentleness no sign of death's astonishment or time's separation shall be imaginable.

# PART THREE
## 1919 – 1924

# 11

# Suffolk
## February – October 1919

*We went, returned,*
*But came with that far country learned;*
*Strange stars, and dream-like sounds, changed speech*
*and law are ours.*
'War's People'[1]

*Joy is here in her terrifying silence.*
Letter to A. H. Buck, August 1919

Between February and October 1919 Edmund and Mary divided their time between the Daines's family home – Deve Cottage – at Cheveley near Newmarket, and visits to Plymouth (described by Edmund as 'a Merk in bricks and mortar')[2] to stay with the Blunden parents. With Mary now four months pregnant, Edmund was anxious about how to set up a home. The financial uncertainties with Christ's Hospital and Oxford had been resolved in Edmund's favour, but there were eight months before the Oxford term started and he felt restless and ill at ease. Life after three years of war had left him weary with delayed shock, and even the countryside seemed unfamiliar and threatening after the 'scene and action that was learned in hell':[3]

*Oaks, once my friends, with ugly murmurings*
*Madden me, and ivy whirs like condor wings:*
*The very bat that stoops and whips askance*
*Shrills malice at the soul grown strange in France.*[4]

He felt numbed and, as so often in his life, he began to look back with nostalgia to a world he had been pleased to leave – for the waters of East Anglia seemed now less intimate than the water of the Ancre,

## PART THREE 1919 – 1924

*When by its battered bank I stood*
*And shared its wounded moan.* [5]

In this mood the idea of an academic life at Oxford was beginning to lose its appeal, as he felt little enthusiasm for following in Merk's intellectually deadening footsteps, and he was equally suspicious of the Oxford University Officers' Training Corps'. More attractive was the lure of literary life and he let no opportunity pass in finding outlets for publication of his poems, confessing to his mother: 'My will is stout enough though my nerves are bad; and I am getting more vigorous when I know something is to be done. We are trying a few poems and articles on the magazines, and hope for the best.'[6] Remembering the pleasure he had taken in reading Siegfried Sassoon's poems at Ypres, he ventured to send some poems to the *Daily Herald*, of which Sassoon was literary editor. He enclosed the following letter, dated 3 May:

Sir,

In the hope that you will notice them in your literary notes, I enclose two chapbooks of verse about which a slight explanation is required. The poems were written at school but not printed until 1916 when I was in France, and I have had no opportunity to issue them until now.

With gratitude not only for your vivacious criticism in *The Herald*, but also for your great efforts throughout the war to bring the ferocity of the trenches home to a public more disturbed about rations than Passchendaele,

I am, sir,
Yours truly,
E. C. Blunden (Scholar-elect, Queen's College, Oxford)[7]

Three days later, he received the following reply:

Dear Mr Blunden,

Send me your *Pastorals* please, plus two more copies of each of the chapbooks. I have only glanced at them for a few minutes, but got an impression of freshness and originality in spite of your juvenile word-crowding and humdrum rhythm. The opening of 'The Silver Bird' is delightful and gave me quite a thrill of surprise – I have had so much bad verse sent to me lately. Come and see me when you are in London – that is, at *The Herald* office. I'm usually there on Tuesdays and Fridays in the morning. In the meantime I will have another look at your poems, and hope they will continue to grip my attention.

When are you going to Oxford? And how old are you? And what did you do in the Army?

Yours very truly,
Siegfried Sassoon.[8]

A meeting was duly arranged, and Sassoon invited Edward Shanks, W. J. Turner and J. C. Squire to join the party at 39 Half Moon Street: 'You will believe that I was at once bewildered and happy, and that I put on my best collar and tie. When I reached Sassoon's rooms, he came forward – a tall young man, almost nervous I thought. . . . I made an attempt to seem used to such illustrious company, but it must have been rather weak.'[9] It was an important meeting for Edmund, for he won the approval of influential figures in London literary circles who were particularly taken by passages from his long poem 'The Barn':

> The barn is old, and very old,
> But not a place of spectral fear.
> Cobwebs and dust and speckling sun
> Come to old buildings every one.
> Long since they made their dwelling here,
>   And here you may behold
>
> Nothing but simple wane and change;
> Your tread will wake no ghost, your voice
> Will fall on silence undeterred.
> No phantom wailing will be heard,
> Only the farm's blithe cheerful noise;
>   The barn is old, not strange. [10]

Most important, it was his first meeting with Sassoon – a meeting which was to develop into a deep friendship over the next forty years. Sassoon was to give his own account of these events in his *Siegfried's Journey*, in which he recalled reading Edmund's poems and 'within five minutes' knowing that:

I had discovered a poet. Here was someone writing about a Kentish barn in a way I had always felt but had never been able to put into verse. I forgot that I was in a newspaper office, for the barn was physically evoked, with its cobwebs and dust and sparkling sun, its smell of cattle cake and apples stored in hay, the sound of the breeze singing in the shattered pane and sparrows squabbling on the roof.[11]

Literary journalism in London was vigorous and lively, and two journals in particular were attracting attention, the *Nation* and the *Athenaeum*. Under the editorship of H. W. Massingham (described by George Bernard Shaw as 'the perfect master journalist'), assisted by H. M. Tomlinson, the *Nation* had won Edmund's favour at the end of the war, partly because its forthright comments had made it a more or less banned publication on the Western Front. The *Athenaeum* was edited by J. Middleton Murry, an old boy of Christ's Hospital.  The two journals were merged in 1921 to become The *Nation and Athenaeum* before amalgamating with the *New Statesman* in 1931. Edmund was quickly drawn into this world, becoming friends with both Massingham and Tomlinson. Closer ties, however, were forged with Massingham's son Harold, and – in particular – with Tomlinson's brother Philip.

In the summer of 1919, however, the preoccupation of Edmund and Mary was the imminent birth of their first child. To their great delight, in the third week of July, a daughter was born – and to mark their delight they named her Joy. She was taken to proud grandparents in Plymouth and then to London on Monday 25 August, as Edmund had agreed to meet both Sassoon and A. E. Bernays – a governor of Christ's Hospital who held 'open house' to Old Blues in London. On the Tuesday morning Joy seemed a little unwell and was taken to a doctor, who diagnosed a minor ailment, and gave Mary some powders for the baby. Edmund kept his appointment with Sassoon and took Mary and the ailing Joy to an exhibition of Modigliani, where he was introduced to the exhibition's promoter, Osbert Sitwell. On the following day he lunched alone with Bernays. Just after 2.00 p.m. Mary noticed a distressing change in Joy's condition, and rushed her to Great Ormond Street Hospital. It appeared that she had been poisoned by contaminated milk. By the time Edmund had been contacted and had reached the scene, Joy's condition had become critical and she was fading fast. A blood transfusion was the only hope and Edmund immediately gave his own blood in a desperate attempt to save her: 'The baby, in her ward, turned when I came to her, opened her eyes, and seemed to know me and ask my pity'.[12] But the situation was hopeless, and Joy – aged just five weeks – died later that evening: 'It was [incredible], to be going off without our Joy; but we did. This was a grief beyond anything I had felt in the War. It has never been quite overcome'.[13] Edmund could hardly avoid seeing a prophetic irony in the title of his poem of 1914, 'Joy and Grief'.

Joy was buried, without a headstone, in a corner of the beautifully peaceful and secluded graveyard of All Saints, Kirtling – a church just outside Cheveley, with a fine Norman arch and a massive west tower looking out over the flat East Anglian landscape.

It was a cruel blow for Mary, already finding Edmund's literary life difficult to adapt to; for Edmund it was to provide another never-fading scar to add to the memories of war and he was often to return to the theme in his poems. In 'The Child's Grave' he recalls visiting Joy's grave with his dog:

> It seemed but as yesterday she lay by my side,
>    And now my dog ate of the grass on her grave.

He imagined asking her spirit what had happened to her:

> since we left her that day
> In the white lilied coffin, and rained down our tears;
> But the grave held no answer, though long I should stay;
> How strange that his clay should mingle with hers!
>
> So I called my good dog, and went on my way;
>    Joy's spirit shone then in each flower I went by,
> And clear as the noon, in coppice and ley.
>    Her sweet dawning smile and her violet eye![14]

The strongest evocation of his grief – strong in its simplicity like Wordsworth's 'Lucy' poems – is the lyric ironically entitled 'To Joy'.[15] Though Edmund's friendship with the composer Gerald Finzi was not to begin until 1947, Finzi had long admired the poem and set it for solo voice[16] and piano – the first performance being given in Edmund's presence at the Finzis' home, Ashmansworth, in 1957, sung by Wilfred Brown, accompanied by Herbert Sumsion. Finzi considered it one of his best songs and his widow Joy recounts that he felt 'it evoked the Suffolk sky where great clouds herald "the breath of the storm"'.[17] The memory of Edmund giving his blood makes lines five and six particularly poignant, and is there perhaps a half-echo of King Lear's grief at losing a daughter in the assonance of 'fall' and 'fool'?

> Is not this enough for moan
> To see this babe all motherless –
> A babe beloved – thrust out alone
>    Upon death's wilderness?
> Our tears fall, fall, fall – I would weep
> My blood away to make her warm,
> Who never went on earth one step,
>    Nor heard the breath of the storm.
> How shall you go, my little child,
> Alone on that most wintry wild?[18]

# 12

# Oxford

## October 1919 – May 1920

---

*Disbanded Generals you might meet,*
*By twos and threes in every street,*
*All now arriving to complete*
*Their interrupted courses.*

'After' Gilbert and Sullivan, drafted autobiographical notes[1]

*We were a nest of singing birds. Here we walked, there*
*we played cricket.*

Dr Johnson on his Oxford days

---

In October 1919 Edmund became – at last – an Oxford undergraduate; and he decided to change from Classics to English. Like so
many of his fellow 'veterans', he found it difficult to come to terms
with the routine of university life. Not that the beauties of Oxford
were lost on him:

The tumult of the war seemed to have been some absurd dream of one's
own. The serenity and the dignity of Oxford stood round me in a clear light.
I was back where I had been in relation to these grey and eminent buildings,
and the learning and courtesy which I felt that they housed, five years earlier,
as a nervous candidate for admission.[2]

Nevertheless, though only five years older than the average fresh-
man, those five years set the war generation very distinctly apart. He
was certainly not to be short of stimulating company and within a few
days he met – on the steps of Queen's College – a young man of
whom he had heard as a poet and literary figure, who also shared his
passion for the poetry of John Clare, Alan Porter. It was to be the first
of several significant Oxford friendships. Many years later, in an unpublished biographical note, Edmund recalled:

110

Alan's appearance was delightful. I have since thought that it might have been invented by Leonardo da Vinci. He was pale and dark, with finely cut features – a mystic in looks, as indeed in himself; and I fancied that he could impersonate Gerard Manley Hopkins, in whose verses he was expert. He walked surrounded with his thoughts, for his lips seemed always ready to smile, and did as soon as he was addressed. Even then, as he was rather deaf, he took a little while to collect what was coming next. He was not tall, but looked well built and travelled speedily. He dressed neatly, primly, and I remember an elegant bow tie, and light shoes. His voice was alto and, as he came from Manchester, he had some northern pronunciation – 'singing', always.

He was from Manchester Grammar School, and had an odd affinity (not opium-eating) with his predecessor Thomas De Quincey. Alan also loved the curiosities of the intellectual world, and I suspect him of leanings towards alchemy. . . . Even in 1919, when he was perhaps only twenty, it would be hard to say that he was unacquainted with any particular writer past or present. As yet he had not found his best way in poetry;[3] and he was in no hurry over it.

We concocted some Imaginary Conversation for a meeting of a literary society in Queen's – in one, I was the speaker representing Coleridge; he took the part of Keats. After a final polysyllabic effort by 'Coleridge', Alan closed the matter by using Keats's words 'Let me carry away, Coleridge, the memory of having pressed your hand' – and he did it with delightful irony in voice and look. He played a great part in Oxford literature during his time, as he was constantly bright with projects. . . .

In the intervals he attended to his proper studies, and I was not surprised to hear that after his Schools the Examiners told him he had set a higher standard than had been known in those papers. But he was a natural scholar, testing all that he was told by severe and patient enquiry. After Oxford, my chances of real meetings with Alan were few. We paid a visit together to W. H. Davies,[4] who sat in a room over a shop, overlooked by numerous portraits of himself. He was not so great an admirer of Clare as we had expected him to be, nor did I discover the poet in him who is so Vaughan-like in many of his lyrics. Alan, who saw him again for a talk, was pleased to illustrate his personality by quoting the following contrast between my early verses and his own work: 'When Blunden sees a blade of grass, he sees all sorts of things, beetles crawling up it and so on. But I *love* it.'

Perhaps I shall remember him longest in some bypath, swiftly stooping to the bank, picking a leaf from a weed and enjoying its scent as he came along again; or similarly in his chair, fastening on some line or passage in an uncommon writer and quoting it with a will.[5]

After leaving Oxford, Alan Porter became literary editor of the *Spectator*, before moving to America to teach at Vassar. In 1919 he quickly introduced Edmund to the Oxford literary circle of the time, which became his regular company for six months. Prominent among the group were the novelists L. P. Hartley and Louis Golding ('a plump little undergraduate, darting in and out, full of literary plans and witty conversation'), together with Hugo Dyson, Edgell Rickword, L. A. G. Strong, Richard Hughes, Arthur Bryant, Charles Morgan and, from America, the poet William Force Stead.

This circle of literary friends[6] was to be widened when Edmund − claiming ill-health − moved into Mona Cottage, a tiny house on Boar's Hill rented from Mrs Delilah Becker, the 'Jubilee Murderess', who was reputed to have murdered her husband with a cobbler's knife in Jubilee year. She was much liked by Robert Graves, who commemorated her in his poems 'Delilah's Parrot' and 'The Coronation Murder'. Though in some ways sorry to leave the activity of Oxford itself, and to have less contact with Sid Steele, the colourful dark-suited and bowler-hatted college porter, the move gave Edmund more space and privacy as well as enabling Mary to join him. And Boar's Hill was populated with writers. Professor Gilbert Murray presided over academic matters; Robert Bridges, Poet Laureate, presided over matters poetic. Just five minutes away from Edmund's cottage was John Masefield (who sympathetically read Edmund's poems in manuscript) and in the cottage in Masefield's garden lived Robert Graves. Also nearby was the poet Robert Nichols. Edmund's relationship with Masefield was always cordial, though never close; his relationship with Nichols was both close and cordial; his relationship with Graves was close, cordial and hostile by turns.

Nichols was not an undergraduate. He was a flamboyant character who never denied the rumour that he had been 'sent down' before the war for throwing a mangold-wurzel at Lloyd George at a political meeting. Edmund had read some of his poetry in the trenches and quickly got to know this friend of Sassoon and Graves, who was 'the uncrowned King of Oxford poetry for that season'.[7] He delighted in the dramatic, and always referred to Edmund as 'Caesar'. Sitting on Boar's Hill Nichols 'radiated his emotional philosophy on the young men in the city; he was a celestial lion-tamer, blandly smiling at the follies of youth':

He certainly drew our attention to the necessity for training our intellect. Once, when he entered my tiny parlour, and laid his hand on some papers on the table, he exclaimed in his loud voice and with a twinkling eye, 'There is too much niggling going on on this Hill'. If he found some manuscript verses lying about, he might scrutinize them, bringing out a blue pencil, with a serious face. From his window lower down the hill he once halted Alan

Porter and me as we were scurrying into Oxford, and compelled us to sit in reverent delay, while he read us excerpts from Goethe's notebooks. In between he adjured us to consider how great a mind addressed us in those pages, and that real writing lay that way.

His slender figure, his thin stockinged legs, his bare head, his musing movement still come over the ridge of Boar's Hill for me. His 'murrey' suit colours the winter greyness. His laugh shatters the fog gathering over bramble-hedge and cabbage-patch there. Perhaps his romanticism was reflected even in his flying and illegible handwriting. It was certainly exciting to look at; it posited the Maestro; it was dramatic. He pretended that he was intensely offended when people confused him with Mr Beverley Nichols,[8] then one of the brilliant figures of younger Oxford. He also carried on an unsubstantial warfare against the poetry of Dr Alfred Noyes,[9] and was proud of a squib (which I bought in Charing Cross Road) containing such lines as

*Peace is here – where is Alfred Noyes?*

The Robin Goodfellow element in his nature was often coming out. When undergraduates performed some scenes from Thomas Hardy's *The Dynasts* – and how wonderfully they recited the poetry and represented the characters! – we took our seats somewhere in the back rows; and presently Mr Hardy made his way towards the front. A mild old gentleman, seemingly detached from his own play and from everything but the courteous meeting with friends gathered for an evening's entertainment. Robert Nichols then came into view, shaking hands with the veteran, bowing over him with a suggestion that it might be Goethe who was welcoming the seer of Wessex. Fate missed a point in not placing R.N. at Weimar when Thackeray and the rest were there.

But equally, as it seemed to me, there should have been a villa for R.N. in the neighbourhood of D'Annunzio.

In 1921 Nichols went to Japan as Professor of English at Tokyo – a significant move for Edmund, as it turned out – and Edmund's contact with him became limited to occasional meetings:

Long afterwards I was busy in my tutorial room at Merton College, when in came Robert. He only came to bless. To declare, also, that no matter what new poets had been rising into fame, there was something to be said for the old ones, the simpler lyrical Georgians, the metrists. He was not so high-spirited as in the old days, and seemed almost willing to become a veteran himself; to rest in his early poetry and in the kind of poetry which had been written during the old War and soon after. There was something very like a tear in his eye as he sat speaking of that hopeful though death-laden time. . . .

He was a creature of nerves . . . for he was an invalid or near that. For my part I remember chiefly his gentlemanly endurance of the poor style in which alone I could receive him at Mona Cottage; and one day there, he was so kind as to read, among other things, that poem of his from which one line seems to toll over his grave:

*'The bell is sounding down in Dedham Vale.'* [10]

Edmund had had contact with Robert Graves before arriving in Oxford, for in July 1919 Graves had written to him after receiving copies of *Three Poems* and 'The Barn' from Sassoon. Graves thought them 'the real stuff', and invited Edmund to contribute to the *Owl* – a new periodical, independent in terms of politics and literary fashion, which Graves was co-editing with W. J. Turner. Edmund offered 'Pan Grown Old', which was accepted, but, at Graves's suggestion, retitled 'A Country God'. In many ways Graves's criticisms of Edmund's poetry were perceptive – he felt that Edmund was too bound to the diction of the past, and wrote too much, too repetitively; but he was also a great admirer and encourager. Edmund was a regular visitor to the cottage which Graves shared with his wife, Nancy Nicholson, and Edmund delighted to remember him as 'a Tennysonian figure, hatless, wearing a sort of shawl round his neck and carrying several volumes under his arm, cycling down to Oxford'.[11] Graves enjoyed the patronage of the influential editor of the five volumes of *Georgian Poetry*, Sir Edward Marsh. When Edmund left Oxford, Graves wrote to Eddie Marsh asking him to befriend Edmund:

May I pass on the Blundens to you as a sacred charge to keep an eye on them? They are a most diabolically proud couple, Edmund especially, and will rather starve than ask for help if they need it. . . . Edmund works much too hard and does too much for charity. He is, on the whole, the 'intrinsically' (whatever that means) best fellow I've met since I left school (Siegfried only excluded) and is going to beat the lot of us as a poet if he goes on at the present rate, and if he learns to let himself go 'all out' a bit more.[12]

Marsh readily accepted the charge, channelling money to Edmund from what he described as his 'Rupert Brooke fund'.[13] It was the beginning of a warm relationship with Marsh, who from this time on was to include Edmund among his already wide circle of patronage.

Relations between Edmund and Graves were soon to become strained – a common enough state of affairs with Graves's friendships. It was probably inevitable that the combination of Graves's confident and somewhat aggressive character and Edmund's quieter, more reflective temperament would prove fragile. Certainly Edmund was to grow weary of Graves's intellectual enthusiasms while Graves became irritated by Edmund's obsessive ambition to become the successor of

Wordsworth and Clare. During the early Boar's Hill days, however, the atmosphere was relaxed and creative.

A mark of Edmund's affection for Graves was the dedication, 'for Nancy and Robert', of his poem 'Almswomen', when it was collected in *The Waggoner*. The poem had East Anglian origins. In the summer of 1918, when Edmund was visiting Deve Cottage, Mary and he cycled out to visit Mary's great-aunt, who lived with a friend in a row of almshouses set back from the road, in Kirtling. Enchanted by the two old ladies, their generous provision of elder-flower wine and the peace which surrounded their Suffolk retreat while the guns roared on the Somme, Edmund settled down that evening to write some couplets in imitation of Pope or Goldsmith, in order to capture the occasion. He intended it as a poetic 'exercise', and 'Almswomen' was the result, written at considerable speed. He read it to the Daines family later that night and was somewhat surprised by their enthusiasm, particularly that of his brother-in-law Jack. A year later it was printed by J. C. Squire in the *London Mercury* and by H. W. Massingham in the *Nation*. The double publication was unintentional but produced a welcome double fee and wider circulation, making the poem for some years a kind of touchstone of Georgian poetry. Graves showed pleasure in it, as did Aldous Huxley and Ralph Hodgson, and the dedication was thus no idle gesture. There were times when he felt burdened by the popularity of the poem, exclaiming to his mother in 1924, 'Why should all my poems be neglected in order that Almswomen may abound? O sentimental condition of humanity!'[14] but he was to recall forty years later that 'years have suggested other topics, other tones; but, like that little daughter buried in the solitary churchyard near the almswomen's garden, this poem comes home to me':[15]

> At Quincey's moat the squandering village ends,
> And there in the almshouse dwell the dearest friends
> Of all the village, two old dames that cling
> As close as any trueloves in the spring.
> Long, long ago they passed three-score-and-ten,
> And in this doll's-house lived together then;
> All things they have in common being so poor,
> And their one fear, Death's shadow at the door.
> Each sundown makes them mournful, each sunrise
> Brings back the brightness in their failing eyes. . . .
> Many a time they kiss and cry and pray
> That both be summoned in the selfsame day,
> And wiseman linnet tinkling in his cage

# PART THREE 1919 – 1924

*End too with them the friendship of old age,*
*And all together leave their treasured room*
*Some bell-like evening when the May's in bloom.* [16]

Association with the world of literature was to be extended further as Edmund joined the circle who visited Garsington Manor, under the patronage of the enthusiastic, generous and eccentric Lady Ottoline Morrell. Garsington had opened its doors to most of the writers and aesthetes of the time, from Henry James and D. H. Lawrence to W. B. Yeats, Virginia Woolf, Bertrand Russell and T. S. Eliot. At the time of Edmund's visits he was more likely to meet John Middleton Murry, Katherine Mansfield, Mark Gertler, Desmond MacCarthy, Siegfried Sassoon, Augustine Birrell and Aldous Huxley.

Contact had already been made with Middleton Murry, for, in February 1920, Edmund had sent an article to the *Athenaeum* on John Clare. Murry was delighted and published immediately. Edmund sent him some poems and received an equally enthusiastic response. Murry wrote a fulsome letter to Katherine Mansfield (whose opinion of Edmund's poetry and John Clare was equally muted) which shows the old Christ's Hospital freemasonry most vividly:

Something rather thrilling has happened. The other day a beautifully written (in both senses) article on the peasant poet John Clare came in to the office. I thought it awfully good, accepted it on the spot, and wrote to the man to say so. He wrote back saying he knew about me, because he was a Christ's Hospital boy. Imagine my excitement. Then I heard he was living in a little cottage near Oxford, married, on nothing a week or thereabouts, sustained by a passion for poetry. He sent me a little book of poems this morning. They are immature, but it's the right kind of immaturity: trying hard at big things: poetry full of the country and of nature. With the book he sent three other poems, again most exquisitely written, two of which I am going to print. Its the real thing . . . this time.

Somewhat surprisingly he picks out the poems 'Wilderness' and 'Chinese Pond' for special praise:

There's no fake about that. . . . That's real knowledge, real vision and artist's use of language: 'Unhouse' for the smoke of damp leaves – how good that is! And the whole thing is exquisite, veiled with an autumn country mist.

The man's (or boy's) name is Edmund Blunden, and he comes from my school! . . . isn't that the real stuff? I'm sure it is. I think he's our first real discovery, and he comes from my school! [17]

But Edmund was about to make his own 'first real discovery'. Together with Alan Porter, he was determined to try and find as much of John Clare's poetry as he could, realising that there was much to be discovered – particularly from the years which Clare spent in the Northampton asylum – than was represented in the 1908 selection by Arthur Symons, which Edmund had taken to the war. Edmund and Porter combed the shelves of the Bodleian Library, looking in copies of the *Gentleman's Magazine* of 1864, the year of Clare's death. A few poems came to light – and Edmund's lifelong pleasure in searching old periodicals for unnoticed poems had begun. Alan Porter found an offprint of an article on Clare's knowledge of flowers, 'Northampton-shire Botanologia', by G. C. Druce. By happy chance Dr Druce was living in Oxford, at 9 Crick Road ('No 1, Parnassus, would have suited our anticipation')[18] and he agreed to see Edmund and Alan Porter and talk about Clare, whom Druce had seen – 'a little dreamy man, staring at the sky'. Druce gave them a letter of introduction to the curator of the Peterborough Natural History Museum, J. W. Bodger, and a visit to Peterborough was arranged for the Easter vacation of 1920.

Edmund, Mary and Alan Porter set out from Oxford station, penniless but full of hope. During the train journey, they found some further Clare poems in three old volumes which Alan Porter had bought in a second-hand bookshop while waiting for the train. On arrival at Peterborough ('a city then more like Bruges than it will be now') they discovered that the city was hosting a horse fair, and virtually all available accommodation was taken up. The proprietor of the Bull Hotel, however, had one spare room and was prevailed upon to convert a bathroom into a bedroom for Alan Porter.

On the next morning they visited the kindly, rosy-faced and mildly surprised Mr Bodger. He gave them the freedom of the museum and unlocked a large cupboard from which spilled out a mass of unsorted papers – the remains of the Clare centenary exhibition of 1893. The excitement was electric: here were thousands of papers. Some were manuscript poems, short, undated, intense poems, mostly unknown; some were transcriptions, including two beautifully bound folios of Clare's 'asylum' poems; some were drafts of Clare's impression of contemporaries – Hazlitt, De Quincey and Lamb.

The only course of action seemed to be to copy the entire collection, and for three weeks of 'happy insanity' the transcription took place, with only brief moments of relaxation in the company of L. P. Hartley:

## PART THREE    1919 – 1924

Our acquaintance with Leslie Hartley took us to Fletton Towers, where his father, mother, sisters and he were kind to us; and another day Leslie took us along the Nene (Clare's river) to his swimming-pool, the Forty-Foot. How icy that water was; but the novelist was in before us; comfortably, and it seemed warmly, beating along over the shoals of immemorial bream who obviously owned those deeps.

Edmund's enthusiasm for tracking down biographical information, and finding insights into writers' work from contemporary sources, was put to the test as he tried to trace some of Clare's relations. One of Clare's daughters, Eliza, married a Mr Sefton and went to live in Spalding – and it was to this home that Clare's widow (the 'Patty' and 'the rosebud in humble life' of his earlier poems) found refuge in her last years. Edmund made contact with Eliza's son, Sam, living in Derby, and they quickly became friends. Sam Sefton was an avid reader ('he looked on a public library with much the same feelings as those of a child surveying a Christmas cake') and had also inherited some of Clare's personal property, including some jottings on the edges of newspapers dating from the time of Clare's escape from the private asylum in Epping Forest. They provided a strange series of contrasts, with stanzas about the heavenly city, the apocalypse and the glory of God sharing a page with the 'small ads' and news of a dull day in 1841.

Sefton also owned a small oil painting of an owl by 'Hilton R.A.' (as Clare had written on the back), the artist who had painted the portrait of Clare which hangs in the National Portrait Gallery. Edmund was particularly taken by the owl and was delighted when, in later years, Sefton presented it to him as a gift. It remained on Edmund's study wall, wherever he went, for the rest of his life. It added to his sense of identification with Clare, which had been apparent in the poem 'Clare's Ghost' and was to reappear as 'The Death-Mask of John Clare'. The poem 'April Byeway', composed in Peterborough at this time, is also addressed to Clare, though he is not mentioned by name:

> *Friend whom I never saw, yet dearest friend . . .*
> *Still stands my friend, though all's to chaos hurled,*
> *The unseen friend, the one last friend in all the world.* [19]

Robert Graves was worried, after Edmund had sent him a letter declaring himself to *be* John Clare, that his identification had become more real than was healthy. He wrote to Edmund:

You identify yourself with Clare because he represents to you the victim of village life, unsuccessful in his attempts to win recognition in spite of the help given him by Old Blues on the *London*. Where Clare failed you are out to succeed and thus avenge him. You have avenged him most miraculously and restored him to popular recognition. His ghost ought to have burned out its discontent. Now I hope you will lose a little of your sense of identity with Clare so that you won't think of madhouses or Mary Joyces[20] or of Clare's pastoralism as an end in itself.[21]

His contact with Sam Sefton confirmed Edmund's view that Clare's first biographer, Frederick Martin, had produced a somewhat melodramatic and sentimental version of Clare's life – in particular the suggestion that Clare's problems stemmed from excessive drinking, the statement that Clare 'pottered in the fields feebly', and that Clare's home – which Edmund considered 'a pretty cottage' – was described as 'a narrow wretched hut, more like a prison than a human dwelling'.[22] Edmund was anxious to redress the balance in his lengthy biographical introduction to the selection of poems which he and Alan Porter published at the end of the year as *John Clare: Poems Chiefly from Manuscript*. It was a selection of nearly 150 poems, ninety of which appeared for the first time – such as 'Badger' and 'The Fox'. It also included 'Ploughman Singing', which Ivor Gurney set for solo voice, dedicating the composition to Edmund in gratitude for his work in bringing Clare to a wider audience. Edmund's fascination with the poetry of the mentally unstable meant that the 'asylum' poems held special interest for him, and he concluded his introduction with his thoughts on the strange, elusive and haunting verses:

His Asylum Poems are distinct from most of the earlier work. They are often the expression of his love tragedy, yet strange to say they are not often sad or bitter: imagination conquers, and the tragedy vanishes. They are rhythmically new, the movement having changed from that of quiet reflection to one of lyrical enthusiasm: even nature is now seen in brighter colours and sung in subtler music. Old age bringing ever intenser recollection and childlike vision found Clare writing the light lovely songs which bear no slightest sign of the cruel years. So near in these later poems are sorrow and joy that they awaken deeper feelings and instincts than almost any other lyrics can – emotions such as he shares with us in his 'Adieu!'

> *I left the little birds*
> *And sweet lowing of the herds*
> *And couldn't find out words,*
>    *Do you see,*
> *To say to them good-bye,*
> *Where the yellowcups do lie;*
> *So heaving a deep sigh,*
>    *Took to sea . . .*

## PART THREE 1919 – 1924

In this sort of pathos, so indefinable and intimate, William Blake and only he can be said to resemble him.

Three years later Edmund was to admit that he was somewhat harsh on Martin, but he still felt hostile to the way Martin 'exaggerated in novelistic vein the humour which Clare in his memories treated his life and sensations.'

The excitement of the Peterborough weeks had whetted Edmund's appetite for literary discovery. He was to recall it all in 1964 in a small pamphlet, *John Clare: Beginner's Luck*, in which he stated: 'literary research, I believe, is what Coleridge in early glory said that poetry is: its own exceeding great reward.' But the excitements of Peterborough were not limited to the discovery of Clare manuscripts, for one of Edmund's fellow guests at the Bull Hotel was to find himself at the centre of the most celebrated scandal of the year – and Edmund and Mary were to become key witnesses.

While Edmund was pacing between the front door and the staircase of the hotel, anxiously waiting to see if accommodation was available, the occupant of Room 15 was relaxing before dinner. He was the famous preacher, Archdeacon John Wakeford, of Salisbury. Wakeford dined alone, a conspicuous figure in gaiters, at a table a little way from the Blundens. Edmund whispered to Mary to keep her hand under the table because she was not wearing her wedding ring – her fingers being too thin to keep it on. The next morning Archdeacon Wakeford paid his bill and left for home. A few months later he was facing a Consistory Court accused of having slept with a young lady at the Bull Hotel on two occasions – one of them being the evening of the horse fair at Peterborough.

Wakeford asked Edmund to appear as a witness and he duly attended the hearing and gave his evidence. It was a bizarre case: the young girl whom Wakeford was supposed to have met in Peterborough Cathedral could not be traced; there was much discussion about whether the Archdeacon wore pyjamas or a nightshirt; the entry in the hotel register appeared in pencil and may have been altered. Edmund was suspicious that his own bill had been confused with that of Wakeford's; he realised that his remarks to Mary on that fateful evening, concerning the lack of a wedding ring on her finger, had been attributed (by a waitress) to Wakeford – perhaps accidentally, but (it was beginning to seem) perhaps intentionally. Edmund believed in the Archdeacon's innocence, but Wakeford was found guilty – to the astonishment of most of those in court; but not entirely to the surprise of the Archdeacon, who 'was aware that not all the assessors were without prejudice'.[23]

The appeal that followed proved to be similarly bleak for the Archdeacon, and the finding of guilty was upheld. The story was taken up by many newspapers, H. J. Massingham in the *Nation* declaring it 'another Dreyfus case',[50] and the journalist and MP Horatio Bottomley produced a film of the events, in which both Edmund and Mary appeared. Mary established a fund to support the Archdeacon, but the Blundens' voice was a minority one; there were few in ecclesiastical circles who shared Edmund's views expressed in the *Nation*:

I, for one, cannot, after my connection with this case, see wherein lies the clinching proof of the Archdeacon's guilt. The adduced proofs seem to me to lead nowhere. The Archdeacon seemed to possess as strong and clear a mind as anyone in England; and I must again ask whether in the official language, 'the delinquency' is not 'lacking in cunning and contrivance' – if we suppose him capable of it. But on the report of the final proceedings, how can we agree with the verdict? 'It is a source of satisfaction to their Lordships,' runs the Press report, 'to find that the views that they entertain are shared by the right reverend prelates who have been good enough to give their assistance on this occasion.' I doubt whether these views will be shared by the public.[24]

With all Edmund's concentration on his Clare work, and his busy activity with his own poetry – contributing to the *Queen's Miscellany*, *Oxford Poetry* and *The Oxford and Cambridge Miscellany*, as well as the London journals, the *Nation*, the *Athenaeum*, the *Owl*, *Coterie*, the *London Mercury* and Holbrook Jackson's *Today* – his undergraduate work was bound to take second place and to loosen its grip. He enjoyed his English tutorials with the Shelley and Peacock expert H. F. B. Brett-Smith, but an increasing amount of his time was spent in playing cricket or visiting Christ's Hospital – sometimes a combination of the two. All this became very clear to Lady Ottoline Morrell, who felt that Edmund should set up as a journalist in London. She was also concerned about Mary, who was feeling isolated from Edmund's exclusive intellectual and literary world. Lack of money was making domestic life increasingly comfortless, and she was now pregnant again, with the emotional strains of the loss of Joy only a few months distant. Some financial security was a priority. Lady Ottoline approached Middleton Murry, and he was delighted with the idea of offering Edmund a job on the *Athenaeum*. Edmund was quick to accept the position and wrote to his parents on 27 April 1920:

# PART THREE    1919 – 1924

Murry, editor of the *Athenaeum*, is taking me on his staff, at a guaranteed wage of £250.00 per annum. I shall be office boy three days a week, coping with all the bad poetry and worse publishers – for this stroke of luck, which means that I can leave Oxford sans degree, sans examinations, sans anything, to begin work when I like, I am (for a ducat) to thank originally, our kindest of friends, Lady Ottoline Morrell.[25]

# 13

# London and Suffolk

## June 1920 – April 1924

*Little Blunden makes me more inclined to label myself
'literary'. For he brings with him his aura of enthusiasm
for literature. He creates a special atmosphere which
inspires me with certainty that I am a privileged person
sharing the mysteries of the noble craft of letters. . . .
When I have spent an hour or two with Blunden I am
agreeably conscious that I have added something to the
treasury of my earthly experience.*
Siegfried Sassoon, Diary, 1922[1]

For a year from June 1920 Edmund was to work from the elegant offices of the *Athenaeum* at 10 Adelphi Terrace, commuting from lodgings in Cricklewood. From June 1921, when the *Athenaeum* joined with the *Nation* under the editorship of the nervously intense, aesthetic 'Il Penseroso' H. W. Massingham, he remained a regular contributor. As always he worked with speed and enthusiasm, writing paragraphs of 'Literary Gossip', reviews of books, and short pieces on subjects as diverse as fireworks, *Crockford's*, Wilfrid Blunt, Dante and Swinburne. It was a happy fulfilment of one side of Edmund, exploring a wide variety of literary paths, showing a breadth of knowledge which would have been impressive in a man twice his age, and channelling his natural nervous impulsiveness into a flurry of writing activity – composing his copy swiftly and energetically at his desk, like some literary woodpecker. Between 1920 and 1924, although only working part-time, he was to contribute over 200 items to the *Athenaeum* and the *Nation* alone. If one adds the publication of individual poems, and his contribution to other journals such as the

## PART THREE    1919 – 1924

*London Mercury*, *Cassell's Weekly* and the *Times Literary Supplement* (with the encouragement of its first editor Bruce Richmond and the 'tall, kind, learned, laughing, gentlemanly' D. L. Murray (Richmond's assistant and, from 1933, his successor), he was to be in print over 450 times during this period. He was never to lose his taste for journalism, and by 1969 his contribution to periodicals (including short notices as well as longer pieces) amounted to close to 3,400 items.

Adelphi Terrace attracted many lively characters. Into the office would come celebrities such as George Bernard Shaw, H. W. Nevinson, Wyndham Lewis and the Reverend 'Dick' Sheppard of St Martin-in-the-Fields. Social life was equally stimulating. At lunchtime Edmund might be the guest of Massingham at Simpson's; at dinner he could be found at the Reform Club as a guest of Sassoon, or at the Chandos with the tall, dark-haired, bespectacled mathematician, scientist, musicologist, writer and boxer J. W. N. Sullivan – 'I doubt whether I have met a more intelligent man.'[2] An atmosphere of 'quiet laughter' reigned, and Edmund relaxed in what he described as 'an intensity of political justice, an alliance of true liberals.'[3]

He was becoming accustomed to the whirl of literary life and the sophistication of London (a city he came to love and know intimately), though his nervousness usually demanded the cushion of company and his financial insecurity made him most often a guest. He would rarely venture into a hotel or restaurant on his own, but in conversation he was confident and at ease. His ability to give of himself meant that he made friends easily, two particularly fruitful associations being established at this period – with Philip Tomlinson and with Siegfried Sassoon.

Philip Tomlinson was a less assured personality than his more successful brother Henry, with whom his relations were often strained. Edmund had a happy friendship with both brothers, but was particularly drawn to the modest, sensitive, shy nature of the short, rather nervous Philip – with whom he shared these characteristics. After her divorce in 1925 from the theatrical producer Leon M. Lion, Kathleen Lion married Philip – and Edmund remained close friends with both of them. As always friendship meant correspondence and several hundred letters were exchanged over the next forty years, during which time Tomlinson left the *Nation* to join, first *The Times*, then the *Times Weekly Review* and finally the *Times Literary Supplement*, in whose offices he was eventually to share a desk with Edmund. They both enjoyed a love of rural pleasures and the backwaters of literary creativity. Edmund described Tomlinson's 'fine mind and affectionate spirit' as among 'the best things in my life',[4] and felt him 'in some lights' to be 'my most intimate friend'.[5] On the publication of *Undertones of War* in 1928 Edmund dedicated it to 'Philip Tomlinson, wishing him a lasting Peace and myself his companionship in Peace or War'.

Edmund's friendship with Sassoon began almost spontaneously at their first meeting. Although ten years older than Edmund, Sassoon had spent his early war around Festubert and to this natural bond was added a shared love of cricket and the work of Thomas Hardy. Entries in his diary during this period show Sassoon very quickly warming to 'little Blunden' and finding his company 'both soothing and stimulating'. To start with, Sassoon was the mentor, introducing Edmund to London literary society and shielding his nervous sensitivity: 'Yes; it is the frailty of Blunden which makes him unique. Perhaps my vanity is flattered by my protective feeling for him. His spirit burns in his body with the apparent fragility of a flame. I want always to be interposing the bulk of my physical robustness between him and the brutish blustering of the winds of the outer world.' But this quickly developed into a deeper meeting of spirits: 'He is one of the rare people in whom I recognize beyond all doubt some comradeship of the mind which leads me outside the exhausted atmosphere of my introspections. With Blunden I am my better self; I feel an intense sympathy and affection for him; but it is a kinship of the mind; the gross elements of sex are miraculously remote.'

On Edmund's side the relationship developed from hero-worship to an intimate friendship. A correspondence of over 500 letters on both sides spanned the next forty years (marred only by a brief period of estrangement) and Edmund was to be a regular visitor at Sassoon's Wiltshire home, Heytesbury. He was particularly struck by Sassoon's dignified bearing and courtesy, often comparing him with Sir Philip Sidney, and imagining him 'in the line – a princely youth emerging from a gray greasy dugout's maw into the upheaval of iron and clay, a sun to face the Sun'.[6] As Sassoon had indicated, 'the gross elements of sex' were never to intrude on their relationship but Edmund's thoroughly heterosexual impulses did not prevent his understanding of Sassoon's homosexual side. When writing to him in the late 1920s he would include Sassoon's friend Stephen Tennant in his greetings, signing his letters 'ever more yours and Stephen's'.

By the summer of 1920 Edmund had prepared a volume of verse for publication – *The Waggoner* – consisting of twenty-five poems, bringing together many which had been published elsewhere, but including five appearing for the first time and others which had been revised. Edmund continued his habit of dedications – individual poems being dedicated, among others, to Siegfried Sassoon, Alan Porter, H. J. Massingham, G. W. Palmer (his old maths teacher at Christ's Hospital) and Joy; the whole collection was dedicated to Mary. The Blunden 'mixture' was beginning to show its pattern – rural observation, water poems, memories of war and a sense of ghostly fantasy. Many of the poems reflected his precise knowledge of country life and terminology, often expressed in dialect words – 'shealings' to describe long flat pebbles, and 'thaive' for a two-year-old ewe. His use of such vocabulary attracted both praise and dissent. Those who disliked it felt it was old-fashioned and a bar to spontaneity; those who appreciated it saw it as a welcome extension of tradition and the mark of a true countryman. Robert Bridges observed:

Since a young poet, Mr Edmund Blunden, has lately published a volume in which this particular element of dialectal and obsolescent words is very prominent, it will be suitable to our general purpose to consider it as a practical experiment and examine the results. The poetic diction and high standard of his best work give sufficient importance to this procedure; and though he may seem to be somewhat extravagant in his predilection for unusual terms, yet his poetry cannot be imagined without them.[7]

*The Waggoner* was published in August 1920 by Sidgwick and Jackson, whose offices were just by Adelphi Terrace and who had published Ivor Gurney and W. J. Turner. It attracted considerable attention. Thomas Hardy and John Masefield wrote appreciatively to Edmund and favourable reviews were printed in *The Times*, the *Spectator*, the *Daily Herald* and the *London Mercury*. Two poems stand out: 'The Waggoner' itself and 'The Veteran'. 'The Waggoner' was a Boar's Hill poem, the rhythms reflecting the slow progress of the waggon along the road, evoking the 'centuries past' as:

> The old waggon drudges through the miry lane,
>   By the skulking pond where the pollards frown,
> Notched dumb surly images of pain;
>   On a dulled earth the night droops down.[8]

In 'The Veteran' (dedicated to Colonel G. H. Harrison) an old man tries to forget his wartime in the pleasure of nature:

> He stumbles silver-haired among his bees,
> Now with the warm sun mantling him; he plods
> Taking his honey under the pippin-trees,
> Where every sprig with rich red harvest nods.
>   He marks the skies' intents,

*And like a child, his joy still springing new,*
*In this fantastic garden the year through*
*He steeps himself in nature's opulence.*

If dreams come to haunt him with the sound of bugles, he wakes only to the sound of 'His bellman cockerel crying the first round'.[9] The whole collection shows a delight in a return to a peaceful countryside and a sense of the healing power of nature as an almost religious presence. This was a theme to which he was to return in *Nature in English Literature* (1929): 'The miracle of Easter has its evidences in every meadow of that bright day, but these seem to be regarded as scenery, worth general reference perhaps, but not in the same spirit of sublimer reassurance as is proper within the four walls of our Church.'

Family affairs were now weighing on Edmund's mind. On a happy note, Mary gave birth to a daughter on 29 October 1920. She was christened Clare, in memory of the poet – and when a son was born two years later he was christened John, so that a 'John Clare' could always be in the family. The birth virtually coincided with the production of the Clare *Poems Chiefly from Manuscript*, which were handsomely printed by a new friend, Richard Cobden-Sanderson, who had set up as a publisher at Thavies Inn. He was the son of the printer Thomas Cobden-Sanderson, who had known William Morris and Burne-Jones and who – as well as being called to the Bar – had studied bookbinding under Roger de Coverley and had set up the Doves bindery in Hammersmith. The concern for the aesthetic nature of printing and publishing was inherited by Richard, a most attractive ideal but one which was eventually to lead to financial collapse. He had published Middleton Murry and William Force Stead and they introduced him to Edmund, where cricket again proved a cementing interest. For the next ten years Cobden-Sanderson was to be Edmund's main publisher.

The publication of the Clare poems also brought a considerable correspondence – throughout his life, Edmund's desk was never clear of letters – and with it a new and fruitful friendship. Walter de la Mare had been impressed by an article by Edmund on Leigh Hunt in the *Athenaeum* in 1920, and now wrote with enquiries about certain Clare poems. The correspondence (in which Edmund observed the common figure of the faithful dog in Clare's poems) led to a warm friendship over thirty years.

In less happy vein, Mary was beginning to feel more and more isolated from Edmund's literary world and she resented his increasing absence from domestic life. It was a difficult atmosphere in which to bring up a baby, and the lodgings in Cricklewood were not particularly congenial. In an attempt to solve this problem, they returned to Suffolk in the early summer of 1921 to lodge with Mary's parents in Cheveley. If it made things easier for Mary, it put extra burdens on Edmund, who was now having further to commute to London – by bicycle and train (he never learned to drive) – and he was deeply involved with his reviewing, in producing a short pamphlet on *The Appreciation of Literary Prose* and in preparing a further volume of poems. He was not finding poetic creation easy, partly because he found the Suffolk summer uncongenial – 'there is not enough hay-making and happiness.'[10] Christ's Hospital approached him to offer a term's teaching, but Edmund wrote somewhat despondently to Hector Buck: 'Mary is against my being away from her for one day and will not agree to my desire in this case. As you know, nothing would please me better than the Summer term at Christ's Hospital and nothing would do me more good. I feel a miserable bag of bones with nerves rattling freely.'[11]

The difficulties of his personal life were highlighted by – and inter-woven with – his relationship with Robert Graves. In October 1920 Graves had written to Edmund congratulating him on the birth of Clare and declaring that 'we miss you two awfully up on the Hill'.[12] Edmund wrote a favourable review of Graves's *The Pier-Glass*, and Graves attempted unsuccessfully – at T. E. Lawrence's request – to arrange for Edmund to review Lawrence's edition of Doughty's *Arabia Deserta*. A visit to Graves twelve months later, however, led to acrimony. On 31 October 1921 Edmund wrote to Sassoon:

I took my new poems down to show Graves a few weeks ago, and he looked on them without much zeal; his critique taking the form of a good many revisions for the worse (which I indulged him, and afterwards expunged), and the general platitude: 'you've written too much'. This view Nancy shared. Nancy annoyed me by upsetting Mary who had been mellowing well, through foolish judgements of me behind my back – e.g. no affection (I don't fawn on Mary); no decency (I don't give Mary all my income but only all her expenses and an allowance). More than that, there was an innuendo about drunkenness. Some time ago I told Robert that my father had over-done 'the pint system'; I told him this, expecting him not to apply it to anything but my circumstances. The failing is now, I may say, almost entirely conquered. Robert, in the most awkward way, blurted out hints about my having a natural bias towards beer; and one day when I went to see a man at Oxford, the three (Robert, Nancy and Mary) solemnly discussed the problems of my returning drunk and of refusing me the house. All because I once confided my father's bygones to Robert.

Graves was upset by the incident and wrote to Edmund:

I wish to record a strange feeling of conflict between us not only based on mutual overwork or unenterprise in seeing each other. I'd like to have that business out with you when possible, but I don't know on what it's based except on the discordance between your home life and mine: I think of you with great friendship and having lost most of my literary friends lately I would not like to lose you without an attempt at reconciliation.
I am certainly as much to blame as you are in this case.[13]

Edmund replied, stressing his indebtedness to Graves, but declaring that he was not a slave to the bottle, and that his relationship with Mary was quite happy. In return Graves sent a letter which included some perceptive analysis of Edmund, highlighting the significance of the tension between the two worlds represented by Yalding and Christ's Hospital:

My dear Edmund
Good for you, a very frank and temperate statement and so as far as I am concerned the conflict is at an end between us. The reported conversation which showed us at Islip as regarding you 'as morally feeble – by heredity liable to lapses with the bottle' is simply false and I wouldn't believe it if I heard it of you. All I have ever said is that you have an 'inferiority complex' (excuse technicality) concerned with your father's shortcomings as I have with my mother's, and the conflict between your father and that sort of context on the one hand, and your Christ's Hospital tradition on the other is a very important motive in your poetry. . . .
The news that you and Mary are happy together makes my heart leap for joy; that was the conflict between us when you were here. I was deliberately imposing a counter-irritant to the people who were trying to make you think of poetry as more important than Mary and Clare. In emphasizing this with too heavy a hand I was wrong and I am sorry. This is the explanation as far as I can feel it and Nancy was adding fuel to the fire, you know her very decided views. We were trying to force things against the natural development in you and our punishment was your sense of pain and isolation resulting in silence and avoidance of us. Well Edmund I am feeling very happy. Send all our tribal affection to Mary whom I for one love most brotherly. About your owings to me. Understand this as my own view of a psychological necessity that if I have assisted you in any given way your assistance to me though it may have taken a very different form must have been no greater and no less. I find my debt to you immense and conclude that the vice versa holds good, that's why I didn't want a break-up.[14]

All was well for the moment, but Graves had touched two raw spots. Edmund was always liable to 'lapses with the bottle' and his relationship with Mary was far from perfect: he was reluctant to admit to either observation.

The new poems which Edmund referred to in his letter to Sassoon were to form the basis of the collection *The Shepherd*, dedicated to Sassoon. Like *The Waggoner*, this was mostly a gathering of poems which had been published in magazines and periodicals brought together to form a volume of forty-four poems with eight new pieces. They represented the pastoral scenes of Boar's Hill ('Spring Night'),[15] the countryside around Christ's Hospital ('The March Bee',[16] 'The Dried Millpond'[17]), some Yalding memories ('November Morning',[18] 'Canal',[19] among others), but were predominantly East Anglian scenes – varying from the description of 'The Poor Man's Pig'[20] and 'The Village Green'[21] near Cheveley, to memories of 'Gleaning'[22] and descriptions of the 'paradise of fungi' which he observed around Newmarket and recorded in 'The Giant Puffball'.[23] But apart from the evocation of country characters such as the shepherd and the mole-catcher, and the detailed description of thistle, longshank and the changing seasons, a more reflective mood is evident. This was a conscious inclusion on Edmund's part. He had a constant fear of being considered just a useful rustic observer and ruefully told Sassoon that he wished to be rid of the feeling that he was creatively impotent except when 'apostrophising a turnip'. He was thus relieved that Graves considered 'Old Homes',[24] published in the *London Mercury* in June 1922, as ending Edmund's 'purely pastoral chapter' – and he shared with Graves a dislike of being labelled 'Georgian'. It was not that he lacked admiration for much of the verse published in Edward Marsh's *Georgian Poetry* series, which he found refreshingly optimistic after the bleakness of war, but he resented the implied escapism and lack of poetic vigour with which the title became associated. He was to be represented by six of his own poems in the 1922 volume, which prompted a letter of advice from Sir Edmund Gosse (who was to meet Edmund a few months later, describing him as looking like 'a dear little chinchilla'):

The laxity of the poets who are called 'Georgian' annoys me very much. Most of them are satisfied to appear in public with slippers on their feet and their braces hanging down their flanks. . . . It is a danger for you that at your very early age you have met with nothing but praise. It is a very serious danger, because you are tempted, by the inconsiderate eulogy of a horde of silly critics, to think anything you write excellent. I venture to say this, because I believe your natural powers exceed those of any other young man of your generation.[25]

Certainly in *The Shepherd* Edmund was anxious to extend his range and polish his diction. He added poems which he liked to describe as writing of 'Experience and Soliloquy' – including 'The Watermill',[26] 'The Earth Hath Bubbles',[27] 'Death of Childhood Beliefs'[28] and 'The Child's Grave'.[29] There were also some new 'war' poems, including 'Third Ypres',[30] and his tribute to his battalion, '11th R.S.R.'.[31] In this poem the mixed reactions to his war experience are again emphasised. His pleasure in recalling his war comrades is vividly evident – in his own copy, he wrote under the poem, 'how *happy* the Battalion was in ordinary country places!' and the poem declares:

> Your faith still routs my dread,
> Your past and future are my parapet.

Yet still the clearest voice asks:

> What mercy is it I should live and move,
> If haunted ever by war's agony?

And this agony, linked with domestic unrest (accentuated by a further move to a small cottage in the Suffolk village of Stansfield, just outside Clare) and recurring bouts of asthma, was beginning to become a cause of concern to his friends and employers. Both H. W. Massingham and H. M. Tomlinson had connections with the ship-owning Runciman family, and they persuaded Edmund to take a voyage to South America on the cargo boat SS *Trefusis*, 'to do something to take away the taste of Stuff Trench'. Later, Tomlinson was to record that 'in spite of his indispensability to his journal . . . we could not bear him on the conscience a day longer'.[32]

Edmund thus found himself, in December 1921, preparing to join the ship which would take him across the Atlantic and up the River Plate to Buenos Aires and back over three months. As he boarded the train to London, he bade farewell to Mary, who 'spent some moments in melancholy visions of my funeral at sea. She hoped these were wrong, and I, beginning to be affected also, hoped so equally. Goodbye to Mary! The curve of the track carried her out of sight.'[33]

If the voyage was intended to exorcise the ghosts of war, it was a marked failure. The solitary hours on board ship – interspersed with literary conversations with the Captain and Third Mate – only fed his introspection. And he defiantly took with him a copy of Young's *Night Thoughts* – the very volume which he had taken to the Somme. No wonder he recorded that: 'still dreams came; the war continued'.[34]

Before leaving, Edmund had been introduced by Tomlinson to the American publisher, G. P. Putnam, who asked for the option of an

American edition of an account of the journey 'ranging where it likes in truth or fiction'.[35] It was published in December 1922 as *The Bonadventure*.

During Edmund's absence *The Shepherd* had been published to much acclaim, and Edmund returned to find that he had been awarded the Hawthornden Prize – the gift of Miss Alice Warrender for the best book published during the year by a writer under forty, and worth £100. Edmund believed that *The Waggoner* in 1922 almost succeeded but was now very glad it hadn't. Sassoon recorded that 'the £100 will be useful to him, though the prize is all bunkum and brings no prestige with it'.[36] It did, however, give Edmund respectability with the Daines family – 'where previously I have walked as the unworthy and slightly crazy husband, I shall now go as the great man'[37] – and the festivities at the Aeolian Hall in New Bond Street on 28 June 1922 were somewhat bizarre. Edward Marsh joined Miss Warrender on the platform, and the prize was presented by John Masefield with speeches by Laurence Binyon and Walter de la Mare. Sassoon recorded his impressions of the afternoon:

At the Aeolian Hall I found myself resenting the existence of various poets and literatures, famous and obscure. Masefield's speech seemed to be a mixture of vaguely pretentious uplift-talk and unsuccessful attempts to be light or impressive. And Binyon was merely diffident and muddle-headed and amiable.

The only bright moment came when Blunden blundered on to the platform, received his cheque, gave two shy and awkward ducks of his tousled head (to Masefield and Miss Warrender) and beat a panic-stricken retreat.[38]

Edmund, however, recalled Sassoon playing a rather more active role:

Sassoon was in good form at the Hawthornden festival, shouting out now and again to the agitation of the nice old ladies round him. He had thought of arriving with a sort of small brass band, but was afraid it would be construed in its opposite significance. . . . The function so annoyed him somehow that he told me he had to be rude to someone afterwards, and at the last moment remembered an invitation to tea which proved a happy hunting ground, for enemies of his and mine were present.[39]

Edmund was to experience the process all over again seven years later when Sassoon was the prize-winner; unable to attend himself, he asked Edmund to receive the award on his behalf.

Sassoon had been spending some time at *Max Gate*, the home of Thomas Hardy, and was anxious to arrange a meeting between Hardy and Edmund. During a visit to Stansfield, a week or so before the

Hawthornden ceremony of 1922, Sassoon had begun to feel a similarity between Edmund and Hardy. He described his visit in his diary:

It was a sunshiny day, and there was little Blunden waiting for me in his shabby blue suit. He had just picked up a first edition of *Atalanta in Calydon*[40] for a shilling in a little shop in Clare. And outside the station sat Mary B. in a smart blue cloak, in a tiny ramshackle wagonette drawn by a small white pony. (A conveyance hired from a farmer and driven by his juvenile daughter). Slowly we traversed the four miles to Stansfield, up and down little hills among acres of beans and wheat. Arrived at Bell Vue, a stone-faced slate-roofed box of a house by the roadside. And for three days B. and I talked about county cricket and the war and English poetry and our own poetry and East Anglia and our contemporaries. While Mary B. (on her best behaviour) produced beef, mutton and pork and several sorts of vegetables for our nourishment. And B. wrote reviews for *The Times* and *The Nation* and *The Daily News*; and I read Clare and Bloomfield and Blunden. And the weather became chilly and it rained on Tuesday and Wednesday; and we drank port by a small fire after dinner. And B. hopped about the house in his bird-like way; and we both received a letter from 'old Hardy' by the same post. And we admired the old man's calligraphy. And we bicycled to Sudbury and lost our road home and had to push the machines across the wheat-fields. And I decided that Mary was quite a good sort after all (in spite of B's critical attitude towards her).

Mary B. has a peasant-like mind which does not interest itself in literature. But she is intelligent, in her own way. She showed considerable adroitness in her creating of a favourable impression with me. And she is an attractive little creature, in her countrified way.

B. is amazingly industrious. And he lives in an atmosphere of intense devotion to the art of poetry. I came away feeling that he is one of the very few men for whom my friendship will never lessen. He is, in fact, almost the ideal friend and fellow-craftsman. My visit has consolidated our friendliness, and I feel that I now understand him completely, and admire him more than ever. I wish I could describe him clearly, but he is difficult to recapture in writing. He has a good deal in common with old Hardy. A simplicity and honesty beyond praise, and a quality of being one with his work to which he has such a noble devotion.

The association was strengthened after a visit which Sassoon made to Hardy almost immediately:

Seeing T.H. soon after my visit to Blunden makes me aware of certain similarities in them. B. of course is sensitive in the same way as T.H. They share a sort of old-fashioned seriousness about everything connected with authorship. Both are fundamentally countrified and homely. Even in outward appearance they have a similarly bird-like quality. Both enjoy talking about

simple things. It is a sublime freedom from sophistication. My own spontaneously affectionate feeling for them both is identical. With each of them I
feel unembarrassed and able to chatter about commonplace matters in a
commonplace way. Two little 'men of genius'. One is eighty-two and the
other barely twenty-five. Yet the difference in their ages seems a mere
tiresome accident (as it is). Only B.'s young promise makes me happy. And
T.H.'s 'time-trenched' decay, despite the load of achievement and recognition which his years have gathered to him, is inexpressibly mournful.

   This affinity of B. and H. is one of the strangest things I have experienced.
Also both are essentially modest and unassuming. [41]

   This visit was to prove successful in arranging that Edmund should
visit Max Gate over the weekend of 15 and 16 July 1922. It was a
pilgrimage which he 'trembled and rejoiced to make', and he was
most struck by Hardy's modesty, youthful zeal and 'Dynastic
Imagination'. [42] They talked of Shelley and Keats, and Hardy reminisced about meeting Browning at the house of Barry Cornwall's
widow, Mrs Procter. Edmund recorded in his diary:

Mrs Procter had given him reminiscences of most of the heroes of the
nineteenth century: she had been introduced by Leigh Hunt to a slackly
dressed youth named Keats, who had left no impression on her otherwise. Of
Lamb: she told T.H. that, after their wedding, Procter and she called on
Lamb, and he, somewhat embarrassed, did not dare to take her into his
untidy bedroom to wash her hands, but instead led the way into the
kitchen. [43]

   Hardy brought volumes from his library for Edmund to inspect –
Young, Abraham Cowley, Thomas Otway and an edition of William
Godwin with annotations which may have been in the hand of Shelley. He could not have found a more enthusiastic or informed
audience. Conversation turned to war, with Hardy trying unsuccessfully to persuade Edmund to write a book on Marlborough, combining it with a survey of old and new warfare.

   Two things particularly stayed in Edmund's memory. One, the
knowledge that Hardy nearly became a pupil at Christ's Hospital, and
the other a walk with Hardy to William Barnes's church, accompanied
by Hardy's faithful dog Wessex, who took an instant liking to Edmund
– an unusual reaction to strangers on Wessex's part. Edmund was
much impressed by Hardy's fitness and his ability to walk 'at a fine
pace'; even more impressive was his ability to urinate 'on the march',
without a pause in step or conversation. 'It was then', declared Edmund, 'that I knew he was a real countryman.' [44] Inside the intimate
church Hardy pointed out the fine calligraphy on the rood-screen – it

was as though they were standing in the parish church at Stinsford, Hardy's birthplace

A year later Edmund took a week's holiday with Sassoon, staying at William Barnes's old house, the Rectory, at Came – a simple, whitewashed, thatched-roof building. They took bicycle-rides around the neighbourhood, and paid daily visits to Hardy for tea at Max Gate, finding him 'in most placid and pleasant mood, remarkable for a *young* man. His talk is a mixture of the trifles with which old age amuses itself, and details of real importance in reading his life – e.g. his first serious reading book (Dryden's *Virgil*), and his zest for discussing smugglers and soldiers.'[45]

Conversation was a little more stilted when they were joined on the Sunday by T. E. Lawrence, dressed in the uniform of a private soldier. It was a curious interaction of characters: Hardy holding forth on literature and war; Sassoon with his gaze fixed on Lawrence; Lawrence fascinated by Edmund; Edmund transfixed by Hardy. Lawrence confided to Edmund and Sassoon that he had 'a poor opinion of Hardy's novels, except the descriptive parts', and that he was astonished at 'the spectacle of Hardy'[46] as an old poet. For Edmund, the days spent at Max Gate were among the most memorable of his life and they formed the basis for his *Thomas Hardy*, 'an account of Hardy's life, and especially his literary life',[47] which was published in 1942. On Hardy's death in 1926 his widow presented Edmund with Hardy's treasured copy of Edward Thomas's *Poems* as a memento of these visits.

The period from his voyage on the SS *Trefusis* until April 1924 was a busy one. He was to write *The Bonadventure* and *Christ's Hospital, A Retrospect*, while planning a biography of Leigh Hunt – a project he had first conceived in the Flanders trenches. His reviewing and journalism were to extend to a further 150 items, covering his favourite romantic poets – but also Matthew Prior, Spenser, the work of the sixteenth-century agriculturalist Thomas Tusser, and poetry on birds. He also indulged his pleasure in fine printing and binding, initiating an association with the publisher Cyril Beaumont in the publication of *To Nature*, a limited edition of thirty-four of Edmund's poems – two-thirds of them new – 'of Honest English song for England sung'[48]. This volume included the first (and less successful) version of 'To Joy' and the first use in 'The Tune' of one of Edmund's favourite phrases, 'the mind's eye'. He also published two poems separately – his tribute to Yalding, 'Old Homes' (dedicated to his brother Gilbert), and 'Dead Letters', published by Holbrook Jackson, which commemorates Thornton Leigh Hunt (the eldest son of Leigh Hunt and virtual editor of the *Daily Telegraph*); Thornton Leigh Hunt's papers had come into the possession of Lady Butterworth,[49] who had sent them to Edmund for his opinion.

Further editing work was also occupying Edmund's time. He prepared a volume of new John Clare poems entitled *Madrigals and Chronicles*, and *Shelley and Keats as they struck their Contemporaries*: both published by Cyril Beaumont at the Sign of the Harlequin's Bat. He also turned to the eighteenth century to edit Christopher Smart's 'A Song to David', together with seven other Smart poems. It was yet another journey down a minor literary road, championing the cause of a mentally disturbed writer: 'Despite such assertions as are often made (that Smart's productions, save one, were worthless). . . the glorious music and painting of the Song to David demand that whatever throws light upon the author should be revived . . . and any labour by which the Song may be made better known will not be fruitless. It should be as familiar as L'Allegro.'[50]

Edmund had also become more involved in the works of another 'troubled' writer, Charles Lamb, and was a regular member of the Charles Lamb Society (originally the Elian Society), an association which he retained for life. It was here that he met the ex-Middlesex cricketer and principal of a mental asylum, Hubert Norman:

I doubt if he could communicate what he knew, except in his actual relations with people whose nerves were in disorder or who had an obsession. Like Lamb, he was inclined to stammer at a meeting. Like Lamb, he was invincibly sensitive concerning 'what wretches feel'. I like to think that he liked us, the Elians. He only saddened when we had to part under the arc-lamps. I shall see him rather at the moment of meeting, when he seemed almost as one who touches land after a shipwreck.[51]

A more intimate friendship was established with the Secretary of the Elian Society, the lawyer F. A. Downing of Gray's Inn. For many years the Downings' house became Edmund's London base, and he was to describe their friendship as one of the chief events of 1922–4. Six years later he was to dedicate his biography of Leigh Hunt to Downing, calling himself 'his unalterable Brother'.

Another regular London venue was the studio of the poet Ralph Hodgson, near Victoria station. Hodgson was twenty-five years Edmund's senior, and was now established as a poet and artist in London (he drew a portrait of Edmund in 1921), after several years in the theatre in New York. A friend of de la Mare and Sassoon, he had founded the publishing house at the Sign of the Flying Fame in 1913, and Edmund was much taken by his typographical expertise and his extensive knowledge of book production. In November 1923 Hodgson introduced Edmund to the Japanese Keats scholar Takeshi Saito, who had been sent to England by the Imperial University of Tokyo – where he was an assistant professor and where he had attended Robert Nichols's lectures. Edmund and Saito were immediately drawn to each other and Saito was to become one of Edmund's most valued lifelong friends, a 'scholar, gentleman and Christian of the first quality'.[52]

Life in Stansfield was active too. Edmund was always eager to become involved in village life: editing a monthly village paper, playing cricket and captaining the football team. He also enjoyed the friendship and patronage of two local characters, the Rector of Stansfield, Canon A. J. Webling (author of several unusual books on spiritualism including *Something Beyond* – dedicated to Edmund – and *The Last Abbot*) and the flamboyant and knickerbockered owner of Gifford's Hall at Denston, A. H. Fass. It was after a cricket match that Edmund was first invited to dine at the Elizabethan hall which Fass had restored, and which housed Fass's books and personally designed furniture. It was the first of many evenings of lively conversation as Fass indulged in his benign 'vision of Merry England' and established himself as Edmund's 'volunteer uncle'. Sassoon was to join them on one evening in July 1923, and he remembered Fass as 'a middle-aged bachelor, pink-skinned, and sandy-grey-haired, grey-eyed and full of cultivated social and antiquarian chat . . . fostering local traditions, herbaceous borders, and rustic recreations'.[53] Edmund's family was growing too, with son John having joined daughter Clare, who was now a:

> *Toddling babe, none looks upon but loves,*
> *And feels life brighter for looking on thee,*
> *Thy gaze I'll remember and treasure as a charm*
> *When cloudy days are come upon me.*[54]

And cloudy days were becoming increasingly regular. He was feeling restless, and this inevitably brought on bouts of asthma ('If I were to write a poem now, it would be all about being buried alive').[55] Four years of part-time journalism were beginning to cloy, and financially he was hard pressed to support his family. He was beginning to look further afield, and the opportunity to change his circumstances came swiftly. In January 1924 Takeshi Saito gave Edmund the news that Robert Nichols was returning from the post of Professor of English at Tokyo and that Saito was commissioned to find a replacement. He suggested that he put forward Edmund's name, adding that Ralph Hodgson was accepting a post at Tohoku University. To Edmund it seemed a God-sent opportunity for greater financial security (£900 a year), and a chance to visit a country he had felt destined to see since childhood. He was to describe these premonitions in 'Omen'[56] and 'Looking Eastward' – in which he recalled a Yalding shopkeeper taking him to a spot where he claimed one could see Japan and 'the mountain' (presumably Mount Fuji) outlined in the Yalding sky:

> Down our street when I was a boy I met a friendly man
> Who took me to the stone-cross steps and said to me 'See Japan'.

Edmund had to confess that he was unable to make this out, but he never forgot the reply:

> He smiled, and said I should find all out, and the words he left me were these:
> I come from my shop to see Japan, and the Mountain, when I please.[57]

Within a month he had accepted the post, and made arrangements to leave for Tokyo in April to begin a three-year contract.

Mary, however, could not be persuaded to share in Edmund's enthusiasm. If the literary world of London was alien to her, the literary world of Tokyo was hardly likely to appeal either. Edmund was determined to go; Mary was equally determined to stay. The tension between them was stretching to breaking point.

On 1 February Edmund wrote to Philip Tomlinson, explaining the situation: 'Hear my sad, mad, glad, bad story. . . . Mary is staying here, she can't grow enthusiastic over foreign parts. She fears the earthquakes and the lingo.' By the same post Mary also wrote to Tomlinson: 'Will you write and tell this man not to go and bury himself in Japan for three years? He refuses to take any notice of my pleadings but says he will proceed with the proceedings. I cannot go – it depresses me greatly. So do tell him what a fool he is for me, if you see him.'[58] Tomlinson tried to act as mediator, but the volatile nature of the relationship between Edmund and Mary is clear in her reply: 'I do not remember saying I disapproved of Edmund building castles in the air. How could I ever disapprove of a thought from such a brain? To me, all his thoughts are pure and real.'[59] Reluctantly they agreed to differ. Edmund was to accept the appointment (taking a young wartime batman named Amos Crick as a 'devoted henchman') while Mary was to stay in Stansfield with the children, now aged just three-and-a-half and one-and-a-half.

Inevitably, having made the decision, Edmund began to have misgivings. He realised that his Leigh Hunt biography could not be completed until his return from Japan, and his letters to Cyril Beaumont and Richard Cobden-Sanderson[60] included references to his coming 'exile', and to the fact that he felt 'thrown out of gear' with 'a state of no state overwhelming him'.[61] He also had to face a round of farewells – a visit to Christ's Hospital, a two-day visit from Sassoon ('three years minus little B. isn't a pleasant thought'),[62] and a dinner in Edmund's honour given by the *Nation and Athenaeum* (presided over by its new editor Hubert Henderson) at the Florence in Rupert Street. H. M. Tomlinson proposed a toast to Edmund, who replied; Leonard Woolf proposed a toast to Japan, to which Takeshi Saito replied; H. W. Nevinson proposed a toast to literature, to which J. C. Squire replied. The whole party then rose to sing 'For he's a jolly good fellow'. Virginia Woolf captured the faintly absurd sentimentality of the evening in her diary entry for Wednesday 12 March 1924:

Last night we dined at Blunden's farewell party, thirty-five covers laid, six or seven speeches made. . . . Some odds and ends of ideas came to me at the dinner. For one thing, how pungent people's writing is compared with people's flesh . . . Jack Squire, fat, and consequential; Eddie [Marsh] grown grey and fatherly. Tomlinson like the hard knob of a walking stick carved by a boy of eight; Blunden, despairing, drooping, crow-like, rather than Keats-like. And did we really all believe in Blunden's genius? Had we read his poems? How much sincerity was there in the whole thing?[63]

On Friday 28 March Edmund travelled to London to board the SS *Hakone Maru* bound for Japan. As he prepared for departure he could look back on a rich life – he had survived three years of war, won an Oxford scholarship, published five volumes of poetry, two books of prose, edited Clare and Smart and become a prolific literary journalist; he had met Hardy, Sassoon, Graves, de la Mare and many established writers; he had married and had fathered three children; he was about to become a professor – and he was still seven months short of his twenty-eighth birthday.

As the ship left harbour, he clutched an edition of Shakespeare's tragedies in one hand as he sadly raised the other in farewell salute to Mary. In reality his separation from her was to be far greater than a mere 10,000 geographical miles.

# PART FOUR
## 1924 – 1931

# 14

# Japan
## April 1924 – July 1927

*I am haunted by a sense of the spirit of Japan – by
Japan in her human expression; of the Japanese scene. I
cannot go for my walk in England without seeming to be
in one moment or another in Japan as well.*
Undated reminiscence[1]

*He is known by everyone to be one of the most English
of English poets and at the same time he could feel with
the Japanese. When one loves one's own land well and
goes down to its deepest roots one inevitably meets the
hearts of mankind. There is no contradiction in it.*
Tomoji Abe 'A Tribute from Japan'[2]

The morning of 1 September 1923 was a warm and muggy one in
Tokyo, the humidity slightly relieved by a rainstorm which stopped at
eleven o'clock. An hour later the city was in flames, having suffered
the shock of a massive earthquake, which was to be followed by a
series of 1700 slighter ones over the next three days, resulting in the
loss of more than 100,000 lives. The university buildings had been
particularly badly hit, and only a handful were left standing – though
the grand old Red Gate had miraculously remained intact, a striking
reminder of the architecture of the Edo period of 1660 – 1868. Edmund was thus to enter a city and a university which were going
through the painful process of reconstruction.

The voyage, via Marseilles, Singapore (where he discovered a copy
of his 1920 Clare *Poems*), Hong Kong and Shanghai, was mostly spent
reading *King Lear*. His obsession with the play began to take the shape
of a personal identification with the tragic hero. The bleak landscape

of war in 1916 had brought to mind the heath scenes, and one of Edmund's earliest war poems – 'A House in Festubert' – suggests the shelter of the hovel and refers to Edgar's 'Prince of Darkness' Mahu.[3] He felt increasingly old before his time and feared mental disorder – though he saw *King Lear* as 'a revelation of the sanity, or inevitable sequence, underlying and co-ordinating what superficially seems incoherence'[4] – and, when in love, he would refer to his lover as Cordelia. The presence of an Edmund in the play was another happy irony. In a letter to Saito written from Marseilles in April he described *King Lear* as 'my perpetual great poem, to which I go almost daily for light and love'.[5]

By the end of April he reached Osaka, from where he travelled on to Tokyo. His initial response was one of excitement as he prepared to follow in the footsteps of Robert Nichols and Lafcadio Hearn, who lived in Japan from 1890, had a Japanese wife, wore Japanese dress and changed his name to Yakumo Koizumi. The senior English Professor, the distinguished philologist Professor Sanki Ichikawa, had arranged for Edmund to rent a small Japanese house in the backyard of his own house, which had previously been occupied by Professor Kochi Doi. Here Amos Crick made him as comfortable as possible – though visitors were confused at the arrangement of using the *tokanama* (an alcove for hanging pictures) as a bed. Very quickly, however, excitement gave way to confusion and loneliness as he tried to come to terms with:

> this strange roof,
> *Beyond broad seas, half round the swaying world.*[6]

Many of his friends in England were equally confused by his wanting to be in Japan at all, and had some difficulty with the Japanese method of addressing letters – a problem which Eddie Marsh solved by inventing the jingle:

> *Blunden does his lyric tricks*
> *Down at Number Twenty-Six*
> *Kitayamabushi-cho,*
> *Ushigome, Tokyo.*[7]

Edmund's first impressions of the university buildings were hardly encouraging. Because of the ravages of the earthquake, he was obliged to move from one 'classroom' to another, either in the undamaged Medical Science building, where he lectured in front of a macabre human skeleton, or in the 'barracks' – single-storey constructions, built of plain boards, with roughly planed desks and benches, and

1 (LEFT) Edmund Blunden's father, Charles Blunden, in naval uniform, 1917
2 (BELOW RIGHT) EB's mother, Margaret, with Edmund (right) and his brother Lancelot *c.* 1902
3 (BOTTOM) Yalding, 1936, drawn by Hanslip Fletcher for *The Sunday Times*, 6 September 1936

4 (ABOVE) Edmund Blunden (seated, centre) as Senior Grecian, Christ's Hospital, 1915

5 (LEFT) H. S. Goodwin, EB's housemaster, 1920

6 (OPPOSITE, TOP LEFT) Blunden at Poperinghe, December 1916

7 (OPPOSITE, TOP RIGHT) 'The Feast of Five': Edmund Blunden with four Christ's Hospital contemporaries, St Omer, June 1917 (standing, l. to r.: W. J. Collyer, H. Amon, E. W. Tice; seated, A. G. Vidler, EB)

8 (OPPOSITE, BOTTOM LEFT) Col. G. H. Harrison, 11th Royal Sussex Regiment, c. 1917. 'His likeness cannot come again in this life, nor can man be more beloved'

9 (RIGHT) Sgt. Frank Worley,
January 1917
'A kinder heart there never was:
a greater spirit never'

10 (ABOVE LEFT)
Philip Tomlinson,
c. 1924
11 (ABOVE RIGHT)
Siegfried Sassoon,
c. 1920

12 (LEFT)
Edmund Blunden at
Garsington Manor,
1924, taken by
Lady Ottoline
Morrell

13  Edmund Blunden drawn by William Rothenstein, 1922

14 (ABOVE)
Farewell gathering
on board *Hakone
Maru*, March 1924
(l. to r.: Mrs. Downing,
Frank Downing,
Nagasawa, Philip
Tomlinson, Mary
Blunden, Ralph
Hodgson, EB)

15 (LEFT)
Edmund Blunden
with Aki Hayashi
in Kobe, *c.* 1925

16 (ABOVE)
EB (centre) with some of
the English School of the
Tokyo Imperial University,
1924–7. Immediately to his left
are Benjamin Brady and
Takeshi Saito. To his right
are Sanki Ichikawa and
Haruji Ogura
17 (RIGHT) Takeshi Saito, 1924.
'A scholar, gentleman
and Christian of the
first quality'.

To Edmund Blunden
with blessings and bon voyage!
from Takeshi Saito
London, 28 March 1924.

18 (LEFT) Mary with Clare and John, *c.* 1929

19 (ABOVE) Sylva Norman, *c.* 1930
20 (LEFT) Annie Blunden, Edmund Blunden's sister-in-law, at Hawstead, *c.* 1930

roofed with zinc sheets. In the heat, the noise of traffic and building-works coming through the windows could be deafening; in stormy weather the rain had a similar effect on the roof. Added to these discomforts was the constant threat of earthquake, when Edmund would have to dive for cover under his desk as glass showered around him. Inevitably it brought back memories of exploding shells.

He was required to teach two courses and chose to lecture on eighteenth-century poetry to the older students (some seventy or eighty) and on the essayists of the Romantic period to a similar number of younger students. He quickly realised that he was often covering entirely new ground – Charles Lamb had never been taught in the university before – and many of his pupils had very little background knowledge. The language barrier was also more severe than he anticipated (he learned only very basic conversational Japanese himself) and he found himself as much a tutor of English Language as of Literature. The monotony depressed him, and he bitterly observed in letters to his father: 'My lecturing goes on like the train between Mark's Tey and Cambridge';[8] 'I feel as if the morning will come when I cry: To hell with Pope! and catch any boat leaving Yokohama.'[9] Tokyo itself, in 1924 a dusty, dingy city of concrete and galvanised iron, offered little in the way of immediate stimulation. The grey canal reminded Edmund of its gruesome twin outside Ypres and he was distressed by the number of diseased stray cats and dogs which roamed the streets; his own unsuccessful attempt to save a puppy – which he christened Moses – being described in the poem 'On a Small Dog'.[10] The lifestyle of Tokyo was also a far cry from the vibrant literary world of London, and feelings of academic and social isolation became acute. He missed beer and cricket; he found that unexpected expenses (£12 for a bath) ate into his salary; his asthma was irritated by the extremes of heat in summer and cold in winter; he felt starved of books and undervalued in the university department. In December 1925 his frustration erupted in a letter to Philip Tomlinson:

The University is about to cease for the holidays, but what it's going to cease I am not quite sure. . . . The full amount of my complaint seems somehow balanced by a desire to do good to the few who are able and willing. If Lafcadio Hearn had survived, all would have been well! He liked them, they liked him, he talked slosh, they liked slosh, and nobody wanted him elsewhere – my main criticism of this appointment is that there is no such appointment! They allow phrases like 'The Chair of Eng. Lit.', 'The Prof. of English Lit. at Tokyo' to circulate abroad; but I am kept out of everything except giving lessons and occasionally a little donkey work. There are several

145

Professors (Japanese ones) and *they* know all about everything – I have no
hand in the general direction of English Studies, the fixing of courses, the
choice and arrangements of books and periodicals, the necessary apparatus –
but damn them, if they don't want, I don't. Only the facts must be freely
recognised. I am talking selfishly – injured dignity, egad! Let's speak of
kippers.[11]

Above all he felt the loneliness of separation from Mary and the
children, and memories of Joy haunted him regularly. In 'A First
Impression (Tokyo)' – a poem significantly more about himself than
Japan – he describes a visitation from:

> The pretty ghost, the sudden sweet
> And most sad spirit of my vanished child:
> From the bare corners of the unknown room
> She peeped with beauty's eyes, till my eyes rained
> Their helpless tears once more; and there, and there
> Was my dead baby battling with dream presence,
> And singing, till I thought I must be mad.

He then imagines Clare and John:

> I saw them in the Suffolk lane; high flowed
> The tide of love and surety in my breast.
> But still, I saw a ghost, and lacked one child. [12]

Looking out over the Japanese shore, he was to record starkly in 'The
Blind Lead the Blind': 'But I know isolation.'[13]

In January 1925 he moved into a room in the Kikufuji Hotel in
Hongo, just ten minutes' walk from the university, where he felt more
independent. It was far from luxurious. His 'cell' was small, consisting
of a desk, two chairs, a bamboo bookcase and a bed constructed from
straw ropes across a wooden frame. Oil stoves provided the only
heating and there was little 'relief from the exuberant cries of the
enthusiastic table-tennis players in the hall. Such inconveniences soon
proved too much for Amos Crick, who booked his passage back to
England.

Yet it was not long before the strangeness and irritations began to be
replaced by a growing understanding and affection for Japan and the
Japanese: 'Japan does not disappoint the stranger; she corrects his
fancies, perhaps a little grimly, and then begins to enrich him with her
truths.'[14] Considerable travelling showed him the Japan outside Tokyo
and the magnificence of the historic city of Kyoto soon cast its spell.
The affinities between the natural beauty of Japan and that of England
also began to reveal themselves, and loneliness was relieved by contact
with the European community: with two teachers (Benjamin and

Meta Brady) and a sensitive and cultured businessman Hans Bernstein in Tokyo; with a linguist Arthur Rose-Innes, a permanent resident, on the coast at Yokohama. Regular visits to Sendai, a little north of Tokyo, brought a reunion with Ralph Hodgson. Here conversation could range widely, for Hodgson – who liked to call himself 'The last of the Fancy' – was an inveterate talker, and had been an amateur billiards and boxing champion as well as a judge of bull terriers at Crufts annual dog show. He could also be moody, aggressive and intolerant. Edmund felt that Hodgson lived on the verge of sanity, but he enjoyed his lively conversation on sport, art and books:

> 'The last of the Fancy' – surely he charms
> Still a few of his kind, with dogs under their arms. [15]

Poetic company was further provided by Sherard Vines, a lively young poet of a Sitwellian flavour, and by the presence of William Plomer – the South African-born poet, novelist and future editor of Kilvert's *Diary*. Plomer had arrived in Japan without a job but with a letter of introduction to Edmund in his pocket. Edmund quickly arranged for him to have a room at the Kikufuji Hotel, found him a position on the staff of an institution with a name 'like the croaking of a frog – the Gwaikoku Go Gakko, or School of Languages'[16] – and used the influence of Ichikawa to secure him a post at the Tokyo Koto Gakko, 'the Eton of Japan';[17] Edmund's generosity secured him another life-long literary friendship.

Constant correspondence kept him in touch with affairs at home. News from Christ's Hospital came regularly from his old housemaster H. S. Goodwin ('his letters have been a lantern unto my feet')[18] and the literary world was reported by such friends as Robert Graves, who effusively declared, 'I sometimes feel a warm gush remembering you.'[19] Visits from British academics also soothed his sense of isolation, the arrival of the critic I. A. Richards resulting in an unexpectedly convivial meeting during which Edmund was surprised and flattered to discover that Richards had much admired his sonnet 'The Deeps',[20] published in the *London Mercury* in September 1925.

The native culture of Japan was asserting its influence too, and particularly its art. On a visit to the Buddhist paintings in the Imperial Museum at Ueno he recognised the power of the scenes of nature in the work of the Zen monk Mokke and the Chinese Emperor Kiso, and he was to extend his enthusiasm to the wood-block prints of the Edo period, admiring the atmospheric world of Hiroshige and Harunobu and the graceful figures in the paintings of Toyohiro. This enlarging of artistic sympathy coincided with a developing respect and affection for his Japanese colleagues. Life seemed almost normal when Takeshi Saito returned from his European travels, for with him there was a meeting of minds and a shared understanding of cultural idiosyncrasies.

Most important was Edmund's increasing rapport with his students. At first he had found them either sycophantic or secretive and withdrawn. He was irritated by their sense of a mystical inheritance which encouraged them to adopt an aura of cultural superiority, but he quickly discovered their thirst for insights into an alien literature linked to a painstaking thoroughness in preparation. If it took him time to come to terms with them, they in turn took time to adjust to his openness and informality, for the contrast in styles between Edmund and Robert Nichols was marked. Nichols was always elegantly dressed and travelled to his lectures by car, accompanied by his wife, from the comfort of the Imperial Hotel. He lectured with dramatic fluency and ended every lecture with a poetry-reading. Edmund walked from his modest hotel, often in the company of his students, shabbily dressed in a battered, ill-fitting coat and a weather-beaten grey hat with its broad brim pulled forward; he carried his notes and books in an antique attaché case. He lectured with deliberate slowness in deference to his audience, and in the breaks between lectures he would join his students for conversation around the coal-heaps outside the lecture room. To a people with a highly developed sense of hierarchy, such approachability from a senior academic from the west was confusing. Few Japanese students at that time could visit America or Europe, and anyone who had done so – known as *yokagaeri* (literally 'one who has returned from abroad') – was particularly respected and admired as a man who brought back culture and learning. Edmund was *yokagaeri* in reverse, and his position was thus even more exalted.

Edmund's gentle, sensitive, 'imaginative sympathy'[21] soon had its effect. His polite courtesy and inability to say no found him making copious notes on the whole of Hardy's *Dynasts* for one student, on *King Lear* for another. Within twelve months he could claim that 'I nowadays do not notice so keenly the points at which Japanese minds, manners and nerves entirely differ from ours. And I think I am a little closer in touch than when I came last year.'[22] It was a growing sense of trust and respect which was fully reciprocated, and it was an understanding which went deeper than intellectual or literary appreciation. Professor Earl Miner of California expressed it perceptively on Edmund's birthday in 1961: 'Though the Japanese may admire or seek out famous people for their fame alone, they are sure judges of those finest qualities which make a person less an Englishman than a citizen of the world, less indeed a person than that which we honour in man.'[23]

Edmund's house and later his hotel room became regular meeting-places for literary conversation, and he found his students' enthusiasm both stimulating and relaxing; he began to look forward to their visits. He founded a Reading Society, with a membership augmented by several 'unofficial' female students, where Shakespeare, Sheridan, Goldsmith, Hardy and Galsworthy were read and discussed, inter-spersed with undergraduate essays on Clare or Wordsworth. He was a keen encourager of student writing too, initiating the English publica-tion of *Twelve Poems* of Haxon Ishii, and ensuring a review in the *Times Literary Supplement*.[24] As relationships strengthened he was able to relax more, and three young Japanese who took him to visit Atami were surprised at his prowess at swimming, and even more surprised to see their professor standing stark-naked at the edge of the pool. It was a slow but genuine development towards a relationship of devoted student and devoted teacher. After three years of teaching the power of 'imagination's commonwealth',[25] he had changed the attitudes and developed the sympathies of a generation of Tokyo English students – and among them were many who were to take eminent positions in Japanese intellectual life: Yoshitaka Sakai, Tamotsu Sone and the novelist Tomoji Abe, who declared that Edmund was 'Japan's best friend: he brings out the best in us'.[26] It was no surprise when Edmund was asked to extend his contract for a further three years. It was equally unsurprising that he found his love-affair with Japan growing from day to day.

As always he fulfilled a punishing schedule of writing and lecturing (in Tokyo and elsewhere) while describing himself as 'Lazy Blunden – that's putting it mildly too, for whenever I turn my mind's eye I am aware of things postponed and neglected'.[27] The little bare room in the Kikufuji Hotel became the cradle for a constant stream of words. Apart from his university lectures, which were written in long hand and prepared for publication, he compiled an anthology of English poetry for his students. He also continued his journalism, sending some sixty new poems to periodicals in England and Japan, and some eighty articles and reviews. He was also heartened to hear that he had been selected as a poet for Ernest Benn's sixpenny series, *The Augustan Books of Modern Poetry*, in 1925.

## PART FOUR   1924 – 1931

During Edmund's early months of depression, Cyril Beaumont had written to him suggesting a series of poems on Japan. Edmund replied that 'Japan, as represented here in Tokyo, is far from inspiring one to poetry – to blasphemy is the direction!',[28] but he was eventually to provide him with twelve poems, published on his return in 1928 as *Japanese Garland*. The poems show his growing sympathy for the Japanese scene, particularly in 'Inland Sea'[29] and 'The Daimyo's Pond'[30] – a small pond within the university grounds to which Edmund often escaped and where 'The Swallows come on swift and daring wings.' Romantically Edmund describes an old man banging a bucket like a drum and summoning the 'secrecies' that lie beneath the shroud of the water; in reality he was emptying slops into the pond.[31]

Beaumont was, however, to receive two volumes from Japan – again for limited circulation. The first represented Edmund's love of minor poets (he had already, with Benjamin Brady, prepared for a Tokyo publisher an edition of poems of the American writer Bret Harte) and his ability to adapt his output to his surroundings. His library inevitably was extremely limited, but he did have an edition of the poems of the eighteenth-century poet Robert Lloyd, 'one of the masters of that genial mystery of reserved elegance'.[32] He prepared an edition of Lloyd's *The Actor* with an introductory essay, which Beaumont duly published. He also sent Beaumont a selection of his own 'principally meditative' poems, including several new ones – many of them 'war' poems – which was published as *Masks of Time* in June 1925. It seemed that the distance from England sharpened the 'strange perspective' of his vision of the melancholic undertones of country life, which was becoming established as the Blunden voice. Six months later he sent *English Poems*, again dedicated to Mary, to Cobden-Sanderson. This included nearly all the pastoral poems of *Masks of Time*, excluded the war poetry and added over thirty new poems, mostly in the sections entitled 'Mind and Spirit'. Many of these incorporate the loneliness of his Japanese existence and the separation from his family:

> And more I ask, and mine it is; – to see
> Sweet faces that are part apart of me,
> The red-lipped mystery of a smiling child.[33]

He was conscious of Robert Graves's warning that he was in danger of writing too much, and was at pains to point out in the preface to *English Poems* that:

In sending forth my collection, I am aware that it is copious, and yet it is not the fruit of facility. I strive for utterance. If half-ideas, verges of shadows and misty brightness, thus find their way into my story, I must often acquiesce, because I know by experience how such visitants come and go, and often, however imperfectly visioned in the first place, do not return again save in low and dispirited murmurings. 'The mirrors change'; the musicians march out of the village.

The collection was on the whole received favourably. In 1961 John Betjeman recalled that:

In Blunden's *English Poems*, which was the first book by a living poet I remember saving up to buy, I found that true tradition of pastoral verse carried on into the present century. Here, without any hint of artiness or escapism, the countryside of Kent was unrolled in mellifluous numbers. I learned many of his poems by heart and can still recite them with their autumn mists, summer cricket matches, sounds of church bells and recollections of eighteenth-century romantic poets.

Blunden puts new life into heroic couplets and uses the old conventional metres of ode forms of men like Gray and Collins to express the England he knew and loved as a boy. But he is never a pasticheur. He is always as original as he is true.[34]

Two further projects were occupying Edmund's time: an essay on the poetry of Henry Vaughan with five of Vaughan's Latin poems translated into English verse (published in March 1927) and a collection of extracts from the nineteenth-century journal the *Examiner*, edited by Leigh Hunt. In Takeshi Saito's extensive library were numerous issues of the periodical, from which Edmund culled articles by or about Hunt, Lamb, Keats, Shelley and Byron. The result was *Leigh Hunt's 'Examiner' Examined*, published by Cobden-Sanderson in July 1928.

Such a prolific output may have seemed remarkable; but it did not include his major literary preoccupation – for sitting at his hotel desk, with just a couple of trench-maps and a few notes, but aided by a phenomenal memory, he was writing *Undertones of War*.

With so much paper-work some assistance was clearly essential and it was provided in an unexpected way. In the early summer of 1925 Edmund was lecturing at a summer school for Japanese teachers of English in the romantic setting of the mountain resort of Karuizawa. A young Japanese lady – seven years Edmund's senior – was attending as a junior-high-school teacher for Nagoya. She was a fluent English speaker, a Christian and a lover of English Romantic poetry; she was also short, plain and unfashionably dark-complexioned. Her name was

## PART FOUR  1924 – 1931

Aki Hayashi. She and Edmund were strongly drawn to each other and she began to visit him in Tokyo, taking on secretarial work.

Starved as he was of female companionship, Aki Hayashi provided him with the romantic attachment for which he so yearned. As always when in love, Edmund poured his passion into a series of letters (nearly a hundred of them in eighteen months) sometimes writing two or three times a day. These letters quickly changed from being addressed to 'Dear Miss Hayashi'[35] to the use of the anglicised form of her name 'My very dear Autumn',[36] and within a few months they are written to 'My Dear Heart',[37] 'Deeply loved'[38] or 'My joy and comfort';[39] they change from being signed 'Edmund Blunden',[40] to 'your deeply longing Edmund'[41] and 'your most fond Eddie'.[42] In a letter of 29 August 1925 he wrote to her:

The love I have for you is truly deep and I cannot reproach myself for it; I shall not grow old and dull over it, but hold you always as my Dear. This is not a declaration against my wife and our years of intimately shared existence, and I am anxious that you should see how we are towards one another; so here are two letters which I had from her this morning just before going out, so please read them and comprehend that side of my life. I must not hurt her, and that is all I can say as a guide to us now. She is looking towards me always, as I read her letters. But still how gentle and beautiful a love has awakened between you and me! I shall rely on it and live on it in many solitary hours  It is a charm to keep me going. I am most distressed that I cannot fulfil all that I ought to Autumn, as things stand now – but you have unselfish patience and a splendid courage. When I was with you, the cares of this hurried and bilious world ceased to touch me. I loved whatever gave me the chance to do some slight thing for you: and, as it has been, so it will continue to be.

A month later his passion had grown:

When we got here in the rain this afternoon I was not disappointed, for your first letter from Nagoya was here. It brightens a dark day, and is really *you*. I think with astonishment and delight of the love you give me, and the suddenness and completeness of it; I am happy in that love and only unhappy in my impatience to have you with me again. You write as though you had seemed rather reserved . . . but I never thought any such thing. . . . your profound companionship gave me new life and new poetry. 'I have offered my heart, my body and everything to you' – dear love, *that* I remind myself of all through the day, and my love seems to grow more and more. Your dear body has but a minor share in our mutual devotion – not to deny or despise physical love; but it is a part of love that could be excluded, and still love would prevail. We are in this world, creatures with bodies; and hence I think

152

it's unnatural to act like hermits or icebergs; but still there's a deeper secret of love to worship most.

> 'Love lives beyond
> The tomb, the earth which fades like dew'.[43]

Most sweet and dear Autumn, how I love and bless you![44]

If his love for Aki was giving him comfort, it secrecy was also causing him unrest:

I have just had a letter from my friend Siegfried Sassoon, the greatest of poets in England now. He closes with the suggestion that I should become a bookseller when I go back and he will provide the capital at the beginning. Alas, my dear, I am afraid he would utterly change his mind, if he knew about *us*; and yet, shall I grieve for that? Even that I could endure, if the worst came to the worst – I hold you so fast in my love and honour, you must be my refuge if ever my friends forsake me. But it will help us, if we can keep a secret.

I don't feel like sleep; so restless and so alone. I have here some Poets whom I love, and long to read their best out to you and share the beauty with you. You dear soul, you have swiftly come into my deepest life. So remain! may envy never harm us. If there is any innocence, it is love; and I cannot help loving you, though far off is one whom I love. This, the common opinion would condemn, but I have spoken the truth. What time may do, I don't know: but you will never pass from me.[45]

His guilt is evident in the poem 'To a Spirit':

> Dear (thus I dare), how I have longed
> To double, treble, nay, to see
> Past computation bloomed and thronged
> The love of thee that raptures me. . . .
> Confused and gross in this my cry,
> Let me not lose thee, loving so.[46]

Letters from Mary only increased the confusion. After receiving one in September 1925 he declared, 'I am torn in two, the reading changed me from well to ill',[47] and in a letter to Aki later in the same month, the problem has become more intense:

As I was getting to bed several letters were brought to me, but not one from you – yet I think there will be one today. There was one from my wife, largely about my friend R. Hodgson at Sendai and some rumours respecting his domestic affairs. Mrs Hodgson was in Tokyo some time ago and my wife says 'Above all keep out of people's way so they cannot blame you for anything that is done; as you know, it would be such a blow for me I could never never forgive you.' This is of course utterly beside the point, so far as

Mrs H. is concerned – it's merely fantastic speculation; but you see how it would apply if my wife knew about us! So be ever patient and strong in keeping our secret – particularly let no one see my letters wherever there is the voice of my love for you. If my wife still looks to me – she does, I cannot doubt it for a minute – think what I owe her.

It's a fine morning and the distance calls: I think of dewy leaves and quiet waters. Autumn is a wonderful season: you have a name that conveys the most subtle charm of this world, this Nature, and this human spirit. I wish we were walking together on some English heath, or looking over the plains of Flanders.[48]

As the months passed, Edmund was having to turn his attention to what he should do after Japan, now that he had decided not to extend his contract, and had handed on the mantle to Arundel del Ré. Sassoon was still suggesting that he set up as a bookseller in Oxford. He told his father that this held some appeal – 'there is no advance on Oxford as a sweet city. My red nose may restore an old tradition in second-hand bookselling, though it may be hard to imitate the glorious illiteracy of some of the pleasantest dealers'.[49] Approaches came from both Cambridge and Liverpool Universities concerning academic posts, but he was anxious to shed 'a strong professional incrustation – a crabbed o'ergathering of dictatorial didacticism',[50] and preferred to take up his old life again 'at a pittance, rather than a fat but public and official job'.[51] He duly accepted an offer to return to work on the *Nation* and the *Times Literary Supplement*.

He was uncertain what he would find at Stansfield on his return. From the autumn of 1925 Mary's letters had become fewer and colder. The thought of his return to England and Mary coincided with a cooling in his relationship with Aki Hayashi, increased by a separation of several months in early 1926 which Edmund spent in Sendai with a sick Ralph Hodgson. On Aki's part this led to increased requests for assurances that Edmund loved her and would fulfil his promise to take her to England as his secretary. On at least three occasions she demanded signed statements to this effect. The possessiveness which had caused jealousy among Edmund's students (who were at a loss to understand the attraction she exerted) was now becoming vividly clear to Edmund himself. Though he always declared that he would not 'withdraw from my promise',[52] 'no matter what opposition is made by anybody',[53] each promise is couched in more neutral terms. In May 1926 he objected:

*Why question me so often?*
*Why rob me of my peace?*

*Have I not shown you my spirit*
*Made you the receiver of my intimate ideas,*
*Entrusted to you the desires of my heart?*[54]

By 17 January 1927, he was asked to sign a bizarre and evasive statement:

In case I should ever marry a second time I should

in all $\begin{bmatrix} \text{probability} \\ \text{likelihood} \end{bmatrix}$ marry Aki.

Edmund kept his promise to employ her as secretary, and to support her financially and undertake all legal responsibility for her, for thirty-four years. To friends she was always referred to as 'poor old Hayashi'; few were aware of the past intensity of the relationship, or even knew her Christian name. It was clear by 1927 that the passion was now one-sided.

Whether or not Edmund expected a sympathetic response from Mary to his 'secret' love for Aki, he was less than sympathetic towards what he suspected may have been a secret love on Mary's part. In February 1927 he expressed his fears to Sassoon:

Firstly, I will say that Mary has several causes of complaint against me in the past, both as to my conduct and my general attitude. Then, let us agree that it must have been in any event a strain for so young and lively a woman to bear three years of absence from her husband, and to keep her path clear. She herself insisted on that absence. I lamented it, but wouldn't coerce her to Japan; I allowed for her as copious an income as I could, and asked for a few services to be done regularly towards the home and myself. The allowance seems to have been too large and perhaps has caused the trouble. What then has been happening? I'll give you some of the things I have been able to make out. I came here in May 1924; up until the summer of 1925 Mary's letters were regular and kind and she attended to the occasional literary and other business which I wanted done. Since then, she has written to me about once in three weeks, very slackly and indefinitely, and at this moment it approaches two months since I had a letter from her. My few requests for little services have been ignored, my many questions unanswered. One letter attacked me because my remittance had been delayed, but she has altogether received much above £300 a year from me and has no just complaint on the whole on that point. Such things as her sending books or newspapers, or presents have been unheard of. . . . All this time many minor indications have led me to feel that Mary has changed in her spirit towards me. I was writing to my Stansfield parson, Webling, who is a devoted soul and ever eager to help me, and I said I heard less from my wife than formerly. This slender and accidental opportunity was seized by Webling who wrote simply that if I wanted 'a resting place' on my return from which to survey my prospects, his house was mine. I replied that I should like him to speak out, and he has done so with admirable fairness of mind, as far as he is able to feel in touch with the situation. From his letters I find that Mary has been telling him the opposite to what she told me. On about the day that she wrote to me practically advising me to stop here and keep supplying the cash, she met him and told him she was strictly commanding me to return. Or again, long after I told her of my certain return she told him that she couldn't get a new home because although I told her of my resignation, I didn't say whether or not the resignation had been accepted. I shan't copy Webling's letter of course, but he gives me to understand that she has been living extravagantly, that I am unlikely to be able to set up my home again with her.

I am now awaiting something more firm from her pen, and my notion is that there is someone else in the plot. Of what stamp, you may conjecture, if you recall how our last evening at Stansfield was interrupted by the arrival of a tipsy gent from Clare to accompany Mary to a dance at Bury. She has let out some brief references to her new 'friends' and it is this corrupt taste of hers in acquaintances which makes me say, that if this chapter of my life is now at an end I get rid of some encumbrances as much as I lose a very promising and gifted housemate. But it is still uncertain what is to happen. I am inclined in any event to live apart. Clare, my daughter, is I think already of Mary's persuasion, and couldn't be trained by me, but I shall want the younger one, John.[55]

It was painfully clear that domestically the immediate future was to be bleak, as Edmund travelled to Kobe on 13 July 1927 to board the SS *Macedoni*, bound for Plymouth, in the company of Ralph Hodgson (on leave from Sendai) and Aki Hayashi. Several pupils came to bid him farewell at the pier, and suddenly Tokyo seemed as inviting as Suffolk, if not more so. All the respect for Japan which had matured over three years, and all the affection he had developed for his courteous, modest, talented and loyal students found voice in his poem 'The Author's Last Words to His Students':

> Forgive what I, adventuring highest themes,
>     Have spoiled and darkened, and the awkward hand
> That longed to point the moral of man's dreams
>     And shut the wicket-gates of fairyland:
>         So by too harsh intrusion
>         Left colourless confusion.
>
> For even the glories that I most revered,
>     Seen through a gloomed perspective in strange mood,
> Were not what to our British seers appeared;
>     I spoke of peace, I made a solitude,
>         Herding with deathless graces
>         My hobbling commonplaces.

*Forgive that eyeless lethargy which chilled*
  *Your ardours and I fear dimmed much fine gold —*
*What your bright passion, leaping ages, thrilled*
  *To find and claim, and I yet dared withhold;*
    *These and all chance offences*
    *Against your finer senses.*

*And I will ever pray for your souls' health,*
  *Remembering how, deep-tasked yet eager-eyed,*
*You loved imagination's commonwealth,*
  *Following with smiling wonder a frail guide*
    *Who bears beyond the ocean*
    *The voice of your devotion.*[56]

# 15

# London and Suffolk
## August 1927 – February 1931

*I have been in a bad state for a year and am now nearly worn out in mind and nerves. I have been considering the pros and cons of returning to Japan where I think I should grow tranquil and be of use.*
Letter to Takeshi Saito, August 1928[1]

*The amount of work before me is enormous. I don't think I wrote so much before I went to Japan, and certainly I didn't write so fast.*
Letter to Aki Hayashi, April 1928[2]

The three and a half years after Edmund's return from Japan were years of restlessness, illness, feverish writing activity, considerable literary acclaim and intense personal unhappiness.

During the return voyage he had pondered long over his relationship with Mary, deciding that reconciliation was impossible – Aki Hayashi or no Aki Hayashi; faithful or faithless Mary. Expecting immediate separation, he was thus surprised to find himself still in love – and to find his love reciprocated. In early September 1927 he confided to Sassoon:

Since I last wrote, my troubles have begun to dissolve and my spirits are a little less tedious. I have seen Mary, and though I still do not understand why she treated me as she did in my absence, her present state and strong affection have persuaded me to resume our life together. She has the greatest wish to do so, and I wish nothing more if things go well. You will not be surprised at this alteration of plan, because you are used to my erratic course – and I am sure you will understand my throwing away all my fiercer and severer notions when you see Mary again. This I say, not out of self-righteousness or from a judgement seat, but simply because her letters to me were so increasingly bad through 1926 and now I am amazed and overjoyed by her excellence.[3]

By the end of the month he was in even more positive mood in writing to Philip Tomlinson: 'I am a curiosity so you will not be bewildered to read that Mary and I are re-uniting almost at once. Not that what I have felt hitherto seems to me wholly unjustified, but her love is so evident, and her spirit so surprisingly remote from what it appeared by her treatment of me before, that I believe all must be well.'[4] And three weeks later, while visiting D. L. Murray at Shoreham, he wrote again to Tomlinson: 'When I got here a letter from Mary was waiting . . . which completely pulled me out of my own blackness and apprehension. She ends "to you I send not only my thoughts, all my thoughts, all my feelings and my affections, my love and my life". Rejoice with me. I begin to find the power of striking out all adverse balances, I assure you.'[5]

In October Edmund and Mary moved a few miles away from Stansfield into a white brick villa in the village of Cowlinge, where for a month or so they made a second honeymoon and Edmund felt that they were 'really beginning life again in a lively colouring'.[6]

Untidily dressed in blue serge trousers bought in the village shop, Edmund became a familiar in Cowlinge – his hat appearing over the hedges of the cottages as he cycled to Ely or Cambridge station, waving to the trees and commending them on particularly fine blossom. It was the world of his poem 'Familiarity':

> Dance not your spectral dance at me;
> > I know you well!
> Along this lane there lives no tree
> > But I can tell.
> I know each fall and rise and twist;
> You – why, a wildflower in the mist,
> > The moon, the mist. . . .[7]

Just a mile away was the thatched and ivy-covered house of Adrian Bell, novelist, countryman, and later to become the first compiler of *The Times* crossword. Edmund and he quickly became friends, walking the Suffolk countryside talking of the poets Robert Bloomfield and George Crabbe. On leaving school, Bell had become apprenticed to a traditional farmer and Edmund enthusiastically discussed the varied methods of ploughing, harrowing or reaping, which Bell recorded in his autobiographical novel *Corduroy*, published in 1930 and dedicated to Edmund. Bell recalled visiting Cowlinge and finding Edmund in:

His cabin-like study in the brick box, leather-walled from floor to ceiling with books. . . . He polished the bindings with shoe polish, and the study walls shone of brown and black leather. There at a deal table I would find him writing *Undertones of War* in his small lucid script with a school pen and a long steel nib . . . the sort of nib that in any other hand than his or a registrar's, dug in and spluttered.[8]

These were happy interludes, but the pressures of emotional confusion at home were causing distress to many friends of both Mary and Edmund. Mary had enjoyed continual support from Ottoline Morrell, from Eddie Marsh (who welcomed Edmund back from Japan with the words 'You *are* rather a pig, aren't you!')[9] and from Mrs Palmer – the widow of Edmund's old maths teacher at Christ's Hospital. Edmund now found his relationship with these old friends was put under strain. People were beginning to take sides.

Sassoon remained a loyal and objective counsellor. He had received several letters from Ottoline Morrell, and was aware of the danger of false rumour. He was anxious not to be involved in 'skeins of inexactitude',[10] and declared that 'the only thing I know is that I am a friend of you and Mary'.[11] At the end of October he warned Edmund:

I have seen too much of this discussing of other people's affairs by people who have too much time on their hands, and I know how pernicious it can become, even when (as in O.M.'s case) the original intention is a friendly anxiety to be helpful. So when O.M. wrote and urged me to advise you to persuade Miss H. to return to Japan, I was at once aware that my flawless friendship (with E.B.) was being threatened. I should like you to show this letter to Mary, so that she may understand that I am being quite open about it all. How can I advise you, or her, when I haven't even set eyes on your Japanese friend? The position is a perilous one for all three of you, but it will not be made less perilous by plottings and schemings – candour is the only remedy.[12]

If this was a testing time for Edmund and Mary, it was an equally difficult time for Aki Hayashi. She was now installed in a London flat, at Edmund's expense, where she was befriended by Edmund's London friends and from where she began to assume secretarial work on Edmund's Leigh Hunt researches, combing volumes of the *Morning Chronicle*, the *New Monthly Magazine* or the *Gentleman's Magazine* for references to Hunt and his circle. This quickly became the pattern of her life. A short, rather plump figure, she became a familiar character in the library of the British Museum, which she visited almost daily, acting as an amanuensis. On visits to London Edmund would take her to an art gallery, or they would go book-hunting, and she became the recipient of several hundred of his letters, in which he repeatedly assures her of his 'deep and unalterable love' and commends her for her courage and devotion. Though marriage was not to be mentioned again, a deep mutual affection was sustained for life.

Edmund quickly found himself returning to the busy rigours of London journalism. His old friendships were re-established and lunches with J. C. Squire or Sassoon at the Royal Palace Hotel became regular occurrences once again. He paid visits to his parents in Salcombe, to the Cobden-Sandersons in Long Crendon, to the Murrays in Shoreham, to Philip Tomlinson in Bushey, Canon Webling in Suffolk or Hector Buck, now teaching at Oakham School before returning to Christ's Hospital. These were welcome breaks from domestic pressure, a privilege which Mary could not share. Visits with Sassoon to Stephen Tennant's home at Wilsford Manor in Wiltshire, provided a refreshing oasis:

This is a sort of earthly paradise – trees, birds, flowers, dogs, reptiles, fishes and all![13]

I am writing this on a seat outside a small circle of trees, with the light wind in the leaves, and a brook passing by. The calls of many birds, some inside an aviary and some on the branches above my head, often make me look about. There is a sunflower in view as big as a kuruma-puller's hat. If this is Autumn, what splendid flowers and bird-music must be here in Spring?[14]

The familiar demands for speaking engagements were also becoming more regular. On 29 November 1927 he found himself sharing a platform with G. K. Chesterton at the Charles Lamb Society. Sassoon was much affected by the occasion, which he described in his diary:

After we'd drunk 'the immortal memory' of C. Lamb, E B (introduced exquisitely by Augustine Birrell – 'he has returned to us from the land of flowers') spoke for twenty-five minutes – a defence and panegyric of Leigh Hunt. He spoke haltingly at times, but there was an unaffected intensity and restraint in his tones, and his (without notes) address was eloquent and earnest. He knew his subject 'by heart'.

As I watched his face – pale, almost gaunt, sorrow-stricken, yet with luminous reflections of his subject passing across it – I was much moved, for it was the mask of a poetic genius, if ever I saw one, and I thought of the death masks of John Clare and Keats. Blunden's profile, with its bird-like beak and small (but resolute) chin, is impressive but not beautiful. Seen full-face, and lit from within as a night-light, he has spiritual beauty and dignity and the structure of the face is magnificent. I shall not forget the angelic loveliness of his fleeting smiles, as he spoke so lovingly and loyally of Leigh Hunt. His eyes were lowered, and he seemed to have forgotten his audience, on whom he had cast a spell. But the nervous continual flickering of his eyelids (and how tired he looked and how harassed!) warned me that all is not well with him. Hardy once said that his first sight of E B was 'like meeting Keats'. Last night he was *Adonais* in the flesh.[15]

The nervous, harassed air was real enough. He was burdened with financial worries, though two benefactors came to his immediate rescue – Sassoon, who had inherited £40,000 from an aunt, sent a generous gift in October 1927 (of which Edmund immediately gave £50 to Aki Hayashi), and the Royal Literary Fund awarded him £500 in February 1928 as the recipient of the Benson Silver Medal, which he received from the hand of Sir Henry Newbolt. His sponsors for this award were Sir Sydney Cockerell and A. E. Housman, whose letter to the committee was verging on the fulsome for a man who was usually economical in his praise:

My Lords and Gentleman,
    Understanding that a letter from me may be of use to Mr Edmund Blunden in an application to the Royal Literary Fund, I gladly take the opportunity of saying how much I admire some of his poetry. His quick and true eye for external nature, and his skill or luck in finding words which convey his own impressions to the reader, are talents in which he is pre-eminent among his contemporaries and noticeable even among English poets in general.
    I ought not to say that he is the best poet who has begun writing within the last fifteen or twenty years, because there may be many with whose works I have not enough acquaintance; but there is none of them for whose poetry, so far as it is known to me, I feel so much personal liking.
    I am, my Lords and Gentleman,
        Yours faithfully
            A. E. Housman[16]

Edmund was flattered by this support and wrote to thank his sponsors. In his reply, Housman told Edmund that he considered the opening lines of 'The Shepherd' quite sufficient evidence of his claim to be a poet:

> *Evening has brought the glow-worm to the green*
> *And early stars to heaven, and joy to men.*

Far more pressing, however, than any financial worries was the steady deterioration of Edmund's marriage. In June 1928 he poured out his heart in a drafted letter to his mother:

I am alone. And yet Mary is in the house. I must tell you that she has been in love with another and a younger man for several years; the fact came to light, though I was previously conscious of it, about a month ago, and today her friend was kind enough to come ,from Ipswich at my request and see me. Things would have been easier if she were not so ill. I did my best to play the man and see their side. It hurt me badly when Mary spoke out quite finally and said she did not love me, for I love her. The progress of the discussion rested chiefly on me. It was roughly decided that M. should go to him, receive support from me (he is in a poor job), and have Clare and Johnny with her. I do not think legal settlement necessary, for it is possible that her new partnership will end in some breakdown and then she will come to me again. Her lover's name is Cyril Keeble; he strikes me as a very sound and quite sensitive and devoted man, and I shall be surprised if he does not look after her in every way. It is only his bad luck he fell in love with a married woman.

I accept my defeat.

Dear Mugg, I am sorry.

– I can now see the paper again, and continue what is to be said at the moment.

Mary hoped that perhaps no decision would be made today, but, as I was agreeably surprised with the demeanour of Mr Keeble, I brought the affair painfully to a point; knowing that it has been a misery on all hands to drag on without candour, without trust, and almost without hope. I can't tell you the dreary gnawing solitude I have myself lived with, or the fiery ordeal of getting my work done and the money in all the time. Indeed, I have lapsed in that, and the splendid gift made me by the Royal Literary Fund has been (to my shame) a 'very present help'.

But what shall I do after this? I am in the dark. I have one unalterable principle left – touching personal affairs – and you may think it foolish, or implying some hidden factor, but I believe you will agree with me. I will not sacrifice Miss Hayashi who was so perfect in her devotion to me in Japan. I am aware that she is in love with me, as other Japanese women seemed in danger of being – one came to the boat at Kobe in tears, who had seen me at school lectures two or three times, and would have gone to the gallows for me! Yet I had no notion of her. A.H. loves me, but without sexual entanglement. So earnest a piety cannot have a grossness in it. Now, I value her, and her happiness: she has had too much unhappiness. I shall, I think, be able to keep her in England to do my work at the British Museum, and if so I shall keep her in good spirits without difficulty by meeting her frequently and seeing that she is not 'an exile'. But if the Home Office refuse to renew her permit to stay here, as they may, seeing what ugly versions were gossiped round about her and me by such cultured villains as Lady O. Morrell, avid for every opportunity of 'knowing' and shining accordingly, or the hysterical Mrs Palmer (who comes here tomorrow), I can only see one way of doing justice to A.H. open to me. That is to resume my dogged career in Japan. In that event A.H. would see to it that I was not starved, ill, or without buttons on my small-clothes. I am her unalterable admirer, as I am of Mrs Barbauld or Queen Victoria – a good woman, and of the highest courage. The Japanese women are in such a tradition that it is almost incredible that one or two of them, like her, achieve such culture, freedom of thought and skill of action. I was so happy that you thought well of her too and received her so naturally and cheeringly. She was profoundly pleased and felt that England was indeed what she had dreamed, as the Japanese will, it would be. But I am not eager to return to Japan, kindly as so many of my old students are, and desirous as they are of having my influence at work among them; neither is poor old Hayashi. I hope therefore that I may stay in England. Emotionally (sad expression for a careful writer! but tonight style is off!) it might be best otherwise, since I love this Mary and shall think of her with savage anxiety. I shall feel she is *in reach* and that's a bitter reflection. Yet my friends, Sassoon, Cobden-Sanderson and his wonderful wife, Phil Tomlinson, H. M. Tomlinson, Kathleen Lion, Old Stead the Chaplain of Worcester College, and some others, all strongly demand that I should hold on in England. (For I have mentioned the other prospect without fully announcing the circumstances.) And I remember with absolute clearness the desire, and indeed appeal, you and my Father expressed at Christmas, that I should not go away again. How I hope my path may be made simple by the Home Office allowing A.H. to remain here!

I must wait quietly for that solution, and meanwhile I ask that when it is time for Mary to attempt her new union, you will receive me. I shall try not to be a burden, and of course can and will pay my footing.

Too tired to say more, except that poor Mary has done her best and has suffered much, being already so enfeebled by illness and strain; she still relies on me.

I feel much as I did in the trenches twelve years ago. Await my next letter soon, do not be grieved too much by this;

    I am always

       your loving Son, the unsuccessful

        Eddie[17]

Immediately, he wrote to Mary in the form of a sonnet – which he apparently never showed her:

> *Dear child, dear woman, all my life's demand,*
> *My only window looking out to heaven,*
> *If I had all bright speech at my command*
> *For you to hear, for me to be forgiven!*
> *But, now in stammering contradictions thrown*
> *I find that tears end all my baffled cry!*
> *To be so near you, Mary, and alone,*

*To fear even to interpret your gray eye.*
*Then feverish misery, swift with ice and fire,*
*Breaks down all will and drives me like a gad,*
*Love's splendid powers at length can raise no higher,*
*Their trembling flame has burned me almost mad –*
*I sink ashamed and breathless from their branding,*
*And wish you, dear, a peace that passes understanding.*

Underneath he wrote:

My love, I am old, strained, hardened; I am a nest of spiritual serpents; but I can still tell Heaven I reverenced you. My faults and vanities have come back to me in pain and terror and solitariness, but I am the father of my wretchedness. What must I do to be saved? You are a woman: your breast is warm and would shelter a starving bird. O help Eddie – [18]

Swiftly the relationship degenerated into angry and bitter confrontation. Though at times Edmund spoke of 'Poor Mary', for whom he 'hoped at some future time to do something', he was more often referring to her 'cruel observations', her 'accusations behind my back'; before long she had become 'a wicked woman' who had had 'scoundrels' as lovers.[19] He reminded her that he had found a sexually explicit letter from an admirer a fortnight after their marriage, and referred to a 'cunning sexual orgy'.[20] For her part, she accused Edmund of drunkenness, of unreasonableness and of bringing back a *geisha* girl from Japan. The bitterness led to nervous illness for both Mary and Edmund, who for over a year rarely woke up without fighting for breath as asthma developed into bronchitis. It was clear that their marriage had reached the end of the road. Edmund spent more time in London moving into a bed-sitter in Talbot Road (where Hardy had once had lodgings). In the spring of 1929 he finally filed for divorce.

There were some bright moments to dispel the gloom. On such was a dinner in February 1929 when he was introduced to the painter Rex Whistler. Afterwards, in Sassoon's flat, Whistler took a pencil and drew a delicate sketch of Edmund's head, working through until 1 a.m. At a meeting next day with Cobden-Sanderson and his partner Kenneth Rae, Edmund initiated the commissioning of Whistler as an artist for Cobden-Sanderson's *New Forget-Me-Not*, an occasional anthology in Victorian style, which was to mark the beginning of the painter's career as an illustrator. Edmund was always delighted by his association with Rex Whistler – and, later, with his younger brother, the poet and glass-engraver Laurence.

To add to all his personal problems, Edmund was working himself into the ground. Between August 1927 and February 1931, he was to complete over 400 more pieces of journalism; in six months he reviewed or 'noticed' over fifty books. In 1928 and 1929 he finished writing *Leigh Hunt's 'Examiner' Examined* and *Undertones of War*, wrote *Nature in English Literature* for Leonard Woolf at the Hogarth Press (which enabled him to champion two more 'troubled' writers, the eighteenth-century peasant-poets Stephen Duck and Robert Bloomfield), and started work on *The History of English Literature by the Poets* – a project he never completed. New editions of the autobiographies of Leigh Hunt and Benjamin Haydon received introductions, as did Lamb's *Last Essays of Elia*. He also prepared a volume of poems of William Collins for a limited fine edition. He had long wanted to pay tribute to the poet whom Dr Johnson had described (in words which Edmund knew by heart and which he liked to think had some relevance to himself) as a man whose:

morals were pure, and his opinions pious: in a long continuance of poverty, and long habits of dissipation, it cannot be expected that any character should be exactly uniform. There is a degree of want by which the freedom of agency is almost destroyed; and long association with fortuitous companions will at last relax the strictness of truth, and abate the fervour of sincerity. That this man, wise and virtuous as he was, passed always unentangled through the snares of life, it would be prejudice and temerity to affirm; but it may be said that at least he preserved the source of action unpolluted, that his principles were never shaken, that his distinctions of right and wrong were never confounded, and that his faults had nothing of malignity or design, but proceeded from some unexpected pressure, or casual temptation.[21]

Edmund's introduction displays his strong sense of the importance of place in a poet's development, and portrays Collins as a fusion of Chichester and Winchester influences; it also emphasises the mixture of romantic imagination and classical formality in Collins's verse: 'he is a poet whose vision extends delightedly over difficult distances, and who hears beyond the voices of the hour the Music of the Grecian Theatre.' As an essay it is a clear example of Edmund's view of himself as a literary critic, anxious to fulfil a sympathetic – almost priestly – role, and following the maxim of Charles Lamb: 'Criticism is at its finest a secondary poetry, and not a private computation; it glows with spirit kindred to that in the created work whence its impulse came; it must have, like poetry, its images, its music and its varieties.' The volume was published in June 1929 by Etchells and Macdonald, the proprietor Hugh Macdonald becoming a close friend.

Edmund was combining this intense writing programme with a busy social life and a considerable amount of travel. A not untypical week in the summer of 1929 saw him having lunch with Hector Buck followed by an evening with Cobden-Sanderson. The next morning he visited his old friend from Japan, Arthur Rose-Innes, before having lunch with Sherard Vines, tea with Sassoon and an evening meeting with Osbert Sitwell. The next day was occupied by a lunch with Philip Tomlinson and an afternoon's cricket at Lord's. In July 1929 he made the first of many pilgrimages to the rebuilt city of Ypres and the battlefields around, and during the same year he also gave lectures at Liverpool and Leeds Universities as well as to the City Literary Institute (published as *Tradition and Experiment*) and to the Shakespeare Association on *King Lear* (published as *Shakespeare's Significances*). The Shakespeare lecture enabled him to bring together many aspects of *King Lear* which had been preoccupying him – particularly the words of the Fool, 'And I'll go to bed at noon,' and their seven types of ambiguity:

I do not wish to rhapsodize over these last seven words, but they impress me with their seven suggestions.
1. They are a sort of tired ironical joke on Lear's late hours.
2. They make a playful complaint that the Fool would like a little food before going to bed.
3. There is a pun on the people's name for the scarlet pimpernel. The weak-bodied Fool with his coxcomb looks like that flower.
4. But, if so, he shuts late. Surely there has been storm enough during the night.
5. There will be a worse storm still; and at once.
6. It is the last time that the Fool speaks during the play. He presages his death, with a secondary meaning in the word 'bed' of 'grave'.
7. He takes off his coxcomb for the last time to please his old friends the audience.

As if all this were not sufficient activity, he also produced two volumes of verse. In May 1928 *Retreat* was published, dedicated 'To Three I Love, Mary, Clare and John'. The title captures the spirit of the poems – a retreat from the pressures of life, and a look over the shoulder to past experiences: to Yalding ('The Complaint'),[22] to schooldays ('Recollections of Christ's Hospital'),[23] to the war ('An Infantryman'),[24] to love ('The Resignation'),[25] to Japan ('Cloud-Life')[26] and to the atmosphere and forms of the literature of the past ('The Age of Herbert and Vaughan',[27] 'The Wartons',[28] 'Nature Displayed'[29] and 'Sonnet on Smart's Song to David'[30]). The collection was the strongest evocation of his constant sense of the backward glance which he had admitted two years previously in 'Unteachable':

> To each his own: I run a backward race.
> I have been wandering distant roads, have striven
> To win new comprehensions; much in vain.
> There's that within me cares not what is given
> By such migrations ....[31]

Edmund sent a copy of *Retreat* to Sassoon, who replied promptly and warmly:

I am so fond of your poetry that when I read it I sometimes find it difficult to believe that you are alive. One doesn't expect the present day to send one a new book by a favourite poet! The end of a rainy day and the day of Edmund Gosse's funeral. My heart is heavy today and so is yours. One Edmund is not enough for me in this weary world, and the fact that there were two was an unfailing joy and inspiration to me.[32]

A second volume of poetry, *Near and Far*, appeared in September 1929, dedicated to William Force Stead. The *Far* was represented by a reprinting of *Japanese Garland*; the *Near* by poems of 'Moods', 'Conjectures' and 'Fancies'. Edmund had been irritated by some of the English responses to his Japanese poems, and justified himself in the preface:

They were blamed here and there for their English tone, and their author was described as an incorrigible 'Briton'. Those, however, who go from England to Japan without succumbing first to Japanesery will find that there is no great gulf between the old experiences and the new. Substitute cherry-blossoms for rose, and rice for bread, and Alps for Chilterns – you do not thereby produce a mystical incomprehensibility.

There was little need to justify the rest of the collection, for it included some of his most popular poems, in particular 'Report on Experience'[33] and the sonnet 'Values'.[34] Both titles suggest the viewpoint of a mature man looking back over his life, as do the opening lines: 'I have been young, and now am not too old' and 'Till darkness lays a hand on these gray eyes'.

At thirty-three Edmund felt twice his age and had experienced what for many men would have been a full life. Both poems, too, take an objective view of past suffering, and though he questions the 'peculiar grace' which can allow for war, he acknowledges that the bitter-sweet experiences of his life have taught him that 'Raindrops may murder, lightnings may caress.' Looking to the future he can see grounds for hope; he 'cannot grieve' but sees that somewhere on the horizon 'are faith, life, virtue in the sun'.

'Report on Experience' is a poem which mixes personal reference and literary allusion. The opening line is a conflation of Shakespeare's line in *Henry VI, Part One*, 'When I was young (as yet I am not old)', and an ironic twist (from negative to positive) of the words of Psalm 37 verse 25, 'I have been young and now am old; yet have I not seen the righteous forsaken.' Edmund was not particularly pleased with the poem during composition. It was, he recalled, 'unpremeditated' and 'almost thrown away'.[35] It became his most anthologised poem:

*I have been young, and now am not too old;*
*And I have seen the righteous forsaken,*
*His health, his honour and his quality taken.*
  *This is not what we were formerly told.*

*I have seen a green country, useful to the race,*
*Knocked silly with guns and mines, its villages vanished,*
*Even the last rat and last kestrel banished –*
  *God bless us all, this was peculiar grace.*

*I knew Seraphina; Nature gave her hue,*
*Glance, sympathy, note, like one from Eden.*
*I saw her smile warp, heard her lyric deaden;*
  *She turned to harlotry; – this I took to be new.*

*Say what you will, our God sees how they run*
*These disillusions are His curious proving*
*That he loves humanity and will go on loving;*
  *Over there are faith, life, virtue in the sun.*

A further 'retreat' was already in Edmund's mind, for the call of Japan was becoming more insistent. The stability of an academic post now seemed preferable to the exhausting life of journalism, even though he had felt exactly the opposite in the summer of 1927. He considered contacting Ralph Hodgson, who had returned to Sendai: 'He has disappeared from my world just like a comet';[36] he 'kept his return very mysterious. He is offended with me but my conscience is clear. He likes, or rather his nature requires, to find offence where only goodness and service was intended. I bless him all the same.'[37]

Several events helped to turn his eyes eastward. Two Japanese friends visited him in London, Professor Hori and Haruji Ogura (whom he took to a memorable party given by Cobden-Sanderson to celebrate the centenary boat-race); frequent letters from his Japanese friends and from William Plomer kept Japan in his mind; constant

contact with his friend J. S. Billingham, a bookseller in Northampton-
shire, enabled a steady flow of cheap editions of English poets to arrive
in Tokyo; and an invitation to take a chair in English came from Keijo
University, swiftly followed by one from Takeshi Saito in Tokyo. By
February 1929 he was almost certain that he would return to Japan in
the following year. Ironically his thoughts of leaving England coincided with his greatest critical acclaim, after the publication of *Undertones of War* in November 1928; perhaps the memory of the hours
spent at his desk in the Kikufuji Hotel fanned the flames. Edmund
could now justly claim to be an established writer, and for the rest of
his life was to be known as 'the author of *Undertones of War*'. Sassoon
remarked: 'You and I are popular prose-men now; but let us always
remember that Poetry is our heavenly spouse. You have the advantage
of me there, for *Undertones* is well stocked with poetry, though I fear
that the majority of your readers will shun that rich appendix.'[38]

At Cobden-Sanderson's suggestion Edmund removed some proper
names from the manuscript before publication (though they remained
in the American edition) and the book went into eight impressions in
two years, with minor revisions for later editions.[39] Its success caused
some difficulty for Cobden-Sanderson and strained his resources considerably. It was warmly received by authors as varied as Arnold
Bennett and David Jones, and fan mail continued for forty years from
all over the world, the poet E. E. Cummings describing it as miracle
filled'.[40] It had its detractors though. Edmund recalled a cricket match
during which an incoming batsman complained that he had written
about the war 'like a child who was happy with a bag of sweets'.[41] A
more sympathetic response came from Robert Graves, who received it
generously, but Edmund was unable to reciprocate when he reviewed
Graves's *Goodbye to All That* for *Time and Tide* a year later. Both
Edmund and Sassoon were incensed at the book, which they held to
be inaccurate and – in the portrayal of the ordinary soldiers – a
betrayal of the fighting men many of whom had seen more action than
Graves. Edmund exploded in a long and angry letter to Takeshi Saito:

R. Graves has published, for money and to create a sensation, a most ugly
and untruthful autobiography. It is the season of gross and silly war books,
and he has succeeded in selling his. But he has lost all the respect that his
recent follies had left in the minds of Sassoon and other old friends. I am
collecting the comments and corrections of those persons concerned, and
hope the British Museum will soon accept a copy in which (nearly) every
page will have corrective marginalia. Mrs Hardy is one of the correctors, via
Sassoon, and many of the soldiers referred to will also be represented. The

War was a great crime, but I shall never forget the general decency and geniality, as well as endurance and unselfishness, of our armies in Flanders. Not often did we achieve great military successes. We met Germany, a very brave and laborious and intellectual nation; and against such power and skill, no nation would have been able to advance without frightful punishment. But, until the last stage, when even German standards failed, there was a high manliness, and a profound cleanness, about the English in Flanders. (Bad language is only a valve, letting off steam harmlessly.) We had so much work to do, so many friendships and loyalties to keep in tune. A man like S. Sassoon would be outstanding anywhere for nobility and ability; but there were, wherever we went, men who could be worthily mentioned with him. We hear that clergymen were rare in Flanders, but there was a religion that hardly needed them, and which they seldom understood. My Colonel, who thought himself a mere 'regular soldier', was a saint without a halo. Every detail of his life would be found to answer his great question: Is this the *right thing* to do? I say all this, because the distortion of men like Graves has been so widely commended; it is equivalent to using the cemeteries which crowd the old line of battle from north to south as latrines. Alas, so many of the best types were killed, sheerly because they were the best; and you may be lucky in twenty bombardments, but the day must come, when mathematics works. Graves knows 'all that', and knows that he saw comparatively little of the front line; it is his own conscience that he is shouting down.[42]

In fact, on 7 November 1929, a week before publication, Sassoon and Edmund spent an evening annotating *Goodbye to All That* (which they subtitled *The Welsh-Irish Bull in a China Shop*)[43] with over 300 corrections and hostile comments in the margins. It never found its way into the British Museum (and Edmund was later to regret being so 'editorial'), but it created an estrangement between Graves and Edmund which was not to be healed until 1966.

The beginning of 1930 marked a new phase in Edmund's life. He had just moved from his London bed-sitter to share a large and isolated farmhouse outside Bury St Edmunds with his 'very gifted but a little unmethodical brother'[44] Gilbert and his German wife Annie. Gilbert had abandoned business in Sheffield, and was anxious to open a private press. For this purpose Edmund gave him the manuscript of *De Bello Germanico*, written in 1918, which Gilbert published in November 1930.

Life at the rambling house, Hawstead, once the rendezvous for a point-to-point, was much to Edmund's liking – the stairs creaked at night, there were moorhens on the lawn and it reminded him of Congelow. Despite the fact that there were several spacious rooms, Edmund chose to use the small attic, with a tiny window, as his study.

Adrian Bell recalled visiting him there, in his 'small garret where he wheezed in the foetid warmth of an oil heater as he wrote, burrowing into literary bypaths'.[45] Annie was looking after Clare and John for the day, and Bell could 'recall her playing the zither to them under a single oil-lamp – with Edmund, rather ill, clutching a shawl round him with one hand and holding up a candle with the other to show me the books on the shelves that lined the wall. It was like the moment that brings down the curtain in a Chekhov play'.[46] Hawstead was certainly an ideal place in which to write about English village life, and Edmund was preparing such a book, *The Face of England*, for J. C. Squire's English Heritage Series, to be published in 1932. The book is a mixture of Suffolk and Kentish memories and fancies, and several characters, such as 'Tatty' in 'National Biography', have Hawstead origins, and the description of the tipsy verger in 'Trouble at Twilight', who coined the word 'symblems' and who extinguished his cigarette beneath his heel on the mosaic floor, records a real experience in Long Melford Church.[47]

Edmund found that he was something of a celebrity in the village and his generous manner brought many requests for help with local activities, which were rarely refused. He was more than happy to comply with the request which arrived with the milk one morning at Hawstead to write a few lines for the autograph collection of Jerome the milkman; equally he was pleased to assist a local farmer's boy who asked for help with the composition of verse and prose. The boy eventually became a priest and received a letter at theological college from Edmund: 'Let your literary and religious life be united, you have admirable advantages and an experience of life as good as Oxford or even Cambridge caps and gowns'.[48] That Edmund should link religion and literature was typical. As he declared to his mother, 'I'm all for Christianity that can write and read'[49], and his interest in the church was more cultural than spiritual. Brought up as a parish chorister and having friends who were priests, he was sympathetic to Christianity but an irregular church attender.

Edmund always enjoyed the company of animals. He had learned to know virtually every kind of fish to be found in English waters, and could recognise most birds. He respected insects and rodent life, was especially fond of rabbits, hedgehogs and frogs, avoided walking on ants and fought a battle of loyalties when mice invaded the attic and threatened his books. He discovered a way of reviving apparently dead bees by placing them on a sunny window-sill in a drop of water; and, when rescuing a bird trapped in a room, he would hold it gently in his hands outside the window as it gradually grew accustomed to the open air again. At Hawstead a tame hen would wander into the house, befriended by Faust the cat, and Edmund was pleased to work at his table while 'Chuck-Chuck' strutted around inquisitively. On her death Edmund admitted that 'the want of that curious companionship has tried me more than I will admit ... no serenity but has its sly, cold undercurrent. I have noticed it more than ever this Spring.'[50] It was an appropriate setting for Edmund to be reading the poetry of the eccentric Victorian Cornish priest and animal-lover, R. S. Hawker. A vivid scene was presented to him one morning in Bury: a boar was tied to a post and held by several labourers, while a drover was sawing off its tusks. The boar was screaming, and, after the operation was complete, was covered in blood. Edmund objected that this was cruelty – but was assured that the tusks were nerveless and that no pain had been inflicted. That evening he recorded in his diary: 'It is time that the intelligence of animals was taken into account in judging cruelty. This boar could see a saw, and could feel his mouth being opened and kept opened for the saw to be applied – to what purpose? That he could not know, and there he was, in mind, at the mercy of the torturer.'[51]

Hawstead provided some domestic calm, for Annie was a solicitous housekeeper and Edmund was never happy without female companionship. There was, noted Adrian Bell, 'something about the little man that made every woman who met him want to protect him from everyone else – and in the end they almost smothered him to death with rivalries of affection.'[52] But, if there was some homely stability, there was no respite from the gruelling pattern of work. He had finally completed his life of Leigh Hunt, which was published in May 1930. It was a handsome volume, including some new silhouettes which Sir William Bull – the befriender in old age of Leigh Hunt's youngest daughter – had shown Edmund. The book was a fine example of Edmund's interest in the circle around writers, and alongside better-known characters such as Cowden Clark are recorded the contributions of Charles Ollier, Vincent Novello, Basil Montagu and Virtue Kent. It was a work which had been in the making for ten years, and was a tribute to the writer whom Edmund described as not for 'all hours' but the ideal companion for 'the slippered mood'.[53]

In February 1930 Edmund began a year's appointment as literary and assistant editor of the *Nation*, in succession to Leonard Woolf. He was aware that the paper was in great difficulties. The economist John Maynard Keynes had withdrawn almost all his financial support, and the new editor Harold Wright knew that he was probably presiding over its death-throes.   Almost immediately Edmund entered into a lively controversy over Middleton Murry's edition of Keats, which led to an extended and acrimonious correspondence in the columns of the *Nation* as Edmund refuted what he saw as Murry's 'ingenious misinterpretations'.[54]

This editorial work once again necessitated travelling to London three days a week, but it also provided a pleasing balance of rural peace and urban activity. In London he had found new friends and acquaintances, including the journalist Richard Church and the short-story writer W. W. Jacobs. In February at the Charles Lamb Society, 'W. W. Jacobs made a speech apparently of unprecedented length for him; it was quite twenty-five words.   He's the quietest modestest man in London. I think that Lamb, if he came to our (his) Society, would instantly seat himself next to W.W.J.'[55] Some travelling burdens were relieved by the availability of Gilbert as a chauffeur, but his car was unreliable and a night spent sleeping on the back seat after a mechanical breakdown made train and bicycle more attractive methods of transport.

With payments to Gilbert and Annie, to Mary, Clare and John, and to Aki Hayashi (who had to be rescued after bailiffs arrived and removed all the furniture from her home), Edmund needed to earn £16 a week to meet his financial obligations; and it all had to be earned by the pen. He continued to provide introductions for anthologies of verse and prose, and to an edition of *The Memoirs of the Late Mrs Robinson*[56] – the actress-mistress of George IV, and the poetess admired by Coleridge. He also continued to produce articles and reviews at the rate of three a week. His poetic voice, however, had deserted him. During 1930 he submitted only three poems to periodicals; the unhappiness of his marriage had smothered the lyric voice. Cobden-Sanderson suggested a selection from the previous volumes, and *Poems 1914–30* was published in December. It consisted of 300 poems, emphasising the problems of editing a prolific and 'occasional' poet. Philip Morrell wrote an acute review in the *Sunday Times*:

It is a handsome volume well printed and well bound but I could wish it had been better edited, for interesting as this book is, I hardly think it does him justice. In the first place it seems to me considerably too long. Blunden has written so profusely and is now so well known we do not want a pious collection of every scrap that has come from his pen so much as a judicious selection of his best work. It may be argued no doubt that almost all his work is of a remarkably high level, but lovers of poetry – as Keats once said in a letter to Bailey – like to have a little region to wander in where they may pick and choose what may be food for a week's stroll in the Summer, but here I find the regions altogether too wide and cannot help thinking that if the book had been cut down, say, to two-thirds of its present length, it would have gained by the process.[57]

Once again Sassoon came to the rescue financially, writing at the end of the year to Hawstead:

Listen Edmund, my income is over £3000 a year. . . . Do please allow me to give you £50 a month for the next year or so. You would do the same for me if our positions were reversed. Try and imagine that it is Shelley that is doing it for you – as he surely would have done, and angels would glorify his name for ever. All you need do is say one word 'yes'. I know how heavy your burden must be, with several people to support. Why shouldn't I wave my wand and dispel the financial anxieties until you have regained your reserves of vitality? And then get thoroughly overhauled by a London doctor. I can't bear to think of you toiling up to London every week in November and December. You have been straining yourself to breaking point and nature is rebelling and warning you with headaches etc.[58]

He was indeed close to breaking point, a brief holiday with the Downings in France being only a momentary respite. The divorce settlement was weighing heavily on his mind. Sassoon had offered to become John's guardian, but Mary had understandably rejected this, and the legal wrangling ground on until, with Mary admitting adultery, the decree *nisi* was granted in February 1931 and six months later Mary was free to marry Cyril Keeble. Edmund felt numbed and old; yet he was just thirty-four.

# 16

# Yalding
## March – October 1931

---

*I am sick to death of the whole [divorce] position; it has
muddled me and worn me down too long, and robbed
me of the energy which ought to have made me a good
poet instead of the shadow of one.*
Letter to Hector Buck, October 1929[1]

*Should my poetry decline, however, I should have much
to do as a curator and investigator of the great and can
see myself as an editor, aged ninety-six, below rows and
rows of weighty works.*
Letter to his father, August 1926[2]

---

If the opening months of 1931 saw Edmund at his lowest ebb, physically and emotionally, they also offered the best chance of recovery by
providing the opportunity of a return to Yalding. His father's retirement coincided with the lease on the old school house at Cleave's
becoming available, and Edmund was able to join his parents and
renew his acquaintance with the countryside of Kent and the banks of
the Teise and the Beult. As he gradually gained strength, poetry
returned; both the melancholic questioning of 'The Kiss':

> *I am for the woods against the world,*
> *But are the woods for me?*[3]

and the objective humour of 'Incident in Hyde Park'.[4]

Divorce proceedings and his appointment to the *Nation* had persuaded him not to return to Japan, though visits from Professor
Ichikawa and Professor Kochi Doi kept Tokyo much in mind. But
new moves were afoot. William Force Stead and Colonel C. H.

176

Wilkinson, Bursar of Worcester College, together with Professor David Nichol Smith of Merton, had been trying to find Edmund an Oxford appointment; and in the spring of 1931 he was elected to a fellowship and tutorship in English at Merton, from October.

The Warden of Merton somewhat patronisingly suggested that Edmund should spend the summer doing some reading in preparation for his teaching, but he had several projects in hand to supplement his *Nation* journalism. A new Clare book, *Sketches in the Life of John Clare*, was completed by March and work was begun on some special items for private presses. A letter of William Godwin with remarks by Edmund was prepared for Fytton Armstrong (the pseudonym of John Gawsworth), published under the title *Tragical Consequences*, and an introduction to 'The Ancient Mariner' was commissioned by the American publishers Cheshire House. This gave him particular pleasure, for with *Shakespeare's Significances* and an article in the *Japan Advertiser* on Herman Melville, he had now paid tribute to the authors of the three works which he felt had affected him most deeply: *King Lear*, 'The Ancient Mariner' and *Moby Dick*. He also brought together forty articles from the many he had contributed to the *Times Literary Supplement* over the last ten years, which appeared at the end of the year as *Votive Tablets*. Edmund described the book, in his dedication to Bruce Richmond, as 'daydreams among my favourite books' and John Skelton and Nicholas Breton happily co exist with Thomas Randolph and Thomas Hood.

The preoccupation of these months, however, was the editing of the poems of Wilfred Owen on which Sassoon had encouraged Edmund to work, feeling too closely associated with Owen to undertake the task himself, as he explained in a letter of Spring 1931:

At Craiglockhart, Wilfred and I talked very little about our experiences of the disgusting and terrible scenes in France. I discouraged him from reviving such memories, knowing that they were bad for him. And little Wilfred was such a modest chap that I never fully realised his imaginative grasp of the scene. I suppose I must some day add my own little commentary on him as I knew him. But I have always suffered from an obscure difficulty in clarifying my friendship with him – perhaps because the loss of him was a shock which I never faced squarely – coming as it did at the most difficult time, when I was emotionally and physically without any foundations.

(As I probably told you, I was not told about his death until more than two months afterwards, and during that period I had not allowed myself to believe that there was an everlasting reason for his not having written to me.) But enough of me – oh EB I cannot get on without you, so be careful of your health.

## PART FOUR   1924 – 1931

The editing of Owen was a time-consuming and complicated problem of establishing an authentic text from a host of variants, but was very much to Edmund's taste; by the autumn of 1931 the work was completed and was published by Chatto and Windus, with an introductory memoir by Edmund based on Owen's letters and on conversations with Sassoon and with Owen's mother. He stresses Owen's position as a war poet, but not *just* a war poet:

He speaks as a soldier, with perfect and certain knowledge of war at grips with the soldier; as a mind, surveying the whole process of wasted spirit, art, and blood in all its instant and deeper evils. . . .

He was, apart from Mr Sassoon, the greatest of the English war poets. But the term 'war poets' is rather convenient than accurate. Wilfred Owen was a poet without classifications of war and peace. Had he lived, his humanity would have continued to encounter great and moving themes, the painful sometimes, sometimes the beautiful, and his art would have matched his vision. He was one of those destined beings who, without pride of self (the words of Shelley will never be excelled), 'see, as from a tower, the end of all'. Outwardly, he was quiet, unobtrusive, full of good sense; inwardly he could not help regarding the world with the dignity of a seer.

Apart from a small edition by Sassoon in 1920, Edmund's was the first wide-ranging selection and for thirty years was to remain the standard text which brought Owen's poetry into popular readership, receiving the widest circulation of Edmund's books apart from *Undertones of War*. He received just fifty pounds for the work. Some of Owen's poems had appeared in 1919 in Edith Sitwell's periodical *Wheels*; though the journal was defiantly anti-Georgian, Edmund's work on Owen brought him into friendly association with Edith Sitwell – a relationship he enjoyed with most of the Sitwell family.

A new enthusiasm was also awakened by regular visits to Keats House in Hampstead. Edmund joined those who were anxious to see it brought back to its original state, supporting the removal of a later extension and the inclusion of the Dilke collection of books from Finchley Road into a refurbished library. He attended the reopening by Lord Crewe in July and the house became for Edmund 'a bride of quietness'[5] in London, to which he made frequent visits under the genial curatorship of Frank Edgcumbe, proudly sleeping in Fanny Brawne's bed on several occasions.

An invitation from Sir Michael Sadler, Master of University College, resulted in a lecture in the Oxford town hall on 'Shelley in Oxford, and His Expulsion', followed by raids on second-hand bookshops to furnish Edmund's college rooms. And then, in the first week of October 1931, he left Yalding for Merton College to spend the next thirteen years of his life as an Oxford don.

# PART FIVE
## 1931–1945

# 17

# Oxford : Merton
## October 1931 – October 1933

---

*Perhaps my greatest trouble is myself, and I write
sometimes in dejection when I should not; but life in
college is a mixture of luxury and privation, and my
shyness has made me slow to adapt myself.*
Letter to his mother, March 1932[1]

*Much in Oxford to like; much to dislike. The burdens
of the life of the place, and the rewards, fall most
unevenly and I have some enemies who hate me for
liberal opinions and some who despise me for
conservative opinions. It is not a job for anyone whose
hopes and previous labour were poetry and good
literature.*
Letter to E.L. Griggs, January 1933[2]

---

Edmund's Oxford years followed the now familiar pattern of alternating stability and upheaval. Having tasted the world of war, Japan, rural England and literary London, he was ready for the stimulation of academic life, and Merton was rich soil within the literary field (a comparatively new discipline in the university), having within its fellowship both the eighteenth-century scholar Professor David Nichol Smith and the colourful Irish grammarian Professor H. C. K. Wyld, as well as the Goldsmith Reader in English, Lascelles Abercrombie – a poet of modesty and sensitivity of whom Edmund grew fond:

> *the brief season of our meetings
> Is on my life most graciously inscribed.*[3]

# PART FIVE    1931 – 1945

The Senior Common Room could also provide plenty of lively and entertaining company apart from its English fellows for it was the college of the lawyer F. H. Lawson and the philosopher (and future Warden) Geoffrey Mure, whom Edmund considered to have 'wonderful intellectual range and capacity. . . . he opens up a question more fully and strenuously than anyone almost whom I know'.[4] Friendships were also quickly formed with the Senior Tutor, Idris Deane Jones, and the Chaplain, Stephen Williams, while two men became his closest Merton friends and colleagues: the Classics fellow Robert Levens and the classicist, literary scholar and former Professor of Poetry, H. W. Garrod (who nearly always wore a hat, even indoors).

Having been allocated rooms on the same staircase as Garrod in Fellows' Quad, Edmund was quickly drawn into the confidence of the formidable scholar, who was as happy to converse about Erasmus or Greek literature as about Keats or the New Testament. Edmund spent many hours in Garrod's rooms – full of books and postcards – with chess, cards (activities during which Edmund was usually a spectator), crumpets, cigars and claret complementing the conversation, interrupted only to take a variety of dogs for walks across the Meadows to the Cherwell. Edmund considered Garrod a kind of model of a university don and remembered him as 'one of the most sensitive and generous people one can imagine living in an old quadrangle among academicals'.[5] The two writers shared an enthusiasm for the Romantic poets and Garrod saw striking resemblances between Edmund and the nineteenth-century writers. On Edmund's forty-fifth birthday in 1941 Garrod wrote to him:

> *Thou wast not born for death – or forty-five,*
> *But with thy books to be exempt from time.*
> *What range possessed you, Edmund, to outlive*
> *Shelley and Keats, unless it were in rhyme?*[6]

Like Edmund, Garrod was a compulsive journalist, a lover of animals and devoted to poetry. A close friendship was inevitable.

With Robert Levens there were different shared interests, dominated by cricket. Levens masterminded a cricket team – the Barnacles – based on Merton, for which Edmund played regularly over many years. After Levens's marriage to Daphne Hanschell in 1932 (a wedding which Edmund attended in his usual shabby suit, unaware of the surprise of the other morning-suited guests) Levens tried to reserve an evening each fortnight for Edmund's company, when Cicero and cricket were equally favoured conversation topics.

If Edmund found the lecture platform something of a burden he found tutoring quite the reverse and quickly formed the friendly rapport with his students which he had achieved in Tokyo. They in turn responded to his informal manner, his endless capacity to listen, his ability to give himself totally in concentration and concern to the person with whom he was conversing, and to his readiness to spend time with them outside tutorials – walking the Oxfordshire country-side or (to conform to proctorial strictures) taking them into Oxford pubs. He treated them not as pupils but as friends and extensions of his family.

Several undergraduates sought him out. An early pupil was Hugh Carleton Greene (later to become Director General of the BBC) who owed his first job in journalism to Edmund's encouragement and backing and who changed from reading Greats to reading English because he was attracted to Edmund's personality, finding him one of the strongest influences in his life. From Christ's Hospital came the talented artist Malcolm Easton and – in later Oxford years – the poet Keith Douglas, who came to Merton as a result of being introduced to Edmund in Hector Buck's rooms. Though Douglas was considered an *enfant terrible* by several of his masters, Edmund found that 'he held no terrors' and considered that 'he should be a brilliant performer in the English Schools'.[7] Douglas for his part found Edmund virtually the only figure of authority in his life for whom he had both affection and respect. Edmund's reputation as a writer and critic attracted pupils too – Alec Hardie, a contemporary of Douglas's who was to become a prominent figure in Edmund's life, wished to be taught by the author of *Undertones of War*, while in the same years Michael Meyer (the future biographer and translator of Ibsen and Strindberg) came from Christ Church, anxious to be taught by the editor of Wilfred Owen; he found in Edmund a most sympathetic mentor. An unusually large number of pupils became English professors: Northrop Frye and Douglas Le Pan in Toronto; Michael Joseph and Jack Garrett in New Zealand; Rodney Bain in Alabama. When Edmund was at Hong Kong University some twenty years later at the instigation of a Merton pupil, Bernard Mellor, he was to be joined by both Alec Hardie and a St Hilda's pupil Mary Oswin (later Mary Visick).

Other pupils were encouraged to become writers or journalists. The American Rhodes Scholar and poet Paul Engle was to set up the prestigious Writers' Workshop in Iowa University, John Barber was to be appointed drama critic of the *Daily Telegraph* and Roger Lancelyn Green was to combine acting and writing. Indeed, during Edmund's time, Merton became a centre of university journalism, providing editors and contributors for *Isis*, the *Cherwell* and *Augury* mostly from the ranks of his pupils. In addition to these students came a regular flow of female undergraduates from Somerville and St Hilda's.

Throughout his Oxford career Edmund's list of official pupils was augmented by a wider circle of undergraduates – predominantly from Merton – who were drawn to his college rooms or to his table at the Bear, the King's Arms, the Turf or the Eastgate. Here could be found Richard Storry, future Professor of Japanese Studies at Oxford (who first went to Japan with Edmund's encouragement), Douglas Grant, who was to take the chair of American Literature at Leeds, the future literary editor of the *Observer* Michael Davie or the biographer and journalist Derek Hudson. From St Catherine's came Laurence Brander, who was to join the British Council, and from Exeter College came the Swedish scholar of Beddoes, H. W. Donner. By 1940 Edmund was regularly in the chair in Oxford hostelries in the company of young poets – most often Keith Douglas, sometimes with Sidney Keyes or John Heath-Stubbs.

With the world of linguistics he had little professional interest (once describing the Anglo-Saxons as 'a race of scribes willing to celebrate any old longshoreman for the benefit of philologers'),[8] though he had friendly contact with J. R. R. Tolkien – then at Pembroke College – and within Merton formed a warm friendship with the future English fellow of Balliol, J. N. Bryson, and with J. A. W. Bennett, who was to become Professor of Medieval and Renaissance English at Cambridge and Master of Magdalene.

Edmund's tutorial manner was not always conventional. Paul Engle remembers having the mysteries of cricket explained to him with the *Collected Works* of Shelley acting as a wicket; tutorials with Michael Meyer were usually held in the Bear. He rarely made his pupils read out their essays and sometimes conducted his tutorials while taking a walk along the Cherwell. The statutory hour was often exceeded and Glen Byam Shaw's step-daughter Jane recalled that it was 'difficult to tear oneself away from such ingenuousness and talent'.[9] It was not that he 'taught' in the traditional sense: he was an accessible fund of knowledge, made literature come alive, listened intently and encouraged creativity. It is difficult to find a pupil who was unaffected by the experience. They discovered what Janet Tomblin described in 1961: 'Despite his gifts and learning, despite that clearer vision distinguishing the poet, you and he are talking on equal terms. For a moment you too are walking on Parnassus.'[10]

In many ways Edmund's university life isolated him from the world outside – a fact which was exaggerated by Merton's particular position. Separated from the High Street and the centre of Oxford by the cobbles of Merton Street, looking out across the Meadows in the other direction – and furnished with a magnificent library – the college was almost a self-contained university in miniature. To an extent this appealed to Edmund, for it enabled him to enjoy the security of the small community which his village upbringing and battalion experience had made familiar. But it also kept him out of the mainstream of political and literary development. The economic restraints of the 1930s were not felt very stringently at Merton high table and Edmund admitted to his mother: 'We eat very good dinners – too good. I hate eating as a fine art. I order permanent bacon and eggs for breakfast and cold beef for lunch'.[11] The constant attractions of contrasting interests pulled him in different directions: a love of academic company and a love of quiet contemplation; the lure of public recognition and the lure of simple life; a desire to popularise as many writers as possible and a desire to dedicate himself solely to his own poetry; a deep love of all things English, yet a great sympathy for the east. It was this inner sense of contradiction which made him restless and mercurial, exemplified by his proud acceptance of election to the Savage Club followed by his resignation a few years later because he felt uncomfortable in the sophistication of clubland. Life in college too seemed a mixed blessing. He liked the comfort but resented the element of regimentation inherent in all communal life, complaining in a letter to Aki Hayashi in October 1931: 'The only thing wrong with my life here, I mean the only oppressive thing, is this being shut in – one's exits and entrances should be natural, casual. But I am looking forward to owning a key which is said to let me in through the Garden, in agreeable solitude.'[12]

Edmund's war experience had given him a seated distrust of politics and politicians, making him generally reticent to voice political opinions. When he did so he laid himself wide open to misunderstanding for he spoke as a romantic idealist and not as a practical thinker. He never entered the arena of party politics, for he never formulated a political code. He was driven by one passion – the avoidance of war. Anything which brought war closer was to be challenged, regardless of the quarter from which it came. In this respect he saw nationalism as the great enemy, for it was likely to breed hatred and extend to 'war-mongering' – a phrase which he always used in anger. Such simplicity was bound to lead him into controversy and during his life he was accused of having sympathy with a number of extreme political opinions. None of the accusations had any validity, for extremism was alien to Edmund's personality. It was his refusal to condemn extremism in others which brought him into conflict with some areas of public opinion but which, by a strange twist of fate, also created the foundation for his success as a cultural ambassador to the east. At heart he was an appeaser, a would-be pacifist who was yet too much Lieutenant E.C. Blunden MC to go the full distance.

He was nevertheless to speak at a peace rally in the Albert Hall in 1935 attended by 7000 people, sharing the platform with Dr Maude Royden and the Rev. Dick Sheppard. Yet he confided privately that 'I fancy even Pacifists are sometimes prone to jockeying, malicious comment, selfishness, superciliousness, and passing by on t'other side. Willing to wound I have commonly found them – but they of course don't wear side-arms.'[13] By 1939 he was to be known as 'a pacifist in a Sam Browne'.[14]

His consistent view – which led to his being consistently misinterpreted – can be seen from contributions to two pamphlets on war published over a thirty-year span. In 1937 his friend Edgell Rickword edited for the *Left Review* a series of statements entitled *Authors Take Sides on the Spanish Civil War*. Edmund's only contact with the war was through writers – whether with Republican sympathies such as Stephen Spender or supporters of Franco such as Roy Campbell. Edmund's contribution was included in the section 'Against the Government' but its tentative tone is evident in the opening line: 'I know too little about affairs in Spain to make a confident answer.' He complains of the 'isolated and flamboyant' way in which the left had worded its manifesto and suggested that 'if one looked *upon the whole* of recent European history' (his own italics) a figure like Franco was a necessity, and he concluded that 'although England may not benefit' from his policies 'I think Spain will'. These may read like the words of a naive political observer; they are hardly the words of an ardent fascist. In 1967 he was to contribute to *Authors Take Sides on Vietnam*, declaring himself, unsurprisingly, against the war. Inevitably he was then suspected of having left views. More controversial was to be his stance towards Hitler in 1937–9, but it was to be a position adopted by a moderate and baffled war veteran and not by a Nazi sympathiser. His general position was clear in 1933 when he declared that 'the

Church of England cannot thrive without reforming their silly minds about nationalism and war.'[15]

Isolation from contemporary movements in literature was more of a chosen stance. He found it difficult to accept poetic 'intellectualising' or obscurity and while he admired the work of Day-Lewis, MacNeice and early Philip Larkin and Ted Hughes, he was less comfortable in the world of Auden, Pound, Eliot or Yeats. In the *Times Literary Supplement* of March 1935 he reviewed Day-Lewis's *A Hope for Poetry*. Commenting on Day-Lewis's assertion that the immediate poetic ancestors of the generation of Auden and Spender were Hopkins, Owen and Eliot, Edmund concluded: 'Those being the ancestors, it cannot be remarkable that their successors present some difficulty of style to the reader who has found Hopkins exceedingly subtle, Owen profoundly ironical, and Mr Eliot surpassingly allusive.' It was a cause of some personal embarrassment that other poets could enjoy what F. R. Leavis described in *New Bearings in English Poetry* (1932) as Edmund's 'simple pieties' while he was not always able to return the compliment, though he often enjoyed the affection and friendship of the poets themselves. Leavis also called attention to 'undertones' in Edmund's poetry which were 'not so simple' and he singled him out from the 'crowd of Georgian pastoralists' as a poet of 'genuine talent'. Edmund was grateful to Leavis for this and, though he did not share his critical standpoint, he respected Leavis's pacifist views and was amused by his 'rubber shoes and Gandhi manner'.[16]

With W. H. Auden it was a similar picture. John Betjeman described a visit from Auden in Oxford in 1926 and recalled him 'appraising my shelves with the sure and precocious literary judgement he had even in his teens. Ah! the usual stuff, he said, but I see you have got something genuine. And he picked out my volumes of Blunden, adding "he's a good poet".'[17] There was, however, little Auden on Edmund's shelves. In the 1930s he described him as 'too derivative' and thought it 'curious that Auden, capable of expressing the beautiful in the Keatsian sense, fights shy of it so often'.[18] Such remarks earned for him the not unexpected scorn of Geoffrey Grigson, who dubbed Edmund 'the Merton fieldmouse'. Yet Edmund had considerable affection for Auden, greatly admiring his metrical skills, enthusiastically supporting the Merton Floats production of Auden and Isherwood's *The Ascent of F6* in 1937 (providing an introductory verse for the programme) and declining to stand against him for the Oxford Professorship of Poetry in 1956, at which time he found himself reading Auden with increasing pleasure.

Similary he took time to come to terms with the poetry of Yeats. His personal contacts were limited to a few brief meetings in Oxford, which Yeats visited several times in the early 1930s, giving a lecture in June 1933 at which Edmund proposed the vote of thanks. For his part, Yeats included six of Edmund's poems in his selection for *The Oxford Book of Modern Verse*, but on Yeats's death in 1939 Edmund confided to Takeshi Saito:

I was not among those who call Yeats a really great poet. . . . I don't find quite as much sign of this rich scene of earth, sea, air as I would wish in his descriptive passages. But Irish poets seldom paint well. They may now and then, but they prefer rhapsodic imagery. . . . My final feeling would be that he was too crotchety and inconsistent for greatness.[19]

This was an opinion he was to moderate, finding considerable pleasure in Yeats's poetry twenty years later – when he also increased his admiration for Ezra Pound – but it represented a point of view which was hardly likely to endear him to those Oxford undergraduates who were enthusiastic readers of the modern poets in 1931. He admitted in 1933 that 'I don't understand what is meant by many of the youth in this city.'[20] He did not share the contemporary enthusiasm for the novels of D. H. Lawrence either, claiming himself to be handicapped by the memory of some of the sexually explicit material which had circulated among his wartime battalion, but he was not unsympathetic to all the 'moderns'. In 1924 a young Japanese student in Tokyo, Tomotsu Sone, had presented him with the early Paris edition of James Joyce's *Ulysses* and Edmund recorded that 'the impression that the unusual book made on me was deep, and the genius of Joyce appeared as a certainty.'[21] William Empson – a fellow enthusiast for the east – he found a stimulating personality and described him in 1931 as 'a man of great possibilities'. It was, however, with T. S. Eliot that the distinction between social affection and literary sympathy became most marked. He held Eliot in high personal regard: a feeling which was reciprocated. (Eliot was also a fellow asthmatic.) Eliot visited Merton, his old college, and offered to publish some of Edmund's poems at Faber and Faber; they had – under the imprint of Faber and Gwyer – included 'Winter Nights' in the Ariel Poems series in 1928. But on the demise of the publishing house of Cobden-Sanderson Edmund had agreed to publish with Macmillan and so had reluctantly to decline the offer. Eliot's poetry, and particularly his drama, remained a more or less closed book to Edmund and he reviewed his work in respectful neutral tones. Eliot's American lectures (1933) had infuriated Edmund and he remonstrated in a letter to Saito: 'His remarks on Shelley are crude and ignorant, on Keats he is deliberately wrong, and he works off his grudge against Coleridge – who has done all that *he* can do, and something more.'[22] But seven years later he described Eliot's visit in warm terms: 'His gentlemanly simplicity impresses and I should like to have the chance of knowing him better. . . . He is one of the finest looking of poets, with something of the American loneliness in his face and ways.'[23]

Edmund's distance from the world of modern literature was part of his distrust and fear of the aggressive – either in personality or on the page. His instinct was always to look towards the lyrical, the hidden, the forgotten – an expression of his philosophy of following 'the glance, the pause, the guess'.[24] It is explicit in the opening lines of his poem 'Lonely Love' (1937), selected by Philip Larkin for his edition of *The Oxford Book of Twentieth-Century English Verse:*

> *I love to see those loving and beloved*
> *Whom Nature seems to have spited; unattractive,*
> *Unnoticeable people, whose dry track*
> *No honey-drop of praise, or understanding,*
> *Or bare acknowledgement that they existed,*
> *Perhaps yet moistened. Still, they make their world.*[25]

In literary terms he adopted a position of critical pacifism, noting in an undated memorandum: 'I conceive that truth needs not to war against error, but to hold her way like the cloudless moon; her argument is her calm brightness.'[26]

In other ways Oxford was a period of expansion and he was able to indulge some cultural enthusiasms. He had long been attracted to water colours (particularly those of Peter De Wint) and to engravings (particularly those of Thomas Bewick, whose autobiographical *Memoir* he was to introduce for the Centaur Classics series in 1961). He now extended his interest in the paintings of Richard Dadd, thus adding a mentally disturbed artist to his list of mentally disturbed writers, and followed the artistic career of his old war comrade Edmond Kapp (who left Hinges in 1916 with Edmund's copy of John Clare's *Poems*). He also took an interest in the work of two contemporary artists, Frederick Porter and Ethelbert White, both of whom had London exhibitions in 1930 and for whom Edmund provided dedicatory poems for each catalogue:

> *Fortune haunts us, moments bloom*
> *Like these, and life's a pictured room,*[27]

and one of White's picture's – a gift from the artist – hung permanently on his walls.

He became a regular visitor to the Ashmolean Museum in Oxford, where he found a close friend in the Assistant Keeper of Western Art, Ian Robertson, a humorous, witty conversationalist and an enthusiast for bronzes, terracottas and ceramics. He also joined the Bach choir (enjoying the company of the genial Director from Christ Church, Thomas Armstrong) and began to make use of his soft baritone voice, surprising some with his vocal solo in a performance of Dryden's *Secular Masque* for the Merton Floats in 1939. He was to develop a particular fondness for the music of Beethoven and Mozart.

He was certainly not isolated in terms of being confined to college or Oxford, for from his arrival in 1931 he was making regular visits to London – to visit F. A. Downing (now established as an engraver), Aki Hayashi (who acted as his seamstress), Philip Tomlinson, Keats House, the Charles Lamb Society or new friends such as the poetically minded Professor of Physics at London University, Edward Andrade. These visits were to be increased when, in 1932, he accepted an invitation to join the committee of the Book Society in place of J. B. Priestley. The Society, the inspiration of Arnold Bennett, had been founded by Alan Bott in 1929 and the committee recommended a monthly selection of newly published books. This meant that Edmund was now to add to his already huge diet of reading and reviewing and was to provide a monthly contribution (usually avoiding novels unless they were reissues of classics) for the next fourteen years. Apart from introducing him to the 'ironical and informed'[28] Bott and to Priestley ('I like J. B. Priestley . . . when he is with me we talk as writers and old acquaintances') it also brought him into contact with the writers Sylvia Lynd ('malicious and gentle by turns') and Clemence Dane. In later years he was to meet Colin de la Mare ('handsome, exquisitely unassuming, a true judge of books and character') and was to extend his friendship with Cecil Day-Lewis ('with his head like Tennyson's and his constant unworded allusion to a world of private jest and mythology'). Other members of the committee were the President of Magdalen College Oxford, George Gordon ('a master of expression, his lightest jokes have the classical touch'), Compton Mackenzie and the novelist Hugh Walpole. He was drawn to the personality of Walpole and wrote a few rough notes of reminiscence some ten years after Walpole's death in 1941:

I am now thinking of Hugh as I saw him, magnificent in bowler hat and massive overcoat, rather like Mr Pickwick in countenance; and if we add the episcopal touch, the poised chin and the ironical eye of a leader in his own world.

About his principal writings I found him exceedingly modest and laconic and one day he told me a little sadly that he was no best-seller in spite of all the appearances of fame. I don't think he meant this because he desired to make more money – he would have given that away in one form or other. He was a little combative on other matters. For example, on his powers as an intellectual. . . .

His speaking voice was delightful; his words came with a purity of accent and modulation which yet seem to linger upon my ear. He could be angry and punitive, and fell on me for saying (with nothing more than mild humour in my mind) that recent novels had not been much to my liking. I wanted something nearer to *Tom Jones*. The voice for once was quite sharp. 'Now Edmund, don't talk such nonsense; you are just like one of the old men in the Clubs.' I remember him raising his voice over some new volume of verse during the war. Cecil Day-Lewis was sitting peacefully enough beside me but Hugh was full of wrath incited by somebody's latest poems. The wrath fell on C.D.L. 'You poets,' Hugh declared, biting his pipe, 'you piped us all onto the parade ground, and now the show begins you are somewhere else.' C.D.L., whose silences are worth *watching*, said nothing.

In the years preceding the war, I came duly from Oxford to the meetings of the Committee of the Book Society, established (and some would say manoeuvred) by Hugh. . . . I was surprised and alarmed to see what London did to a man like Hugh. He was apparently full of rumour and fantasy. He varied from month to month, rather like the gaslamp in *Pickwick Papers*, flaring up and dying down. I saw an able and generous man at the mercy of all that wild neurotic flux of 'news' and 'what the real people are saying' which infests a super-subtle metropolis from time to time. I wish that this fever in the world's great cities might begin to find its physicians. .

The last time that we met, I perceived that some physical effect was upon him. . . . It was for Holbein to depict him then. Not the slightest apprehension that he would die soon afterwards crossed my mind. I had him alone, as it happened, for a while. He had a Sainte-Beuve in him. He was sentimental, learned and witty. I urged him to write a biography of Hartley Coleridge. A life of Hartley Coleridge by Hugh Walpole, living as he did at moments in the lakes, would have been a romance superior to all fiction – at least to all Hugh's earnest and prolific series of fictions.[29]

Of greater personal significance was a meeting with another member of the Book Society management, for in Hugh Walpole's Piccadilly flat in 1932 Edmund was introduced to a tall young man who had spent two years as an actor at the Old Vic and the Lyric Hammersmith, two years as an office-boy at William Heinemann's publishing house, and was about to become a director of the publishers Jonathan Cape. He was Rupert Hart-Davis. A friendship was established which was to become one of the most important in Edmund's life and – inevitably – lead to a correspondence of hundreds of letters on both sides. They were to share the pleasures of book-hunting, fishing, cricket and theatre-going for forty years and Rupert Hart-Davis was to join that inner core of intimate friends which included Siegfried Sassoon, Takeshi Saito and Philip Tomlinson. In June 1932 Edmund wrote to Sassoon: 'Rupert Hart-Davis is a great discovery to my mind; he has much brightened my old age, and I am sure you would like him at once.'[30] Edmund was indeed to introduce them and thus initiate another influential literary friendship.[31]

To add to the pressures of tutorial duties in Oxford, of financial worries and of business outside Oxford (he was still contributing virtually every month to the *Times Literary Supplement*), he now found himself bombarded with invitations to speak at literary societies or with requests to pass opinions on the work of younger poets such as A. L. Rowse and Dannie Abse. He was often to be seen carrying files of papers – even to cricket matches – which included letters and manuscripts from aspiring writers. Regardless of the quality of their offerings they all received detailed and personally written replies. In November 1931 Edmund once again corresponded with Sassoon:

Who should appear lately but Rex Whistler and his young brother? So I went to Balliol, and we took tea and all was delightful. I was much struck, as on former occasions, by Rex's countenance; it is a face varying between a blankness and a second-sight, a glorious light. That I think may be said of his poetic brother, who has a different cast of features but when allured by a theme is as vivid as a sunset seraph-cloud.[32]

Following this, Laurence Whistler sent some of his poems to Edmund for his comments. He received a closely written reply, full of encouragement and detailed, constructive suggestions.

All this left little time for social life though he always made time for his wide circle of friends. Life was becoming exhausting and the fear of having no time for his own writing was threatening. After only eight weeks in Oxford, he was wondering if he had made the right decision in accepting the fellowship. He complained in a letter to Aki Hayashi that he had to attend meetings in Oxford on three consecutive evenings, then spend a day in London before returning to Oxford to have tea with Mrs Robert Bridges and thus would 'not be able to attend to my own work'. He continued: 'Indeed I much wish that I had been left alone to arrange my affairs and not brought here. There is nothing but good nature about me generally but my whole way of living and working doesn't agree with the present idea.'[33]

And there was more pressure to come with his appointment as the annual Clark Lecturer at Trinity College Cambridge for 1932, involving a series of seven lectures intended for publication. It was obvious that he was accepting too many engagements to give him time to prepare properly; yet still his inability to say no prevailed. In the first week of February 1932 – in addition to his college teaching – he gave a lecture at University College London on Monday and spoke to the Literary Society of University College Oxford on Wednesday. On Thursday he gave a Clark Lecture in Cambridge, attended a party in London on Friday and addressed a society in Merton on Saturday evening. He also wrote at least three lengthy personal letters and sustained his quota of – on average – one or two articles or reviews each week. By the end of the month he had given two more Cambridge lectures, three more Oxford lectures and a lecture at Westfield College London – lectures which he admitted were prepared 'on my nerves and alcohol'.[34] He was clearly overworking and exhaustion brought on bouts of asthma. He complained in letters that 'my head burns, my body shakes – and yet I am not getting things done.'[35] He was also finding himself being invited to endless lunch-parties 'which are so pleasant and yet so difficult to me . . . and I am not very neat at refusals.'[36] He felt uncomfortable as an Oxford figure and complained that 'even going for my glass of beer becomes a sort of passage through Oxford and its entanglements. . . . I want to be *free*, so to speak, not on show all the time.'[37]

He chose Charles Lamb as his subject for the Clark Lectures, finding him a difficult character to pin down: 'I prepared several fine-meshed nets, but he was through like an elver every time. I sought him but he was nowhere to be found. This is very like my life as a whole.'[38] Ruefully he regretted that his world was handicapped with a twenty-four-hour day and he confessed his failure to master the acoustics of the hall of Trinity. It was not Edmund at his best. When I. A. Richards visited him in February 1932, Edmund confided to Aki Hayashi that 'from Richards's friendly remarks I gather that my lectures . . . aren't thought a success, but I guessed it as you know.'[39]

Edmund's theme was to distinguish Lamb from his circle as the 'reasonable Romantic' who had too often been:

fobbed off as a contemporary of Wordsworth and of Keats who liked roast pig, puns, dogs'-eared books, whist, artificial language, writing for magazines, quotations and parodies; who disliked churches, Goethe, the Lake District, philosophy, punctuality, Shelley's voice, sanity, Scots, Jews and school-masters. If it is so, it is not surprising; for nobody has been more ingenious in professing unimportance than Lamb, except Lear's fool.

He presented Lamb as a poet, prose-writer and critic. But he also portrayed him as a man 'greater even than his writings' – as the man of whom Coleridge said, 'his heart is as whole and as one as his head.' The lectures were published as *Charles Lamb and His Contemporaries* – with the eccentric misprint in the first sentence of 'solecism' for 'solar system'.

Despite the muted reception which the lectures received, Edmund enjoyed his visits to Cambridge, not least because he could re-establish his friendship with I. A. Richards (then a fellow of Magdalene) and his wife Dorothea, being relieved to discover that 'any possible uncertainties as to whether the *Principles of Literary Criticism* might harm mutual understanding vanished happily.'[40] At Trinity he was able to renew the acquaintance of A. E. Housman and he recorded that on 24 February 1932 he sat next to Housman after dinner, 'talking of Shelley and Jane Williams. Housman surprised me by saying, "Jane wasn't married to Williams; Jane" (with a benevolent severity) "was living in sin". I hadn't known that.'[41]

The dejections and punishing work-schedules of 1930 – 31 were not particularly conducive to poetic activity, but Edmund decided to bring together some privately printed material, adding a few new poems, to produce a selection marking his thirty-fifth birthday on 1 November 1931 – appropriately called *Halfway House* – though it was not published until 1932. It combined, with some additions, two previously published single volumes: *A Summer's Fancy* (which had been written in Yalding in 1921) and *To Themis*. The latter collated *On Several Occasions* (including 'A Shadow by the Barn', much admired by Sassoon) and a series of four poems on famous trials including 'Shelley v Westbrook'. Rather bitterly (after memories of divorce proceedings) Edmund acknowledges that 'my increasing acquaintance with lawyers as well as literary critics rather frightens me from further escapades in this direction.'[42] Both earlier volumes had been published by Cyril Beaumont and were illustrated by Randolph Schwabe in a manner, declared Edmund, 'vastly to my liking'.[43] The remainder of *Halfway House* is predominantly melancholic, reflecting the quotation from Henry Cary's translation of Dante which appears on the title-page:

> *In the mid way of this our mortal life,*
> *I found me in a gloomy wood astray.*

The sense of gloom and melancholy is most strikingly clear in Edmund's birthday poem entitled 'November 1, 1931', which paints in its opening lines the restlessness of his life and the ever present memories of Ypres.

> *We talked of ghosts; and I was still alive;*
> *And I that very day was thirty-five:*
> *Alone once more, I stared about my room*
> *And wished some ghost would be a friend and come;*
> *I cared not of what shape or semblance; terror*
> *Was nothing in comparison with error;*
> *I wished some ghost would come, to talk of fate,*
> *And tell me why I drove my pen so late,*
> *And help with observations on my knack*
> *Of being always on the bivouac,*
> *Here and elsewhere, for ever changing ground,*
> *Finding and straightway losing what I found,*
> *Baffled in time, fumbling each sequent date,*
> *Mistaking Magdalen for the Menin Gate.*[44]

The collection was admired by Masefield and favourably reviewed in the *Oxford Magazine* by Graham Greene.

Domestic and personal affairs were now also weighing on him. His sister-in-law Annie was established uneasily at Yalding and was more and more relying on Edmund's support. Annie and Gilbert had briefly separated and Annie was caring for Gilbert's son. Over the next difficult months of temporary reconciliation, Edmund felt that they both needed him as a 'Siegfriedian brother'[45] and he was anxious to maintain the idea of *his room* in their house. Annie, eight years older than Edmund, constantly looked to him for comfort and company; she never looked in vain. He regarded his relationship with her to be similar to that between Mrs Mary Unwin and the poet William Cowper, who wrote in the late eighteenth century:

> *Thy needles once a shining store,*
> *For my sake restless heretofore,*
> *Now rust disused, and shine no more,*
> *My Mary! . . .*

*But well thou play'dst the housewife part,*
*And all thy threads with magic art*
*Have wound themselves about this heart,*
  *My Mary! . . .*

*Partakers of thy sad decline,*
*Thy hands their little force resign;*
*Yet gently press'd, press gently mine,*
  *My Mary!*[46]

In a letter from Merton in February 1932 he confided: 'In that poem you may see Annie and me. To such a degree does Cowper's case seem mine that last December here, sitting alone, thinking that Annie is no longer young and that time races us on into age, I already felt an old, old, man, and I wept and wept.'[47]

There was one bright light in his life. He had been aware for over a year that a young lady in London – a reviewer for the *Nation* and a writer of somewhat unusual and undistinguished novels – was in love with him. She was Sylva Norman, an Armenian (she had changed her name from Nahabedian) who came from Manchester where her father worked in the textile trade. Sylva and her two sisters had shown considerable enterprise: Dora going into films, Rita setting up a dancing school, while Sylva – with no university education – had engaged in wide reading (particularly in the Romantic period) and had established herself as a free-lance writer in London.

She was a small, determined woman with distinctly Jewish-looking features of which she felt self-conscious, a cheek scarred from a skiing accident and a shrill, unmusical voice. In later years she became sadly bent despite her obsession with physical fitness, shown in daily bouts of energetic skipping, and her stringent diet left her worryingly thin. Professional portrait photographs of 1931, however, accentuate a graceful profile and sensitive eyes.

Still bruised from divorce from Mary and worried that his nervous exhaustion and restlessness would depress any partner rather than be soothed by a relationship, Edmund shrank from any new involvement. But Sylva was persistent. Edmund was also concerned about the effect that a new affair would have on Aki Hayashi and Annie, while Dorothea Richards (a friend of Sylva's) had warned Edmund of Sylva's conventional family background. He felt torn in all directions, but by the beginning of 1932 he succumbed to Sylva's advances. In February he wrote her his first love letter:

Since I first saw you, my dear, I have understood that you felt for me a beautiful kindness; and you have been in my mind as a bright and happy presence all the time. Whatever happens to me, I shall not be deprived of you in spirit. Now you have honoured me with your particular love. I have been in a fever of delight and despair since you kissed me and told me. I should have come to you a long time ago to win your kiss and you, but for the danger that I feared, and fear, in my involving your liberty and your finest emotions in my life. I remained apart, and did not even write, I can't say with the hope (for my hope was exactly opposite) but with the perception that you would find your thoughts of me lessening, and so go safe and free. And on my side, as I briefly told you, there are long-sustained loyalties, for which I have had to fight and to' risk much, and which I should do an ugly thing to desert now. I mentioned Annie. Without my constant care and deep affection, she would find this world only a slow torture. In her earlier life she has been bitterly wounded again and again. She looks on me as her salvation and promise to that end. To her I owe most of the calm and sweetness which I have had for the last four years. To her I talk almost always. . . . She is in love with me, I think; and she is not the only one. . . . The other one who loves me is Aki Hayashi. . . . I have wished that she would find somebody to charm her, but she cannot: all her view is – the miserable E.B., by her invested with light and glory. She is a child (though not a young woman and having no special allurements but character); to injure her by throwing her aside is unthinkable, and I am the more concerned to do well by her because she suffered much in her younger days. I shall hardly need to ask you again not to ascribe those relationships of mine to a sensual passion. God knows, my married life might have driven me to any adventures which may be. The essential position is as I have now disclosed it; and for the sake of those whom I name, I have more than once already, with some care, retreated from the probabilities of new romances! but I did not, till now, feel myself damned and flayed by my dilemma. I was content to retreat and oblivion followed; for I judged in time. One or two (I thought) awaited a glance or a word – but I could not.

The summary is that having repressed my gift of love, having resigned myself to a less marvellous secret, what am I at thirty-five? an ancient. What have I to offer you, what grace anywhere near that you showed me? I dream a moment or two into your love, am with you in heavenly weather, you are mine and I am freely yours, and for the moment nobody else is considered; we would do such things. But what, in everyday reality, I could bring you is what you have read here; and I am not sure that after that you will be at the trouble of reading further. If you are reading still, think that besides these matters I am pretty well played out, the quantity and variety of the demands on my wits is too great without a real sustained rest, and my body worries me with one or two weaknesses. Think too, I am not writing all about myself, but to serve you. . . . I would see you the happiest woman in this world. You make me intensely happy – but then the light dies off. I do not know what you will make of this situation. And I should lose all the good I see in life if through me at length you should come to feel defeated, and worse off than ever. It is something, that I should be suddenly able to share my thought with you in this way; even if you went from me now for ever.

Do not do that! Be near, even though what I've said should make you too fear love.[48]

And so began another of Edmund's correspondences, which was to extend to over 1100 letters or postcards (and he could write on a postcard what most would write in a letter) over forty years. He was to write to Sylva almost daily during the opening months of 1932, some-times twice a day, timing as well as dating his letters – many of which were written in the early hours of the morning after an exhausting day. His letter of 8 February (after a week-end visit to Sussex with Sylva) is typical:

My dear Vision,
    Your letter was at the top of my morning budget when I hurried out at the sound of the messenger on my staircase. Thank you with all my heart for it. I should have had a bad day without it. As the state of my nerves . . . is liable to be shaken by almost any problem now, even trifling things, you won't be surprised to hear that since Saturday I have hardly slept. I stayed up and tried to be busy last night till four, then I went to bed, – no use; only, I have had you in my arms, and I dreamed awake that I still had, only in utter serenity and simpleness. . . . When you said that you had never loved any one before, I believed you, as the earth receives the rain – I then had to see swiftly how I could do least injury to your inward light and delicate, long bravery. These considerings are all ungodly – I am utterly sorry that they arise; there should have been only love and love.
    But one thing you know: were all else lost, your E.B. would be at your command and you should allow him to be a part of your world though that world only included three or four final human beings. Let me be more than the phantom of Sussex Downs![49]

Constantly Edmund warns her of his state of nervous instability and advises her against involving herself in the affairs of a man whose financial, working and emotional life seemed so precarious. He admits to feeling 'half alive' and accepts that 'it is probably true that I have dual personality, though I don't know from *inside*: and I have heard that my poetry shows it.'[50] He was also aware that some in Oxford felt that he was spending too much time on non-Oxford affairs, though he claimed, 'I do not think I fear Oxford's many tongues . . . but I fear myself.'[51] He again invoked the picture of Lear and Cordelia as an image of his love relationship, seeing himself as the 'foolish fond old man' despite his being only in his mid-thirties. But he was quickly being drawn into a relationship which was to prove irresistible. Watching a performance of *Romeo and Juliet* with Peggy Ashcroft playing opposite Christopher Hassall, he found the balcony scene too powerful to watch detachedly and he complained that fate had introduced Sylva 'so late'[52] in his life. In the twilight hours in his Merton rooms he tried to include her in all his past experiences – particularly those of wartime – usually with the assistance of a glass of whisky:

I have put you into all I have done whenever the remembrance returns. A tune came dancing into my head this minute, it danced me over to South America, and there you were in the lunch room at the top of the tower, glancing at the Plata's great waters in the sun far below, and then I think your eyes returned to me. And that became Calais, and your window was opening on the old Staple Hall archway and I was just admiring your forehead in profile – but that was last night too; and then too I caught you by the little cold spring of Hamel in the middle of the Somme battle (that spring took some destroying), where I went alone, and drank – how did you get here, miss? September 1916 – why, what a grown girl you are but let me tell you, this place is the devil's, they flay it every hour from Beaucourt and Grandcourt – let me carry you out of it quick, but – a kiss first, we're alone, that blood-stained stretcher won't peach. Kiss me long, long, long; for next time you see me I shall be a lost man whose kiss is not that boy's, but half curst or more than half.

Yes, tobacco, whisky, worry, bad thinking, bad muddling – they spoiled something.[53]

On other occasions his letters include verses set in France or Flanders – illustrated by sketch maps of the area – where Sylva appears at the end of a description of a shell-shocked Festubert road:

> *And you are come, and there is need of you,*
> *As much as on that track of blood and dew,*
> *O you shall conquer, dear, and the weak day*
> *Shall even yield you grace and roundelay.*[54]

He also wanted to share that part of him which felt spiritually Japanese, a March rainstorm taking him back not only to 1917, 'but also into bamboo – shadows, Buddhist eaves, Wistaria nooks, the soft-breathing time of early Summer in Japan. . . a rain that quietly unites Festubert and Fuji'.[55]

In addition to reassuring Annie that her life 'will always be in my list of faithful cares'[56] (and fending off the advances of a young American poetess), he had to face the problem posed by Aki Hayashi. Suffering from severe bronchitis coupled with a bout of malaria, she now realised that Edmund's real affections were turned elsewhere and she was in a state of intense dejection. Edmund tried to resolve the problems in a letter of 7 March 1932, using the formal tones of tutor to pupil and revealingly suggesting that his relationship with Sylva was not one of passion:

Although I may ask much of you in regard to letting me live my life as my new emotion and vision suggest it, yet you will know that I have a strong affection for you and that your place in my world is yours always. . . . You would be surprised, perhaps, how often I bless you with words spoken to myself, sometimes to others, because I think of you as a pattern of courage and goodness. Woman or man makes little difference to me nowadays, apart from Sylva N. – and I am stirred by her not so much by feminine qualities as by general genius of which she has a share. My tiredness does not disappear, indeed my late illness is not quite gone.

The letter did little to put her mind at rest. She wrote in depressed vein and suggested that Edmund's payments to her were falling behind and were barely adequate when paid in full. On 9 March Edmund replied in what he described as a short letter (over a thousand words):

It is not fair to me . . . that I am to be the only object and support of your total personality. . . . You forget the number of people who rely on me generally or in particular matters of friendship or literature or influence. . . . Already I pay out so much for you (and others) that I am always hard up and always overworking. . . .

I am afraid you have grown so possessive, and so much in one idea, that you will not really act unselfishly about me should 'I ask much of you.' I may ask you to be absolutely content with working for me, and with having my friendship and my continued care and trust: to avoid all attempt at a love affair with me; to behave quietly and respectfully towards me, as a secretary should; to expect that I shall not visit you alone as much as I have done. In short, should it become possible for me to marry Miss Norman, I ask you to show your gratitude to me, and your love for me, by treating that with the greatest reverence and good will. As you know, such a step on my part would not mean that your living in London and serving me is to be altered. You have my promise, and I mean it. . . . if you fail me now, I shall have one more black page in my life's story. Have I had enough? You know it. . . . I hope you will only think of getting well and letting me do so too, for I am half in pieces.

Her hopes of marriage now faded for ever and she surrendered to the inevitable – meeting Sylva in November 1932 and establishing a respectful friendship. She sublimated her affections in an intense schedule of work for Edmund, chasing references and copying extracts (mostly in the British Museum or the Newspaper Library at Colindale) for the next thirty years. Hardly a month passed without her receiving a request to find sources for Edmund's latest literary enthusiasm, his encyclopaedic knowledge, acute memory and researcher's instinct directing her to the pages of such journals as the *Country Spectator, Blackwood's Edinburgh Magazine,* the *Morning Advertiser,* the *Examiner,* the *Morning Chronicle,* the *London Review, The Times,* the *Athenaeum,* the *Spectator,* the *Literary Gazette,* the *Westminster Review,* the *Gentleman's Magazine,* the *Quiver.* or *Fraser's Magazine.* For particular characters the search would become more local – when Edmund was chasing information about Shelley's friend Thomas Hogg, she was despatched to Durham to search copies of the *Durham County Advertiser* and the *Darlington and Stockton Times;* when Keats's friend Charles Armitage Brown[57] was the subject of the moment, copies of the *New Monthly* had to be combed together with any journals of the period from Plymouth; for Shelley she was sent to the pages of the *Windsor and Eton Express,* the *Buckinghamshire Chronicle* and the *Taunton Courier.* These were tasks that she performed willingly and with great care, declaring to Edmund that 'I would rather be at your service starving, than do any other work for any other people in any country'.[58]

On Edmund's side he kept his promise to support her for life, meeting her regularly on his visits to London. As the years went by she became more of a recluse, feeding scraps to the birds which came to the window of her lonely rented room as she suffered increasingly from diabetes. Her letters became more and more a catalogue of fears and complaints and she lived almost entirely on her memories of her association with Edmund.

Throughout the remainder of 1932 and early 1933 Edmund continued his frenetic round of tutorial, university and journalistic business; even the most selective list of his engagements and contacts during these months paints a picture of almost uninterrupted activity. He became a regular supporter of the Bodley Club and the Film Club within Merton; of the English Club and the Japan Club within the university. He often found himself in the chair at these gatherings, introducing such speakers as 'our piebald contemporary Richard Aldington: now an excellent author, now a dervish'.[59] He was also meeting an endless stream of old friends and new acquaintances, being visited by Sassoon (often bearing gifts of pictures), by 'the excellent but too diffusive Shakespearean interpreter'[60] G. Wilson Knight, and

203

by visitors from Japan. In Oxford, friendships were formed with Christopher Hassall at Wadham and Nevill Coghill at Exeter College, and he began to spend an increasing amount of time in Christ Church with the 'incomparable Padre' H. M. Irvin (who had moved from Merton), with the ancient-historian R. H. Dundas ('an example of modest humaneness and fine benevolence'), with 'the excellent librarian'[61] J. G. Barrington-Ward, or with two future Vice-Chancellors of Oxford, J. C. Masterman and Kenneth Wheare.   He maintained his contacts with John Masefield, visited his Suffolk mentor A. H. Fass, established a friendship with the Clare scholars John and Anne Tibble, visited John Buchan at Elsfield and extended his association with the Sitwell family. Dinner invitations came from the Professor of Poetry Ernest de Selincourt ('a gentle, classical type and genial to a degree') and from Kenneth Clark of the Ashmolean – where he met 'the gentle nymph-like Mrs Clark', Professor Beazley ('of Greek vase fame'), John Sparrow ('a noble youth') and the artist Henry Lamb ('the résumé of those striking faces that Italian painters choose').[62] November 1932 saw him in Aylesbury as the guest of Frank Pakenham, where he first met John Betjeman, while breakfast in Merton in February 1933 found him in the company of Julian Huxley ('a naturally candid young man, who described H. G. Wells as a cockney Voltaire,).[63] Further literary parties in Oxford and Cambridge brought him regularly into contact with a host of writers and scholars.

Financial commitments continued to demand sustained literary activity, as maintenance for Clare and John, payments to Aki Hayashi and Annie (with additional help for Gilbert's son), together with the rent for Cleave's, swallowed virtually all his Merton salary. He prepared an introduction for James Thomson's *The City of Dreadful Night*, published by Methuen, an essay on Matthew Arnold for H. J. Massingham's *The Great Victorians*, and was pleased to have written four reviews and two articles in one week in May 1932 – a month in which he also addressed a League of Nations dinner in London and societies in Oxford at St Edward's School and St John's College. School lectures were now being regularly added to the round of universities, with Highgate, Wellington, Maidstone, Burford and Christ's Hospital all being fitted into these months.

His relationship with Sylva both soothed some of the frenzy and increased nervous exhaustion. A visit with her to Alfriston in Sussex in the spring of 1932 (the source of the poem 'Argument in Spring')[64] finally convinced Edmund of his love and he saw the respite from academic life as similar to war leave. He explained to her: 'You did something for me by being with me which only The War did before. Don't laugh at the apparent horror, I mean War showed me common things as infinitely intimate and precious . . .';[65] 'You see why the war to me does not always mean the worst. But the next one would. Let's have no more.'[66]

Such associations were to be increased in the summer of 1932, when Sylva joined Edmund on a visit to the battlefields of France around Cassel, Amiens and the Somme, where 'the river valley is fresh and beautiful with countless wild flowers and clear sparkling streams.'[67] During this visit he formed a warm friendship with the Professor of English Literature at the Sorbonne, Louis Bonnerot. An invitation to lecture at the Sorbonne in February 1933 resulted, and Edmund was to contribute to *Etudes Anglaises* on six occasions under Bonnerot's editorship.

The French visit of 1932 was to be recorded in what was probably Edmund's least distinguished literary venture – a description of the journey thinly disguised as 'almost a novel' with Sylva as co-author. It was entitled *We'll Shift Our Ground* and subtitled *Two on a Tour*. It consisted mostly of a dialogue between Chloe and Duncan (who became S.N. and E.B. in an epilogue), engaging in arch literary conversation and contrived humour. It was published in 1933 by Cobden-Sanderson and dedicated to the Bonnerots.

Perhaps contrived humour was all that Edmund was likely to manage. When separated from Sylva he felt dejected and listless. His daily letters to her – written on any available paper, often the backs of railway timetables or exam papers – frequently included verses and references to *King Lear*, but they also became more passionate as she was addressed as 'curious peach',[68] 'wild strawberry' or 'shining star'. He imagined himself as a pike devouring Sylva the roach – though at times he preferred to see himself as 'gudgeon rather than pike';[69] she is seen as both 'bewitcher' and 'victim'. Sylva was reticent about the relationship developing into something too physical for she had fallen in love with Edmund's intellect and creativity. Edmund sounded an anxious warning note: 'I cannot love you only for your mind; I am not so superior an intellect.'[70]

There were moments of agreeable relaxation: visiting the North Oxford Liberal and Working Men's Club for darts, shove-halfpenny, quoits, billiards and beer; taking Clare and John to the Canterbury Cricket Week; playing a weekly game of cricket in the summer months; enjoying country walks with colleagues or pupils, often with Derek Hudson, who provided a meal afterwards. But more common were fits of depression and exhaustion. The constant travelling was wearying – despite the opportunities which train journeys gave for letter-writing and reading ('Adam Smith is good railway reading')[71] – and a missed train in May 1932 meant a sleepless night in the waiting room at Paddington station. He found evening solace in reading Vaughan ('that friend of midnight thought')[72] and annotating Ford and Tennyson ('looking into texts and scribbling parallels seems to do me good'),[73] but the tensions between Annie and Sylva and his strained relationship with his brother Gilbert were weighing heavily on him. His attempt to find a London home for Annie caused bitter resentment from Sylva over the expense and – after Edmund had taken Annie to Calais for a week end, sharing a hotel room with her – Sylva accused him of loving Annie more than herself. He thus found himself in conflict with friends and family, walking back from Maidstone to Yalding in rage one evening after a bitter argument with Gilbert, and he was forced to admit that he was 'not a subtle tactician in personal matters'[74] and became 'violent under provocation'.[75]

His mood coincided with a morbid interest in literary suicides, and he started planning a possible anthology. He was particularly struck by a series of coincidences which he discovered in the death of Leigh Hunt's grandson Bryan. He described them in a letter to Sylva:

Consider:      1. Leigh Hunt who lived proclaiming the benevolence and beauty of books.
               2. Carlyle, who said that books were a university, and who may be called the founder of the London Library.
Then picture:  3. The reading-room of the London Library. Enter Leigh Hunt's grandson, finding himself alone: Shoots himself among the books; not quite dead, he makes sure with another shot.
               4. An old man comes in and discovers Leigh Hunt's grandson. The old man is Thomas Carlyle.[76]

Edmund suspected that he himself might not 'have a long course ahead of me . . . perhaps it's the sense of so little having come of my thirty-five years hitherto',[77] and by October 1932 he exclaimed wearily, 'Alas, how Oxford terrifies this tired exhausted mind.'[78]

Such emotional and physical strains began to take a visible toll. What little sleep he could manage was interrupted by nightmares of war, and he was turning increasingly to the relief of tobacco and alcohol. When playing cricket he complained of being breathless after a single run between the wickets and found keeping wicket against fast bowling on uneven grounds a painful strain. His eyes were troubling him (though he avoided visiting an optician, preferring to experiment with other people's spectacles), he began to have bouts of deafness, his asthma was ever present, the nervous movements of his hands became accentuated[79] and he was badly shaken in a car accident when returning from a visit to Broadstairs with Robert Levens. None of this checked the flow of engagements, and November 1932 saw him on the platform at Royal Holloway College, a few weeks before a period of enforced rest in Princess Beatrice Hospital for treatment on his veins. His surgeon was James Johnston Abraham, who had studied English Literature under Edward Dowden and who was writing a biography of Dr Lettsom – the eighteenth-century surgeon who had once been introduced to Dr Johnson. Edmund gave the book a review as a leading article in the *Times Literary Supplement* in October 1933 and commemorated both physicians in the poem 'To Dr I. Lettsom' (1934). Typically for Edmund, even a visit to the doctor became a literary occasion.

The weeks of recuperation after his operation paved the way for a more tranquil period, enabling him to compile a volume of poetry in lighter tone, including twenty-five previously unpublished pieces. The opening poem was dedicated 'To Sylva' and the collection ranged from a parody of a Book Society Committee meeting ('Chapters of Literary History')[80] to 'Country Conversation',[81] in which a lane, a meadow and a windmill see themselves under threat from an increasingly urbanised world. He also experimented with short four-line pieces, moving between the delicate observation of 'Lark Descending'[82] to the witty objectivity of 'Sentimental':

> *I gather from the survey of*
> *The Ultimate Review,*
> *God showed too much sentiment*
> *In making bluebells blue.*[83]

The selection was published as *Choice or Chance* in 1934.

In late 1932 Edmund began work on a *History of English Literature Since 1866* for Chapman and Hall (a project which was never completed), and he also continued his interest in translation. His early schoolboy French exercises had been followed by an original piece of French verse, *La Girouette* (later translated as *The Weathercock*), written at Ypres in 1917 and published by the Ulysses Bookshop in 1931, as well as by some material for Cyril Beaumont's *The Birth and Death of Scaramouch* in 1924. In 1933 he translated eight of George Herbert's Latin poems for *Essays and Studies*. This classical vein was to be continued in 1955 with Latin translations of poems by Donne, Herbert, Crashaw and Milton for the *University of Toronto Quarterly* and by a translation of Marvell's 'Hortus', published in *Eleven Poems* (1966). His translation of Greek was to be Aeschylus' *Prometheus Bound* – not to be published until 1967 in *A Review of English Literature*. In 1960 he was to engage in his only foray into Japanese translation – two short four-line poems on blood transfusion, written on the occasion of the Eighth Congress of the International Society of Blood Transfusion in Tokyo.[84] On the surface it seemed an exotic and eccentric exercise but the memory of the events surrounding Joy's death in 1919 had not been dimmed by the passage of forty years.

In 1932, however, he was more concerned with encouraging Sylva's literary career, suggesting that she take over two of his own possible projects – studies of Coleridge's favoured novelist Mrs Benet and of James Morier, the nineteenth-century author of *Hajji Baba*. In January 1933 he declined an invitation from the Oxford University Press to edit the correspondence between Shelley's friend Thomas Hogg and Jane Williams. Humphrey Milford asked if Edmund could suggest an alternative editor: 'Someone with one-third of your scholarship, one-sixth of your wit, one-ninth of your goodwill would do for me.'[85] Edmund steered the job towards Sylva, as well as providing her with his notes on his visits to Max Gate for her contribution on Thomas Hardy for *The Great Victorians* (1932) and presenting his essay 'Fall in, Ghosts' (on a Royal Sussex regimental reunion) for her volume of *Contemporary Essays* published in 1933.

Life was beginning to take on some sense of stability. Or that was certainly how it seemed as Edmund left Oxford to spend a few summer days in Yalding. On 4 July 1933 he wrote two letters to Sylva. The next morning he took the train to London and at three-thirty in the afternoon went to Willesden registry office, where he and Sylva were married.

A reception at Rupert Hart-Davis's flat was followed by a three-week honeymoon in Brittany (during which Edmund wrote three times to Aki Hayashi). On their return Edmund and Sylva moved into a flat at 19 Woodstock Close in North Oxford: Siegfried Sassoon having paid the first year's rent as a wedding present. It was a pleasant location and the presence of Graham Greene in an adjoining flat provided literary companionship – leading to a visit to Chipping Campden with the young novelist, who recalled lively conversation coupled with an excessive intake of parsnip wine.[86] Edmund and Sylva were to move into Greene's flat when it became vacant two years later.

Despite the calm that had at last entered Edmund's personal life, but signs of the old restlessness were in the shadows. Late in September 1933 he wrote to Sylva from Yalding, ending with the cryptic words: 'All my love ever, marriage or no marriage; in verse or reverse.'[87] There were to be several reversals in both domestic and national life over the next twelve years.

# 18

# Oxford and Germany
## October 1933 – September 1939

---

*In happy hours, some hours, I spring;*
*From dense unhappiness I sing;*
'Invitation', 1936[1]

*Germany was a very pleasant experience and a sad one;*
*for everyone, Nazi or not, is so decent, so fair, and even*
*now so inclined to treat an Englishman with special*
*kindness. I am afraid I can't admire our public mood*
*and manners toward that country, nor can I rejoice that*
*encirclement political and commercial has caused them*
*any difficulties in their ordinary life.*
Letter to Rupert Hart-Davis, August 1939[2]

*I am pretty sure we shall be spared an international*
*disaster.*
Letter to Aki Hayashi, August 1939[3]

---

For the first six years of his marriage to Sylva, Edmund enjoyed a more
ordered routine than he had for a decade. Each March he attended the
Southdown Battalions' Dinner – usually providing a poem for the
menu and often proposing a toast. Every summer he joined the
Barnacles' cricket tour of Sussex, went to a Test match at Lord's and
visited Sassoon in Wiltshire – where in 1933 he again met Geoffrey
Keynes after a gap of ten years, and established a lasting friendship.
During each university vacation he visited Yalding, saw Clare and
John and spent a week with Annie – who moved to houses of which
Edmund had taken tenancy, first at Blue Bell Hill near Chatham in
1935 and then in Tonbridge in 1939; she took Edmund's library with

her at each move. He also made an annual pilgrimage to the war battlefields and cemeteries of France and Flanders, from 1936 onwards in his official capacity as adviser to the Imperial War Graves Commission.

His new room in St Alban's Quad at Merton remained a meeting place and a kind of headquarters for pupils and friends and his immensely wide social circle inevitably made him a popular choice as a godparent. In December 1933 Sassoon had married Hester Gatty and, on the birth of their son George, Edmund became a godfather for the first time. It was an office he was to hold for Robert Levens's son Andrew, for a young Japanese pupil G. S. Kishimoto on his conversion to Christianity, and – in later years – for the children of several of his pupils.

Lecturing demands continued unabated. In Oxford his weekly lectures were gaining popularity and the audience needed to arrive early to be assured of a seat. Lectures outside Oxford ranged from visits to the Bank of England Literary Society to meetings of the Royal Literary Society, and extended to Bristol (on *Edward Gibbon and His Age*, published in 1935), Hull, Newcastle, Sunderland, Reading, Nottingham (as the guest of Professor V. de Sola Pinto) and Durham (as the guest of Professor Claud Colleer Abbott). By 1942 he had addressed a society in virtually every Oxford college.

His desk was always heaped with papers; coping with his correspondence was almost a full-time job. (He hated the telephone, suggesting that 'the noise of that instrument will give the Devil an idea for our future.')[4] His weekly quota of reviews and articles was sustained and he fulfilled his monthly Book Society obligations in London, but he was growing concerned about his prose style. A review of *Votive Tablets* in the *Oxford Magazine* had complained of its awkwardness and Edmund felt that the quotations justified the criticism. He confided to Sylva that he was 'ashamed . . . not to have acquired some agreeableness in writing',[5] but the increased stability of his domestic life now enabled him to write with a more relaxed and fluent pen.

He certainly gave himself plenty of practice, for in early 1934 Jonathan Cape published *The Mind's Eye*, a collection of essays (including seven new ones) on 'Flanders', 'Japan', 'England' and 'The World of Books', while between 1934 and 1936 he was preoccupied in fulfilling a long-held ambition – the writing of a life of John Taylor, who with his partner James Hessey had been the early publisher of Keats, Clare, Landor, Lamb, Hazlitt, Coleridge, de Quincey and Carlyle. Edmund had long enjoyed quoting Carlyle's declaration that 'Ten ordinary histories of kings and courtiers were well exchanged against the tenth part of one good History of Booksellers,' and the project had received the vigorous encouragement of H. W. Garrod.

Apart from recording the stormy but paternal relationship between Taylor and his clients, the book enabled Edmund to enter into the speculation surrounding the identity of Junius, the pseudonymous author of letters of political invective published in the *Public Advertiser* between 1769 and 1772, with Edmund strongly backing Taylor's belief that the author was Sir Philip Francis. The biography was published in 1936 under the title *Keats's Publisher* and was dedicated to Rupert Hart-Davis. It represented Edmund's most scholarly work and remained the academic achievement which gave him most satisfaction.

Never happy to be restricted to one literary activity he co-edited with E. L. Griggs a book of essays on Coleridge (contributing an essay himself) in 1934 – a year that also saw the publication of *Charles Lamb, His Life Recorded By His Contemporaries*, which included much new material and was prepared for Leonard and Virginia Woolf at the Hogarth Press.

Biography was fast becoming his most favoured prose reading and writing, and several more possible subjects suggested themselves to him. In 1937 he re-read Hogg's life of Shelley and described Hogg as 'a fantastic liar' whose biography of the poet was 'really the worst of all the crimes committed against that fair spirit'.[6] He began to plan a book which might redress the balance. A similar reaction to E. K. Chambers's life of Coleridge initiated preparations for a Coleridge biography[7] – a project which was never completed – while a conversation with Sir Sydney Cockerell at Heytesbury (in which Edmund was told that Hardy was treated by his mother as a 'little boy' even in his seventies) sowed the seeds of a possible study of Hardy.

The summer of 1937 saw Edmund once again in the role of a midwife to a literary discovery of some importance. His old friend William Force Stead had been entrusted by a descendant of Christopher Smart, Colonel Cawardine Probert, with the manuscript of an unknown Smart poem dating from around 1760 – the *Jubilate Agno*. Stead had been in a nervous state for some time and the problems presented by the editorial work threatened to delay the preparation of the manuscript for publication. Like Stead, Edmund was convinced of the poem's importance and thought it superior in parts to *A Song to David*. He was fascinated by its movement from 'incoherence to intense beauty',[8] was struck by its Blake-like qualities (and was intrigued by the possibility of Blake having read it). He spent a considerable time attempting to decipher its allusions, his knowledge of birds, fish and flowers proving invaluable. He gave Stead constant encouragement and the poem was published as *Rejoice in the Lamb* by Jonathan Cape in 1939. The poem's full antiphonal quality was not made clear, however, until W. H. Bond's edition published by Rupert Hart-Davis in 1954. It quickly became accepted as part of the eighteenth-century poetic canon, particularly after Benjamin Britten's musical setting of parts of it in 1943; it is difficult to remember that it first came to light as late as 1937. It was not to be Edmund's last association with Christopher Smart. He searched all his life for an early copy of *Smart's Hymns for the Amusement of Children* – a rare unsuccessful bibliographical challenge – but had to be content with introducing a new edition for Basil Blackwell in 1948.

Predictably, a short period of relative tranquillity heralded a period of restlessness. He began to feel the need to 'shift his ground'. Merton had extended his fellowship, but he was receiving invitations from several quarters – a year's lecturing in America, a professorship in Scotland, another in Australia, a third in Japan. It was the Japanese approach which tempted him most and he explained to Saito that he longed to return, yet he did not want to leave England: 'I only want to be in two places at once.'[9] He wanted to escape from his teaching commitments; yet it was the aspect of Oxford which he most enjoyed. He was at his peak in the lecture hall; yet it was the activity which exhausted him most. His married life had given him a sense of security; but Sylva's refusal to start a family was causing a strain in their relationship.

These tensions were reflected in *An Elegy and Other Poems*, his next volume of verse published in 1937 and dedicated to Henry Donner. The title-poem was composed as a tribute to George V on his death in 1936, and Edmund was to address royalty again in January 1937 in 'Verses to H.R.H. The Duke of Windsor' on his abdication:

> *Only for this, maybe, I write:*
> *Distressed that service rich and bright,*
> *So willing, unpretentious, should*
> *So soon meet such ingratitude.*[10]

Another curious royal association was reported in the Sunday press of May 1936 in an article describing the near arrest of the Prince of Wales as a spy on the Canal Bank of Ypres in 1917: 'He was brought to Battalion H.Q. where lieutenant Edmund Blunden all alone received him.'[11] This, as Edmund declared, was 'passing strange', for he had no recollection of the event at all.

For the most part, *An Elegy* evokes a mood of uncertainty and foreboding – clear in the poems' titles – presenting the 'Present Discontents'[12] of a figure moving 'for ever between Now and Then'[13]. Most tellingly, the third section consists of ten 'First War Poems' all written between 1934 and 1937. The threat that a new war was to break out was such a terrifying prospect that Edmund refused to accept its possibility, however tell-tale the signs. His mind went back to 1916 – 18, to 'Nights before Battle',[14] as if the very fact of recreating the horror of those days would convince all sane minds of the folly of 'Recurrence'.[15] Yet, ironically, the old heroism came back to him too. The cruel contradictions are described in the poem 'Can you Remember?':

> *Yes, I still remember,*
>   *The whole thing in a way;*
> *Edge and exactitude*
>   *Depend on the day. . . .*
>
> *New-old shapes for ever*
>   *Intensely recur.*
>
> *And some are sparkling, laughing, singing,*
>   *Young, heroic, mild;*
> *And some incurable, twisted,*
>   *Shrieking, dumb, defiled.*[15]

He found it particularly difficult to disentangle foreign politics from foreign friendships. After the Japanese attacks on China in 1937 he wrote to Saito:

We are all of us much worried by the storm on China. I don't understand the beginning of it, and few here do, but the tendency is . . . to condemn the Japanese military faction. My feeling is that great military interest anywhere is almost certain to need (biologically, as it were) a practical experience. Here, we have tried it all; and . . . I believe that the 1914 – 18 experience has left us wiser. I believe equally that the Far East will learn by the present struggles, and will emerge cooler and finer. Am I wrong? It is only part of my main notion, that the general advance of humanity is not absolutely contemporaneous, and that criticism must be cautious about dates. The English howls against Mussolini in Africa were raised by those who thirty-seven years ago would have applauded any English inroads into uncivilized Africa. There are still many here who are living in the seventeenth century, and on the other hand Shelley is still ahead of 999 in a thousand of us. All the same, the sooner they stop flinging explosives in China the better. I do not want to read *Undertones of War* by Takeshi Saito.[17]

Edmund's attitude towards Germany in the period immediately before the outbreak of war brought him into considerable controversy and he seemed unconcerned about the inevitably hostile reactions to his often unguarded remarks. He had no sympathy for Nazism but he had great affection for the German people and believed that the ordinary man had no desire for war. He stubbornly held to the belief that the German leaders were equally unwarlike – as late as August 1939 he interpreted a speech of Göring's as showing 'the strongest reluctance to start a war'.[18] In July 1939 he remarked that 'Hitler has done his bit'[19] for Germany and only in late September did he admit that 'Hitler is offering us a seven year's war if we like it!'[20]

He distrusted the opinions of those who had no personal experience of war – who saw it only as an 'abstract conflict' – and he was angered by what he described as the 'war-mongering' of Churchillian rhetoric and the language of newspapers such as the *Daily Telegraph* 'blowing up flames for us all to roast in'.[21] Constant contact with Germany, and concentration on those things which could unite the two nations, seemed to him essential – and he saw nothing more unifying than literature, the life-blood of 'imagination's commonwealth'.[22] He thus went to Germany four times between August 1935 and August 1939, travelling with Paul Engle on one occasion, casting himself in the role of a cultural ambassador. It was Edmund at his most gullible.

In August 1935 he lectured in Munich, Frankfurt and Koblenz. The compliment was returned in 1937 when eight German professors attended one of Edmund's Oxford lectures. In April 1937 he and Sylva travelled to Göttingen, Marburg and Heidelberg where, at each venue, Edmund delivered a lecture on 'The Englishman's Discovery of War', tracing a literary line from Hamlet to Hardy's *Dynasts*. Sylva kept a diary[23] of the tour which reflects a gradual loss of innocence as the days progressed. An early entry reads: 'The fact that Hitler once dismissed the Jews, we must leave as a feature of internal politics. . . . Do we imagine the Jews will be wiped out? There shall be no such respite to their increase.' Such implied anti-semitism was not an attitude adopted so vigorously by Edmund. He had several Jewish friends and was to have a Jewish son-in-law, but he did retain a suspicion of the Jewish race as a whole, feeling that in some ways they had vulgarised modern society, and they became not infrequent targets of half-humorous attack in his letters and diaries. Sylva's stance may have stemmed from her own national self-consciousness. In 1932 Edmund had written to her: 'Do not be shy, my dear, of your race. . . .

215

To me beauty is the sum of ancestral hopes and selections. I never saw any face but I thought of grandparents.'[24]

During the early part of the lecture tours, Sylva seems persuaded of the German desire to avoid war. She records Professor Löhde's exclamation: 'In England your papers are always talking of the next war and the probability of war. Here we never speak of war at all.' By the time they had reached Heidelberg as the guest of Professor Jensen ('the man we had been warned – even by Germans – was so ardent a Nazi') she was less enchanted. She described her host as:

. . . a small Dictator, who kept dotting every 'i' on every scrap of information he could give us – about our programme, about the way to lecture, about the architecture of his town . . . about the number of minutes he would leave us to wash and settle down before returning to us . . . an *anxious* Nazi; no ease of dictatorship helped his obvious and strenuous efforts to do right.

For Edmund's part, he was always keen to turn the conversation away from politics to literature (even being prepared to discuss the German enthusiasm for Kipling), but Jensen's obvious disapproval of Edmund's evening drinking habits were a cause of considerable irritation.

The experience did not prevent Edmund from returning to Germany two months later to attend Dr Hans Grimm's congress of authors at Klosterhaus in Lippoldsberg on the banks of the Upper Weser; he was to attend again in August 1939.

It was an idyllic setting for a symposium of poetry: a dozen German poets reading their work – with a handful of foreign visitors – against a sunny, rural background. Most of the writers were veterans of the Western Front, including Paul Alverdes, who had been shot through the throat at La Bassée in 1915, so Edmund felt he was among members of his own club. There were bizarre touches. Edmund's German was very limited, so many of the readings were lost on him; on his second visit he engaged in conversation in Latin whenever it was possible. He recorded his 1937 visit for *German Life and Letters*, significantly stressing the beauty of the summer skies, the blossom of the hollyhocks and the Dürer-like quality of the setting and figures. He failed to note the threatening undertones of the perfectly trained military band which goose-stepped into the courtyard; nor did he catch the full irony of the closing moments of the gathering as the orchestra played the Dead March from Handel's *Saul*. The account presents a striking picture of a benevolent poet smiling over an occasion which he could only half understand. His feeling that a literary gathering in a setting similar to Glyndebourne was typical of Germany in 1937 or 1939 illustrates the dream which he clung to; the alternative was a nightmare which he feared he might not survive. His often repeated view that war would be avoided was as much a hope as a belief, and he regularly returned in his memory to 1916–18. He began to make use in correspondence of his store of postcards of pre-1914 Ypres as if he was reminding all who saw them of the destructive power of war, and on impulse would go to Belgium for a week end visit to the battlefields with Sylva or Ian Robertson.

It was a strange fact that Edmund should gain a reputation for extremism when it was the least likely manifestation of his personality and the characteristic which he most distrusted in others. His description of Lord Vansittart's *Black Record* – an immensely popular anti-German pamphlet of 1941 – was typical. Edmund saw it as 'An unconscious portrait of an extremist, a man flown with wrong passion, and many will have found an opportunity accordingly to affirm the need of moderation and the reference to actual history.'[25] His admiration was for C. R. M. F. Cruttwell's *History of the Great War*, and in particular for the opening paragraph of its Epilogue, which begins: 'War between great states . . . cannot now be regarded as 'an instrument of policy'. It becomes inevitably a struggle for existence, in which no limit can be placed on the expenditure of men and money, no objectives can be clearly defined and no peace by an agreed compromise attained.'

In May 1937 Edmund entered a more public forum. The University of Göttingen – founded by George II in 1734 and opened in 1737 – had invited several foreign universities to attend its bicentennial celebrations. Oxford decided not to send representatives and Edmund wrote a vigorous letter to *The Times* deploring the decision to be absent from a cultural event at what was 'almost an English foundation'.[26] Though he claimed to receive far more private approval than opposition, the letter sparked off plenty of attacks. He complained in a letter to the novelist and playwright Enid Bagnold: 'One always gets the stick for such attempts . . . . my letter drew on me the wrath of strange and dreary correspondents from most parts of Europe, and I have had other instances. There is also the private intimidation game. Both my wife and myself have been addressed and spoken of as Nazis.'[27] None of this upheaval interrupted his busy social schedule, nor stopped his pen.

A new admirer, Lord Carlow (killed in May 1944), offered to publish privately a collection of poems under the title *On Several Occasions*. It was, as Edmund described it, 'a bit of luxury printing' and was issued in April 1939. Sixteen poems appeared for the first time and though some of them summon the ghosts of war ('To Wilfred Owen and His Kind',[28] 'In West-Flanders',[29] 'In the Margin'[30] and 'At My Writing Table'[31]) a pastoral element is predominant. Surprisingly he did not include poems of this period which expressed his despair at the thought of a second war, for poems such as 'War Talk: Winter 1938',

> They're talking of another war,
> They say some things I've heard before [32]

had to wait another two years for publication. In the *Times Literary Supplement* of October 1938, however, he did declare his hand in 'Exorcized':

> Twenty years had nearly passed since the War called
>     Great had roared its last,
> And some were talking, men who fought the Somme
>     before their twentieth year:
> They talked of echoes, shadows, hauntings not so easily
>     exorcized,
> They granted Time had healed grim wounds, and yet
>     these watchers recognized
>         One stubborn and total fear. . . .

The fear was of a dream that:

> 'The Armistice has all gone wrong. While we were
>     out of the abyss,
> It seemed heaven's mercy, faked you see, merely to add.
>     new death to this:
>         The War is on once more.'
> Twenty years had nearly passed, and while these watched,
>     they saw aghast
> That giant enemy of sleep, that ghost which summed the
>     worst they knew
> Come creeping into waking thought, creeping and
>     gathering like a storm
> About the summer's loveliness, a vaster, more inhuman
>     form.
>     The dream was coming true.
>
> Back to your madhouse, child of hell: too many of us
>     know you well. [33]

The dream came true on Sunday 3 September 1939. Edmund was at Woodstock Close in the company of Laurence Brander when the declaration of war was announced on the radio. Edmund wrote in his diary that evening: 'We walked in Port Meadow, anywhere, and back past Binsey and Godstow. The aspens shone, the river was illuminated with white columns of clouds and sapphire sky-reflections. The wild hops are thick in the hedges . . . . I saw all at Klosterhaus where I was so much one of the family in a clear light.'[34] They returned home via the Dewdrop where, Brander recalled, 'we drank in the bitterness to come.'[34] That evening Edmund wrote to his mother: 'So the impossible has happened . . . we are again to blow up old friendly Fritz and vice versa.'[36]

The next morning Edmund met Kenneth Wheare walking into Christ Church and was reassured that he saw negotiation with Hitler as a future possibility. Such a chance was what drove Edmund to draft a letter to the leader of the British Fascist Party, Sir Oswald Mosley, in mid-September 1939 – a letter which he apparently never sent. Amazingly he saw Mosley as a peacemaker:

With party politics I have never had any connection; but I was struck when I was in Germany during August, by the momentary hope which people shared when your name was mentioned. I believe that any movement known to have your backing would be of great interest there. But I venture to appeal that you would stand for peace here, not simply as a leader whom everybody knows, but as a spokesman beyond the party boundaries . . . concentrating the thoughts of all who see unspeakable disaster ahead unless peace is still the central consideration.

To such as myself, who still feel as though they had only yesterday escaped from the Somme, Passchendaele etc., the planned recurrences to the same sort of business are a source of scarcely expressible bewilderment.[37]

The pacifist voice was clear a month later in a letter to his mother: 'I still regard murder as murder no matter how boldly hidden up in steel helmets and rolls of honour.'[38]

Having criticised the British Government and failed to condemn Hitler publicly, having paid regular visits to Germany and apparently holding some respect for Mosley, it is little wonder that he was suspected by some of having Nazi tendencies. Nor perhaps was it so surprising that with an Armenian wife and a German sister-in-law, and having had a Japanese lover, he could see war as a 'family quarrel' and be doggedly deaf to the calls of nationalism. What was surprising was that he took so long to see its destructive manifestations in others. Once he had accepted the inevitable, he contented himself with encouraging an attitude which he had adopted in 'Stanzas: Midsummer 1937':

## PART FIVE    1931 – 1945

*Yet if it chance*
*That England long advance with swelling sails,*
*Then be not proud.*[39]

His diary entries reveal his despair:

My one real concern for the war now – for I do not stand with those who think Hitler the sole cause of happiness or otherwise – is to see it end. I may have a right to think this way after my own years of experience in the bewilderments of active service . . . I am baffled by such indifference to the fate of common people . . . the War Cemeteries and the hard truths they enunciate (oh those endless, endless graves of mere boys) have not been visioned for a second by the 'war-worshippers' . . . who will no doubt allege that they are going to fill up many more of the sort to save future generations from filling up any more of the sort. Playing with pebbles, and infinity . . . . oh for a Commission for the living!

He retreated to his Merton rooms and brooded on the possible fate of Annie and Aki Hayashi – and on his increasingly cooling relationship with Sylva.

But unknown to Edmund he had attracted the attention of another female eye. A young English undergraduate from St Hilda's twenty-two years younger than him, had attended one of his lectures on war poetry – advertised with a misprint as 'war perjury'. She was instantly drawn to the sad eyes of the lecturer. Being a cricket enthusiast she went to the Barnacles match against Sassoon's Heytesbury eleven on the Merton ground in 1938, and watched Edmund play; her attraction was strengthened. After the sudden death of Lascelles Abercrombie later in the same year, a memorial service was held in Merton Chapel. Edmund was sitting in the nave, his gaunt face caught in the candle-light, while the funeral march from Beethoven's A-flat-major sonata played in the background. From across the aisle he was being watched by the same young lady, who knew from that moment that she was in love with him. She was Claire Margaret Poynting.

# 19

# Oxford: War
## September 1939 – May 1945

---

*If you were to ask how I got through some of the mud
and filth and blanks of 1939– 40, I should name
young Claire Poynting.*

Letter to Siegfried Sassoon, November 1940[1]

*I am an ordinary Englishman of modest position, of
simple family tradition, and of an exacting patriotism.
My country means much to me, and I do not want to
see her driven by want of intelligence, or at the bidding
of inferiors, into a devil of a mess. Neither do most
Germans.*

Diary, 10 October 1939

---

Claire Poynting was brought up in Manchester. Her father had read
Greats at Balliol and joined the Indian Civil Service, returning before
the Great War to assist in the organisation of Belgian refugees. It was
while he was engaged in this work that he met and married Margaret
Wilkinson – by coincidence, she was twenty-two years younger than
him. He was a literary-minded man, had won a university French
prize, and was a collector of poetry. Being a firm believer in women's
education he encouraged Claire's enthusiasm for English, shown in
her growing interest in the work of Robert Browning, and supported
her entry to Oxford – using a legacy to pay for her fees. Apart from
poetry, Claire's main passion was cricket. She was a regular attender at
Old Trafford and was a member of Lancashire Cricket Club. With
these interests and the fact that St Hilda's undergraduates regularly
went to Edmund for eighteenth-century-literature teaching, it seemed
that destiny was bringing them together.

## PART FIVE   1931 – 1945

Edmund was not to remain unaware of Claire's attentions for long, and he found himself in a particularly susceptible position after Sylva joined the army and was stationed away from Oxford. At first he shared the Woodstock Close flat with Sylva's parents, until relations with his argumentative mother-in-law grew so strained that he escaped to lodge briefly on Boar's Hill with an Indian family (the Palmers) before moving back into Merton, to larger rooms in Fellows' Quad once occupied by the philosopher F. H. Bradley, where he was virtually living the life of a married bachelor. The stage was perfectly set for a new romance. Tutorials only served to increase Claire's devotion and she took every opportunity to be in Edmund's company. When conversation turned to cricket, he lent her a copy of John Nyren's *Young Cricketer's Tutor*; on returning it, she enclosed a few verses urging Edmund to consider writing a cricket book. He was duly flattered, and the lines formed the opening of the preface to *Cricket Country*; she had successfully broken through his first line of defences.

One autumn evening in 1939 as Claire was walking from Oxford station, thinking of Edmund and trying to come to terms with her feelings, she looked up and saw him crossing the road to greet her. Plucking up courage she asked if she could come and see him, and he invited her to call at his Merton rooms. Their relationship developed speedily, despite the difference in age (at twenty-one Claire was just two years older than Edmund's daughter Clare, now an English undergraduate at Somerville), as the tell-tale sign of feverish letter-writing on Edmund's part bore witness. By early December Claire had become 'Clairissima – the name Claire was a remarkable choice. . . . The clearlight in your whole body. . . . I never saw anything so radiant and so entire.'[2] By the end of the year he was declaring that:

You have beaten me, dear Visitant. . . . You must be right in thinking me a complex creature. I don't want to talk much more about myself, but the effect of all my experiences . . . has been to produce the most intense though usually masked sensibility. I suffer – but you have perceived this – the dreariest pangs, and I am blessed with the most brilliant and radiant melodies: and you won't mind me saying that that's where you live.

But one point: I used to warn Sylva years ago 'to fly my paths, my feverish contact fly' – do you, my dear Juvenile, think of your life, and be sure I shall await that day when you find your happiness clear of all such muddle. I'll know.[3]

Gradually the regularity of the correspondence increased from a weekly diet to daily and then twice-daily letters. Over the next five years Claire was to receive more than 1200, often written on the

222

interleaves of Greek Testaments or similar scraps of paper, in which the picture of Lear is repeatedly evoked – 'I kneel to you as Lear to Cordelia.'[4] Edmund's health remained precarious and by early 1940 he was struck by an attack of pleurisy. With Sylva away, Claire became both nurse and companion. Their love quickly deepened.

The late evening was Edmund's favourite time for reading and the war years found him increasingly turning to Shakespeare, but also to Langland, Dryden, Thomas Shadwell, Herrick, Wordsworth and Matthew Arnold, as well as the works of Lucretius (a gift from Claire) and Hesiod. Sitting alone in his Merton rooms he would put down his book and take a walk in the Fellows' Garden, from where he could see the lights of St Hilda's tantalisingly just out of reach; in the early morning he would meet Claire for a dawn walk through the Botanical Gardens or Christ Church Meadows. From early days they talked of marriage and planned a family, envisaging a daughter Margaret and a son Edmund. By the end of 1942 they had secretly exchanged unofficial rings, and in January 1944 Edmund reminded her:

Yes my love, it was not many days after our first real meeting when I asked you if you'd marry me if we could, and you said yes at once, and it was a triumph in me. How often have I lamented that I was not then free, for we should then have moved straight on and by now you would have been with Margaret and probably her Brother and me and we'd have had four years of our own with a great deal of their particular happiness and lovingness and experience.[5]

On hearing rumours of Edmund's new love, Sylva rushed back from her army barracks at the first opportunity and Edmund confessed everything. The news was not all black for Sylva, however. Her strong possessive nature rebelled against sharing Edmund's affection, but there was some relief in not having to supply all his emotional needs. For the first few years they were able to live in a precarious *ménage à trois*. Aware of Edmund's desire for children, Sylva knew that her platonic relationship was not sufficient for him. She accepted the necessity of Claire in Edmund's life but wanted her own position (of married companion rather than lover) to be maintained. Between November 1939 and February 1940 Edmund's diary charts her fluctuating moods:

Sylva knows, and knowing me is not afraid, or angry or hopeless: but our life can go on. . .

Poor girl, somehow fascinated by the active life, which is so full of flaccid passages. Her complexity is only reduced to one glorious simplicity by mountains and wintersports – that's a psychological history. . . .

With Sylva one encounters the artist – the experience nine times out of ten is scarcely complete before the interpretative passion is tapping away. A tragedy.

The romance was kept secret from all but a few close friends, and Edmund remained candidly honest with Sylva, telling her in March 1940: 'I have a tendre, almost amounting to a passion for Claire. You are always wanted, and I am only polygamous now and then in the tide of times.'[6] He was now faced with an emotional juggling act similar to that which he had faced with Annie and Aki Hayashi. He told Claire that 'I swear that I am not by nature unkind to any' but he was also aware that 'I complicate everyone who gains my love.'[7] He explained that Sylva 'lives with me as fitfully as the wind rattles my door . . . [she] is a child, angry, who floats off suddenly on some errand of fantasy, and darts in again full of adventure, and longs to love and hasn't time to.'[8] If marriage were to become possible he wanted Sylva's position to remain and asked Claire in 1943 that 'You will let me sometimes give her a walk and a call at the local. . . . she at least realises that she does not know what the strength and demands of a love of soul and body are; she admits that [when] this love's absence runs through all relationships between a man and a woman, [it] impoverishes and exhausts.'[9]

And the war also brought its impoverishments and exhaustions. From 3 September 1939 Edmund kept a diary in order to record the progress of the war and his reactions to it, sublimating his desire to voice his feelings by a daily cathartic exercise of the pen. With a few brief intervals he maintained the diary for three years. Its pages give the clearest picture of Edmund's ambivalent political position and reveal a gradual if reluctant acceptance of the aggressive nature of German intentions. In the early months he refused to condemn Hitler's political manoeuvres, complaining that slogans such as 'He's got to be stopped' were considered 'one of the laws of Nature like Guinness is good for you'. Whatever gloss may have been put on Hitler's action in Poland, Edmund maintained that 'he did not want to be the first to strike out in the *Western* war, and he has not been.' He described a speech of Hitler's as 'marvellously honest and humane', characteristics which he attributed to Hitler's having had war experience while 'our leaders (it is true that Churchill once commanded a battalion in a rest-cure sector for a few days) are not in touch with people like me.'

Slowly, by mid-1940, he yielded to the conclusion that invasion was likely: 'For to that, the speedy overthrow of other nations must have been considered a stage. . . . But whatever comes, let us hope that the true virtue and clear spirit of England will find their way into the new world.' Such a hope may sound distinctly close to pacifism, yet he declined an invitation to speak at a Peace Pledge Union meeting because he was unable to adopt such a stance. Several of his pupils were conscientious objectors and he was sympathetic to their position – being accused by some in Oxford circles of having corrupted them – but his diary records that 'the arrival of war makes conscientious objection unreal' and he was quietly confident that, if he were to raise a battalion himself, most of his pacifist pupils would join. He was ready to admit as early as the winter of 1939 that a *short* war might even be beneficial – *if* it produced a speedy solution. It was the style of war which was at the root of his unease. The skills and comradeship of the trenches were one thing; a propaganda machine at work at home was quite another. He half wished to be back in Belgium defending the area he knew so intimately, and bitterly observed to Rupert Hart-Davis that he would like to take some of his accusers for a few nights' patrolling among the shell-holes of Flanders. Lack of any specific activity was perhaps the most irksome thing of all, and by March 1944 he was complaining to Claire, 'It *does* vex me a bit that this War did not employ me, not because I think of war any more gladly than you know but since it has crashed down again I ought perhaps to have been somewhere on my prowl.'[10] His strongest criticism continued to be directed at the rhetoric of hatred and what he saw as enthusiasm for war, or a lack of understanding of its horrors. His opinion of George Bernard Shaw, whom he had hitherto regarded as 'a skilled journalist', was raised considerably because 'he always refused to *rejoice* over war';[11] it was an attitude which described Edmund exactly.

Everything in his mind was related to the experience of 1916–18 and as almost every day in the diary is an anniversary of a First World War action the events are dutifully reconstructed. The fear that his young Merton colleagues might be cheered on their way to some scene as ghastly as Passchendaele – or even worse – provoked the most sarcastic observations: 'if dead men are the chief flooring of a smashed trench, presumably everyone is satisfied, and liberty maintained.'

His reading too was coloured by war preoccupations. A visit to the home of the Hertford College lawyer C. H. S. Fifoot, who lived in what was traditionally believed to be Chaucer's house, sent Edmund back to Chaucer's *Tale of Melibee*, where an old man warns youth of the difficulties of controlling or stopping war once it has started – and is silenced; a reading of John Selden's seventeenth-century *Table Talk* provided a striking example of national prejudice in the Englishman's depiction of the Saracens after the crusades as men with 'huge, big, terrible faces (as you still see in the inn signs of The Saracen's Head) when in truth they were like other men'; from Dryden he copied out the stark couplet:

> *Or what can wars to after times assure*
> *Of which our present age is not secure?*

He did not always hide behind the secrecy of his diary. His door at Woodstock Close was knocked on more than once for black-out irregularities ('what can an airman see 6000 feet up at 250 m.p.h.? Glow-worms beware!').[12] He also signed a public letter of appeal to Lloyd George to offer an alternative to Churchill's position and in April 1940 he once again wrote to *The Times*, this time to object to the indiscriminate bombing of German cities:

For some time past there has been talk . . . of the usefulness, the necessity of bombing the 'business' parts of German cities – for instance the station at Cologne as demarcated from the Cathedral across the way. Should such attacks be undertaken by us, the results are not hard to forecast. There will be the killing and wounding of civilians. Things of beauty, the property of mankind rather than the nation which preserves them, would be destroyed. As for 'teaching the Germans a lesson', there would be only the increase of bitterness . . . and . . . distaste for democracy.[13]

That his position should lay him open to the charge of being unpatriotic was the sharpest cut of all. He considered that his life and writings clearly showed the opposite and he proudly asserted in his diary that 'above all I need and I adore the English language.' He still believed that his wish to serve Germany as well as England might not be regarded as treachery but was aware that he must be ready for any retaliation to be taken for Sylva's and his German friendship and visits. And such action was not slow in coming. By mid-1940 Sylva had been shouted at while shopping in the Oxford market and called 'a fifth-columnist' and a 'traitor to your country'. In July of the same year Annie's Tonbridge home was raided by police, who removed all Sylva's letters to Edmund and searched the house from top to bottom. It looked as though Annie might be interned. A few days later the police returned and solemnly went through all Edmund's books ('which may have had educational value for the policeman engaged')[14], and it was clear that Edmund was also under suspicion. By the end of the month he was summoned by the Warden of Merton, Sir John Miles, who had:

. . . had word from the police that they had reports about me and my Defeatist Talk, that he had also had protests and one anonymous letter. I was supposed to be wanting the Germans to win and to have said that I hoped Hitler would come here etc. . . . I replied that I was not surprised at such things and told him all I could and incidentally answered his suggestions that (it was said) I was unwilling to do what I could for my country, mentioning that I had written to my old C.O. not a week ago on the matter. That pleased him and he said he would write to the police accordingly. He was glad I was not taking up some terrible position: and he would tell the police I would gladly come and see them.[15]

The next week Edmund went to Worcester College to see Colonel Wilkinson ('an old Cavalier, and one of my towers of defence in a naughty world')[16] who had become commanding officer of the Oxford Officers' Training Corps and who had arranged for Edmund to become a map-reading instructor with an honorary commission. Once again Edmund found himself in uniform – which he pointedly wore on his next visit to Tonbridge. After a week's training at Wellington Barracks he began his regular routine of instruction, which was to be his war activity for the next four years. Many of his officer-cadets remembered his lectures as the most enjoyable part of their training, filled as they were with literary anecdotes and a general history of cartography, augmented by imaginative exercises in the more agreeable parts of the Oxfordshire countryside. He was also called upon to participate in more elaborate exercises such as the one he described in November 1942:

We – the Mobile column – set out early for Chiselhampton, quite attracting notice as we went (guns and tanks as well as common motor vehicles), and passed Garsington which gave me cause to sigh a little – but where is that not likely round Oxford? – and so to our mock battle between the Baldons and Dorchester. Leafy avenues of trees, red cottages and white villas, and children at gates and mothers at thresholds drew my attention from my business, but in the end I hobbled along towards the scene of victory over paratroops. . . . One little thing I liked: a whiskered Colonel was holding a post mortem on the exercise at the edge of a thin wood, with several officers close round, when I saw a fat field vole run on his usual course right through the group of boots and safely into his disturbed residence.[17]

Edmund still did not feel completely safe and sent the first volume of his diary to Claire because he did not want it to be read 'in the interests of freedom by some Churchillian spy-maker; some things in it do not concern the national safety.' The diary ends abruptly in mid-1942, partly perhaps because Edmund was tired of 'retrospective tunnellings' and felt he had said all that he wished to on 'war rather than this war'. He feared he might be witnessing the ruin of western civilisation and felt particularly for places such as Rouen or Bayeux 'which cannot exist if bombarded for a few days in the modern style. It is not possible to replace them. They are personalities.' The German bombing of Coventry in November 1940 removed for him any distinction between the combatants in terms of 'civilised' behaviour. He refrained from further outbursts but maintained the stance of a reluctant soldier who steadfastly refused to hate his enemy.

'Some of the things' he recorded which did not concern the national safety included a record of his love for Claire and a striking picture of wartime Oxford.

In most respects the university was only superficially affected by the war. Its numbers were dramatically reduced, the average age of the dons inevitably increased and many colleges found themselves playing host to servicemen – in Merton to Canadian airmen. The noisy skies above Oxford were mostly threatening only in passing and were usually heralds of violent activity in London or further north. These changes tended to increase the feeling of a club-like intimacy among undergraduates and dons alike. Extra administrative tasks were required and Edmund became Principal of Postmasters (Merton scholars), college fire-watcher and finally Sub-Warden. He also became more reliant on the social life of the college, cementing his friendship with Nichol Smith, whom he found 'such a straightforward lover of life, including books, and so natural in his pleasure',[18] and with H. C. K. Wyld, whose private behaviour he preferred to his public image: 'he is immeasurably better in his own room than in company; he there finds no trouble in being the mild humorist, he recollects carefully – among several people he strikes an attitude and endeavours thunderbolts.'[19] Dinners at high table became more enjoyable too, and he acquired a taste for such donnish games as selecting which autograph manuscript one would most like to have been sent by a writer, receiving general approval for his choice of Milton's L'Allegro and Il Penseroso. At one dinner a guest engaged Edmund in vigorous conversation on the First World War and ended by warmly encouraging him 'to read the work of Blunden'.

Above all Edmund was increasingly spending time with H. W. Garrod, for while he distrusted Garrod's opinion on college matters ('he tells me one lie a minute')[20] he could discuss the progress of the war with him without fear of recrimination. He was impressed by Garrod's reading and close observation of political events, noting that he had correctly predicted the date of the declaration of war and had stated in October 1939 that 'Germany will outstay us economically but will lose the war politically.'[21] He found Garrod a most stimulating literary critic – 'often perhaps wrong (and whimsically inclined)' but 'always learned without pomp, subtle without obscurity, and *alive*'.[22]

In addition to Common Room friendships Edmund was also welcome company for the college servants, and his relationship with Claire required the discreet understanding of the two college porters, Arthur Major and Arthur Innes. On being invited to tea with Innes one Sunday, Edmund was somewhat overwhelmed by his reception: 'He received me with the air of the Mother casting her arms about her sailor son, and produced rather special bread and jam as well as his celebrated tea. He amused himself, and me, with some drollery on Merton Authorities, and I believe looks on me as an antidote to the haw-hawering that is let loose occasionally.'[23] Similarly he was at home in the local of his old scout Tom Redman, being introduced to his friends – 'men of some consequence, grave and correct of speech, steady consumers of pints'[24] – and relaxing in the college buttery, enjoying the conversation of Penny, for fifty years a college servant and lover of cricket.

As well as meeting official visitors to college – including Sir William Beveridge, Max Beerbohm, Duff Cooper and the Shakespearean scholar E. K. Chambers – he continued to open his door almost daily to many friends and writers who 'called in passing'. In February 1941 he was visited by the eighty-five-year-old Margaret Woods, who had met nearly every literary figure of her lifetime and had sat on Tennyson's knee as a child. A more abrasive meeting occurred a few months earlier when the pioneering birth-control advocate Marie Stopes visited to express her views on 'exterminating Russia' and accused Edmund of being rude in claiming to have no opinions on 'the art of poetry' and refusing to say anything more than 'I like reading poems.'[25] In 1944 he also began to visit the novelist Joyce Cary, who was temporarily living in Oxford and with whom he could talk of 'Ireland, Germany, America, Russia, Turkey, Eton and Shelley'.[26]

PART FIVE    1931 – 1945

Within the university his friendships and contacts continued to extend in all directions. A walk through Magdalen Grove might result in an invitation from E. H. W. Meyerstein to look at manuscripts of Chatterton or Landor; emerging from the University Parks he could visit Leonard Rice-Oxley, the English fellow at Keble. On his way to the Bodleian Library, New College increasingly provided the company and friendship of Lord David Cecil – who was to introduce him to the eccentric Lord Berners, remembered by Edmund as like 'a nice old oil lamp with a white globe, comforting the room'.[27] Dinner invitations continued as before the war – Paul Grice at St John's introducing him to the President, Austin Lane-Poole, who conversed on Hardy and the First World War; Colonel Wilkinson at Worcester ('what an air of permanence and handsomeness over everything there')[28] regularly inviting him to dine and talk of 'books and birds, of otter and hedgehog',[29] with a game of bowls to end the evening. (It nicknames were used, a partnership between Wilkinson and Edmund became a pairing of 'the Horse and the Rabbit'.) The Dean of Wadham, Jack Thompson, was an old Merton friend and Edmund particularly remembered an evening with him and the Warden of Wadham, Maurice Bowra, when he enjoyed:

. . . the capacity to view all that passes *with a private mind*. Wit is not dead because of an emergency! how excellent and how repugnant to some I have met. . . . Bowra is one of the men on whom I would base a claim to English pre-eminence: so learned, so keen, so just. It seems to me we would do well to appoint other very brilliant and even capricious young men to such Wardenships, which leave them brilliant and make them philanthropic. Dr Thompson was exceedingly interesting on the scientific side of the war as well as the scandalous.[30]

Very little seemed to have changed since 3 September 1939 and certainly not the pace of Edmund's life: one day in June 1940 saw him lunch with Bruce Richmond, watch – and review – a Dryden play in the afternoon and address a society on Max Beerbohm in the evening; one week in September saw the publication of two book reviews, a poem and an article; on 25 November he lectured on Lamb and Keats in the morning, on map-reading in the afternoon and on seventeenth-century religious elegance in the evening. At lunch he was the guest of the Principal of Somerville, Helen Darbishire, together with the modern linguist Enid Starkie and the Jewish artist Bernard Meninsky. Edmund's recollection of this meeting reveals his latent anti-semitic instincts: 'Meninsky is a Jew, and at once I felt my indignation against

Jews for their share in bringing a catastrophe reduced. Were they all as impartial and sensitive as he!'[31]

The war years also saw Edmund taking a more active interest in the affairs of the Bodleian Library, becoming a committee member of the 'Friends', which brought him personal satisfaction in January 1943 when he sold some Clare manuscripts to the Library on behalf of Sam Sefton. His mind went back twenty years: 'In 1920 I remember approaching Mr Craster in the Library and asking him if there were any manuscripts by Clare there. "Clare", he answered, "Clare. And where do you expect to find any manuscripts by Clare?" Well, today, he was the Chairman, and he almost registered excitement when I laid my packet and descriptive letter before him. It is an odd life, things often form a story.'[32]

The feeling that university life should go on unchanged as much as possible both pleased Edmund and made him feel a sense of guilt. A chance lunchtime meeting with C. S. Lewis in the Eastgate helped to establish a perspective: 'I told him I admired his strength of mind in delivering his lectures despite the strain of war. He said: "Do you know *The Peterborough Chronicle?* I found in it the very best motto for the job: 'Throughout these evil times, the Abbot retained his abbacy.'" This quite warmed up the chilly morning.'[33] Edmund certainly retained his position as tutor and if anything exercised his role more extensively. But while he became an anchor for many of the pupils who passed through his rooms at all hours of the day, they became equally indispensable to him. He found being surrounded by the 'faithful, young and true'[34] a necessary reassuring stimulus – for he was rarely a solitary by choice. Undergraduates could easily lure him to a hostelry for extended conversation, and his room became a favoured venue for party, society meeting or wedding breakfast. The company of his pupils, regularly represented by Michael Meyer, Alec Hardie, Douglas Grant, Mary Oswin and Bernard Mellor, was augmented by his daughter Clare and her Somerville friends, by Claire and her St Hilda's friends and by a young aspiring actress living in Masefield's old house on Boar's Hill, Joan Appleton (who was to marry Douglas Grant). She made a striking impression on Edmund: 'For clear beauty like to the clear in highest sphere I never saw the equal of Joan Appleton. . . . I can gaze on her sad slender countenance as one might on the morning moon, or some first primrose under budding hedges.'[35] He also found himself acting as adviser and poetic encourager to his pupil Keith Douglas.

## PART FIVE    1931 – 1945

Although he had enlisted as soon as war was declared, Douglas was not called up for another year. He was an aggressive personality, much concerned with himself; he was also sensitive and artistic, energetic and impatient. Edmund quietly accepted these contradictions and became Douglas's principal mentor, much to the surprise of many at Christ's Hospital who 'scarcely credit my claim to have some controlling influence over that poetic planet'.[36] It was a strange relationship: Douglas impatiently keen to enter the arena of war, Edmund anxious to avoid it at all costs. But Edmund was quick to see Douglas's talent, championing his cause with the *Times Literary Supplement* and attempting – unsuccessfully – to persuade T. S. Eliot to publish a selection of poems.

Douglas's artistic talents came to the fore in his designs for the Merton Floats' production of Dryden's *Secular Masque* (in which Edmund played Chronos opposite Joan Appleton's Diana) and Fielding's *Tom Thumb* (in which Edmund played Merlin). It was an interesting choice of entertainment, and very much Edmund's own idea, moving from Fielding's satirical views of moralistic tragedy (reminding Edmund perhaps of the political rhetoric he so despised) to Dryden's dismissal of Mars's claims for the achievements of war. After the performance, Douglas sent Edmund an envelope elaborately decorated 'in the manner of Rex Whistler. . . setting forth Diana and Chronos as the Lady and Lord of misrule'.[37] From the Middle East, Douglas wrote regularly to Edmund, enclosing poems for comment and entrusting him with a manuscript of *Alamein to Zem Zem*. It was the violent power of Douglas's poetry which Edmund admired, both the ironic bite of 'Security' ('which much delighted my rebellious spirit')[38] and the haunting premonitions of death in 'I must see what war is like', 'The beast on my back' and 'I fear what I shall find.' He saw these as some of the finest poems which the war produced.

Edmund recalled Douglas as:

. . . a bespectacled undergraduate, with an oddly weather-beaten face, unexpectedly slow speech, and a desire to please. . . . He was of middle height and strongly built and mostly wore a green sports jacket and green corduroy trousers . . . his hair was thick and long and flamed with a bronze tint. . . .

Perhaps there is a tale of woe, or I shall be getting that in a letter after term ends. It is one of Keith's natural afflictions that although he for his part always makes the case absolutely clear . . . inexplicable frustration attends him . . . . In one aspect he was a child, expecting the world to be a neat arrangement of attentive apple-trees, all ready to stoop their branches to him and place oranges in his hand; but in another way he was a resolute and masterful character, as outspoken as he was keen in judgment . . .

His book *Alamein to Zem Zem* is uncommonly good . . . but it was necessary to go through it carefully before publication, for the number of violent and painful comments on identifiable people was unusually large. I think Keith would strike out the epithets 'violent and painful'. . . .

Just before D Day Keith was visiting Oxford but I only heard of his being in town when it was too late. . . . I was told that he talked away as if the 'haunting' was not there; and he talked with his usual wrath about other people, myself included. . . . But who would complain of him, especially after his experiences in desert warfare, for being rather embittered and 'seeing through' us?[39]

In June 1944 Douglas was killed in Normandy by an exploding mortar shell. Immediately Edmund wrote to Douglas's mother, who joined Mrs Owen and Mrs Vidler as bereaved mothers with whom Edmund regularly kept in contact. That such talent as Keith Douglas's should have been extinguished only confirmed the destructive waste of war in Edmund's eyes. It was not to be an isolated incident. A month later came the news of Rex Whistler's death, another Normandy victim. Edmund expressed his sadness to Sassoon: 'What a cruel work of fate, and so unfair since he was one of the true lovers of peace and did so much with all his gifts to enrich the world of peace. I can imagine that he performed grandly in the front line, and if these things must be I wish he had been with you or me in such experiences. We shall not see a better artist.'[40]

Bitter reminders of the First World War took the form of survivors who were now claimed by the Second. James Cassells ('we were as David and Jonathan') and 'my old friend Sergeant Davey – he had been a gentleman's servant and was infallible in courtesy: even when a shell had just killed two men with him, and he was in a half-dazed and shocked state, he was correct as at the pay-table.'[41] Even a coincidence of names in *The Times* obituary column would send his memory back to France, as he explained to Claire:

I find the name of Guy Compton, who was in my company in 1916 and who was an extraordinarily brave youth; he left us and was killed in 1917. I can still see and hear him returning from bombing a German trench and (to his own horror) killing a poor old spectacled fellow who was creeping round a corner with awful anxiety. So you see how the years pass, for I am really not much more fit for this world than I was when I gave Compton a drink and listened to his passionate and half-weeping story. That was at 'Port Arthur', which I haunt still (perhaps they don't know what it is, at the estaminet there, that disturbs the silence).[42]

And there were deaths unconnected with the war, such as Virginia Woolf's: 'It's ages since I saw her and then she got me to dine so that her nephew might talk of nature poetry to a practitioner – he too is dead, young Julian Bell. She had a way of changing suddenly from grave intellectual and social bearing to a rather vibratory wildness and high-pitched gaiety.  Poor lady.'[43]

Despite these moments of depression, the general tenor of his life was brighter. He was physically fitter than for some time (apart from a brief illness in early 1942), being watched over carefully by the genial Irishman Dr McQuillan, but Edmund attributed his calmer frame of mind to the presence of Claire, who had become for him 'a fulfilment of all that is good in the world . . . a child, and yet in the communion of spirit she is all that I can conceive woman may be. There is that serenity, that calm which in the end men seek from women.'[44] Edmund always associated Claire with nature and the countryside and the war years saw him extending his walks in and around Oxford, regularly exploring Sutton Courtenay, Cumnor, Hinksey, Culham, Clifton-Hampden or Islip, often in the company of pupils or friends together with Sylva and whenever possible with Claire. They became familiar figures in the local hostelries, though Sylva's fussy dietary habits were a source of mixed bewilderment and irritation to Edmund. He also took an active part in country life, helping at harvest-time on the farm of a New College tenant, Mr Ellis of Stanton St John.

Rural regeneration was to become reflected in his poems. The months leading up to the war were not rich poetically for Edmund and he welcomed the suggestion of Macmillan that he produce a volume of *Poems 1930–40*: a collection of 200 pieces, only twenty-six appearing for the first time (including eight new 'First World War' poems), with most of *On Several Occasions* being reprinted. He also paid tribute to a number of individuals: to his friend Arthur Rose-Innes on his death in Japan in 1938 ('In Memoriam A.R.I'),[45] to Joan Appleton ('To J.A.' and 'After a Masque'),[46] to his daughter's friend Madeline Bishop ('Pastoral to Madeline')[47] and to Claire ('To a Friend').[48] The collection was dedicated to H. W. Garrod, 'a master of critical encouragement', and received a mixed critical reception – the review in the *New English Weekly* being entitled 'Recollected in Too Much Tranquillity' while the *Times Literary Supplement* published its notice under the heading 'In the True Tradition'. After the accusation of Nazism it was with a wry smile that Edmund saw himself described in the *Birmingham Post* as 'a Left Poet'. *Poems 1930–40* also represented a publishing break with Richard Cobden-Sanderson, who had finally closed business. He had published eighteen of Edmund's books over twenty years, happily accepting even those which would clearly have only a very limited circulation. Their friendship continued over the following years.

If the 1930–40 anthology reflected a degree of creative stagnation, then 1940 itself marked a new phase of pastoral energy which was to be evident in his 1944 collection *Shells by a Stream*, whose first poem acknowledges that 'I hear fresh hours appeal'. The book is a poetic diary of his love for Claire from her early Oxford days to the brief time spent in teaching posts before she joined the army in 1942, being stationed in Derby. Edmund always liked to recreate specific pastoral scenes in his poems and each collection can be read as a kind of gazetteer of his walks and travels at the time. In Rupert Hart-Davis's copy of *Shells by a Stream* Edmund wrote, 'maybe each Bard should be compelled by act of parliament to express his acknowledgements to the parishes which have supplied his scenery,' and then identifies the origin of several individual poems – recording walks along the banks of the Beult at Yalding, the Medway at Twyford and the Cherwell in Oxford as well as other Sussex, East Anglian, Oxford and Derby settings.

And it was not just his own poetry which was occupying his time, for he was compiling an anthology of military and naval verse for Colonel Wilkinson and preparing the 1815–37 volume of the *Oxford History of English Literature* for Bonamy Dobrée – though both projects were eventually abandoned. He delivered his short book on *English Villages* to Collins in 1914 before beginning *Cricket Country*, which was completed by 1944, while for Macmillan he was writing *Thomas Hardy*, appearing in early 1942. The Hardy volume was typically idiosyncratic (infuriatingly so for Desmond MacCarthy, who reviewed it for the *Sunday Times*), tracing three aspects of Hardy's life and their effect on his writing: the influence of war (noting that Hardy was twelve at the time of the Duke of Wellington's death), the importance of Hardy's classical education and his love of London. Considerable space is given to contemporary reviews, and he eccentrically chooses to give detailed accounts of only two novels – *A Pair of Blue Eyes* and *Two on a Tower*. Three chapters are devoted to poetry, two of them to *The Dynasts* alone – a reflection of the conversations he had enjoyed at Max Gate, as recalled in the dedication: 'To Siegfried Sassoon, remembering other days in the homes of William Barnes and Thomas Hardy'.

Claire's absence from Oxford made Edmund restless and he found the lines of Coleridge acutely apt:

> *I mix in life and labour to seem free*
> *With other persons pleased and common things,*
> *While every thought and impulse tend to thee*
> *And every action from thy influence springs.*[49]

Partly to compensate for this but partly as a perennial necessity, Edmund surrounded himself with the company which naturally gravitated to him. He needed companionship to chaperone him through the day and there were always those in addition to his family, pupils, colleagues and other friends who fulfilled this function. He knew them as his 'permanent men' and during 1939–45 three in particular played this role, as war commitments allowed: Ian Robertson ('without him Oxford is dry sand'),[50] Laurence Brander ('about the most modest, gifted man I know')[51] and an Australian cricketer from Adelaide University who had taught science at Christ's Hospital before becoming Assistant Director at the Oxford University Delegacy for Teacher Training, F. W. Wagner ('his companionship is my best consolation').[52] On most days one of the three would join Edmund for lunch in a favourite Oxford pub such as the Old Tom ('a pleasant drowsy nook . . . with barrels in full view of the thirsty').[53] With Brander – an enthusiast for Thomas Hood – shove-halfpenny and bar billiards punctuated the conversation; with Wagner (always known as 'Wag') conversation was often cricket-based, and he became the dedicatee of *Cricket Country*. In Ian Robertson's company Edmund several times visited Iffley, where the colourful John Bryson lived in baronial splendour surrounded by paintings by Ford Madox Brown and D. G. Rossetti, and played host to a variety of artistic and literary guests.

Opportunities to travel outside Oxford soon presented themselves. A tempting but unsuccessful invitation came from John Betjeman, acting as Press Attaché at the British Embassy in Dublin, to visit Ireland, where Edmund was assured that he had 'very warm admirers in Sean O'Faolain and Frank O'Connor' and where 'your presence would be a comfort and a joy'. Letters from Betjeman,[54] addressed to 'Dear and best of living poets', were liberally illustrated by sketches of church interiors with umbrellas nestling in racks at the ends of pews, and evoked nostalgic memories of England and Oxford: 'Oh God to be in England! Oh God for a nice whiff of paraffin oil and hassocks. Yes, even for a glance at [C.S.] Lewis striding tweed-clad to Headington.' Edmund did, however, journey to Scotland on two occasions to visit Alec Hardie in Kircudbrightshire. Here he relaxed in the comfort of the thick-walled, grey stone house with its ivy-covered porch, surrounded by trees and looking out on to moorland and mountain, with brown heath under mother-of-pearl skies, and en-joyed being driven into Dumfries by green sports-car, or taking the family Airedale for walks before returning to the luxuries of tobacco, Younger's ale, whisky, biscuits and chocolate. He established a relationship with Hardie's parents, similar to that which he formed with Mrs Douglas and Mrs Owen, only in reverse: on the death of Hardie's mother, Edmund composed a poem which is inscribed on her grave in Forfar cemetery; on the death of his father in 1950, Alec became from time to time an extra member of the Blunden household.

Lecturing engagements began to increase in number again, taking Edmund twice to Cheltenham as well as to London for two prestigious occasions: a lecture in October 1941 on Thornton Hunt to the Royal Society of Literature, published as *Leigh Hunt's Eldest Son*, and in 1942 the Warton Lecture at the British Academy, published as *Romantic Poetry and the Fine Arts*. He also maintained his non-nationalistic stance by making himself available for as many international cultural initiatives as possible. In Oxford he made the acquaintance of a Polish film-making colleague of Dora Nahabedian, Sigismund Bakanowski, and Edmund offered to do anything he could for the Polish cause. In April 1940 he attended a dinner at the Randolph Hotel in honour of Dr Kawai, a Japanese 'travelling ambassador' who had just visited Italy and was on his way to meet Hitler. One of the Japanese party stressed the strength of Edmund's influence on the literary life of Japan – and a little while later Edmund noted in his diary that 'the East may call me again.' Through the agency of Joan Appleton's father, Edmund had lectured to Indian students visiting New College, and an Indian connection was to be extended with Laurence Brander's appointment as Eastern Intelligence Officer in the Empire Department of the BBC in 1941. Edmund was invited to join the panel of broadcasters giving talks for Indian students of English literature. He gave his first broadcast – on Thackeray – in January 1942, being first taken to lunch by Herbert Read at the Reform Club. The Talks Producer for the Indian Service was George Orwell, with whom Edmund quickly established a cordial relationship, describing him as 'an Etonian worthy to rank with Rupert [Hart-Davis] – and

that as you know is an eulogy indeed'.[55] Edmund continued to broadcast throughout 1942, after which Orwell arranged for him to take
over the role of chairman for the 1943 series, when Orwell introduced
Edmund's talk on Hardy and Edmund returned the compliment for
Orwell's talk on Shaw. The broadcasts also provided the occasional
company of William Empson, with whom Japan as well as poetry was
common ground.

To add to Polish, Japanese and Indian associations, Edmund found
himself in April 1943 back in the Aeolian Hall in London for a
poetry-reading in honour of the French, arranged by Osbert Sitwell,
and held in the presence of the Queen and the two princesses. The
audience was a suitably distinguished one, and the readers included
T. S. Eliot, de la Mare, Masefield, Edith Sitwell ('wearing a green
turban like a laurel wreath'),[56] Vita Sackville-West ('who recited in
her empire-building accent')[57] and H.D. (the poet and novelist Hilda
Doolittle). Edmund began the readings with 'The Spell of France'[58] –
the only poem read on that occasion which made any reference to
France – and during the interval was presented to the Queen, who
engaged him in long conversation. At the end, the Queen 'nodded
farewell to the company and gave me a nod on my own'.[59] Six months
later a similar occasion was arranged in the Wigmore Hall for the
United Aid to China Fund, when Edmund shared the platform with
Louis MacNeice, Cecil Day-Lewis, Kathleen Raine and Anne Ridler.

In November 1944 it was the turn of Russia, and a group of writers
under the patronage of J. B. Priestley met at Claridge's to pledge
support for better relations between London and Moscow. More
memorable for Edmund was a visit he paid on the same day to
Maurice Buxton Forman (son of the nineteenth-century scholar Harry
Buxton Forman), who had inherited his father's books. It was a perfect
kind of occasion for Edmund and reads like a reconstruction of a
meeting between Coleridge and Lamb. After lunchtime conversation
over 'a hundred things about Keats and Shelley'[60] they retired to the
library to inspect the collection of Keats and his circle. A discussion of
Keats's letters followed in which Buxton Forman was 'alert for any
trifling novelties, and I could produce one or two,'[61] before Edmund
left with the loan of several unusual Shelley items in his bag.

The phrase 'Many visitors!' which opens the diary entry for 22
November 1940 might well apply to any day during the next five
years. Some, like Hector Buck, came to play cricket; some, like
Christopher Hassall, to talk over a lunch-time: some, like Hugh
Macdonald, to talk all day. Visits from his family became more regular

too. His relationship with his daughter Clare blossomed from proximity and when she married an old Mertonian, Philip Ross, at the synagogue in Marylebone in October 1943, their home became a welcome retreat, for Clare remained 'a winner; she always was, even as a tiny girl: the steady eyes insisted on an honest and proud reply.'[62] Relations with his son John were also restored. John had joined the navy before being struck by tuberculosis in 1943, and a visit just before this was remembered as 'very agreeable and affectionate. We might have been together for years, so easily did the hours pass.'[63] Most agreeable of all was Edmund's reconciliation with Mary. She had written to him at the outbreak of war, begging him not to volunteer and subject himself again to what she had seen him suffer twenty years before. She visited Oxford regularly to see Clare and report on John's progress, and Edmund's diary gratefully recorded that 'the bitterness between Mary and me has gone and we feel much as in early happy hours. It is hard to believe that we ever were at war.'

The same could not be said about his relationship with Sylva. As Claire became more and more the central part of Edmund's life it was impossible for Sylva to maintain the position of wife, even if only in name. When she and Edmund were in company the strain became exaggerated, with outbursts on both sides becoming increasingly common. It was clear in which direction things were moving as Edmund for the third time in his life introduced a young lady to all the varied strands of his past. Claire met Edmund's parents and both Annie and Aki Hayashi; she was taken to Christ's Hospital and stayed in Brighton when Edmund was attending a Southdown Battalions' dinner. She also had to become familiar with Edmund's literary world and somewhat nervously she was taken to Heytesbury to meet Sassoon and to Henley to meet Rupert Hart-Davis, who remarked of Claire afterwards, '*that is the girl E.B. should have married.*' On her side, Claire had introduced Edmund to her friends and cousins, Dick and Joan Chamberlain, and taken him to meet her mother – who, Edmund recorded, 'showed excellent grace in meeting her daughter's married lover'.[64]

By mid-1943 Edmund was certain that his future lay with Claire and that his Oxford days were over. He wanted to escape from the official routines of the university and return to the life of a writer, for he had felt 'intellectually badly off – my trouble is a rustic or even mystic tendency'[65] and he concluded that academic life 'yields no imagery, no native vocabulary, and it deprives one of the chance to gather them where they grow.'[66] He thus resigned his Merton fellowship with effect from January 1944 despite hints that an Oxford professorship might be waiting for him, and suggestions from his Christ Church friends that a non-teaching studentship was a possibility there. He also resisted overtures from the British Council to take up a chair àt Ankara University, and in February 1944 he joined Annie at her house in Pembury Road, Tonbridge, while Sylva shared the Woodstock Close flat with Suzanne Galarza, the former wife of the writer Leo Walmsley. It was another characteristic, impulsive action for he was giving up financial security with no firm prospects of any regular income. As the Warden of Merton pointedly exclaimed, 'Oh, you have thrown your bonnet over the windmill, Mr Blunden![67]

Edmund now decided that he must give Sylva official grounds for divorce, and contacted lawyers. Inevitably a literary connection emerged and their solicitor was Atherton Powys, a cousin of the writer John Cowper Powys. Under his direction, on the evening of 12 February 1944, they booked into the Dorchester Hotel in London. A few days later Edmund wrote to Sylva:

I hope that the letter I am writing will not be a shock to you, though I cannot write without a mixture of feelings. At least I do not think that it will come as an entire surprise to you since we have so often discussed our married life, and both of us have been aware of its becoming a deep strain on us both. Circumstances, private and general, have not lessened that: and I believe you will agree that the past four years have made it especially nervous and exhausting. So I have resolved on taking a step which should enable you to bring these difficulties and the unhappy situation as a whole to an end. I enclose the bill from the hotel at which from February 12th to the 14th I stayed with Claire Poynting. If you could cause enquiries to be made at that hotel, I believe you could obtain further evidence which would lead to your being able to take action and allow us both to begin things again in our own paths . . . .

You will know that I have not moved in the way this letter tells you without remembering many happier passages of our lives in former years and being still really grateful to you for a great many affectionate loyalties and endeavours. I am only sorry that these have not been able to characterise our marriage throughout and that it should have fallen into a state of discontent and discord.[68]

Sylva's reaction could not have been more generous. She responded to Edmund's letter:

I can't pretend that it hasn't made me unhappy, and finally quenched any hope that any clouds might blow over so that we might settle down happily again together . . . . this letter of yours has finally disillusioned me, and left me no reasonable course except to do as you wish. It is no use trying to keep you 'officially' when your whole being is centred somewhere else. Heaven knows there is little enough happiness in life, especially when one is no longer very young. If you believe you still have a chance of catching a spark of it I shall not stand in your way.[69]

To Claire she had been equally selfless:

I do wish most heartily, for Edmund's sake and for your own, that all may go smoothly. You and I both believe that we are acting as we are to promote his happiness – and in your case it implies your own happiness as well . . . I feel as I ever did for Edmund, and shall not stop loving him in my own weak way . . . if you can get out of that Derby circus and live a Christian life and become a devoted mother, then I think the sun may shine on you both.[70]

Such reasonable understanding characterised her relationship with Edmund from then on, a fortnightly correspondence being maintained almost unbroken for over twenty years until her death in 1971. Perhaps the most remarkable sign of her generosity was the dedication in 1954 of her most successful book *Flight of the Skylark*, on Shelley's literary reputation, to 'Edmund and his Claire in lasting friendship'.

The months waiting for divorce proceedings, which Edmund spent in Tonbridge, were mostly dedicated to the writing of a biography of Shelley. As usual, Tonbridge life both suited and irritated him. He liked the compact but cosy house with its resident animals and birds – cat, dog, canary, chickens and rabbits – and he was just five minutes walk from the Angel cricket ground and a similar distance from the local pub. But Annie (threatened with yet another woman in Edmund's life) was becoming more possessive, and the presence of lodgers increased the sense of claustrophobia, resulting one evening in a fist fight between Edmund and a Canadian soldier. Quieter moments were provided by visits from old pupils and friends and from new acquaintances such as the poet Andrew Young, who delighted Edmund by declaring that there was no such thing as 'poetic technique' and by being unaware of the existence of the Book Society. Locally Edmund was quickly in demand, as he had been in East Anglian days, and it was not many weeks before he was invited to talk at Tonbridge School, where Claire's brother Bob had recently been a pupil. It was a moving occasion, for a group of boys stayed behind afterwards to talk to Edmund of peace and war and he confessed to being close to tears 'to think of these kind youngsters and the promise they have in them for a decent tomorrow'.[71] Outside Tonbridge he was also fulfilling what had now become routine demands, and regular visits to London for lectures or meetings of the Charles Lamb Society or the Book

Society (for whom he introduced an edition of Jane Austen's *Persuasion*) all kept him from his desk. Other absences were courted – he celebrated his forty-eighth birthday with a visit to the theatre with Michael Meyer to see Ralph Richardson in Ibsen's *Peer Gynt*, and spent three days at Heytesbury with Sassoon, talking over burgundy until the early morning and bringing home a gift of Lionel Johnson's *Poems 1895*, a book 'agreeable in every way'. One rather eccentric enthusiasm led to a visit in July 1944 to Hurstbourne Priors, Lord Portsmouth's estate just outside Basingstoke where an experiment in 'land settlement' was in operation – a kind of communal rural life, using old-fashioned techniques of farming and land development. Edmund was delighted with the scheme, staying with Lord Portsmouth and enjoying his conversation, pictures and books – and the woods, hills, streams and water-meadows on his estate. It was reminiscent of Shelley's visit to Cwm Elan. Edmund had already, in 1943, edited *A Return to Husbandry* – a pamphlet dealing with alternatives to 'Commercialism and Mechanization', which gained the approval of the Archbishop of Canterbury, William Temple – and at Hurstbourne he met an old friend, J. E. Hosking, who had been the proprietor of a seed-growing firm near Ashford. Together they planned a further volume of essays in husbandry, published in 1945 as *The Natural Order*, and Edmund contributed an essay for the centenary catalogue of Hosking's company, Eastes and Loud. He must be one of the few poets and Oxford dons to have written for a seed catalogue.

Early in May 1945 an invitation from the *Times Literary Supplement* to join the staff as an assistant editor provided just the kind of permanent journalistic opportunity which he was seeking, and he accepted the post from June. The appointment also enabled him to write occasionally for *The Times*, for which he provided leading articles on Swift and A. E. Housman, and he was also to repay a compliment to the scholarly assistant editor C. W. Brodribb – who had composed a Latin translation of Edmund's 'Exorcized' in the *Times Literary Supplement* of 1938 – by introducing a memorial volume of Brodribb's poems after Brodribb's death in 1945.

Also by early May, Sylva and Edmund were granted a decree absolute. The inevitable publicity which resulted, with reports in the local press, caused some awkwardness in Oxford circles and made Edmund an infrequent visitor for some time. A fortnight after the divorce, on 29 May – six years after their first meeting – Claire and Edmund were married at Tonbridge Registry Office. It was a bright, sunny day and Mugg and Pugg arrived from Yalding with flowers from Cleave's garden for Edmund to give to Claire, suspecting correctly that Edmund would have overlooked this. The wedding group consisted of a party of ten, including Claire's mother and Rupert Hart-Davis, but not including Annie, whose absence Edmund had engineered for the day; all catering arrangements, including the making of the cake, were in the hands of Alec Hardie. The honeymoon was a typical Blunden arrangement for it was to include a talk to boys in Hector Buck's house at Christ's Hospital before Edmund and Claire were able to relax as guests of Alec Hardie's father in Scotland. It also provided an opportunity for Edmund to buy Claire the official engagement ring which he had previously forgotten.

Since arriving in Oxford in 1931 Edmund had published nine prose works, six volumes of poetry and a thousand contributions to journals. He had given hundreds of lectures, exerted a considerable influence in the university, endured a war and married twice. The next twenty years were to offer many changes in his life but little change in its pace. The vital change was to be the company of Claire. Since leaving school he had never felt fully secure either physically or emotionally; now he felt assured of complete understanding. Until 1939 the women in his life, whether lovers or not, had too often been expressions of only part of his life – Mary representing the spirit of rural England; Hayashi the spirit of Japan; Sylva the beauty of the intellectual life. Annie, in early days, had been a symbol of the pleasures of domestic comfort. In each case he had been used to some degree – by Mary to achieve respectability; by Hayashi to come to England; by Sylva to enter the literary establishment; by Annie to gain homely reassurance. In consequence, Edmund had been able to give only a part of himself in return. From Claire he received a total gift which surpassed any analysis of representative elements. It was the fusion of body and soul which he had sought for thirty years, and he had now achieved the desire which he had first recognised five years earlier:

I should like to capture Claire and have her here, for she is like some clear horizon, like my first view of the sea coast as a child, a better light and day.[72]

# PART SIX

## An Interlude:
### *Preoccupations*

# 20

# Book Collecting

*He was the most accomplished book-hunter I have ever
known — ever more knowledgeable than my beloved
Edward Garnett, since his range went further back. He
knew every edition of every book, important or obscure,
the handwriting of every writer and of many lesser
individuals, and he had a diviner's instinct of where
treasure might lurk.*

Rupert Hart-Davis, 'A Personal Introduction' to
*A Bibliography of Edmund Blunden,* 1979

*I cannot profess to be a genuine collector of books, I
know nothing of positive bibliography; small books, I
call octavos, and large ones quartos. Folios I seldom
carry home, out of a growing sympathy with my weary
body. But so far as my preferences in size and weight are
satisfied, I am a willing rescuer of books.*

From 'Bringing Them Home',[1] 1930

From the first childhood explorations into the cupboards of Congelow
in Yalding, through the variety of the Christ's Hospital library and
chance discoveries of volumes in ruined houses on the edge of battlefields in France and Flanders, to the sophistication of Oxford
libraries and hours spent in second-hand bookshops, Edmund was
never without the company of books – which he treated with the
same affection and respect as he did people and animals; they became
his friends. He was not an impulsive collector, for he imposed rules on
himself in terms of size, price and association and rarely bought a

'new' book. He collected for two reasons: to build up a 'working' library and to rescue volumes he felt others would ignore. He believed that an adequate library of English literature could be established without paying more than sixpence a volume in 1920 – a price he allowed to increase to two shillings and sixpence in 1930 and ten shillings in 1950 – and by this means he created a library of 10,000 volumes by 1965. Copies of books sent him for review, which amounted to several hundred during his lifetime, he gave to Aki Hayashi to sell in order to supplement her income.

His collection clearly reflected his own preferred reading. (In reply to the often asked question, 'What is your favourite poem?', he usually suggested Marvell's 'The Garden', Shelley's 'The Question', Collins's 'Ode to Evening' or de la Mare's 'The Listeners'). His working library included 39 Chaucer volumes, 200 Shakespeare, 50 Milton, 40 Dryden, 70 Pope, 75 Swift, 50 Addison and Steele, and 90 of Dr Johnson. His Romantic collection included 150 Coleridge items, 100 Shelley, 80 Keats, 70 Lamb, 70 Wordsworth and 25 Clare volumes. More interesting were his 'rescued' minor poets, so that eight editions of Charles Churchill, seventeen of Samuel Rogers, twenty-eight of Christopher Smart, twenty-five of William Collins, ten of Francis Quarles, eighteen of William Barnes and twenty of Edward Young happily share the shelves with their more eminent contemporaries. Abiding by his rule of not paying more than a few shillings for any volume, he was prepared to wait several years to rescue a desired item from some dusty barrow or cobwebbed cellar, rather than pay over the odds.

In an article for the *Book-Collector's Quarterly* in 1930 entitled '*Bringing Them Home*' (reprinted in *The Mind's Eye*), he declared his preferences in collecting. He was not slavishly attracted to first editions (though a few pence secured a first edition of Voltaire's *Candide*, which his keen eye uncovered in the damp cellar of an Ipswich shop in 1929),[2] knowing that the fourth edition of Mrs Gaskell's biography of Charlotte Brontë was the one which included 'the reviews that meant so much', and that the third edition of Bunyan's *Pilgrim's Progress* was as rare as the first. Of more interest to Edmund were binding and typography (a Paris edition of Maria Edgeworth being purchased for its typeface), and he had an unfashionable preference for cloth bindings of the early and mid-Victorian period – both the restrained productions of Lamb's son-in-law Edward Moxon, and his more flamboyant contemporaries – partly because as a child he had read Izaak Walton in such a binding, 'festooned with golden creels and rods and lines and trout and bullrushes'.[3] He was particularly attracted to an 1896 Leipzig edition of *Dichtergrüsse*, feeling when he held it that he was 'handling perfection; the maze of green, gold, terra-cotta, fawn, blue, red-brown of circles, arcs, twirls, stars, trellises, of rose-buds and violets and apple-blossoms, however, mechanically pro-duced, has a spirit in it all which speaks.'[4] Two other volumes were rescued for their binding:

I would show as a quiet triumph a book in every way accordant with my desires – *The Letters of Rusticus on the Natural History of Godalming 1849*, by Edward Newman, naturalist and printer. It is tall, thin (but not emaciated), and bound in bright red slightly ridged cloth, upon which is embossed at the back a series of chain-designs, and on the sides an embroidery a little more complicated. At the back, the one word RUSTICUS, so done in gold as to have just the suggestion of being rather made from twigs than from steel types, looks from the bookcase. I can only say 'Well done!' when I see human achievement so clear within its particular and well-understood limits, and I feel happy and encouraged. Or, next to it, I might have disturbed again *Rowe's Illustrated Cheltenham Guide*, a little book of about the same date, and looking as perennially fresh in its pale blue linen (again made distinct with an impressed pattern of intertwining flowers). This guide is like one of those trinkets that lie sweetly still in escritoires. It is printed in light-blue ink, with engravings of houses and crescents and fashionable life in a lively black on every page; often, indeed, all the print is surrounded with the artist's garland-ing, as a summer-house under sycamores.[5]

Edmund's greatest pleasure was finding books with associations. Sometimes this might mean buying a volume of a lesser-known mem-ber of a distinguished writer's family, and he added to his S. T. Coleridge collection forty-five volumes by other members of the Coleridge family. More often he would detect the handwriting of an author or buy a particular edition because it had been owned by another author; he believed that he had Lamb's copy of Milton, and Byron's copy of *The Rolliad* – with some verses in Byron's hand.

Unlike many collectors he annotated his volumes copiously, usually in pencil. One snowy winter's day in 1923 Edmund had been taken by Canon Webling to a booksale at an old farmhouse in Suffolk, and filled a waggon full of 'first editions and many unusual but excellent books by authors who had unfairly been forgotten'.[6] In many of them the previous owner had followed the example of Charles Lamb and made marginal notes, which delighted Edmund and encouraged him to do the same. His annotations were varied. Sometimes they reflected his precise eye for detail and accuracy: he would correct indexes and footnotes. In an extensive bibliography of Blake he would query the colour of the binding of a particular volume, because his memory suggested that the entry was incorrect. It was this encyclopaedic knowledge of books and editions which prompted his friend and fellow bibliophile Sir Geoffrey Keynes to hang a William Rothenstein sketch of Edmund at shoulder-height by the fireplace of his study, so that Edmund's eye could be checking the details of his writing. For similar reasons Lady Mander (who wrote on many Romantic characters under the name of Rosalie Glynn Grylls and came to know Edmund well) referred to him as 'E.B.[2], standing for Encyclopaedia Britannica and Edmund Blunden'.[7]

Often his annotations reflect impressions of a book or record thoughts prompted by the text, giving cross-references to other poems or poets in the margin. On the title-page he would write out a bibliography of a minor writer, carefully recording dates and editions. After his visit to Hardy in July 1923 he recorded Hardy's and Sassoon's comments on William Barnes in his copy of *Poems of Rural Life*, as well as listing twenty-six of Barnes's prose publications and the fact that Hardy had visited Came Vicarage just before Barnes's death and 'bore away this last saying: The sparrows are pulling my thatch to pieces. I shall have to have it attended to it I'm afraid.' As he found more information he would update the entry – adding to his Barnes notes in 1938 and again in 1946.

A flyleaf might record why a particular volume was bought. In the front of an 1801 edition of the poems of the Reverend William Lisle Bowles, he wrote:

This volume has a place in the Shelley bookcase. At pp. 92–106 it contains the poem on 'Cwm Elan' dedicated to Shelley's uncle Thomas Grove, with a picture engraved from a drawing by Mrs Grove, the sister of Mrs Timothy Shelley. At the moment I am to enquire if (as I imagine) the poem and picture appeared in quarto in 1798. Coleridge imitated some of the lines in it. And I dare say Shelley in boyhood read it and bore some things in his memory.

In one of his *Melancholy Hours* Kirke White pointed out what I think has been forgotten, that Bowles practised the rhyming couplet with a freedom such as blank verse obtains. There is evidence for this claim of metrical innovation in the poem 'St Michael's Mount'.

Sometimes he would suggest further work that might usefully be undertaken on a minor writer. In H. L. Howard's 'Joseph and his Brethren', of 1824, Edmund identifies the author as Keats's friend, Charles Wells, and adds:

A rare book. 'That degraded Wells' – J. Keats. M. Buxton Forman possesses the immense letter signed *Amena* by which Wells deluded the amorous Tom Keats into going a fool's errand. It seems hard to connect the author of that practical joke with the author of this Scriptural Drama – See Dorothy Hewlett's 'Adonais'.

I wish I had leisure, and the MSS, etc. for a careful study of Charles Wells. What of his shorter poems? They might have the opulence and singularity of some of the intermittent fine things in 'Joseph'. Would M.B.F. assist from his South African retreat? Are there no descendants from this literary Wells?

His pleasure in finding annotations by other hands is exemplified in his copy of W. Mason's 1807 edition of Thomas Gray:

This was Henry Milton's copy, but who was he? Some of his notes may still be useful, in doing what Johnson said Criticism disdains to do: and finding some sources for details in T. Gray's poems. It is true of Mason's *Gray*, as of many books partly superseded, that one can't afford to neglect it. Mason knew Gray as nobody since could, and expresses his memories and impressions as though for Gray to hear him. This is not to deny that Mason misused Gray's letters in the manner described in L. Whibley's edition.

Occasionally the history of finding a particular volume is revealed. Edmund had long championed the cause of Henry Kirke White, the poet who had died aged twenty-one in 1806, and of whom Edmund wrote in *Notes and Queries* in 1948, claiming that he had exerted an influence on Keats and Shelley. He collected ten volumes of Kirke White and noted in the eleventh edition of 1825:

On our march to the battle of the Somme in 1916 I left behind at a farmhouse where I stayed one night, a copy of this Edition; and it has taken me fifteen years to replace that copy. Yet, whereas I paid sixpence for that book in 1915, I got this one for threepence in a time of elevated prices. This edition is a useful one, for it contains not only the usual 'works' of K. White but the supplementary, issued by Southey in 1822 and scarce. Some of these are superior to any of the first pieces collected.

Apart from individual poets – for, with the exception of Fielding, Sterne, Thackeray, Dickens, Scott and Hardy, novelists are less well represented – Edmund also collected anthologies (580 volumes) and periodicals (350 volumes) as well as classical authors (particularly his favourites: Xenophon, Cicero, Homer and Horace), books on water colourists and natural history, and booksellers' catalogues, which he was constantly trying to persuade the *Times Literary Supplement* to review. His annotations of anthologies point out where treasures lie, or suggest new themes for collections; the notes in periodicals indicate where, for example, a memoir of John Clare can be found in a copy of the *Gentleman's Magazine* for July 1864. Nearly every volume is marked in some way. Unusual books are particularly heavily annotated. In an eighteenth-century edition of Latin poems by members of Christ Church, *Carmina Quadragesimalia*, he notes that Coleridge was an addict of the unusual pieces of wit and poetry on philosophical problems such as the possibility or otherwise of a vacuum, whether a quantity is infinitely divisible or whether colour exists in the dark. Edmund translates a selection of such questions as well as rendering some light-hearted Latin verses on city public houses into rhyming English couplets.[8] He also declares that the book has been 'readable at times when almost all other books failed'.

Similarly he 'introduces' his copy of Henry Slack's *Marvels of Pond Life* 1861:

Henry James Slack, 1818–1896, journalist. Edited: *The Intellectual Observer* 1862–8, president of the Royal Microscopical Society 1878, of the Sunday League 1897; author of the *Ministry of the Beautiful*, 1850 *The Philosophy of Progress in Human Affairs*, 1860 and the present work which reached a 3rd ed. in 1878. Ed. with W. B. Hodgson the memorial edition of the works of W. J. Fox, 12 vols. 1865–8. I am not sure if it was he who long preserved the letters of P. B. Shelley to Elizabeth Hitchener. In the preface to his life of Shelley, E. Dowden thanks Mr Henry J. Slack for the use of them. E.H.'s solicitor was named Slack, I think, and she deposited the letters with him when she went abroad and did not reclaim them(?).

He lived at Forest Row, Sussex. There is an appreciation of him in one of the volumes of recollections by R. C. Roach Smith.

His annotating habits also extended to the books of his friends. He was always ready to inscribe their copies of his own books with personalised dedications in verse or prose, taking as much care over the layout or calligraphy as over the content. He also occasionally made notes in other books, which would only be discovered when the owner next consulted the particular volume. Such was the case in Francis Warner's copy of Shakespeare's *The Phoenix and the Turtle*. Some months after a visit from Edmund, Warner found an intriguing suggestion for a reading of the notoriously contorted syntax of one couplet:

> *To themselves yet either neither,*
> *Simple were so well compounded.*

Edmund had underlined 'To' and written in the margin, 'The argument and the metrical plan seem to suggest that this should be Two, with a comma after themselves.' And then, characteristically, he added as though he were writing a letter, 'Sorry if this is nonsense – Edmund.'

Whenever possible he would 'raid' a second-hand bookshop and record his success afterwards. In February 1929 he bought what appeared to be Beddoes's copy of Wordsworth's *Poems* (four volumes 1820) and Southey's copy of his own *Joan of Arc* – both for a shilling; but on the same day he extravagantly parted with eight-and-sixpence for a copy of the eccentric eighteenth-century miscellany of university verse, the *Oxford Sausage*. In Oxford his chief fellow bibliophile was Colonel Wilkinson of Worcester College; in London it was Rupert Hart-Davis. His favourite haunt became the barrows of the Farringdon Road in London. So confident was he of success that he would take a suitcase on such expeditions, and rarely went home without its being filled. On a not untypical day in April 1931 he found an 1819 edition of Christopher Smart, a 1765 edition of William Collins, *Coleridge on Method* and a copy of Goldsmith's *Vicar of Wakefield* illustrated by Mulready, for a grand total of eightpence.

After the Second World War he was introduced to the bookseller Edward Finneron, a cricketer, patriot and bibliophile who had been a sergeant-major in the same Guards regiment as Rupert Hart-Davis. Edmund began a regular correspondence with Finneron, who supplied him with volumes of poetry which he found 'unsaleable' in his Woking bookshop and who kept a wary eye open for particular requests. Edmund was thus able to extend his collection of the work of the eighteenth-century novelist and poet Charlotte Smith[9] (an appreciation of whose work was an unfulfilled ambition) to two dozen volumes. In a signed 1804 edition of her *Conversation Introducing Poetry* he records:

Wordsworth mentioning that he takes a stanza from 'St Monica' which he calls 'a poem of much beauty upon a monastic subject, by Charlotte Smith', calls her 'a lady to whom English verse is under greater obligations than are likely to be either acknowledged or remembered. She wrote little' – he's not quite right there – 'and that little unambitiously, but with true feeling for rural nature, at a time when nature was not much regarded by English poets, for in point of time her early writings preceded, I believe, those of Cowper and Burns'. This hint should be acted upon by some student of the poetry. As in the present instance, some of Mrs Smith's poems must be sought in her novels, tales and other prose works.

As Edmund was constantly on the move, his library also made its peripatetic course – growing larger at every move – through East

Anglia, Yalding, Oxford, Chatham, Tonbridge, Virginia Water and
finally resting at Edmund's last home, Hall Mill, Long Melford. For
the long stretches when Edmund was abroad, in Japan or Hong Kong,
his books were sometimes cared for by others. In 1955 Rupert Hart-
Davis found himself giving them a home in his small flat in Soho
Square; it took three men eight hours to complete the operation of
carrying them in and they stayed there for six years. For a while they
found sanctuary with Edmund's daughter Clare at her home in Clare,
Suffolk. After Edmund's death they had a few years' sojourn at Radley
College, Oxfordshire, before being sold to the University of Ohio at
Athens, Ohio (the home of Edmund's old friend and Shelley editor
Neville Rogers), where the civilised Head of the English Department,
Bernie Fieler, agreed to keep the library intact.

Edmund was always happy among his books, which surrounded him
like a comfortable nest. This sense of retreat colours his poem 'In a
Library'[10] (1933) but the sense of excitement and pleasure which his
reading and the company of his books gave him is best captured in the
opening lines of 'The Two Books' (1941):

> *Come tell me: of these two books lying here,*
> *Which most moves heart and mind to tenderness,*
> *The one approaching its three-hundredth year,*
> *The other a recruit fresh from the press?*
> *The one well honoured down the years, and still*
> *Trusty to light our pathway, poise our view,*
> *And this as yet uncrowned, which may fulfil*
> *As great a task through centuries strange and new?*
> *In both you find one nature, one appeal,*
> *And that antiquity and this young birth*
> *Share the same glory, equally reveal*
> *Man in his wisest, luckiest hours on earth.* [11]

# 21

# Cricket

*The game itself, if it is found in its natural bearings, is only the agreeable wicket-gate to a landscape of human joys and sorrows and is greatest where it fades away most imperceptibly into their wider horizons.*
Cricket Country, 1944

*He can bat, he is a natural batsman, and even now I could turn him into a very formidable player. His defect is that he stops his forward stroke and doesn't follow through, turning on his left hip. He is inclined to stab at the ball, but, make no mistake, he could become a fine batsman.*
Letter from C. B. Fry to Clifford Bax, on Edmund's batting, June 1947[1]

There was never a time in Edmund's life when cricket was not a central consideration, as player, spectator, writer or meditator on its more philosophical aspects; the mixture of athletic challenge, civilised behaviour and competitiveness without brutality never lost its magnetism. Whether played on village green, club square, county ground or Test wicket, the game revealed its unique secrets. Even in Japan, starved of regular competitive cricket (though he played for the English in Japan against an Australian side in 1949) he would set up stumps on any available piece of ground and give himself 'a net' – in the company of any willing British visitors. In Hong Kong too, where there were more opportunities, he never missed the chance of a match. His letters were filled with cricketing references and it became as frequent a conversation topic as war memories. The two became nicely combined on a September morning in 1961 when Edmund was a guest of Sassoon's at Heytesbury, in the company of Dennis Silk, who recalls:

Siegfried seldom left his bedroom before lunch and Edmund and I went for a walk in the Wylie valley. He thought the rolling downs much like Picardy and began to lay out his trench network: the command post here, the listening posts there and there; the communication trenches should follow that contour and must not be overlooked by that eminence across the valley. As I listened to him I stooped to pick up an enormous horse chestnut lying in the grass beside the lane. Edmund's quick eye discovered a distant Hereford bull across a neighbouring field. He became eager and excited: 'See if you can reach that bull with that chestnut.' Anxious to please my hero and very much on my mettle I wound up and hurled the chestnut. It landed between the bull's front legs and startled it a little.

'Excellent, excellent,' cried Edmund. 'Right into the bull's gloves'.[2]

As a player Edmund inherited some of the wicket-keeping skill of his paternal grandfather and the bowling finesse of his father, and throughout his playing career he continued his schoolboy habit of batting without gloves. Though he was never to be more than a competent player, he progressed from the Yalding Second eleven, and the Christ's Hospital first eleven, to play regularly for a variety of clubs. In his undergraduate days he had played for a team based on Garsington Manor (for whom he also played football) and when living in East Anglia he played for his villages – Stansfield and Cowlinge. His literary connections found him playing for Sassoon's team on the private ground of Heytesbury House (where Sassoon fielded on the boundary so that he could leave the field when bored) and he played for J. C. Squire's side the Invalids, of which he became president. Publishing connections provided invitations for a variety of cricket matches when publishers played authors, or authors played against the National Book League. In 1938 he played for Jonathan Cape against the Alden Press at Oxford, opening the batting with Rupert Hart-Davis. Reporting the match the *Tatler* recorded that 'Edmund Blunden knocked up a sparkling forty-six not out, and afterwards kept wicket with such proficiency that he only let three byes get past him.' After the Second World War he played regularly for the publisher Billy Collins, as well as taking part in more exotic matches such as a Keats – Shelley eleven versus Hampstead.

A series of matches were played between the Authors (whom Edmund usually captained) and the National Book League, first at the

Pearl Assurance Ground at New Malden and then at Vincent Square in Westminster (the National Book League usually being captained by Sydney Goldsack and later by Professor Jack Morpurgo), and also between the Authors and Publishers – usually at Marlow. The qualification for representing the authors was fairly elastic, but the players must have 'appeared in print'. This meant that 'authentic' writers such as the novelist Nigel Balchin, the historian, broadcaster and commentator Chester Wilmot and Edmund's old pupil the journalist Michael Davie could be joined by first-class cricketers such as I. A. R. Peebles, P. G. H. Fender and Douglas Jardine. On one occasion Peebles recalled that Edmund had put him on to bowl:

He allowed me to bowl a few laborious overs and I was pleased and grateful when a Publisher struck a gentle skier to mid-on where our leader had stationed himself. But regrettably the ball fell to earth on an unoccupied space, for, weighed down by the cares of captaincy, he had forgotten to change over with the rest of the field and so was still stationed roughly at old-fashioned point.[3]

A festival match, in which Edmund captained an 'All-Parnassus' team against the National Book League, was played in 1947, with C. B. Fry umpiring and Sir Pelham Warner as chairman of the selectors. Indeed, it was Edmund's proud boast that he had once captained a team containing four former Test captains. The authors' matches also brought him into contact with the cricket writer R. C. Robertson-Glasgow – the legendary 'Crusoe'. Edmund had been with him at the end of his playing career, and on his death recalled 'Dear Crusoe, joyously friendly and amusing. I thought he had said some private adieu to his own cricket career and I am glad that I took him to the nets in what may have been his last game.'[4]

When Edmund's friend and old pupil Hugh Carleton Greene joined the BBC in 1940, invitations arrived to join the BBC's team of Bushmen, but Edmund's longest and fondest association was with the Oxford side the Barnacles, based on Merton College and directed and captained by Robert Levens. Edmund played regularly for them from 1931 until the war (the period in which he was playing his best cricket) and intermittently afterwards. The Barnacles could boast a more than competent standard of cricket, and a most distinguished array of scholarly talent. Besides Edmund and Robert Levens, regular players included two Oxfordshire cricketers – Paul Grice (scholar of Merton, later Fellow of St John's Oxford, and Professor of Philosophy in California) and Jack Linnett (Fellow of Balliol and Queen's Colleges, FRS, later Master of Sidney Sussex College Cambridge and Vice-Chancellor of the university). These were joined by the Merton Chaplain Stephen Williams, Jack Thompson (later Fellow of Wadham), Donald Thompson (later headmaster of Chigwell School), Max Reese (later to become a Shakespearean scholar) and Edgar (Bill) Williams (later Fellow of Balliol and, as Sir Edgar Williams, Warden of Rhodes House). From the St John's fellowship came H. W. (Soccer) Thompson (who became Sir Harold Thompson, FRS, chairman of the Football Association); from the Queen's fellowship came Tony Woozley (later Professor of Philosophy at St Andrews and in America). Three more future knights were Barnacles – Denys Page (later Master of Jesus College Cambridge), Laurence Kirwan (later Director of the Royal Geographical Society) and Hugh Greene (later Director General of the BBC). There can have been few cricket clubs that could field four future knights, two fellows of the Royal Society and six professors, including two heads of Cambridge colleges. The home team would occasionally be augmented by visitors, Siegfried Sassoon and Hector Buck being Edmund's guests from time to time.

Described in Edmund's *Cricket Country*, thinly disguised as the Paladins, the Barnacles played on Oxfordshire and Berkshire village grounds during term time, but toured Sussex in the summer vacation – a tour which Edmund rarely missed – always playing a memorable game against Ditchling (where he once took three wickets for nought in one over) and also against Horsham – giving a chance for an annual visit to Christ's Hospital. He was also frequently called upon, in his Oxford days, to play for Colonel Wilkinson of Worcester College or J. C. Masterman of Christ Church – recalling in 1940 that 'scarcely a season has passed without my keeping wicket to J.C.'s windmill bowling.'[5] In one week in 1951 he captained the Authors, played for Colonel Wilkinson (batting with Jessop of Hampshire for one ball, before a declaration) and scored twenty-four for the Barnacles against Moulsford. Cricket was yet another time-consuming activity in an already overcrowded life.

Having been brought up on the boundaries of two counties his loyalties were somewhat divided and, though his first love remained Sussex, he followed the fortunes of Kent with almost equal interest – the names of L. E. G. Ames, B. H. Valentine, H. T. W. Hardinge and Colin Blythe occurring as often in conversation as those of M.W. and F. W. Tate, or George Cox, father and son. Two influential friendships were established, one from each county: Charles Marriott of Kent becoming a regular correspondent and visitor; C. B. Fry of Sussex becoming a keen encourager of Edmund's batting. Both Marriott and Fry acted as hosts to Edmund at Lord's, as did Edmund's literary agent A. D. Peters (who once invited Edmund to his private box to watch a day's cricket with Terence Rattigan) and Sir Pelham Warner. Edmund's account of the first day of the Second Test at Lords against Australia in 1930 (which Australia won by seven wickets, with Bradman scoring 254) appeared in the *Nation and Athenaeum* and records his delight in the skill of such players as Hobbs, Grimmett, Woolley, Hendren and, in particular, Duleepsinhji.

It was Kennington Oval, however, which was the stage for two particularly dramatic cricketing occasions. The first was the memorable Fifth Test against Australia in August 1938, when England declared at 903 for seven, with Hutton making 364. Edmund was present on the second day. As was so often his habit after memorable occasions, he recorded his impressions a few days later, on a scrap of paper:

The play opened, after about half an hour's delay through rain, with the England score at the unusual figure of over 300, one man out. Tall, slender young Hutton and well-filled Leyland (who had an injured thumb and shoulder) went on with their stand, and gave a perfect display of the dead-bat against O'Reilly's spin. It was necessary, for Hutton particularly haunted by fieldsmen squatting almost at his toes. Besides the wicket was not so horribly harmless as had been alleged, and more than one faster ball from O'Reilly or Waite flew up over the wicket keeper's head – and reach. Fleetwood-Smith had no luck, once, when he beat Leyland, but the ball jumped over the bails. The field on the off was packed with great judgment (and the expectation of a lifted shot from a not-quite half-volley), but the batsman would not be deceived. Four hundred went up and then Leyland, seeing that a fieldsman had let the ball slip away a yard or two, called a second run, hared along in recognition that he shouldn't have gone, and was run out (187). He turned shyly as he walked off, to say goodbye to a partnership of 382.

This brought Hammond in with lunch not far off, but he appeared indifferent to that point and slashed away at the expense, mainly, of Fleetwood-Smith. The brilliance of his beginning strangely disappeared after lunch when he refrained from his surprise strokes and, one thought, was not quite seeing the ball: no wonder, the light being poor all day and dismal at this stage. Runs were made, but with difficulty – the fielding being arranged to allow singles and little else; the outfield making boundaries none too easy except for sharp cuts and glides. O'Reilly maintained his bogey-man run and his variation of flight with his usual genius. Hutton finished every stroke, whether for runs or not, as before the eye of all cricket history. 500 up. But I was not altogether surprised when Hammond stopped a ball from Fleetwood-Smith with his pads, in uncertainty, and was out for fifty-nine. Then Paynter, looking awkward, did much the same to O'Reilly, and was out for nought; and, in the gloom and drizzle, Compton was bowled by Waite after a pleasant moment of practice. So, at five o'clock, England had 555 for five which made some of us remark on the possibility that in spite of Hutton the total might be under 600. The Australian gift for changing the position suddenly, and holding on to a new opportunity, is sufficiently familiar.

But Hutton was watching the ball still, in the ghostly light, scarcely giving even a chance for a faint l.b.w. appeal all day; and Hardstaff came in to imitate his complete control, and to add one or two fierce, elegant shots which might have passed a ring of fifty fieldsmen. Hutton moved at his own pace, though weary, into the 290's, where he had no pretence of doubting his ultimate arrival at 300. The batsmen exchanged a word as he approached that score; it was plain that when it came, they'd appeal against the light, and as soon as Hutton advanced the necessary single, they did – and the umpires agreed immediately. It was about 6.15 and the marvellous thing about the day was perhaps that the vast rain storms travelling over the ground had not prevented play altogether. The score was 634 for five, and Hardstaff had forty of them. For my part, Hardstaff's performance was as great an achievement as any of the others; and the next day of course he went on to 169 not out. He arrived at a very nervous moment and played with ease and foresight, now and then with a touch of splendour – but that showed how rarely even the Australian change bowlers gave anything away.  Fleetwood-Smith flung up a good many full tosses but not many of them looked safe to batter at. The scoring was reduced to a minimum by the placing and speed of the field; I saw some overs which would have produced a dozen runs against most fielding, and yet yielded nothing. Many of the finest shots were picked up at once, and to score it was almost necessary *not* to make these rapid strokes, but to push the ball gently. The running between the wickets was highly intelligent.

Hutton, since I last saw him, has acquired a flowing beautiful style, which may mean that in a short time he will become a fast-scoring as well as a wonderfully secure batsman. His body and bat were as one being. It is astonishing, and disturbing, that he and the others who in this innings fought it out with the world's most searching bowlers, and probably fastest fieldsmen, should have been discussed as if they had not quite behaved themselves: and as though the wicket was beyond any bowler's hope. It was very good, but the Australians themselves failed on it. And the light, as I have said, was much against the batsman on Monday. Hardstaff has been blamed for being slow on Tuesday, when raising the score to 903 for seven; Wood (whose game was to lash out) has been praised for his lively knock. But of the 106 put on by these two, Wood's share was fifty-three, and Hardstaff (not out at the end) also fifty-three. Let us suppose that had Mr McCormick been included in the Australian side, the wicket would have been much less perfect to the minds of the English censors: and perhaps our score would have been farther from the fabulous 1000 mark. But such batting as the team showed, such a concentration of judgment and accomplishment, won't occur very often: the Australians had it at Lord's a few years ago; this was England's turn. Why grumble? The Australians didn't. It now remains for Bradman to beat the score of 364 – or perhaps Brown can do it.

Similarly he recorded his impressions of the Fifth Test match against the Australians in August 1953, when England won by eight wickets thanks to the bowling of Bedser, Trueman, Lock and Laker:

So there we were, at Kennington Oval, ready to see the finish of the Test Match which should at least yield a victory to Australia or to England. It was all curiously lucky. A noble-minded friend had offered us not only tickets, but a choice of dates; and for some invisible reason we have preferred the fourth day, little guessing that it would be the intense last one. The morning was cool, the air not quite still but secretly astir, and I found my thoughts wandering away from London, to a carp-pond with a little stream bubbling into it from a mossy sluice. We were seated quite high in the pavilion stand. With their usual stumpy dignity, the two umpires walked forth to their places.

Then came the Australian team, with Hassett's cap and Morris's bright hair catching my eye; and then the two English batsmen. Hutton should have been one of them, but an odd error of his the evening before had deprived us of that great opener. Still, like two soldiers advancing on a special duty, Edrich and May appeared to know their austere way very plainly. It was easy for people to say that only ninety-four runs to win, and nine wickets in hand, gave England an almost complete security; but as you know, 'security is mortal's chiefest enemy'.[6]

Edrich was playing as though to continue the classical 1900 to 1910 school of batsmanship, and his tall partner was almost as correct . . . Even with these runs and these defences, I was sitting or hovering in some torment. Johnson had bowled a ball or two which popped up fantastically from the awkward length; and when Lindwall obtained a rest, it was Miller who was running up with the ball at the pavilion end. Miller, perhaps, in 1953, had grown somehow metaphysical over his cricket. He sometimes seemed to explore nature for a method which was never discovered before. But he is a sort of genius to make a dream on the cricket ground come true. He now sent up 'Miller's mixture', twisted cunningly and with quick palm and finger. The manner in which he turned to whip down, was delightful; 'the wind bloweth where it listeth'. And soon Miller had May out, but, to be sure, he owed it partly to the unexpected catch and the late trap; it was four runs? Another day perhaps, but now it was 'out'.

So May went away into the pavilion; a sad cricketer for a moment, but he had done well by any standard. But he, too, may have had it in mind that to the Australians this wicket's fall might be an inspiration. The distance to go was little more than forty runs, but these had to be actual. Compton came in, and the illustrious Middlesex partnership of so many matches was renewed. I did not count how many fielders stood around Compton's crease; it felt like the ghosts pressing round Aeneas, and presently Lindwall was firing away again. Edrich appeared, by now, to forecast and to order the events; and when the clock reached the lunch interval England had a hundred runs or so safely recorded.

Edmund's remarkable memory for detail enabled him to hold cricket statistics in his head, and he knew the full initials of most first-class players, past and present. It was this which often baffled his Japanese audiences, when they overheard conversations with visitors such as Richard Hughes of the *Sunday Times*, and the confusion is wittily described in the poem 'Cricket, I Confess'.[7] Among all the great names, two were pre-eminent for Edmund – Warwick Armstrong of Australia and W. R. Hammond of England. Of Armstrong he wrote:

He made a bat look like a tea-spoon, and the bowling weak tea; he turned it about idly, jovially, musingly. Still, he had but to wield the bat – a little wristwork – and the field paced after the ball in vain. It was almost too easy. W. W. Armstrong sat down while they fetched the ball. If I were to write a Dictionary of Cricket, I would enter in the Index: Armstrong, W. W., see Grace, W. G., and Grace, W. G., see Armstrong W. W.; and it might not be forgotten in the text that Armstrong could bowl – ever so easily, ever so amiably. . . .[8]

Hammond was eulogised in verse, attracting Edmund's highest accolade:

> *Not to have seen him leaves us unaware*
> *What cricket swiftness, judgment, foresight truly are.*[9]

While Edmund's association with the first-class game was mostly that of a spectator he did write two pieces for the Marylebone Cricket Club. In 1937, for the special MCC edition of *The Times* in honour of its 150th birthday, Edmund contributed an article on cricket books; for the MCC *Book for the Young Cricketer* fourteen years later he wrote a short essay on cricket and poetry. He was also invited to give one of the speeches at the pre-Test match dinner at Leeds in 1967, though ill-health prevented him attending. When Sassoon replaced[10] an early gift of a first edition of Nyren's *Young Cricketer's Tutor* with a similar copy signed by Cowden Clarke, Edmund felt that the book deserved a more exalted home and secretly presented it to the library at Lord's.

Considering all this, Edmund remained somewhat disappointed never to have been elected to membership of the MCC.

It seemed inevitable that he would eventually write a sustained piece on cricket and he received encouragement from two sources. One was his friend Milton Waldman, Assistant Editor of the *London Mercury*; the other was Claire Poynting (the Cordelia of the pages of *Cricket Country*), who had written to Edmund in verse:

> *Have you not ever felt the urge to write*
> *Of all the cricket that has blessed your sight?*
> *Is there no inspiration in the names*
> *Of those that play our best of summer games?. . .*
> *The summer evening sound of bat and ball*
> *Haunts through your verse – but is that to be all?*
> *You 'seek and serve a beauty that must die' –*
> *Must cricket's beauty then unwritten lie?*
> *Cricket should dare you take your pen and write*
> *'Worthy the reading and the world's delight.'*
> *Dare you among your writings leave but one*
> *Of this your 'worship in the summer sun'?* [11]

From these promptings came *Cricket Country*, published in 1944, which quickly sold 25,000 copies and kept its popularity for many years. It is an unusual cricket book, donnish in its approach. Edmund includes a section on painters of cricket scenes, and suggests a team of cricketing poets including Cowper, Crabbe, Byron, Keats, Bridges, Conan Doyle and Sassoon, with Francis Thompson umpiring, Gerard Manley Hopkins scoring, and Leigh Hunt and Mary Russell Mitford among the supporters. He revels in the names of crickets clubs, finding them a pastoral poem in their own right:

The I Zingari, Free Foresters, Blue Mantles, the Band of Brothers, the Invalids, the Hampshire Hogs, the Devon Dumplings, Harlequins, Authentics, Barnacles, Perambulators, Incogniti, Wanderers, Yellowhammers, Grasshoppers, Quidnuncs, Sussex Martlets, Somerset Stragglers, Derbyshire Friars, Brighton Brunswick, Thespids, Stoics, Cryptics, Cyphers, Nondescripts.

At the heart of *Cricket Country* is the English village and its cricket team, for they were extensions of the simple life. In the sophisticated pavilions of Hong Kong he would often 'sigh for the simpler wooden hut and The Mothers' Union bringing tea'.[12] Edmund had already painted this scene in 'An Ancient Holiday' in *The Face of England*, and in *Cricket Country* the text comes alive when the 'unofficial' game is being celebrated – the game he knew from Yalding, 'for in our village

and our county the game was so native, so constant, so beloved
without fuss that it came to me as the air I breathed and the morning
and evening.[13] While the great have their praise, it is the unnamed
who are the real heroes, of the book (as they had been in *Undertones of
War*) and in particular 'the ever unsuccessful player' who 'comes up
afresh for execution, Wednesdays and Saturdays':

The happiest face I ever saw on a cricket ground, the happiest exclamation I
ever heard there, belong to a still more distant day of sunshine. Then also my
post was behind the stumps, and then also the last batsman (he was about to
join the Army for the old war) came to the crease in faultless flannels but
without any hope. However, he immediately cracked a yorker served up to
him away into the country, and was about to run, but I said, 'Don't bother –
Boundary.' He smiled like a new sun and cried out, 'Good Egg!' He repeated
the feat, and that, I think was all, but it was enough. The expression which
he used has ceased to be heard, so far as I have noticed, but to me it will
remain the gladdest of all glad phrases – 'Good Egg! – Jolly Good Egg', the
only word for that supreme moment. . . .
   I have known cricketers who, as far as my observation went, practically
never scored a run, nor were called on to bowl, nor took much part in the
rest of the proceedings; and yet they were always present, always eager.[14]

In an undated memorandum Edmund tried to define the attraction of
the game, and he asked:

What, then, is the secret of its unique magnetism? It is no new question, and
all the oracles have failed to give the conclusive answer. The aspects are too
many for that. The main one is surely the beauty which, in general, belongs
to the king of games; for his season is Summer, his arena is an expanse of
green, his men go in their shifting design upon that greensward in white. . . .
Upon this scene the action is itself beautiful, if the athletic brilliance and
fluency of the human body is ever so. . . . This is the outward show of
cricket; and to this it adds an intellectual exercise. I have known those who as
spectators of grand matches, pursuing with all their minds the moves and the
occurrences 'in the middle', have left the ground almost as weary as if they
had been playing the whole match. Such mental fascination is bound to result
in literature one day. The game is a contest of a number of abilities and
possibilities. It is a science, it is a wheel of fortune, and a drama of personalities and intentions. No warriors in the clouds fight a more distinctly
innocent war than the cricket teams and their anxious partisans; the action is
real enough – but what is this reality, where victory is as gentle as the western
sunbeam on the weathercock at the close of play? It is all a poem, a vision, a
philosophy.[15]

# PART SEVEN
## 1945 – 1950

# 22
# The *Times*
# *Literary Supplement*
## May 1945 – December 1947

*I shall never lose Claire now. . . . I love quite a few and some I shall never see again: but I would live with Claire for a thousand reasons, and one is that she is my home.*

Diary, January 1942

> *There was a hope – but I have forgotten,*
> *For now is hope fulfilled;*
> *And, watching your bright brow this moment,*
> *I have no house to build.*

'Fulfilment',1944[1]

In June 1945 the rather cramped offices of the *Times Literary Supplement* in Printing House Square became Edmund's second home and on 7 July, twenty-four years after his first review, he composed his 340th contribution – a figure which was to rise to over 600 during the next two and a half years. Offprints record subjects varying from Thackeray to Harriet Shelley, from Milton to the literary forgeries of T. J. Wise. Edmund was pleased to be able to claim association with every editor since the paper's foundation – Bruce Richmond having handed over to D. L. Murray, who was in turn succeeded by Stanley Morison – and he was now to enjoy the friendship of two later editors, Alan Pryce-Jones and Arthur Crook. His greatest pleasure, however, was to find himself sharing not just an office but a double-sided desk with Philip Tomlinson. Together they composed their weekly leading articles and reviews, punctuating their writing with lunchtime visits to the Baynard Castle and evening calls at the Temple Bar, where the regular company included J. B. Priestley, J. C. Squire, J. B. Morton and John Betjeman. Vigorous consumption of beer one lunchtime resulted in Tomlinson's falling across the office table, his hands sliding outstretched so that his hair covered the central inkwell. Edmund, anxious not to disturb his partner, gently divided the strands of hair without waking their owner, and quietly dipped his nib into the inkwell between the parted locks.

On Claire's leaving the army in July 1945 she and Edmund took a flat in Earl's Court Square, where life became – by Edmund's standards – considerably more relaxed. Lecturing demands were reduced to monthly engagements, and writing deadlines became less insistent, with introductions to editions of Sterne's *A Sentimental Journey* and *The Life of George Crabbe by His Son*, an essay on 'Elegant Extracts' for a *Festschrift* in honour of David Nichol Smith's seventieth birthday, a tribute to George Gordon of Magdalen College Oxford, together with a short pamphlet for the Council for the Church and Countryside being comfortably fitted around his Shelley researches over an eighteen-month period. Visitors became fewer too, but there was to be no such respite from correspondence, which continued to receive a prompt and generous response. When Michael Meyer wrote to request a reading-list for a projected thesis on the minor nineteenth-century writer Edward Thurlow, he might have expected a few lines of encouragement and half-a-dozen suggestions; instead he received a list of over forty possible references (with most of them dated, from memory) which typically ended with an apology for sending only rough notes and guesses because 'my books are almost all away' and 'I have no exact list at hand.'[2]

Within twelve months, Edmund and Claire moved out of London to a rented house in Virginia Water. When the dustman informed them that he wanted to sell his house a little further down the road, Edmund agreed on the spot to buy it for a thousand pounds and thus provide a small family home for Claire and for their daughter, who had been born just before the move. She was named Margaret, as Edmund and Claire had planned since 1940, but joy at her birth was inevitably intermingled with painful memories of Joy's death:

> *My darling, what a power is yours*
> *To make me weep, after such years;*
> *For twenty-seven years at least*
> *Are gone since your brief coming ceased, –*

> *And still you force my hopeless tears*
> *And still your fate dwarfs all my wars.* [3]

Remembering the parting look of bewilderment in Joy's eyes he begged that she would:

> *Look not thus ever, tiny wretch,*
> *Dear child of long ago; we bring*
> *A second self with whom your span*
> *May round, with Margaret now you can*
> *Make fun of things, feed, call and sing,*
> *Tease, tantalize, adore, bewitch.* [4]

Coincidences continued to obsess him. He noted that Margaret's birthday was the anniversary of Shelley's expulsion from Oxford, but there was another local connection which was to lead to a striking and unnerving experience. For a few troubled months in 1813 Shelley had lived at Bracknell in a large Georgian house called High Elms. Edmund, eager as always to visit places with literary associations, went there one summer afternoon with Claire. The house had become a furniture store and stood in substantial but overgrown grounds. As they walked through the French windows into the tangled garden, they recalled Shelley's unhappiness in the house and sensed an atmosphere of oppression and distress enveloping them, coupled with a vivid ghostly aura. For Edmund it was a common enough experience, for he had felt the presence of Clare when working on the Peterborough manuscripts and had been aware of the figure of Hardy in his Merton rooms when he was writing his study of him – a sensation described in 'Thoughts of Thomas Hardy'.[5] At Bracknell it was a shared experience for both he and Claire were suddenly aware that they were being watched and were then pursued noisily and aggressively down an alley of hazels. They turned and scrambled up a high bank to escape, before nervously looking back over an entirely deserted garden:

> *Not but some shadow of despair*
> *In this dark purple ominous*
> *From that high summer beckons us;*
> *And such a shadow, such a doom*
> *Was lurking in the garden there.*
> *We could not name the incubus,*
> *Save that it haunted Shelley's home.* [6]

It was a typical example of that poetic sensibility which can invest the passing moment with a timeless quality. The point at which:

# PART SEVEN    1945 – 1950

*quiet place and day*
*Disclose for a flash the boundless, timeless play.* [7]

The importance of place in a writer's life had always fascinated Edmund, and the influence of Sussex on Shelley's development was to be stressed in his life of the poet which appeared in the spring of 1946. Tracing his childhood from Field Place to Eton, he also emphasised the significance of Shelley's classical education and the breadth of his reading – Spenser, Elizabethan drama, Milton, Gray, Chatterton, Wordsworth and Coleridge in poetry; history, travel, Bacon and the Bible in prose. He painted Shelley as a figure of the Age of Romance, surrounded by visionary poetry, thrilling fiction, projects for reform, scientific passion, flourishing music and fine art, and all the bewildering influences of a revolutionary world. It was a sympathetic and vivid portrait of a lively and independent mind and it became Edmund's most popular biographical work (being warmly reviewed by Humphry House) and included some of his finest prose in the description of the deaths and funeral rites of both Shelley and Edward Williams.

In many ways 1946 had been Edmund's happiest year and it was fitting that it should end with a memorable celebration for his fiftieth birthday on 1 November. After a BBC broadcast in Edmund's honour (instigated by Roy Campbell) had been cancelled, he was free to accept an invitation to the private dining room of the Garrick Club as the guest of seven literary friends – T. S. Eliot, Walter de la Mare, Cecil Day-Lewis, William Plomer, Rupert Hart-Davis, Philip Tomlinson and Stanley Morison, Sassoon being unable to attend. Seated around a candle-lit circular table, in front of a blazing fire, surrounded by paintings by Zoffany on the walls, they enjoyed a six-course dinner with burgundy from Sassoon's Heytesbury cellars to accompany roast pheasant. After the meal Rupert Hart-Davis proposed a toast to 'Edmund Blunden and his modest shining genius',[8] and read a poem of Sassoon's written for the occasion. Before a similar poetic tribute was read by William Plomer, Cecil Day-Lewis stood to read his birthday poem, referring to Edmund as:

> *One who was never at home with*
> *Pomp or pretentiousness.*
> *Here is a loving-cup made from verse,*
> *For verse is your favourite of metals.* [9]

The celebration was both a moving personal tribute to Edmund and a vivid picture of his literary stance – happy to share the company of old and young, caught between the modern and the traditional: sitting, as he was, between Eliot and de la Mare, flanked by Day-Lewis and Plomer. It was an evening which he always remembered with pride and in a letter of thanks to Rupert Hart-Davis for 'a golden evening' he promised that 'I shall be talking of it even more than of the Battle of the Somme, the innings of 224 by R. H. Spooner, the pike I hooked on a sullen winter afternoon at Cheveney and the greatness of Colonel Harrison.'[10]

One dark shadow, however, was falling across his life. While he was enjoying the happiness of a new marriage, Sassoon was suffering the bitterness of a disintegrating relationship – and in 1945 Hester moved into her family home in Winterbourne near Salisbury. Edmund's visits to her became a source of considerable irritation to Sassoon, despite Edmund's reassurances that his own marital experiences prevented him from taking sides or listening to malicious gossip, and he reminded Sassoon of the neutral position which he had adopted over Edmund's arguments with Mary. In July 1947 Edmund wrote to Heytesbury regretting that Sassoon seemed 'disinclined to see'[11] him – a situation which he reluctantly accepted with patience in deference to Sassoon's ill-health and low spirits. Sassoon promptly replied (to 'Dearest Edmund') that such a breach was impossible after 'twenty-seven years of flawless friendship'[12] but he felt that Edmund considered his attitude to Hester to be unreasonable. The rift grew greater over the next months with Edmund sadly watching what he saw as Sassoon's 'egotism defeating his invention and imagination'.[13] For nearly three years correspondence between them was halted and invitations ceased; it was an estrangement which Edmund felt particularly deeply.

The quieter months which Edmund had been enjoying since May 1945 were inevitably to be only a brief lull, for demands to play a more public role soon sought him out. He had been tempted by an invitation to take up a professorship in China or Korea – and even more by a similar approach from Paul Engle in Iowa – though his obligation to the *Times Literary Supplement* prevented acceptance of any of them. But more insistent calls were making themselves heard. Paradoxically, his refusal to hate his enemies – the very characteristic which had brought his patriotism into doubt in war – was now counted an essential ingredient in the waging of peace. He found himself a guest at a Buckingham Palace garden party in July 1946, with a second invitation arriving in the following year, and he was then summoned to the Foreign Office. He was informed that a United Kingdom liaison mission was to be sent to Japan and that he was invited to become a member. The recommendation had come from a combination of those familiar with the Japanese literary and academic circles such as Vere Redman – who was to be the mission's counsellor – and experienced diplomats such as the Ambassador to Japan, Sir Alvary Gascoigne, and a future ambassador John Pilcher. They were all acutely aware of Edmund's special position in Japan and convinced the Foreign Office that he was the ideal person to take on the work of cultural adviser. He promptly accepted the post, having gained generous leave of absence from the *Times Literary Supplement*. Events had transformed Edmund from a suspected traitor into an ambassador for his country; the irony was not lost on him.

It was a prospect which excited and pleased him, particularly since he was able to take his family with him, and he was impatient to begin a work of reconciliation which he felt especially fitted to achieve. It confirmed the encouragement received from a visit to Printing House Square in 1945 from a tall young man, Lewis Bush. After teaching in Japan before the war, and then being taken prisoner by the Japanese, Bush was to return to Japan in 1947 to become a prominent broadcaster and journalist. He quickly became a firm friend of the Blunden family and acted as Edmund's literary agent in Japan. His message to Edmund in Ward's Irish House in Fleet Street in 1945 was simple: 'You must go back to Japan. They, and we, will need you more than ever in the days to come.'[14]

The idea that literature could heal wounds which politics could not was a notion which Edmund now believed more strongly than ever. After the bombing of Hiroshima and Nagasaki in August 1945, he confided to his brother Lance:

I am more convinced that the overwhelming of Japan in this manner (for it is now generally admitted that they were hardly able to hold out three months, *without* Atom bombs) will have strengthened the feelings of all the Orient from Persia onward that the Western Civilisation is *the* barbarism. . . . So any of us who can help at all in reviving the message of men like Shelley and Henry Vaughan should not miss any opening.[15]

Edmund saw his Japanese mission as just such an opening.

One person who was likely to be less enthusiastic about the project was Aki Hayashi, now to find herself alone in London while Edmund returned to Japan. She must have looked back with some sadness to her arrival in England twenty years before.

The last few months of 1947 were spent in official briefings interspersed with pleasant social occasions – an introduction from Rosalie Mander to Shelley's direct descendant Sir John Shelley-Rolls which

21  Edward Blunden, 1929

22 (ABOVE)
Coleridge 'A' House
Cricket Team, Christ's
Hospital, 1915.
EB, captain, is centre.
On his right are
A. R. Creese and
C. L. Fox. Front left
is Hector Buck

23 (LEFT)
Edmund Blunden
walking out to open
the batting, with
Rupert Hart-Davis,
for Jonathan Cape
versus the Alden
Press, Oxford, 1938.
In deference to EB,
Hart-Davis also
declined to wear
batting gloves

24 (ABOVE) The Barnacles *v.* Ditchling, 1939 (back row, third and fifth from left: F. P. Grice and J. W. Linnett; seventh from right, A. D. Woozley; front row, first, third and fifth from left: Rev. C. S. C. Williams, Edgar ('Bill') Williams and Robert Levens; second, fourth and fifth from right: EB, J. N. C. Thompson and the Ditchling captain, Kenning)

25 Edmund at the crease, Marlow, *c.* 1940

26 Edmund Blunden listening to a test match with Siegfried Sassoon and Dennis Silk, Heytesbury, *c.* 1961

27 (LEFT)
Edmund Blunden in
Tokyo, *c.* 1947

28 (BELOW)
Bronze monument
to Edmund Blunden,
Central Library,
Hiroshima

29 (RIGHT) Edmund Blunden
being greeted by Chou En-Lai,
Peking, 1955

30 (BELOW) Edmund Blunden's
Hong Kong study, drawn by
Lo King Man

The Study.

31 Edmund Blunden and Claire
with Margaret, Frances, Lucy and
Catherine, October 1956

32 (RIGHT)
Edmund Blunden,
drawn by Joy Finzi,
1952

33 (BELOW)
Edmund Blunden
with Richard Burton
and Robert Levens at
a celebratory party
at the Victoria Arms,
Oxford,
after his election
as Professor of
Poetry, 1966

34 (ABOVE) Edmund
Blunden on a visit
to Oxford as
Professor of Poetry,
c. 1967

35 (LEFT) Edmund
Blunden at the
double wedding of
his daughters,
Lucy and Frances,
summer 1971; the
last picture

resulted in lively conversation and inspection of Shelley relics; a dinner at the Waldorf in honour of Philip Tomlinson. More important
was a friendship which developed after Edmund had been commissioned to write an Ode for St Cecilia's Day to celebrate the festival of
the patron saint of music at the Albert Hall on 22 November 1947, for
his musical collaborator was the composer Gerald Finzi.

By 1947 Finzi was established as one of the most sensitive English
songwriters, particularly when setting English pastoral poetry. Edmund
was somewhat perplexed by the problems of composing words for a
musical setting on the grand scale of oratorio, but his rhetorical ode
needed little revision to make it suitable for choral ensemble. Its first
performance was to be given three weeks after Edmund had set sail for
Tokyo and he was to wait until November 1950 for a repeat performance. It was not a memorable occasion; the appalling acoustics of the
Albert Hall meant that Edmund hardly heard a word of it. But more
important than the music was the friendship formed with Gerald and
his wife Joy. Frequent visits were made to their beautiful Berkshire
home at Ashmandsworth on the Newbury Downs, where Edmund
delighted equally in Gerald's fine library[16] and his preservation of rare
fruits – especially unusual strains of apples – in his spacious garden. Joy
was an accomplished portrait-artist and her skill was to be shown in
three fine drawings of Edmund's head,[17] her penetrating perception
highlighting the story to be told in his expressive eyes – the reason,
presumably, why he was to be drawn or painted by at least seven
artists. Finzi was to add Edmund's poem 'Harvest' to his setting of 'To
Joy', both to be included in the song cycle *Oh Fair To See*, and further
literary and musical collaborations were to be enjoyed after Edmund's
return from Japan.

On 6 November 1947 Edmund, Claire and Margaret boarded the
SS *Strathnaver* bound for Yokohama via Algiers, the Suez Canal,
Colombo, Singapore and Hong Kong. On his first journey to Japan,
Edmund had read Cowper's poetry; on this voyage he read his letters.
Deciding to concentrate on prose he also chose the work of Chaucer,
Sir Thomas Browne, Milton, Boswell, Coleridge, Shelley and Dick-
ens. From his classical shelves he selected Aeschylus – savouring his
writing on the sea – and Ovid, whose poetry he found particularly
refreshing – 'how striking his contrasts within a few syllables! His
verses are like the leafy and fruitful branches in a gentle breeze!'[18]

Five weeks later he was taking the train from the harbour at Kure
to Tokyo and, looking at the familiar scenery, he felt a quiet confid-

ence about the task ahead of him as he made his diary entry for 16 December:

Where do mountain and plain form such alliance of minute and patient cultivation? . . . what I formerly felt of the diligence and wisdom of rural Japan is increased now. These are the true patriots, tilling every foot of their inheritance and finding places also for the chrysanthemums and the flowering evergreen by their doorstep. What millions of daikon roots are now hung beneath their eaves. . . . I am coming back to Japan after twenty years which divide me from the youth I possessed. . . . Many imaginings of the meetings with old friends here who have equally undergone that change fly through my mind as the train flies through the misty night. At least I assure myself that they will rejoice to see me come with my Claire and Margaret.

# 23

# Japan

## December 1947 – May 1950

*It has often been said that the greatest merits of the
occupation period in Japan were the dispatch of General
MacArthur from the United States and Professor
Blunden from the United Kingdom. True it was. I
could be a living witness for it any time . . . because I
have been so lucky as to . . . learn that true
humanity . . . was a straight way to bring heart to heart
relations beyond racial and rational boundaries.*
Mikio Hiramatsu, Edmund Blunden: *A Tribute from Japan, 1974*

> *And so we walk, and beauty reigns once more,
> Beauty not quarrelling over East and West.*
> 'Japan Beautiful',1953[1]

Edmund always knew that his second Japanese visit was going to be a
success; how much of a success he could scarcely have foreseen.
Immediately on arrival he embarked on a kind of royal progress
through the country from Asahigawa in the north of Hokkaido to
Kogoshima in the south of Kyushu, when everywhere enthusiastic
audiences (mostly students) packed in their hundreds – on at least one
occasion in their thousands – into university lecture theatre, school
assembly hall, civic building or Buddhist temple, to hear him talk on a
variety of literary subjects. He found them eager to discover western
culture and hungry for intellectual stimulation; he saw his own role as
a cross between Aristotle and Matthew Arnold. His original year's
contract was quickly extended to eighteen months, which was in turn
extended to twenty-four months, requiring him to repeat his cir-

cuitous travels, by the end of which he had delivered in excess of 600 lectures: an astonishing average of five a week if spread uninterrupted over 120 consecutive weeks. Though some were repeated, a majority were prepared or adapted for specific occasions, with more than a hundred being written out in longhand – often in the early-morning hours – to form a collection which was published as textbooks for Japanese students in the universities of Keio (*Favourite Studies in English Literature*), Waseda (*Influential Books*), Hosei (*Sons of Light*), Kyoto (*Poetry and Science*), together with Tokyo Woman's Christian College (*Some Women Writers*) and Tokyo University (*Addresses on General Subjects*, followed by *Chaucer to 'B.V.'* and *Shakespeare to Hardy* – the last being reprinted fourteen times between 1948 and 1970). Although they were intended as simple introductory talks for those who were non-fluent English speakers (Edmund described them as 'woolly homilies') their construction took as much time as more advanced lectures and they needed to be delivered with particular care. As translation was frequently required they often lasted two hours.

Such a schedule required both sensitivity and stamina, two qualities which Edmund was able to provide in remarkable quantities. In 1924 he had shown considerable compassion for the victims of an earthquake which had shattered social and academic life in Tokyo; now he showed the same imaginative sympathy for the victims of a political, economic and cultural earthquake which – particularly after the devastating events at Hiroshima and Nagasaki – had shattered every section of Japanese life. Wherever he went he received an enthusiastic welcome from friends made twenty years earlier. Some were old colleagues – Kochi Doi now in Sendai and Haruji Ogura and Sanki Ichikawa in Tokyo; others were former pupils – Eishiro Hori and Tamotsu Sone, who had both had their libraries destroyed in air-raids, which had also claimed the lives of Hori's wife and daughter; Tomoji Abe was now a respected novelist, Torao Uyeda was directing the influential academic publishing house of Kenkyusha, and Yoshitaka Sakai was established as a university teacher in Tokyo. The pattern was repeated throughout his travels where former pupils were mayors of cities, headmasters of schools or professors of English, and regular visits were made to the lively Yukichi Nakamura at the city library in Osaka. Many contacts were formed within the universities in Tokyo – notably with Saito's son-in-law Masao Hirai – but most pleasing of all was a reunion with Takeshi Saito himself (his library had miraculously survived the war), who was now the leading figure in Japanese English studies. For several months after Edmund's arrival,

Saito would privately take him on one side and apologise for Japanese actions in the war – proof, if any were needed, of Edmund's particular suitability as a healer of wounds.

Throughout their stay Claire and Edmund lived within the compound of the British Embassy, where they enjoyed the support and relaxing friendship of the families of Alvary Gascoigne, who was to introduce Edmund to General MacArthur, and of Vere Redman, a genial and rather Churchillian figure, responsible for Edmund's schedule. Life may have seemed hectic in Oxford days but the pace was even more demanding in Tokyo. The doorbell and telephone brought hourly requests from aspiring poets and writers wanting help with publishing or translation, from compilers of textbooks and dictionaries, from journalists seeking interviews, editors commissioning articles or students enquiring after opportunities for scholarships to study in Britain. All received a patient hearing. Edmund was also having to play the role of a public figure, attending receptions or dinners as the guest of the official welcoming party for official guests such as Prince and Princess Ri of Korea, and he established easy relations with the Japanese royal family, spending some time with the young Crown Prince Akahito. There was inevitably some jealousy and suspicion among the ranks of professional diplomats over Edmund's exalted position in the eyes of the Japanese, for expressions of respect and affection were very open. At virtually every function, grand or informal, he was besieged by those who thrust forward a book to be inscribed, a card to be signed or a *shikishi* (a piece of special thick paper) on which Edmund was expected to compose a few extempore lines appropriate to the owner. Some formed part of *Records of Friendship* (1950) commemorating a visit to Kyushu and in 1967 Takeshi Saito traced a further seventy, privately published as *Poems on Japan*, but these pieces were almost certainly far from being an exhaustive collection. Being thrown into this kind of public arena was not to Edmund's taste and was accepted in part because he knew that the anonymity of his *Times Literary Supplement* desk was waiting for him in London. Suggestions from his friends in England that his name was being mentioned as a likely successor to the Poet Laureate thus filled him with 'deep alarm'.[2]

Japanese life was a series of contrasts; constant reminders of the past jostled with hopes for the future. Depressing stretches of ruin in the cities were balanced against the beauty of the Japanese landscape and its striking views of lake and mountain. These seemed to Edmund to be reflections of the contrasts of sentimentality and aloofness within the Japanese character and he noted that 'the Japanese poet is as sensitive as the Japanese war-monger is loud, and he writes with the shyness of a passing breeze.'[3] He was aware too of the contradictions he had noted twenty years earlier, as he observed in a letter to Philip Tomlinson:

If only these attentive and beauty-loving Japanese understood cricket! I am a little tired of the endless 'we Japanese' attitude: they mostly turn every subject round until once more the world is all Japanese if all had their rights – and yet I do not know whether this is not an American weakness also. The extraordinary culture of the Englishman, when he is cultured at all, comes out more the more I live away. I, for my own part, am ashamed of my rawness and dullness in his company. . . . is it a merely psychological necessity that a people like the Japanese should forever be muddling round in the hopes of painting Japan as a mystical supremacy? They are up against it there! The country is glorious, but by comparison with England and France it is unvaried. They have Fine Arts, but not creative powers. They have ingenious minds, but not reflective: i.e. they copy all that the Western world has given, or rather what they see is useful, but they never really comprehend that the Western world gives as well as bargains. I am not disgruntled, for the personal life here is exceedingly gentle and honest; but I am surprised to find my impressions of a rather primitive society, dated 1926 say, still obtaining. Yet, if that were not so, my function would not flourish. The audiences which sit through my lectures and demand that they should be long lectures, are there because they know I am an old friend of Japan. All agree that their regard for friendship is beyond praise. A man like Takeshi Saito knows all that I have said.[4]

Edmund's own life fluctuated between extremes too, with intense periods of lecturing interspersed with quieter moments of relative rest. Travelling remained frequent and exhausting: within ten weeks of arriving in Japan, he was in Hong Kong giving a series of lectures and staying as the guest of the Governor; on his return to Japan he was soon in Kyoto, giving thirty lectures in a fortnight. In something like despair he exclaimed to Lance: 'Life is lately one infernal scramble . . . but I have three goldfish here, given to Margaret, who remind me that we all live endlessly hurrying around a small prison and emitting bubbles.'[5] He found the round of social activity exhausting too – 'all these silly parties, with their savage din and senseless dialoguing'[6] – though he was intrigued to meet, at an Embassy lunch, the colourful Mrs Morrow Tait who, together with Mr Townsend of Cambridge University, was flying round the world in a single-engined wooden plane: 'She is a young woman with a torrent of fiery hair and considerable candour, and I should have liked to call D. G. Rossetti's attention to her for he has painted her without knowing it; but I suspect she would not identify the name of D.G.R.'[7]

Two Tokyo venues provided opportunities for fulfilling his duties in more relaxed circumstances. On his retirement from Tokyo University, Takeshi Saito had become President of the Tokyo Christian Woman's College – Tokyo Joshi Daigaku – and here Edmund became a regular visitor, composing a college song and enjoying the peace of the spacious grounds. On later Japanese visits he was to stay in the comfort of the college's Reischauer House. Just outside Tokyo was the beautifully situated Jiyu Gakuen (literally, School of Liberty) founded by the remarkable Mrs Motoko Hani in 1921 as a Christian secondary school for girls. It quickly developed into an entirely self-supporting community, the pupils sharing the duties of management – including cooking, book-keeping and budgeting; there were no servants. Over the next forty years it was to become fully co-educational and take pupils from primary school age to university level, while still retaining its original ideals. Its graceful setting and unique atmosphere of calm co-operation became a favourite retreat for Edmund. He had first visited the school in 1924; two days after his arrival in Japan in 1947 he returned. He was to give several talks to the students and become a regular and welcome visitor – the affection of the school being shown on a visit in 1963 under the principalship of the founder's daughter Miss Keiko Hani. Edmund took Francis Bacon's phrase, '*Abeunt Studia in Mores*' (Education becomes real life) as the theme of his talk to the young lady graduates, and wrote the words in chalk on a blackboard. They were never erased – and twenty years later the blackboard remained untouched; Edmund's handwriting treasured for future generations.

Within the Embassy grounds he could also find relaxation, taking an evening walk with his dogs Pippa and Tessa by the moat which surrounded the compound. His sad account of Tessa's death in his diary entry for Good Friday 1949 suggests that he might have neglected his potential as a novelist:

This day, with spring sunshine and blue skies and blossoms opening all round us, our charming little dog Tessa was killed. I was working in my study and was getting quite interested in the biography of Mrs Siddons and Edmund Kean, when poor Claire came in – and in a low voice told me that Tessa had had an accident and was dead.

Her body was on the couch in the front room. She was still warm, and I half thought she was alive. No mark; no blood; her tongue just a little

279

protruded, her eyes closed ('in endless night' poor dear). Just Tessa, as she has been – but dead.

She had gone for a walk with Claire and Madeline Redman and Madeline's dogs Bella and Ondine – and all crossed the road somewhere but Tessa saw another dog and turned back . . . and a car ran over her. Then she got back to the pavement (how?) and suddenly barked as if in trouble, and almost instantly died. The girls brought her home in their arms. Ondine tried to arouse her, but Bella seems to have known what the truth was.

The story of Tessa is that the Goodmans found her in the street and gave her a home and then Mrs Goodman offered her to us and we took her in, only in December last. She soon adopted us and was happy and played with everyone old and young. She insisted on sharing our bedroom and my study, and I can hardly work without her sleeping assistance there on the grey sofa while I dip my pen into the ink here. She was young and a little jealous. . . . Not many days ago Margaret brought in a new green leaf from the creeper on the terrace. Claire was soon waited on by Tessa, who was offering another leaf for her part.

All the household came to say goodbye to this little dog as she lay on the study sofa, then the Cook-san and the boy E-chan dug her grave in the corner of the garden where she often met the other dogs of the Embassy, and Claire meanwhile sewed her into her shroud of sacking. Claire at last carried her forth and with Hatsue-san and Keiko-san buried her and planted flowers on the grave and placed a stone on it.

And so all at once this member of our household is gone for ever.

The smaller animal world was catching his attention too for he was becoming increasingly interested in insect life, noting that 'the closer I watch the insects, especially when they are in a bit of trouble, the more I think *individual* life is everywhere,'[8] and complaining that 'the Americans seem resolved on draining the moat. I found that this is what they are doing in a democratic manner in this country, which is not theirs. I should like to join a Mosquito Protection Society.'[9]

Outside Tokyo his most pleasurable escapes were to Hokkaido with Saito, to Kyushu with the two-year-old Margaret as a travelling companion, or to Saito's cottage in the cool hills at Karuizama. It was here that he had first met Aki Hayashi; now he took Claire and the family – which had grown in May 1948 with the birth of Lucy, to be joined a year later by Frances. For Edmund, though, rest rarely meant inactivity, and his retreats to Karuizama were almost exclusively dedicated to writing. His lecturing commitments prevented him from sending more than half-a-dozen articles to the *Times Literary Supplement* but he contributed a monthly piece for Japanese journals, usually *Studies in English Literature* or the *Rising Generation* – under the influential editorship of Professor Rintaro Fukuhara. Also for Japanese readership he compiled a collection of verse and prose on Japanese topics published as *A Wanderer in Japan* and an edition of Shelley's *Defence of Poetry*. For the British Council he compiled a pamphlet on John Keats – and he was to add *Charles Lamb* to the series in 1954 and *War Poets 1914–18* in 1958. His main preoccupation, however, was struggling with his volume of *The Oxford History of English Literature* (it was not dubbed 'O HELL!' for nothing), finding it almost impossible to strike a balance between narrative and factual information; he felt almost certain that his efforts would not be acceptable to the editors, and this indeed proved to be true. More satisfying was the planning of a biography of Coleridge (a project which was never completed), a weekly request for references being sent to Aki Hayashi at the British Museum. He was also able to include news of her family, and he tried to arrange for her to receive John Clare's magnifying glass (which had been given to Edmund by Sam Sefton) to help her failing eyesight. He was not neglecting his poetry either, and in August 1948 he sent Macmillan a collection of nearly fifty poems to be published as *After the Bombing* a year later, dedicated to his literary agent A. D. Peters – who had represented him for twenty years, with the friendly assistance of Margaret Stephens and Michael Sissons. While some complained of outdated vocabulary in the collection, others noted a change of direction and pointed to a more contemplative, questioning, metaphysical tone. Edmund had subtitled the volume *and Other Short Poems* and the two shortest, elegies on a hedgehog and a snail, are as understated yet keenly observed as any previous poems. The vocabulary too, especially in 'The Snail', is distinctly contemporary:

> Under the bus wheel comes the tiny snail
> With all the touch of exquisite accord
> Which drew it through the showery world, with all
> The accomplished painting of that rounded shard.
> A child's eye drooped, so gleamed the ring-bright shell,
> And then the time was up, the thing occurred:
> Softly the huge car stopped, with a wheel as still
> As that slain mystery, hardly discernible.

By early 1950 Edmund felt that the call of England and his commitment to the *Times Literary Supplement* could be ignored no longer. The Foreign Office were reluctant to lose him but realising that he could not accept a further extension to his contract they approached the poet and scholar G. S. Fraser, who agreed to take the appointment and spent a month with Edmund and Claire to acclimatise himself.

As Edmund prepared to leave he could look back over an outstanding period in which he had, for a second time, touched the hearts of
the Japanese in an extraordinary way. He was to continue to write for
Japanese journals and to contribute to *Festschriften* for the next fifteen
years, and was to make five further visits between 1955 and 1965.
Often on these occasions his old friend from Keio University, Professor Mikio Hiramatsu, was his host; on other occasions he confirmed
his warm association with Hiroshima, establishing a firm friendship
with the Chaucerian scholar Professor Michio Masui. His 1964 visit
took him to the celebrations in Tokyo for the 400th anniversary of
Shakespeare's birth, where he deepened his acquaintance with Father
Peter Milward of Sophia University. As always, he was constantly
requested to lecture, talk or inscribe poems and he was welcomed and
fêted in return – a particularly lavish dinner being given in his honour
in 1964 in the Zen Temple in Tokyo.

Honours began to be heaped on him. He received the Order of the
Rising Sun in 1963, and was elected to honorary membership of the
Japan Academy in 1950. He was only the third Englishman ever to
have been given this honour, which was almost exclusively given to
eminent scientists – indeed he was given membership in the company
of four physicists, inlcuding Albert Einstein. Literary gifts were to
come his way as well. In 1950 four former Japanese pupils presented
him with a publication entitled *Eastward*, consisting of nearly forty of
his poems in holograph facsimile on handmade paper, and in 1974 – at
the instigation of E. W. F. Tomlin, who had been the British Council
representative in Japan and cultural counsellor to the Embassy – a
volume *Edmund Blunden: A Tribute from Japan* was published as a
memorial. Most remarkable of all were the physical memorials which
were erected throughout Japan between 1950 and 1975 in the form of
commemorative tablets inscribed with Edmund's poetry, on the islands
of Hokkaido, Honshu, Kyushu and Shikoku. Every August in the
coastal town of Ito on the Izu Peninsula, a ceremony is held to
commemorate the visit in the early seventeenth century of the first
Englishman to land in Japan, William Adams of Gillingham in Kent. A
stone plaque records the event and next to it stands a large stone
engraved with a poem 'To the Citizens of Ito' – the engraving perfectly capturing Edmund's handwriting – which Edmund composed on a
visit to Ito in July 1948, looking forward to greater English – Japanese
links. Just above the town of Sendai, north of Tokyo, is the famed
beauty-spot of Matsushima. At its highest point, looking out to the sea
through the tall trees, stands a five-foot stone engraved with Edmund's

poem 'Matsushima', with a Japanese translation below. While commemorative stones are traditional Japanese memorials, what is particularly remarkable is that they should have been placed in so many locations, and to commemorate an Englishman in his lifetime. Two memorials, however, were to wait until after Edmund's death. Just opposite the city of Hiroshima is the Island of Miyajima – a beautiful shrine, whose great arch, or *Torii*, stands majestically marking the entrance to the Inland Sea. It was a favourite place of Edmund's and on a visit in 1959, the bicentenary of the death of William Collins, he composed a short poem in the style of Collins's 'Ode to Evening', asking for a permanent home 'Among the pinewoods on the mountain side'. The poem is now engraved on a black marble stone, designed by Professor Sato, by the steps leading to Hiramatsu Park – where the island offers its most beautiful view. According to Buddhist belief Edmund's request has been fulfilled, for some part of his soul will remain in the monument for ever. In Hiroshima itself, in front of the new Central Public Library opposite the striking castle and the Park of Peace, is a bronze monument designed by T. Suzuki, which has inscribed on it the words of encouragement which Edmund incorporated in his poem 'Hiroshima' (later set to music by the Master of the Queen's Music, Malcolm Williamson), which concentrates on 'Not what has been but what will be'. The tablet has a Japanese translation of the poem by Bunsho Jugaku and an embossed relief of Edmund's head by K. Entsuba. The prospectus for its construction listed over eighty individual and group sponsors, and the monument was unveiled on 3 August 1975 in the presence of Mayor Araki of the city. It stands as a remarkable tribute to an Englishman from the citizens of a devastated city. As Father Peter Milward recorded of Edmund in the *Japan Times* in 1976, 'in Hiroshima too, his immortal spirit is forever enshrined.'

In December 1947, Edmund had arrived in Tokyo with two suitcases; on the morning of his departure in May 1950 he was weighed down with packages of gifts and presentations. As he left the Embassy to be driven to Yokohama, a group of fifty or more Japanese lined the drive and silently bade farewell as though they were attending a funeral. Once again Edmund had achieved by the quiet strength of his personality, and by patient understanding, a quite remarkable public and personal success. By concentrating on the cultural links between nations and by avoiding political divisions he had made lifelong friends in a land only recently laid low by war with the west. He became to many Japanese their image of England and the English. It was something of which his successor George Fraser became acutely aware, writing in 1952:

As for Professor Blunden, I think the warmth with which he is regarded by his friends in England equals that which is felt by his friends in Japan. He has that very rare quality, a genius for being loved.[10]

# PART EIGHT
## 1950 – 1964

# 24

# The *Times*
# *Literary Supplement*
## May 1950 – September 1953

---

*There's something the matter with this country, and with
literature, when a way can't be found for keeping you
with us. It's a disaster, and past understanding.*
Letter to E.B. from H.W. Garrod, August 1953 [1]

> *Life is a sheer stampede, and I am really a tired
> old hawk.*
> Letter to Leonard Clark, June 1953 [2]

---

Edmund's return to England was a return to old friends and old habits
of journalism. The house in Virginia Water, though too small for a
family of five, was situated in a corner of agreeable rural naturalness
from where book-raids on Windsor were easy local expeditions. After
sixteen months, however, Edmund and Claire moved into their home
in Tonbridge – giving Annie the tenancy of the Virginia Water house
– where there was room for both family and books and where Edmund could once more feel at home in his native Sussex and Kent. He
resumed his position on the Book Society (this time including novels
in his monthly reading) and returned to his desk at the *Times Literary
Supplement* composing weekly copy which was to bring his total of
contributions to nearly a thousand by the summer of 1953, and he
often deputised as editor – for no extra salary. One sadness was that he
was not to enjoy the company of Philip Tomlinson, whose absence
had been forced by increasing illness, and this removed what had been

one of Edmund's principal incentives to return. On a happier note came news from Laurence Whistler that Sassoon had been talking of Edmund with great affection and that a healing of their three-year rift seemed possible. Edmund responded immediately, was invited to Heytesbury, and reported that 'the spell was snapped'[3] and that their old friendship was fully restored – never to suffer a further breach.

As the months passed, the old patterns of a crowded life returned too. Visitors from Japan became familiar figures in Tonbridge and lectures to the Japan Society joined renewed requests for talks to schools in Maidstone and Windsor – where he was the guest of his old Merton pupil and editor of poetry anthologies, W. G. Bebbington. Edmund's postbag now contained so many requests for help from aspiring writers that he was finally – and very reluctantly – forced to produce a printed letter regretting that pressure of work prevented him from entering into such correspondence. There were new elements too, and he was not untouched by signs of some public recognition in England. His Japanese work was rewarded by the award of the CBE in 1951 and he was flattered to find himself becoming a 'collected' author: not only was Rupert Hart-Davis compiling as complete a set of Edmund's publications as possible, but he was also being collected by a most colourful character, Major Trevor Moilliet – retired soldier, former greengrocer and ardent Blundenophile. Edmund was also to see the first British selection of his poetry and prose appear in October 1950, published by Rupert Hart-Davis and edited by Kenneth Hopkins, a writer and critic with whom Edmund had corresponded in Japan after a brief London meeting and who was now to become a regular lunch time drinking companion. New associations were also to be formed with Leonard Clark, a schools inspector and tireless organiser of poetry workshops, which he tirelessly persuaded Edmund to attend as a guest speaker – and with the librarian of Pembroke College Cambridge, Matthew Hodgart. In London Edmund was to find himself invited to an evening with Neville Cardus ('more than a cricket writer and music critic – an authority on the whole intellectual life'), and entertained by the companionship of the journalist and broadcaster John Arlott, when conversation could range with equal ease over poetry or cricket. He was quickly settling into the hectic social and intellectual life which he had enjoyed in London both in the 1920s and immediately before his second Japanese visit.

Other aspects of his work began to develop in new directions. In 1950 he travelled to Normandy with Douglas Grant on behalf of the Imperial War Graves Commission and followed this with a memorable visit to Italy with Claire in 1952; over the next ten years his editorial work for the Commission was to lead to publications on naval memorials in England and the memorial to airmen at Runnymede, together with records of memorials as widespread as Belgium, Germany, Greece, Crete, Malta, Scandinavia, the Faroe Islands, East Africa, Tunisia and Hong Kong. At home he constantly involved himself in the affairs of Christ's Hospital, whose quatercentenary celebrations in 1953 provided him with his first opportunity to try his hand at a dramatic piece, resulting in *The Dede of Pittie*, a pageant-like portrayal of the school's 400-year history – performed both at Horsham and at the Fortune Theatre in May. Edmund himself made a brief appearance as Bunny in the scene set in the trenches in 1914 which, as Jack Morpurgo noted, 'might have been *Journey's End* had we not known that it was *Undertones of War*'.[4] The success of the venture gave Edmund the idea of a dramatic representation of the life of John Clare, but it was an idea which remained unrealised.

A month after the Christ's Hospital celebrations a second musical association with Gerald Finzi was incorporated in 'A Garland for the Queen' – a programme of Music for the Eve of Coronation Day – when Edmund's poem 'The White Flowering Days'[5] was performed in Finzi's setting for mixed voices. A further Blunden–Finzi project was to be fulfilled in the same year, for both were devoted to the memory of the composer–poet Ivor Gurney. Finzi had long championed the cause of Gurney's music and for some time had been urging Edmund to produce a selection of his poems. Sensing that this would be achieved only if Edmund were removed from his other literary commitments, he invited him to Ashmandsworth and vacated his study – usually a jealously guarded sanctuary – keeping Edmund in virtual isolation for a week until he had assembled a selection of nearly eighty poems with an introductory memoir. It was clearly a far from ideal arrangement for the choosing of poems culled from complicated manuscripts, full of variant readings – some in difficult handwriting, some typewritten – with many dating from Gurney's troubled asylum years. Edmund was later to regret the speed of the volume's compilation and the selection of too few 'Asylum Verses', but it was for some time to provide the only available text of Gurney poems, and Edmund's textual choices sometimes look more logical than later more leisurely considered editings. The introduction was a typically sculptured prose-evocation of Gurney's fragile temperament and his lyrical and at times idiosyncratic metrical beauties: 'His poetry has its sweetness but also its sharpness and severity, or what he calls "patterns like earth-sense strong" – something of the gargoyle against the flying cloud'.[6] The memoir was written in one morning, virtually without pause, and needing no correction. On the flyleaf of his own copy Edmund recalled his meeting with Gurney: 'I see him yet, and hear him too – singing and playing to "a naked frosty sky."' Beneath this he added sadly, 'this volume had no future.'[7]

A more commercially successful venture was an edition of *Selected Poems* of Shelley, prepared at the same time as the Gurney volume, which quickly ran into nine reprints and sold nearly 40,000 copies. Edmund's association with Shelley was to be further extended through friendship with the Pickwickian Shelley editor Neville Rogers, and his association with Keats through meetings with Keats's biographer Robert Gittings. A visit to Rome had brought the twin associations together at the Keats-Shelley Memorial – and laid the foundation of friendship with the curator of Keats House in Rome, Vera Cacciatore and her poet husband Edoardo. From 1950 Edmund was to contribute on sixteen occasions to the *Keats-Shelley Memorial Bulletin*.

Despite such varied and busy activity it was not long before his innate restlessness began to stir him to think of further changes of scene and work. He was finding constant reviewing both monotonous and financially cramping, and he was feeling the pull of the past. Worries over the health of Philip Tomlinson, Annie and Aki Hayashi sent his mind back to first meetings, and the deaths of Eddie Marsh, H. J. Massingham and F. A. Downing (with whom relations had been strained in later years) similarly evoked nostalgic memories. A further shadow was to fall in November 1951 when, after a brief illness, Pugg died quietly in Yalding – with Lance at his bedside, to whom he whispered his last words: 'Thank you.' It was an emotional visit to old homes and haunts which Edmund paid at the funeral, though it was lightened by the familiar sight of the eighty-six-year-old sexton Mr Basden digging a deep grave in the churchyard, incongruously going about his work bowler-hatted in the pouring rain.

After only a year at the *Times Literary Supplement* Edmund's thoughts turned again towards academic life and he was pleased to accept nomination in February 1951 as Professor of Poetry at Oxford – the only professorship which is decided by the votes of MAs. But, on discovering that Cecil Day-Lewis was also a candidate, Edmund instantly withdrew from the contest, determined not to stand against a friend. He travelled to Oxford to cast his vote for Day-Lewis, warmly congratulating him when he was duly elected. It was a typical gesture of generosity and forbearance on Edmund's part, particularly as the opportunity presented itself at a time when he would probably have been most able to do himself justice in the chair.

A year later, seeing no academic opening at home, his attention was focused once more on the east. His old pupil Bernard Mellor, now Registrar of the University of Hong Kong, had approached him in 1949 as a possible candidate for the vice-chancellorship of the university. Edmund declined on the grounds of his dislike of administration and his discomfort in fulfilling the role of a ceremonial figure. When the chair of English became vacant in 1953, Mellor came to England to persuade Edmund to accept the appointment. The offer, which included a free house and unlimited tenure, provided just the kind of financial security which he needed and he agreed to an initial period of five years, thus unwittingly removing himself from opportunities within the new British universities. It was another impulsive decision similar to his acceptance of the Japanese professorship thirty years earlier. On this occasion he had the dubious benefit of the unnerving advice of an acquaintance in a local pub, who had a reputation as a fortune-teller. In earnest terms he warned Edmund against accepting the job, giving him unequivocal assurances that everything would 'end in tears'. Edmund understandably decided to ignore such apparently ungrounded warnings.

Stocking his cases with volumes of poetry, he prepared for the now familiar five-week journey and for the absence from friends and England – leaving behind a tearful Aki Hayashi on the platform at Waterloo station. The voyage itself was to be less relaxed than on previous occasions, for a British Council lecture was arranged for the two-day stop-over in Colombo, interviews had to be prepared for arrival in Hong Kong, and his young family kept him more than occupied on board ship. In a letter to Lance he painted a bleak picture of the liner's swimming-pool:

I cannot describe the horror. In the allotted cistern a quantity of seawater slams and foams to and fro over a slippery floor as the ship moves in the wind, and a herd of young with a good many overfed parents flops about in the tidal violence. All shout and shriek at the top of their voices. I am sometimes compelled to go in, nominally as caretaker to our three. . . . Am reading Cowley's long poem about David, which perhaps nobody else in the world is doing this September.[8]

And so in late September 1953 Edmund found himself in the east for the third time. Casting his mind back to 1924 he could picture himself as a vigorous young man stepping into unknown territory.

## PART EIGHT  1950 – 1964

Now he was returning to a world which was becoming as familiar as Oxford or Yalding; but he was returning after sustained, nervously exhausting activity, and he was beginning to feel every one of his fifty-six years.

# 25

# Hong Kong
## September 1953 – May 1964

*No living Englishman has done more, by hard and devoted work and by being his unique self, to link the English imagination, at its inspired and compassionate best, with that of the Far East.*
William Plomer, Daily Telegraph, September 1963

*No longer so hourly drawn back to an ancient year or two of war intensity: but I must expect . . . a recurrent voice from that time. I am nothing now, and John Clare's fate is much like mine in a way – Mary, who first went into that world of lights and shadows with me, is dead – Mary: A most beautiful woman . . . but few will remember. How shall I forget? These new times must be welcomed, and already Claire and I have been together nearly twenty years.*
First page of diary for 1958

*When I was young I hoped that one day I should be able to go into a post office to buy a stamp without feeling nervous and shy: now I realise that I never shall.*
Conversation with Rupert Hart-Davis, 1956[1]

In 1955 Edmund published a poem entitled 'A Hong Kong House'[2] (later to become the title of his last major volume of new poems), which evokes the sounds and sights of his Hong Kong home. It creates a haunting atmosphere of tantalising movement, while the title suggests domestic comfort, security and retirement to a private world of contemplation – looking out on to a garden whose life is similarly ambivalent: where 'trumpet-purple blooms' blaze majestically but where 'no kind root' or sweet flower can find a permanent home and where dove or dragonfly are welcome but temporary visitors. It was an apt metaphor for his Hong Kong days, which were to consist of many public successes and triumphs, but were also to mark a gradual withdrawal from both creative and academic life – and it was increasingly to become a retreat to uncertainty and self-doubt, punctuated by bursts of frustrated anger, as the world around him became ever more burdensome, 'etched with many rings'.

The house itself, a square colonial-style structure with tall, spacious rooms and elegant verandahs, nestled on the edge of one of the many steep inclines which zigzagged up the university hill like a staircase and commanded a picturesque view through trees to the deep-blue waters of the bay and the hills of the islands beyond. It was not long before 3 University Path became synonymous with warm hospitality given freely to the many eminent visitors who called on their journeys east and to the many university students who quickly discovered that their professor's door was always open to his pupils. A procession of spirited young female undergraduates came to the house for tutorials in the cosy book-lined study and would sometimes join other students for a literary evening at which Edmund particularly enjoyed giving dramatic readings of Dr Johnson with Claire taking the part of Mrs Thrale. It was the familiar world of Oxford and Tokyo once again and represented the more cultured face of Hong Kong. Another view was evident from his office in the faculty building, where the immediate sight was endless rows of Chinese houses with their perpetual lines of washing, heralding the bustling, colourful, commercial world whose claustrophobia could become as choking as Edmund's asthma.

The contrasts and contradictions were to extend both domestically and professionally. The house was comfortable and the services of a cook, a housekeeper and an amah Ah-ling (commemorated in 'The Sleeping Amah'[3]) meant that the family – to be completed by the birth of Catherine in September 1956 – could enjoy a degree of luxury which was unprecedented. It began to look remarkably like a reincarnation of life at Congelow, with four young girls (the eldest not to reach teenage years until 1959) making their presence firmly felt. The Yalding habit of nicknames was repeated too, Margaret being invariably known as Margi, Frances as Fan, and Catherine as Beano, only Lucy keeping her name unshortened. Animal life was represented by Anatole – a pet mouse kept in a cage on the verandah and solicitously cared for by Edmund – and by a procession of cats headed by Ham, the most senior, who added to the homeliness but whose fertility meant that many hours were spent by Edmund in the ventilation space beneath the house, coaxing kittens from its recesses. An atmosphere of happy relaxed security prevailed; at times of depression, however, the sense of so much activity and the presence of so many lively, younger females around him intensified Edmund's feeling of isolation and the threat of old age. Similarly his office was to become the centre of a thriving department under his leadership, with many devoted colleagues and pupils, but it was also to become a symbol of irksome administrative duties and academic politics with which he had no sympathy, but which were not to leave him unscathed.

Edmund was immediately attracted to the university itself, finding an agreeable atmosphere somewhat akin to an old grammar school – even if its rigid sense of hierarchy based on length of service was a less attractive similarity – and enjoying the vitality of a young university which was mirrored in the dedicated attitude of its students. The biggest drawback was the lack of second-hand bookshops, and requests for volumes to be sent from home were regularly directed to Rupert Hart-Davis or Edward Finneron, either for his personal use or to augment the rather meagre supply on the shelves of the English Department – whose library he transformed (supported by the tireless efforts of the librarian Dorothea Scott) and on whose walls is appropriately hung a commissioned portrait of Edmund by Douglas Bland.

The English Department soon began to look like a home from home, for two lecturers were old Oxford acquaintances: Mary Visick, who had been a pupil from St Hilda's, and Alan Green, a language specialist to whom Edmund had been official tutor at Merton. By 1955 they were to be joined by Alec Hardie, and a year later Claire was to join the department as an assistant lecturer. With Bernard Mellor as his next-door neighbour Edmund was thus surrounded by five former pupils and the association was to be strengthened through two of his Chinese colleagues: Margaret Yu, whose father and brother had been at Merton, and Anne Choy, who was to do postgraduate work at Oxford and become, by Edmund's introduction, part of the Levens household. The familiar establishment of affection and respect among his pupils was soon evident as they discovered him to be:

> *Willing to give whatever art I know*
> *To some new theme or old one newly springing,*[4]

and he quickly created friendships – with a postgraduate Lily Chan (the 'L.C.'[5] of the poem of that title) and in particular with two of his students, Chau Wah Ching and Yung Kai Kin. The former was to teach in Canada and devote almost all his free hours to cataloguing Edmund's library and to compiling a complete edition of Edmund's poetry. His early death in 1987 took away one of Edmund's most devoted followers. Yung Kai Kin was to settle in England and after a brief period as curator of Dr Johnson's birthplace at Lichfield (during Edmund's presidency of the Johnson Society in 1967) he became Registrar of the National Portrait Gallery, one of Edmund's favourite London haunts. It was the gift of encouragement which was probably Edmund's greatest strength as a teacher, and just as he had been sensitive to the particular needs of his Japanese students, so he adapted his approach to those in Hong Kong. He felt acutely aware of the danger of their becoming isolated from both the rich culture of China and that of the west, and he thus took every opportunity to help them to travel, securing postgraduate university places in America or Britain for several of his pupils.

With the arrival of Alec Hardie both university journalism and drama were bound to flourish and Edmund was quick to lend support to the university literary journal, *The Chimes* (which devoted its August 1964 issue to him), and to encourage the work of his pupils such as Yeung Ngai Hin and the writer, artist and musician Lo King Man. The frequent productions of the dramatic society, the Masquers, became something of a family affair with Alec Hardie as director, Claire as costume-manager and Edmund supplying verse prologues for the programmes of six productions, as well as appearing on stage himself as Adam in the 1958 production of *As You Like It* and as the Baron in a Christmas pantomime. His association with the Masquers also brought him into contact with a wide circle of students, including a young Indian hockey player, Harnam Grewell, who after a Cambridge degree became an eminent member of the Hong Kong civil service and remained a loyal friend. Grewell was also an enthusiast for war literature and together with Yeung Ngai Hin took Edmund on a tour of the concrete trench network in the New Territories, which had served as defences in the Sino-Japanese war. With their criss-cross patterns and names like Shaftesbury Avenue and Piccadilly Circus, Edmund was quickly taken back imaginatively to Festubert, the Somme and Ypres.

Despite his lack of enthusiasm for official functions there were several at which Edmund's presence was required: an annual celebration for the Japanese Emperor's birthday at the Repulse Bay Hotel; a monthly lunch party for Old Blues in Hong Kong; dinner-parties at Government House; a royal visit from Princess Alexandra in 1961 to celebrate the university's Golden Jubilee – to the official history of which he contributed two chapters. But in other respects life was more insular, centring on the university campus and the English Department, where he was given devoted service from the secretary Sheila Yuan. In his teaching and lecturing he concentrated on Shakespeare and the Romantics, his ever-present fascination with textual and biographical details being shared with his colleague Barbara Rooke (a Coleridge specialist) as well as his many correspondents on Shelley matters: Sylva, Neville Rogers, Rosalie Mander and Louise Boas of Massachusetts (who paid him a visit in Hong Kong). Indeed his correspondence was probably at its most extensive during this period, for in addition to a host of other letters he was writing at length each week to Sylva, Aki Hayashi and Rupert Hart-Davis. Further stimulation was provided by contact with colleagues outside the English Department – with the cricket-loving Professor of Chemistry John Driver and with the Professor of Geography S. G. Davis. He also formed a friendship with the Vice-Chancellor Sir Lindsay Ride (composing a celebratory poem for his wedding in 1954), while visits to Government House offered the company of the Governor Sir Alexander Grantham and, in particular, his successor – the convivial and witty Sir Robert Black and his vivacious wife.

It was indeed company which he sought most after the ease with which he had found it in Oxford and London, and he therefore took special pleasure in greeting visitors who arrived with almost monthly regularity throughout his Hong Kong years: Japanese friends such as Takeshi Saito, Sir Vere and Lady Redman, Hans Bernstein and Lewis Bush; his former Oxford friends and pupils Michael Meyer, Paul Engle, Richard Storry and Douglas Grant; visiting academics including the Vice-Chancellor of Cambridge Herbert Butterfield, Oxford biologist Alister Hardy, Matthew Hodgart from Cambridge, and Kingman Brewster from America. From the publishing world came Billy Collins, while visits from the violinist Maurice Clare and the pianist Angus Morrison were augmented by actors on tour, enabling him to meet Celia Johnson, Sybil Thorndike and Sir Lewis Casson. Most pleasant for Edmund was the company of other writers, and a chance to renew contact with Vera Brittain at one dinner-party was followed by an invitation to dine with Vita Sackville-West and Harold Nicolson. Other literary opportunities were offered by the personal visits to University Path of Alec Waugh, John Arlott, D. J. Enright, Somerset Maugham and, on two particularly enjoyable occasions, Graham Greene, whose wide-ranging conversation he recalled with enormous pleasure, though he declined Greene's invitation to soothe his asthma by visiting Macao to smoke opium.

Edmund was also to travel considerably himself. Journeying east, in addition to his five Japanese visits (always involving extensive rounds of lectures, recordings, speeches and the composition of articles and impromptu verses) he was also invited to Formosa and gave a lecture-tour in the Philippines, where John Pilcher had become ambassador. (The visit to Manila was not without its drama for on the first morning Edmund broke his set of false teeth, which were miraculously repaired just minutes before he was due to deliver his lecture.) The most influential visit, however, was to be northwards to China in December 1955. Originally planned as an informal visit by individual members of Hong Kong University to view Chinese educational developments and to make contact with academics, the idea soon grew into something more formal, with the twenty-strong party – still travelling as a group of individuals rather than a delegation and offering a cultural rather than a political face – becoming guests of the People's Association for Cultural Relations with Foreign Countries. For three weeks they travelled through China, escorted by their hosts and journeying mostly by train, noting the sharp contrasts between the primitive agricultural world of the centre of the country (where water-buffaloes and donkeys pulled tyreless carts) and the splendour of the ornate buildings of Peking. Edmund was elected leader and spokesman for the group, inevitably finding himself required to deliver speeches at formal dinners and to give interviews in the elegant suite provided for him at the Peking Hotel. Receptions at the British Embassy as the guest of the Chargé d'Affaires Con O'Neill, a Balliol English graduate whom Edmund had met at *The Times* offices, and lunch with the young Third Secretary (and future Foreign Secretary) Douglas Hurd were fitted round visits to university departments, law courts, the Great Wall and the Ming Tombs. On 23 December an unexpected invitation was extended to meet the Prime Minister Chou En-lai at the Winter Palace. All were aware that it would be a meeting requiring considerable diplomacy, for Chou En-lai had been publicly attacking Hong Kong after an incident in which a bomb had allegedly been placed in a Chinese plane. The visitors sat on three sides of a square in the large main reception room of the State Administrative Council in the company of more than a dozen ministers and officials, with

Edmund sitting next to Chou En-lai on the fourth side. For nearly three hours, over the inevitable clink of tea-cups, the Prime Minister asked and answered questions in a frank and easy manner, impressing Edmund by his mental and physical energy as well as his humour. Claire noted that in the course of the close questioning 'the poet was never once worsted by the diplomat,' and another observer described Edmund's quiet skill as like 'Bailey batting against Lindwall'. Much to the surprise of the People's Association Chou En-lai paid an unscheduled visit to the caviare-and-champagne party given to the Hong Kong guests on Christmas Day, spending a considerable time in further conversation with Edmund.

On his return to Hong Kong Edmund was bombarded by the press and obliged to write several articles for newspapers. As always his prime concern was to avoid political controversy; inevitably he failed. The *Hong Kong Standard* sharply attacked him for the mildness of his criticism of the Chinese regime and demanded that those who, like Edmund, used their classrooms to disseminate Communist propaganda should be expelled from Hong Kong. The wheel had turned full circle: in 1937 Edmund had been dubbed a Fascist; in 1939 a Nazi; now, apparently, he was a Communist.

His official statement, printed in *The Times* of London on 31 December 1955, was hardly controversial:

I can think of nothing more interesting in the Far East at present than even a brief view of the experiments in the reconstruction of a nation of 600 million people.

We found among our hosts, and might judge that this feeling was general, a tranquillity about work which is now distributed to all kinds of people; but we would not say they are living in any utopian daydream. They repeatedly reminded us that, especially in this early stage, there must be many imperfections in their schemes. Although preservation of antiquities cannot be the first object of a movement directed towards a utilitarian stage, we were deeply impressed by the remarkable restoration and renovation of many famous memorials of earlier China. We were repeatedly and cordially desired to make our visit a habit, and the Prime Minister himself urged strongly that we should extend our present visit on a future occasion.

Edmund and Claire acted on Chou En-lai's final suggestion and revisited China in March 1964.

Journeys were not, however, to be confined to the east, for Edmund was to make five visits to England in seven years. Sometimes they were brief official visits, as a delegate to a conference of English professors at Jesus College Cambridge in the summer of 1956 under the chairmanship of E. M. W. Tillyard, where a warm association was formed with Douglas Grant's colleague Norman Jeffares, resulting in Edmund becoming the recipient of an honorary doctorate from Leeds University in the spring of 1962. In June of the following year he was a guest at a dinner at Skinners' Hall in London in June 1963 to receive the Companionship of Literature from the Deputy Prime Minister R. A. Butler on behalf of the Royal Society of Literature. The presentation was made after a dinner attended by over a hundred literary figures, presided over by Lord Birkenhead, with Edith Sitwell, Evelyn Waugh and Aldous Huxley being similarly honoured at the same occasion. Two longer periods of leave enabled him to enjoy more extended European travels during the second halves of 1957 and 1961, journeying with Claire and the children via Athens and Rome, where he was joined briefly by Sylva. Typically he filled his diary with social occasions, lectures, poetry-readings and cricket matches, weaving visits to family in Kent, Devon, Manchester and Scotland around War Grave Commission business in France and Belgium, and taking his daughters to see Christ's Hospital. On both periods of leave he was to spend a week at Heytesbury with Sassoon, who on one day in July 1957 took him on a memorable visit to Monsignor Ronald Knox. In the month before, he had been taken by Joy Finzi to Winchester, where he paid homage to Jane Austen, Edward Young and William Collins; and in 1959 he was to provide an introduction to the catalogue of an exhibition in Winchester College Library to commemorate the 200th anniversary of Collins's death. In October 1957 he paid a visit to Stratford-on-Avon to see a performance of *The Tempest* and dine with the producer Glen Byam Shaw, and in the same month he was to speak at the Radley College Literary Society, an occasion which was to provide an incident strikingly similar to that at the '*Abeunt Studia in Mores*' lecture at Jiyu Gakuen and again illustrate the kind of hypnotic poetic aura which surrounded him. His hosts at Radley were Peter and Elizabeth Way. Having grazed his finger, Edmund unwittingly left a bloodstain on the cover of the armchair in their sitting room. Elizabeth Way, struck by the sensitive frailty of Edmund's demeanour, refrained from removing the stain – which remained like some religious relic until its natural disappearance.

If the pattern of activity was hardly restful for Edmund it was equally demanding for his hosts – most often Rupert Hart-Davis in his small flat in Soho Square, Joy Finzi at Ashmandsworth, Clare Ross in London and Suffolk, or Claire's cousins Joan and Dick Chamberlain in

Wimbledon. Wherever he was, visitors were naturally attracted or enthusiastically invited – in London he was seeing more of the poet James Reeves and regularly meeting Aki Hayashi in the London Museum Tavern; staying with Joy Finzi provided the company of an old Christ's Hospital friend, the publisher Max Martyn of Hamish Hamilton, and his wife Evelyn. When travelling with all the family, these demands were exaggerated; but even when he was alone there could be difficult moments, as Rupert Hart-Davis recounted in August 1956:

On Monday E.B. had some friends in for drinks at my flat. He had asked everyone he'd seen, but couldn't remember who they were, so we waited anxiously, and presently welcomed a second-hand bookseller from Woking, an out-of-work journalist from Brighton, two Chinese lawyers, my daughter (who happened to be in London), an enormous girl who used to be in the B.B.C. repertory company, my secretary (to whom E. had taken a mild fancy), Arthur Crook (who does all the work on the T.L.S.), the female representative of some American publishers, etc. As soon as it was decently possible I took my daughter off to dinner and a movie.[6]

It was only a few days before this that news came that Mary was in hospital suffering from leukemia. Edmund was anxious to see her but found that his busy schedule prevented him from doing so; within a few weeks of arriving back in Hong Kong he heard that she had died. His failure to visit her at the end brought back horrible reminders of his delayed arrival at the bed of Joy, more so when he learned that as Mary slipped into a final coma, she was heard to whisper, 'Bring me my little Joy. Bring me little Joy'.

Edward had always associated Mary with Cheveley, close to the country of the poet George Crabbe, and he immediately wrote a sonnet at the back of his edition of Crabbe's poems:

> Dear Cheveley Mary, thou art gone; and I,
> Once all amazed for thee, must soon pass by,
> My Mary – one together we would look
> Where Crabbe had served in widespread Wickhambrook,
> And many scenes observed. The rustic mind
> Attracted both and all that it designed;
> Besides, you may recall how once we two
> Tied a love-knot that nothing would undo.
> Mary, the rest let others tell; my child,
> My vision when I came from the war's wild . . .
> I cannot call you perfect, nor you me;
> And yet we are wed to one eternity.[7]

## PART EIGHT   1950 – 1964

Edmund's return journey to Hong Kong at the end of 1957 was to be an active one for he was to give lectures in India and Bangkok on the way. After arriving in Bombay to find that his lecture had been cancelled, he travelled to Delhi where he was the guest of the High Commissioner Malcolm MacDonald (an old Queen's College man whose company Edmund greatly enjoyed), who was turning the verandah of the imposing Embassy into a gallery of modern Indian paintings and medieval sculptures. Edmund described him as 'one of the best great men anywhere'.[8] From Delhi Edmund travelled on to Allahabad and Calcutta, being much amused by the transport provided – light aircraft which seemed to be propped up against hedges like bicycles. His literary connection with India was to be extended in 1961 when he joined the Indian Committee for the Rabindranath Tagore Centenary in commemoration of the Nobel Prize-winning poet (inevitably Edmund provided a commemorative poem) and he was to attend the Hong Kong première of the film *Mother India* in the following year (which also meant providing a poem for the programme) – though he somewhat wryly observed that the film showed considerably 'more gore than Tagore'.[8]

Such a hectic schedule was relieved by visits to the variety of islands which lay just off the Hong Kong mainland: exploring the beauties of Lamma Island with S. G. Davis (to whom the poem 'Lamma Island' is dedicated[9]); enjoying the curved, stone streets and pink, green and primrose-coloured houses of Macao; resting in the holiday house at Cheung Chau, admiring the colourful markets stocked with melons and eggplants, and sharing the evening company of toads and lizards. At home he could relax with Alec Hardie or Bernard ('Bunny') Mellor – 'a most valuable counsellor and ever a private friend' – but he was becoming more drawn into an inner world. He felt geographically and emotionally isolated; he realised that his young family were not part of his old world of memories; his identification with Lear returned. Almost daily came news of the deaths of friends from earlier days: from First World War years he lost Frank Worley and Colonel Millward; from early London days de la Mare, H. M. Tomlinson, Middleton Murry and Ralph Hodgson; from Oxford days H. W. Garrod and Colonel Wilkinson; and these were joined by Joyce Cary and Roy Campbell (whom he liked to remember as a 'literary Sheriff who sometimes came in to clear up the burg').[10] In 1956 had come the news of the untimely death of Gerald Finzi from cancer (he is commemorated in the poem 'For a Musician's Monument'[11]), which had also claimed Annie in 1955. These provided constantly recurring moments of depression, emphasised in March 1955 by the death of Phil Tomlinson – 'I do not feel that he has entirely gone from me, his quiet spirit having seemed to be somehow in my life though I might not be seeing him regularly'[12]. One morning in 1962 Claire found Edmund leaning on the fireplace in the sitting room, his head lowered, staring at the floor: the morning post had brought the news of Aki Hayashi's lonely death from a cerebral haemorrhage. Just as he had written of Mary's association with Cheveley, so he was to sketch, in his diary on a visit to London a year later, a stanza in memory of Aki:

> Strange that the absence of but one,
> A quiet, weary, ageing one,
> Should so estrange this so familiar town;
> Her trudging, once so burdensome
> To me with thoughts ahead, and time
> But scanty, now I think's become
> Why I with crisis grappling fell not down;
> Her grumbling now (no great storm then)
> Would make this corner live again.[13]

Despite the closeness of his family, Edmund was beginning to feel solitary; and for the first time Claire was feeling the disparity in their ages.

To the casual observer Edmund remained a successful man enjoying a world of frenetic activity and a degree of public acclaim. Behind the closed doors of 3 University Path, however, a different story was slowly unravelling itself.

It was clear that the constant travelling was an outward expression of an intense inner restlessness which was to find expression in alternating bouts of frustrated impatience and depressed listlessness from which alcohol was increasingly to become the first avenue of escape. He felt hemmed in by the claustrophobic heat of Hong Kong and the equally close atmosphere of university politics. The humidity drained his energy; the dry heat inflamed his asthma. Physically, mentally and emotionally he felt as low as he had in the trenches of the Somme and Passchendaele, which he revisited almost nightly in dreams from which he awoke shrieking and shaking. His teeth troubled him, his eyesight was fading, his appetite was deserting him, and the steep walk from home to faculty exhausted him. Unable any longer to be a sure judge of the speed of a cricket ball, he broke his collar-bone while facing quick bowling. He gave up cigarettes but complained that this increased his impatience. A brief spell in hospital revealed that asthma had severely damaged the blood circulation in his chest, which could be controlled only by cortisone. The result was a change in Edmund's features which changed from the sharp outlines of a darting sparrow to the puffed-out contours of an owl.

Physical worries were merely a cover for deeper psychological worries, for he was harbouring secret fears – of losing his poetic powers, of losing his mind. In January 1959 he recorded a dream: 'a brown hop garden (winter, some poles standing) and a dark lake. I said with great joy, "I have my poetry back again."'[14] But it was to remain, for the most part, a dream. And the picture which he had conjured up was the setting of 'The Midnight Skaters' when, beneath the dark waters of the lake, death was at watch.

He began to feel a relic from a poetic past. The award of the Queen's Gold Medal for poetry in 1956, while a pleasing honour, seemed too much like a reward for completed services. Similarly, though the welcome publication in 1956 of *Poems of Many Years* – a large selection of Edmund's poetry chosen and edited by Rupert Hart-Davis – included twenty pieces composed since 1949, the weight of 'many years' was becoming too intimately felt. *A Hong Kong House* was to provide evidence of almost eighty poems written between 1951 and 1961, but they were composed spasmodically and were predominantly elegaic or occasional. Few stand comparison with Edmund's best, though one is conspicuous both for its technical skill and for its portrayal of Edmund's feeling. In 'Dog on Wheels'[15] a toy Airedale finds itself, like Edmund, left alone in the study while the young members of the household go about their life, 'free-wheeling' while the dog is restricted to its fixed axle. Looking with sympathetic affection at the toy, Edmund tries to breathe life into its battered and motionless body, as he would wish to revitalise his own poetic voice. And the process is not wholly unsuccessful, though cruelly it leads to sadness:

> But as I shut my desk and say goodbye,
> Downward droops a disappointed eye.

Edmund's disappointment with his poetic powers was to extend to a loss of confidence in his prose too, and he reduced his output of articles and reviews to the modest (for him) average of one a month. The frustration of being unable to find an appropriate vocabulary combined with a sense of rapid ageing resulted in uncharacteristic outbursts of passionate temper, released by alcohol, often directed at Claire. The bitter sadness of regret the following day only served to increase the desire to escape again down the same spiral path.

A more creative escape was to bury himself in editorial work (as he had predicted to his father years before), compiling a Tennyson selection but concentrating on the neglected 'unimportant' writers whose 'melody and sidelight' he had celebrated in his preface to *Poems of Many Years*. He found a ready collaborator in Bernard Mellor, for whose edition of *The Poems of Sir Francis Hubert*[16] Edmund provided an introduction. Together they compiled three companion volumes of poems from the seventeenth century onwards which were rarely found in anthologies. Many of Edmund's favourite minor poets were thus brought together – *Wayside Poems of the Seventeenth Century* giving room for such as Mrs Aphra Behn and Gertrude Thimelby; *Wayside Poems of the Early Eighteenth Century* providing a public voice for Hetty Wright and Moses Browne; while *Wayside Sonnets 1750 – 1850* allowed the likes of John Bampfylde and Joseph Hucks to reach a wider audience. Edmund had also made contact with another enthusiast for minor poets – the genial and bearded J. Stevens Cox. From his private Toucan Press in Beaminster, Dorset, came a regular flow of material about local writers. For his series on Wessex Worthies Edmund was to contribute a pamphlet on the eighteenth-century sonneteer Thomas Russell, who died at the age of twenty-six; for a companion series of Dorset Worthies he provided a piece on the eighteenth-century author of 'Lewesdon Hill', William Crowe; and in 1964 he was to add to the series of Hardy marginalia with *Guest of Thomas Hardy*. In other areas he also embarked on some unusual topics. Respecting the scientific origins of the university he contributed articles to Hong Kong journals on 'Engineering and Poetry' and 'The Family Physician in the Seventeenth Century' and gave the Jubilee Congress Lecture in 1961 on 'English Scientists as Men of Letters'.

His frustration at his loss of creativity and the weariness of his depression were made worse by a growing dissatisfaction with the policies of the university and the directions being taken by the English Department. As early as February 1957 he had angrily pointed out in his diary, 'I hate the whole silly university insipidity. Not the young – no – no.' Six years later he felt he was being pushed aside by the authorities and was unhappy about what he saw as the growing influence of linguistics at the expense of literary studies. Although his tenure had been enthusiastically extended in 1958 it seemed unlikely that any further extension would be offered after another five years, despite the staunch support of Sir Lindsay Ride – indeed, a new ruling that retirement should be statutory at sixty-five seemed directed at both Edmund and Ride (who had both just passed that age), despite assurances which had seemed secure in 1953. In terms of age Edmund was not sorry to be giving up responsibilities, but in private memoranda[17] he described himself as a 'disappointed man' who had committed academic suicide by accepting the Hong Kong chair. He was still firmly supported by his inner core of colleagues, but he felt by 1963 that he was simply 'playing out time'. To the future he looked with uncertainty. He had decided against a British Council lecture tour of Australia because he did not feel physically strong enough, though the lack of readily available drugs made staying in Hong Kong equally difficult. He had agreed to stand again in 1956 for the Oxford Professorship of Poetry (hearing from Alan Pryce-Jones that there was support for him) but, discovering that Auden, Wilson Knight and Harold Nicolson were also candidates, he withdrew – and then discovered that his nomination was too late in any case. By 1964, aged sixty-seven, retirement seemed the most attractive plan, and when Sassoon offered to pay two-thirds of the price of an old mill house in the Suffolk village of Long Melford, he accepted with some alacrity.

Few except his most intimate circle were aware of the tensions beneath the surface and to the world at large he remained the quiet, selfless, cultured public figure and the dedicated, generous, learned, sensitive teacher. This was made fully clear by the private publication of *Edmund Blunden, Sixty-Five*, presented to him on his birthday in 1961. It contained messages of greetings from over eighty friends from all over the world – from eminent writers to undergraduate pupils – compiled by three of his students as an expression of their 'supreme debt of gratitude'. In return he dedicated *A Hong Kong House* to the students and colleagues 'who have so encouraged me for nearly a decade to share life and letters with them in the University of Hong Kong'. Yet again he had been an exceptionally successful literary ambassador to the east. This was made unambiguously clear by an anonymous writer of a letter about Edmund to the *South China Morning Post* in January 1974:

He lived among us for eleven years; he taught many of us who are now teachers in our turn, and he will not be forgotten by the hundreds of people to whom he was 'the Prof' and a rare friend.

We treasure the books he gave us ('Here, have this' he would say) annotated in his beautiful italic writing, and the memory of his home, always open to us, and the tutorials in which he gave us something of his scholarship and his understanding.

Edmund Blunden had no 'subordinates': the idea was one he never accepted.

306

He had only friends – teachers, students, secretaries, clerks, messengers, domestic staff. . . .

We who teach hope, as best we can, to pass on ... a little of what we learned from him of literature and of life.

I sign myself with pride
A STUDENT OF EDMUND BLUNDEN

# PART NINE
## 1964 – 1974

# 26

# Long Melford and Oxford

## May 1964 – February 1969

*I cannot understand why I have in my seventieth year
become so much of a barbarian. At home, though I do
not cease to love all (and when all are not there I grieve),
every small trouble drives me wild and sets me off roar-
ing. I let things drift and hardly care. . . . My asthma is
checked by kind Dr Stewart's various pills, but I have a
suspicion that these make me take much more beer than
I used. I don't always want anything stronger, but I find
sudden 'compulsive' wishes for whisky, gin and the rest,
and these if satisfied obliterate my thinking and memory.
How great a burden I lay on Claire, and to some extent
the girls because of this! Moreover I lose the name of
action. . . . Disorder naturally vexes me . . . now I
create it and am indifferent; or I drink it out of
sight. . . . But no more for the moment, I chiefly have
to 'be sober and keep vigil'. And forget about old age.*
Personal memorandum, 1966[1]

The mill house at Long Melford stands just to the side of the long
main street at the edge of the estate of the moated Elizabethan Melford
Hall at the north end of the village. A little way above, on slightly
higher ground, stands the magnificent 250-foot-long fifteenth-century
perpendicular church, its restored tower looking out over the picturesque village-green backed by old almshouses. To the side of Hall
Mill runs a small stream arched by an elegant brick bridge, just a short
distance away from the medieval Bull Hotel.

311

It was a comfortable family home and the proximity of Edmund's daughter Clare, together with Adrian Bell, Edgell Rickword and Geoffrey Keynes, as well as the closeness of Cambridge, provided the possibility of a choice of either social activity or quiet retreat. Inevitably his presence attracted attention and local residents soon knocked on his door to bid him welcome. One such was a poet and admirer from Oxford days in the 1920s, Phoebe Carter, who was to act as Edmund's secretary; another was Jim White, a young schoolmaster and enthusiast for the poetry of the First World War, who quickly became a friend and drinking companion. Within the village, too, Edmund became something of a celebrated figure and before many months had passed he had compiled a new guide-book for the church, calling attention to the unique small stained-glass window above the north door depicting three rabbits (an image, perhaps, of the Trinity) always known as the 'Rabbit Window', which caused Edmund some personal amusement. It was not long, either, before a small edition of his poems, selected by Jim White, was on sale in the church porch on behalf of the restoration fund, to be followed by a further volume in 1969. Visits to Cambridge enabled him to renew some old friendships as well as to establish new ones, and he was offered dining rights at Peterhouse (where Sir Herbert Butterfield, who had visited him in Hong Kong, was Master), at St Catharine's (where Francis Warner, a new young friend and Old Blue, was teaching) and at King's. His association with King's was strengthened after a private lunch with E.M. Forster – arranged by Francis Warner – at which the two old writers reminisced at ease about the English countryside before the First World War.

The immediate preoccupation before moving into Hall Mill had been the celebrations in May 1964 of the centenary of John Clare's death. Edmund had visited Clare's birthplace and grave with Yung Kai Kin and Alec Hardie in 1961 (making a special effort to visit the grocer's shop in Stamford which had been owned by Clare's loyal friend Octavius Gilchrist); now he was to return to Northampton, Peterborough and Helpstone, giving a talk in Northampton and a second one at the Aldeburgh Festival which was to form the basis of *John Clare: Beginner's Luck*, printed for Edmund's seventy-fifty birthday in 1971. It was to be the last publication of an original piece by Edmund and appropriately appeared almost exactly fifty years after *John Clare: Poems Chiefly from Manuscript*.

There were to be many more requests for lectures. A visit to Clacton in January 1965 for a commemorative talk on Louis MacNeice was followed in June by a visit to the East Suffolk Education Committee at Belstead House for a course of lectures on Marlowe, and a sitting for an oil portrait by Vera Curtis.[2] Such occasions caused him considerable anxiety, for he was finding his memory as unreliable as his eyesight, and fear of public functions brought on fits of nervous worry evident in his handwriting, which grew ever more shaky. In this state he regularly sought refreshment at the Bull, where he became a familiar customer, moving comfortably in the company of the locals, and impressing his daughters by engaging in lively conversation one lunchtime with the visiting disc-jockey Pete Murray – though afterwards Edmund had to admit that he had no idea what a disc-jockey was.

The combination of alcohol, high blood-pressure, nervous anxiety, breathlessness and fading sight made him unsteady on his feet and apt to fall – the genial Jim White delivering him to the door of Hall Mill one evening after rescuing him from the river bank. He was clearly in no state of health to undertake exhausting travel or public engagements, but the call of Belgium and France became increasingly insistent. He was to pay seven visits to old war haunts within three years, attending the 1965 golden jubilee celebrations of Toc H with the organisation's founder Tubby Clayton, to whose sensitive, absent-minded and private personality he felt strongly drawn.[3] On other occasions he was to return in the company of Claire, Alec Hardie and Yung Kai Kin, as well as with Margaret and a veteran commander of the Western Front, Brian Dickson. If such travel left him physically exhausted he was more devastated by his lack of poetic inspiration. He complained that he had written nothing worthwhile since Hong Kong (the *Eleven Poems* which Francis Warner was to select in 1966 included the only eight from this period which Edmund wished to preserve) and was thus particularly encouraged by the enthusiastic response to his poem 'The Meadows for Ever', which he offered to Thomas Braun's and Stephen Medcalf's *Christ Church Meadow* in defence of the Meadow's threatened desecration from the building of a road across it in 1965.[4] It was a matter close to Edmund's heart and a fitting subject for what was one of his final poems. He was, however, to find himself chosen as a subject for a collection of poems for the Bodley Head's series of verse for young readers in 1968, when Cecil Day-Lewis chose and introduced a selection entitled *The Midnight Skaters* with illustrations by David Gentleman. It was a series to which Edmund had contributed a Clare selection, *The Wood Is Sweet*, in 1966 (with illustrations by John O'Connor) and he was to edit a Wordsworth

313

selection *The Solitary Song* in 1970 (with illustrations again by David Gentleman). There was to be little relaxation in the production of introductions for other authors' books, as he provided them for Frederic Manning's account of the First World War, *Her Privates We*, for Brian Gardner's anthology of 1914–18 poets, *Up the Line to Death*, for a biography of William Collins and for editions of the poetry of Robert Bloomfield and Keith Douglas. He also wrote a dedicatory poem for *Twelve Poems* of R. H. Mottram, and another for Lord David Cecil's *Homage* to Ruth Pitter. These projects were interspersed with an essay on 'Random Tributes to British Painters' for *The Saturday Book* and contributions to *Chambers' Encyclopaedia* and *The Dictionary of National Biography*.

Many of these commissions were taken on in part for financial reasons, as the demands of four daughters and a sizeable house were ever threatening. For these reasons too he continued his literary journalism, despite finding intense reading uncomfortable, providing reviews and short articles for the *Times Literary Supplement*, the *Daily Telegraph* and the *Western Mail*, on seventy-five occasions in the first three years after his return to England. For Claire the calls of family and finance were equally strident and she took up part-time teaching at Sudbury Girls' High School, while Margaret began an English degree at King's College London (providing Edmund with a wonderful opportunity to introduce her to the delights of book-hunting in the Farringdon Road) and Lucy moved to Cambridge during the week, staying with Francis and Mary Warner while attending the Perse School; Frances and Catherine remained Edmund's companions at home. It was hardly a relaxing world and Edmund's patience with teenage children was fast running out.

If he could have chosen for himself he would have retreated to his bookroom by the end of 1965, moving quietly from there to the Bull and back, enjoying the life of a freelance belletrist. But he reckoned without yet another call upon him – a call which he was in no fit state to answer but which was to prove irresistible: the Professorship of Poetry at Oxford.

There can be few more puzzling events to outsiders than Oxford's procedure for electing its Professor of Poetry. Anyone can be nominated providing that they have the necessary sponsors, and voting takes place on two days in Oxford, with any MA of the university being eligible to vote. The professor is required to give only three lectures a year during his five-year tenure, for which he is paid an annual salary of £350. Like the Poet Laureateship it is viewed by some as an honour

314

more than an academic post. Being decided by the votes of MAs the choice usually reflects a fairly conservative attitude; the result does not always fill the undergraduates with great enthusiasm – as far as they are concerned the chief requirement is that the professor should be able to lecture well and preferably be available to aspiring university poets.

For many years the election had passed by as a more or less routine Oxonian ritual, but things had changed in 1951 when the colourful Somerville don Enid Starkie decided to campaign for her favoured candidate Cecil Day-Lewis – even to the extent of engaging in door-to-door canvassing. She was rewarded with signal success, which was repeated five years later with a flamboyant campaign for W. H. Auden. Oxford's dreaming spires suddenly became the setting for activity more suited to an American presidential election.

With the retirement of Robert Graves in 1966, Edmund was approached by Enid Starkie to stand for the chair. All Edmund's instincts were against it. He knew in his heart that his lecturing days were over and his inability to travel easily from Suffolk meant that he could never be a readily available Oxford figure. He privately confided to Sassoon that he did not consider the election to be a sensible one and he wrote to Enid Starkie declining to stand. But he reckoned without the formidable energy of a seasoned campaign-manager and he was begged to reconsider. He had stood down in favour of Day-Lewis in 1951, in favour of Auden in 1956. Now he had no personal friend to compete with, for the only other nominee was the American poet Robert Lowell. Edmund's sense of patriotism was kindled and he began to see the professorship as a chance to reach the higher ranks of the Oxford hierarchy, which he felt had never fully recognised him. He was also sympathetic to Enid Starkie's half-recovery from serious illness and hated as always to say no. He reconsidered and accepted nomination.

Immediately the factions were drawn up, Maurice Bowra – claiming extreme distaste for the whole affair – becoming the spokesman for Lowell, Enid Starkie campaigning even harder for Edmund, warmly supported by Francis Warner (now at St Peter's College) and by the writer Joanna Richardson, who had received considerable help from Edmund in her Keats researches. The candidates themselves were both somewhat bewildered: Lowell in America musing on the eccentricities of English university procedure; Edmund in Suffolk taking some comfort from the news that Ladbrokes gave odds of 5−4 against his success. The fact that odds were available only emphasised the very public arena into which Edmund had unwittingly stepped.

315

Posters began to appear in the streets of Oxford; letters supporting or attacking each candidate flooded the local and national press. Richard Burton and Elizabeth Taylor – in Oxford for Nevill Coghill's production of *Dr Faustus* – publicly supported Edmund. The Lowell camp published a list of some fifty nominators; the Blunden camp replied with a list of over 300 – though twenty-seven turned out not to have the required qualifications, including the Bishop of Bermuda and the Archdeacon of Macclesfield. Most bizarre of all was the fact that, when challenged, Bowra could not quote a single line of Lowell's poetry; Enid Starkie was equally unable to offer a single line from Edmund's.

On the two polling days – 3 and 5 February 1966 – intense media attention, including television cameras, was focused on the Sheldonian Theatre. In the days immediately before voting it had become a one-horse race – Lowell, the forty-nine-year-old modernist, would completely overthrow the outdated sixty-nine-year-old Blunden. But Oxford preserved its reputation for the unexpected. Many of Edmund's old friends and admirers saw the election as an opportunity to repay past kindnesses and they were joined by coachloads of Blunden voters from country cricket clubs and rural parsonages. The final count was Lowell 241, Blunden 477. Edmund was elected by a 236 majority, the highest poll and the largest majority ever recorded. A celebratory party at the Victoria Arms in Marston was attended by a crowd of well-wishers including the Burtons. Edmund was, for the moment, the best-known poet in England.

The locals at the Victoria Arms were impressed too. When the party was over he stayed with them to discuss fishing opportunities in the Cherwell and the price of beer. Their response was the request, 'Don't take him away from us: he talks our language.'[5] They were right – the public bar was now more Edmund's home than the lecture theatre. He retired to bed that night basking in the glory of his new recognition. But it was to be short-lived. The prestigious academic cap was soon to become a crown of thorns.

The immediate effect was a blaze of publicity – film-crews and reporters visiting Long Melford – and a doubling of his already over-weighty postbag. Four days after his election he wrote to Sassoon:

There was no thought in my mind of competing for Robert Graves's vacant chair but Enid Starkie, having heard that Robert Lowell had been put up with some attitude of overwhelming success (not his fault), decided to do something. We (Enid and I) have long known each other, yet scarcely had a conversation. Anyway, Enid was determined and especially as we knew how ill she is, it was agreed. Several wonderful friends – especially in Oxford – did all they could, and on Saturday evening I found myself 'in the chair'. Since then, need I say, torrents of letters and telegrams . . . and manuscripts for me to read . . . have kept me pretty busy.[6]

One letter was particularly welcome, for Lowell wrote to congratulate him on his success and to declare that 'I've admired your poetry for years, and rather felt as though an old friend were being set against me, when this controversy began to boil. I really should have withdrawn when you entered, but somehow didn't through inertia.'[7]

A further pleasant outcome was a reconciliation (after thirty years) with Robert Graves who, at the following year's Encaenia (the university's annual ceremony to commemorate its benefactors), sought Edmund out from all the assembled dignitaries and shook him warmly by the hand, saying, 'You're the *one* person I really wanted to meet.'[8]

The spectre of lecturing was mercifully postponed for a time during which he engaged in a two-week Arts Council poetry-reading tour of the North-west and the Midlands in the company of the poet Vernon Scannell. A warm friendship quickly developed between the cricketing Great War veteran and the professional boxer, who had served in the Middle East and Norway in the Second World War. They shared war memories, poetic enthusiasms and a taste for beer, and Edmund remembered these weeks as some of the happiest of his later life. For Scannell's part he recalled Edmund as 'the most modest, courteous and generous man I have ever met or will be likely to meet and it was impossible not to love him'.[9] He recorded the tour in a sonnet written for Edmund, entitled 'Meeting in Manchester':

> *Manchester sustained its long sad jest.*
> *The mild monsoon that's drowned so many scores*
> *Sighed like slow surf on cold deserted shores,*
> *But I wore comfort like an extra vest*
> *And hoped that you were just as warmly dressed*
> *While at that table, neither mine nor yours*
> *But briefly ours, we talked of our two wars,*
> *Of books and games with undiminished zest.*
> *Almost it seemed to me that you and I*
> *Were equals – sharing, as we did, a taste*
> *For poetry and drink, revering the pen,*
> *Though both had known war's splendour and its waste –*
> *Precious illusion of equality,*
> *Best gift from best of soldiers, poets, men.*[10]

## PART NINE   1964 – 1974

On Edmund's return the full nature of his Oxford commitment became clear and his nightmare began. He confided to Michael Meyer that he felt like some half-blind cricket professional who found that he was unexpectedly required to open the batting. Not that he had lost all his platform presence, as George Fraser had found during Edmund's lectures for the Clare centenary. Fraser recalled him lecturing 'without notes, with strange, inhuman bird-bright eyes, fitting his lecture together, straw by straw, twig by twig, like a bird's nest'.[11]

For his Oxford lectures Edmund clung to the familiar themes of Romantic poetry, war poets and Thomas Hardy, but found it increasingly difficult to order his thoughts or even to engage in any sustained reading. His nervousness and fear of public failure almost brought him to a state of collapse. On the lecture platform there were moments of near farce – fumbling with his papers and academic dress he managed to place his notes inside his mortar-board, which he then placed on his head. As the months went by, the torture became greater and the audiences dwindled. By a cruel stroke of fate he had been given his most public English platform at the moment when he had least to say and was losing the power to express himself.

A few weeks after the inaugural lecture in May 1966 his doctor insisted on Edmund's spending some days in Papworth Chest Clinic, for nervous exhaustion had inflamed his asthma; it became the pattern of his Oxford visits, as he was to suffer some kind of collapse after each lecture. For convalescence in the summer of 1966, Edmund and Claire explored the Ancre valley, taking the little train from Amiens to Albert, looking out on to the sun-drenched landscape of the Somme. Almost immediately after their return they were back in northern France and Belgium, visiting Verdun and Ypres with Alec Hardie and Yung Kai Kin. Edmund seemed stronger and prepared himself for the celebrations of his seventieth birthday in November, which was to be marked by the Arts Council with a poetry-reading and the cutting of a gramophone record of a selection of Edmund's work read by Cecil Day-Lewis, his wife Jill Balcon and the actor Carleton Hobbs; the list of sponsors for the recording exceeded 300 names. But on the evening before his birthday, Edmund fell and hurt his back, finding himself on 1 November in Bury St Edmund's Hospital. Claire and the family were forced to attend the festivities without him, and Rupert Hart-Davis read his prepared eulogy to the empty chair that Edmund should have been occupying.

The routine of Oxford visits, trips to France and bouts of illness continued through 1967; and other worries were pressing. For

318

eighteen months Sassoon had become increasingly unwell and Edmund found visits too painful for both parties – Sassoon had become irritable, moody and difficult to hear. In June of 1967 Mugg died peacefully in her one-hundredth year. Intimations of mortality seemed all too clear.

The professorship, however, relentlessly brought invitations for talks or lectures outside Oxford. In March 1966 he gave the Tredegar Memorial Lecture to the Royal Society of Literature on Wordsworth, and in July of the following year the Presidential Address to the English Association on a typically whimsical title, 'A Few Not Quite Forgotten Writers?' In the same year he was also to lecture at the University of Kent and at the Cheltenham Festival, and give a speech to the Johnson Society at Lichfield, in which he included his own translation of Dr Johnson's Latin poem addressed to the editor of the *Gentleman's Magazine* in 1738. All these events meant tiring journeys, usually by train, unless he was driven by Alec Hardie, who stayed for extended periods at Hall Mill.

Within Oxford there were engagements both formal and informal. The less formal non-university occasions were distinctly more pleasurable – a lecture on Shakespeare in the town hall, a talk to the monthly lunchtime meeting of Oxford bank managers where his 'simple yet penetrating personality was felt by all', and an evening spent with the appreciative patients of Littlemore Hospital, all enabled Edmund to show his best relaxed style. The more formal obligations of joining the Encaenia procession and delivering the Latin Creweian Oration caused more worry, though he was proud to have composed a Latin oration for his first Encaenia which required only little adaptation from the Public Orator. When not involved in official functions he visited Merton (where he was an honorary fellow), sitting for a portrait[12] by Charles Stitt which Nevill Coghill had commissioned for the Senior Common Room, and spent an increasing amount of time in St Peter's College, which had given him honorary membership of the Senior Common Room and where he found a welcome from a group of undergraduates whose tutorials he often attended and contributed to, and in whose rooms he could relax, talk and drink informally, away from the public eye.

In the privacy of Long Melford his state of health was causing deep concern to Claire. Nightmares and war memories were becoming more frequent, the dread of lecturing increased the desire for alcohol, and his rages grew more violent. His precarious balance precipitated a further series of falls, which resulted in his tripping over the doorstep on returning from the Bull one evening, and crashing down the stairs of Hall Mill after angry exchanges. He began to feel isolated from his family, growing jealous of their youth and fearing intrigue behind his back; at times he felt possessed by an alien personality.

In August 1967 Edmund and Claire were back in Flanders and in the following month Edmund was again at Toc H headquarters in Ypres. On his return he was met at Sudbury station by Jim White, who was to drive him back to Long Melford. During the drive Edmund was informed of the news which he had been secretly dreading: while Edmund had been in Belgium, Sassoon had died at Heytesbury. Suddenly there seemed little left to live for.

He gave his Oxford lecture in the autumn but on returning to Hall Mill he collapsed in the kitchen. He was rushed to hospital suffering from concussion, which left his memory unreliable and affected the pattern of his speech. He struggled through yet another lecture in the spring of the following year and then, with a sense of immense relief, he resigned the professorship. Some in Oxford circles attacked him for being feeble.

The next six months became a subconscious process of reviewing the varied strains of his life and setting them in order. A visit to the Star and Garter Hotel in Brighton (where he had stayed with Claire in 1940) marked his farewell to the Royal Sussex Regiment, followed by a final trip to France and a meeting in the Bull with Lindsay Clarke, one of the principal characters in *Undertones of War*. Edmund seemed almost able to say 'Goodbye to all that.'

While in Amiens in 1966 he had written his last poem; for the Clare centenary celebrations he had completed his prose writing; in July 1968 he wrote his final contribution for the *Times Literary Supplement* and laid down his pen.

Mugg's death had closed a Yalding window; Catherine's enrolment at Christ's Hospital Girls' School provided a comforting sense of continuity. Visitors from Japan and Hong Kong kept the east in view. A sad visit to Joy's grave at Kirtling was balanced by a happy family Christmas with the company of Clare. (His son John and family had moved to South Africa.) A lunch at Romano's in London provided a shared birthday celebration with Sylva and memories of thirty years before; Margaret's marriage to Mark Miller in June 1968 focused thoughts on the present and the future.

After another fall in February 1969, Edmund visited Margaret, who had moved to Wales. He was driven by Alec Hardie in company with Yung Kai Kin, travelling slowly through the Wye valley, stopping at

Tintern Abbey and later visiting the grave of Henry Vaughan. It was to be the last of Edmund's much loved literary tours, and indeed to be his last journey outside Suffolk. On his return to Long Melford he withdrew behind the doors of Hall Mill, following his own summons in 'A Swan, a Man', written a few years earlier:

> *Into the house, recall what dead friends say,*
> *And like the Ancient Mariner learn to pray.*[13]

# 27

# Long Melford
## February 1969 – January 1974

---

*His world now is timeless and events seem almost
irrelevant but his smile for all of us, and his friends,
shows how affection is still there and it brightens us all.*
Letter from Claire to Rupert Hart-Davis, May 1971[1]

> *The great rage,*
> *You see, is kill'd in him.*
> King Lear, Act IV, scene VII

---

Almost from the moment of Sassoon's death a new calm seemed to enter Edmund's consciousness. It was as if the spectre of his own death could now be faced without fear, and the release from the burdens of public duties took away the frustrating sense of inadequacy which had haunted him. Slowly the inner rages subsided and the white-haired figure walking in the garden smiled again with his characteristic gentleness – as he fed his bacon-rinds to the rats, on the grounds that they were the senior residents and were relations of his old verminous comrades in the war-trenches. His family watched him with growing unease, especially after a cerebral spasm in May 1969 left him in a state of semi-consciousness for three days. Sylva and Clare arrived to find him sitting quietly by the window, and he confided to Jim White that during his coma he had 'visited a country of birds'. From that moment on he slowly became an observer rather than a participant in the world around him and his now husky voice became less and less heard.

Events and time became blurred. When being driven to Aldeburgh one afternoon, Edmund fell asleep in the back of the car. On arrival, he awoke to see the lines of little houses on the sea front – reminiscent of Gallic villages – and like Lear he enquired, 'Am I in France?' He spoke in French for the remainder of the day.

For Claire, now aged fifty-two, life was becoming increasingly difficult. She had given up teaching to spend more time at home, and the award to Edmund of a Midsummer Arts Prize of £1,500 in 1971 relieved some of the inevitable financial worries. But earlier in the year she had fallen off her bicycle and broken her ankle – a fracture which required surgery and which refused to heal quickly, leaving her a semi-invalid for almost six months, forcing her to miss family celebrations at the Bull for Edmund's and her silver wedding. Some help was essential and was provided by a friend of Claire's in Long Melford, Hilda Anderson, who came to Hall Mill to act as nurse for extended periods and within a few days gained Edmund's affection and total trust.

He still received a few visitors, including his old infant-school teacher from Yalding, Mrs Mitchener, who was brought by her son on three successive summers. One of the last and most welcome guests was Vernon Scannell, who arrived in the summer of 1971, bringing the poet Ted Walker with him. Scannell was struck by the sense of 'energy in repose' in Edmund's features and described him showing them his treasured picture of an owl which he had been given by Sam Sefton:

We stood there for some time, fixed by the owl's stare. Then, as we turned away, Edmund said, in his faint, crepitant whisper, but quite distinctly, 'He's a good old owl . . . .'

We exchanged farewells and. . . . I got into the car and we drove away.

We were silent for a few moments. Then Ted spoke. 'He's a good old owl,' he said.[2]

The summer of 1971 also marked Edmund's last public appearance, at the double wedding of Lucy and Frances in Long Melford church. Another personal thread had been happily woven, though he had to say an immediate farewell to Lucy, who moved to live in Belize.

As the months passed he became an increasingly silent figure in the house, communicating almost telepathically with Claire, sitting quietly in his favourite chair in the kitchen – where, a year later, he smilingly held his new granddaughter, Lottie Miller, in his arms.

Gradually he retired to his bedroom as his mind became more confused; he seemed only half aware of the news of Sylva's death. He became a thin figure moving slowly between the bed and the window, looking out towards the church. It was in his chair at the window that

## PART NINE 1964 – 1974

Claire found him on the morning of 20 January 1974, the Eve of St Agnes, quietly slipping into a coma after a sudden heart attack. As she put him into bed, Hilda Anderson entered the room and Edmund looked up and smiled. Clare arrived with her daughter Caroline, and Margaret, Mark and Lottie lay on the bed beside him as he slowly faded into unconsciousness. Later in the day, Claire was sitting in the room with Frances when she heard Edmund's breathing change. She gently slipped her arms around him as his old grey eyes closed in final rest.

His grave was dug in a quiet and beautiful corner of Long Melford churchyard, headed by a simple stone commemorating the 'Beloved Poet' with the opening lines of his poem 'Seers' engraved around his name:

> *I live still, to love still*
> *Things quiet and unconcerned.*[3]

The day of the funeral, on 25 January, was a fine wintry one, and a simple service – at which Catherine read Edmund's sonnet 'Values' – was conducted by the rector. As the crowd of mourners gathered outside, the sun appeared briefly and shone on the fine stone exterior of the old church. Among the group standing by the side of the grave was a small unobtrusive figure: he was Private A. E. Beeney of the 11th Royal Sussex Regiment, who had been Edmund's runner at Ypres and Passchendaele. Stepping forward he let fall from his hand a wreath of Flanders poppies which fluttered down on to the coffin in fond and final salute.

# EPILOGUE

---

*So passed away one of the most beautiful personalities that I had ever known.*
Sir Geoffrey Keynes, 'The Gates of Memory', 1981[1]

*Life always did appear difficult to me, yet I was rather keenly urged towards some sort of leadership in it.*
Letter to Claire Poynting, February 1942[2]

---

With someone as widely loved as Edmund had been it was inevitable that warm tributes would be paid to him from a wide variety of sources.

On 7 March 1974 a memorial service was held in St Bride's Church, Fleet Street, at which John Betjeman read the lesson and a moving address was given by Rupert Hart-Davis – who described Edmund as 'absolute for friendship' – and which ended with his reading of 'Values', a poem which incorporates the voice of Edmund probably more than any other single poem:

> *Till darkness lays a hand on these gray eyes*
> *And out of man my ghost is sent alone,*
> *It is my chance to know that force and size*
> *Are nothing but by answered undertone.*
> *No beauty even of absolute perfection*
> *Dominates here – the glance, the pause, the guess*
> *Must be my amulets of resurrection;*
> *Raindrops may murder, lightnings may caress.*
> *There I was tortured, but I cannot grieve;*
> *There crowned and palaced – visibles deceive.*
> *That storm of belfried cities in my mind*
> *Leaves me my vespers cool and eglantined.*
> *From love's wide-flowering mountain-side I chose*
> *This sprig of green, in which an angel shows.*[3]

# Epilogue

A month later a service of thanksgiving was held at Christ's Hospital, when Francis Warner read eight of Edmund's poems and Jack Morpurgo gave an address. In Japan the monuments at Hiroshima and Miyajima were followed by a stone carving of Edmund's head which was installed in the library of Tokyo University, facing one of Lafcadio Hearn. Hong Kong University was to offer its tribute some years later with the establishment of a Blunden Memorial Lecture.

It was to be eleven years before full recognition was to come his way in Westminster Abbey, when he was to join fifteen other names on a memorial in Poets' Corner to First World War poets. Here, fittingly, his name will for ever be found alongside that of Siegfried Sassoon.

But perhaps the ceremony which would have given Edmund most satisfaction was the dedication of a memorial window engraved by Laurence Whistler, in the church of St Peter and St Paul in Yalding in 1979.[4] After a reading of some of Edmund's poems by Vernon Scannell, the address was given by Dennis Silk. He read from a letter which Edmund had written to Pugg some fifty-five years earlier: 'Hopping is over. I smell Yalding distinctly. That shadowy ripeness hanging in the air, the smoke permeating from the Kells, the jerseyed bin men and mittened pickers in the further gardens – I must see it again one day.'[5]

In a sense, Edmund had returned home. After many homes and many hauntings he could say as he had written in his poem 'Homes and Haunts':

> It is not wholly past, the time enrolled
> In registers grown old; those records lie
> Outside the playhouse of the inward eye,
> And life's a story not so simply told.[6]

EDMUND

*I live still*

BLUNDEN

*to love still*

1896 ~ 1974

*things quiet*

BELOVED

*& unconcerned*

POET

Simon Verity's design for EB's gravestone, 1917

# Notes and References

## Abbreviations

| | |
|---|---|
| A.H. | Aki Hayashi |
| B.K. | Brownlee Kirkpatrick, *A Bibliography of Edmund Blunden, Oxford University Press, 1979* |
| C.M.B. | Mrs Claire Blunden |
| H.R.C. | Humanities Research Center, University of Texas at Austin |
| *P.M.Y.* | *Poems of Many Years*, Collins, 1957 (B.K. A135) |
| R.H.-D. | Sir Rupert Hart-Davis |
| S.N. | Sylva Norman |
| S.S. | Siegfried Sassoon |
| *The Poems* | *The Poems 1914–30)*, Cobden-Sanderson, 1930 (B.K. A35) |
| *U.O.W.* | *Undertones of War*, Penguin, 1982 (B.K. A28) |

References to quotations from Edmund's published material are to the most readily available sources, rather than the first appearance. Several poems are available in *Edmund Blunden, Selected Poems*, ed. Robyn Marsack, Carcanet, 1982.

Full bibliographical information is available in B.K.

Provenance of material (except where noted): Letters to C.M.B., A.H. and S.N., in the possession of C.M.B; Letters to R.H.-D. and Philip Tomlinson, in the possession of R.H.-D; letters to and from S.S. and all Blunden diaries, at H.R.C.; letters to Takeshi Saito at Meisei University Library, Tokyo; letters to Hector Buck in the Bodleian Library, Oxford.

## PART ONE 1896–1915

### 1 Ancestors

1 Letter, 16.9.41.

2 Information from a conversation between the author and Edmund's sister, Mrs Phyllis Pritchard.

3 Quoted in Sir Rupert Hart-Davis's memorial address for Edmund, St Bride's, Fleet Street, 7.3.74.

4 *Diary of Virginia Woolf*, vols 2 and 3, ed. Anne Olivier Bell, Penguin, 1981, 1982.

5 Siegfried Sassoon, *Diaries 1920–1922*, ed. Rupert Hart-Davis, Faber & Faber, 1981.

6 Letter to Edmund (in typically eccentric format and calligraphy), 15.12.28, in possession of C.M.B.

7 Accounts of the astonishing burial-alive of Mrs William Blunden, after a heavy drinking bout, can be found in *History of Basingstoke* by F. J. Baigent and J. E. Millard (1889). The incident appears to have been familiar to

Jane Austen for it was a favourite story of Lady Jane Bertie, first mother-in-law of Jane Austen's brother James. Lady Jane's sister-in-law was the daughter of Mrs William Blunden.

8　Letter transcribed in Edmund's hand among papers at H.R.C.

9　Letter to S.N., 27.9.33.

10　An obsession with Shelley began with Edmund's earliest reading. Kirkpatrick lists over sixty entries concerning Shelley in her Blunden bibliography. Shelley moved to Great Marlow in 1817.

11　*Memoirs of the Verney Family*, vols 1 and 2, ed. Frances Parthenope Lady Verney, vols 3 and 4, ed. Margaret M. Verney, Tabard Press, 1970.

12　Letter from Lady Verney to Edmund's mother, 21.10.19. In the possession of Mrs Phyllis Pritchard.

13　Letter, 7.3.24. See note 12.

14　Letter, 2.1.12. See note 12.

15　Correspondence between Tyler and his wife is in the possession of Mrs Phyllis Pritchard.

16　The Liberty and Property Defence League was a small political group which emphasised individualism and upheld the rights of small business in the face of increasing municipalisation.

17　Leigh Hunt was another of Edmund's obsessive literary loves. Nearly forty Hunt items are listed in Kirkpatrick's Blunden bibliography.

18　See *Who's Who of British Members of Parliament*, vol.2, ed. M. Stenton and S.Lees, Harvester Press, 1978.

19　Edmund's mistaken belief that Henry Tyler committed suicide led to a fanciful theory that he would have been buried on the edge of the cemetery in 'unhallowed ground'. In fact Tyler's death certificate records his death from diabetes and his burial certificate records interment in a communal grave – not uncommon for cholera victims during epidemics at the time, though inexplicable in Tyler's case. The family's apparent neglect of his memory remains unexplained.

20　Charles Lamb was never far from Edmund's thoughts. There are over fifty entries concerning Lamb in Kirkpatrick's Blunden bibliography.

21　Edmund probably identified with John Clare more than with any other single writer, and some forty-five relevant entries are listed in Kirkpatrick's Blunden bibliography.

22　This observation is written in Edmund's hand on the title-page of his own copy of his own edition of *Poems by Ivor Gurney*, Hutchinson, 1954 (B.K. B167), in possession of C.M.B.

23　*The Poems.*

## 2　Yalding

1　Letter to S.S., undated.

2　*English Villages*, Collins, 1941 (B.K. A69).

3　'Old Homes', *P.M.Y.*

4　Autobiographical notes at H.R.C.

5　Unfinished ms.memoir of his father at H.R.C.

6　*A Hong Kong House*, Collins, 1962 (B.K. A156).

7　Ms.autobiographical notes in possession of C.M.B.

8　'Country Childhood' from *Edwardian England 1901–14*, ed. Simon Nowell-Smith, Oxford University Press, 1964 (B.K. B256). Ms. of first draft in possession of C.M.B.

9　Charles Blondin (1824–97) crossed Niagara on a tightrope – also blindfolded, on stilts, with a wheelbarrow and with a man on his back. Captain Matthew Webb (1848–83), the first man to swim the English Channel, died attempting to swim the Niagara rapids.

10 Letter from Miss Christabel Eyre, daughter of the vicar of Framfield, at H.R.C. Quoted in a letter from Edmund to his brother Lance, 27.2.53. In possession of Lance Blunden.

11 The training ship *Mount Edgcumbe* at Saltash.

12 Letter to his brother Lance, 8.10.53. In possession of Lance Blunden.

13 'C.E.B.', *P.M.Y.*

14 'Leisure', *P.M.Y.*

15 *Ibid.*

16 *English Villages.* See note 2.

17 *P.M.Y.*

18 'Country Childhood'. See note 8.

19 'Water Sport', *The Poems.*

20 Letter to R.H.-D. 1.2.54. Edmund shared, from an early age, Hardy's identification with his landscape in novels such as *The Return of the Native* and *Far from the Madding Crowd*. Later he preferred Hardy's poetry. Kirkpatrick records more than thirty entries on Hardy material in her Blunden bibliography.

21 Letter to his mother from Ypres, 28.7.17.

22 'Country Childhood'. See note 8.

23 *Ibid.*

24 'Masquerade', *The Poems.*

25 'The River House', *To Nature*, Cyril Beaumont, 1923 (B.K. A14).

26 'Epitaph', *P.M.Y.*

27 'Country Childhood'. See note 8.

28 'The Nameless Stream', *P.M.Y.*

29 'Leisure', *P.M.Y.*

30 'Country Childhood'. See note 8.

31 'Cloudy June', P.M.Y.

32 'The Yellowhammer', *P.M.Y.*

33 *P.M.Y.*

34 *Ibid.*

35 *Ibid.*

36 *Ibid.*

37 *Ibid.*

38 See note 4 above

39 See note 5.

40 *P.M.Y.*

41 'Old Homes', *ibid.*

42 'Country Childhood'. See note 8.

43 *P.M.Y.*

44 *The Face of England*, Longmans, 1932 (B.K. A43)

45 From article on his father in *SS Peter and Paul*, Yalding parish magazine, Dec. 1951 (B.K. A115).

46 *Ibid.*

47 Letter from father, 27.2.33, in possession of R.H.-D. Copy at H.R.C.

48 'Country Childhood'. See note 8.

49 *P.M.Y.*

50 Hence Francis Warner's poem 'Bells', dedicated to Edmund: *Collected Poems 1960–84*, Colin Smythe, 1985.

51 'Country Childhood'. See note 8.

52 *P.M.Y.*

53 *A Hong Kong House.* See note 6.

54 Anecdote supplied by Lance Blunden.

55 *P.M.Y.*

56 *Ibid.* 'Forefathers' first published in the *Nation*, June 1920.

57 'Country Childhood'. See note 8.

58 *P.M.Y.*

## 3   Christ's Hospital

1 Letter to Hector Buck, 11.11.20

2 Coleridge was constantly in Edmund's consciousness, and Kirkpatrick's Blunden bibliography lists some forty relevant entries.

3 Leigh Hunt, *Autobiography.* See *The Christ's Hospital Book 1553–1953*, ed. Edmund Blunden, Eric Bennett, Philip Youngman Carter and J. E. Morpurgo, Hamish Hamilton, 1953.

4 Lamb's 'Christ's Hospital Five and Thirty Years Ago', *Essays of Elia.*

5 *Cricket Country*, Collins, 1944 (B.K. A76).

6 Orbilius Pupillus, who taught the poet Horace.

7 Leigh Hunt, *Autobiography.*

8 See note 4.

9 Coleridge, *Table Talk.*

10 Letter to George Dyer. See *The Christ's Hospital Book* (note 3).

11 Autobiographical ms. in possession of C.M.B.
12 See note 4.
13 Supplied by Hector Buck.
14 Philip Youngman Carter, *All I Did Was This*, Sexton Press, 1982.
15 *The Poems*.
16 'My First Housemaster', *The Blue*, May 1956.
17 See note 11.
18 Supplied by Hector Buck.
19 *Ibid*.
20 *Edmund Blunden, Sixty-Five*, ed. Chau Wah Ching, Lo King Man and Yung Kai Kin, Hong Kong, 1961.
21 Ms. in archives at Christ's Hospital.
22 See note 11.
23 Gilbert White (1720–93), priest and distinguished naturalist, was the author of *Natural History and Antiquities of Selborne* (1788).
24 Originally 'A Prologue', *The Poems*.
25 See note 11.
26 From Shelley's 'Ode to the West Wind'. See 'S.E.W.', *The Blue*, June/July 1944.
27 'S.E.W.', *The Blue*, June/July 1944.
28 Anecdote supplied by Hector Buck.
29 See references to Merk in *Barnes Wallis*, biography by J. E. Morpurgo, Ian Allan, 1981.
30 In the archives at Christ's Hospital.
31 Presumably Edward Lytton (1831–91), poet, rather than his father, the novelist Edward Bulwer-Lytton (1803–73).
32 Ms. notes on back of a large brown envelope. In possession of C.M.B.
33 Letter, 28.2.15, in possession of Mrs Phyllis Pritchard.
34 In the archives of Christ's Hospital. Timothy curiously misspells Edmund's name as Blundon.
35 'Epicedium', *The Blue*, March 1919.
36 H.R.C.
37 *The Blue*, June 1974.
38 Letter to Sydney Matthewman, 5.8.22, H.R.C.
39 See note 37.

40 J. E. Morpurgo (1918– ) was Professor of American Literature, University of Leeds, 1969–83, and Director General, National Book League, 1955–69.
41 W. J. Cullen was an Irish rugby international, capped in 1920. T. N. Pearce (1905– ), the cricketer, was captain of Essex, 1946–9. D.R.W. Silk (1931– ), captain of Cambridge University Cricket Club, 1955, obtained blues for rugby and rugby fives and played cricket for Somerset, 1956–60. He was Warden of Radley College, Abingdon, from 1968.
42 *The Christ's Hospital Book*. See note 3.
43 See note 11.
44 *Ibid*.
45 Notes entitled 'Some Writers of Our Time' at H.R.C.
46 'Mr Kipling Reconstructs', *Nation and Athenaeum*, 28.4.23.
47 See note 45.
48 Introduction to *The Unending Vigil, A History of the Commonwealth War Graves Commission*, Philip Longworth, Constable, 1967.
49 See note 11.
50 *Ibid*.
51 *Ibid*.
52 Quotation from 1 Peter 2:17, always read as a lesson in the Christ's Hospital leavers' service. It has become a kind of unofficial school motto.

## PART TWO 1915 – 1919

1 Letter to his mother, 31.3.[18], H.R.C.

## 4 Training
## August 1915–May 1916

1 *Edmund Blunden, Sixty-Five*, ed. Chau Wah Ching, Lo King Man and Yung Kai Kin, Hong Kong, 1961.
2 Keats was another of Edmund's passions. He wrote over fifty

articles or reviews related to Keats material. T. Richards was one of those who objected to the unseemly rush to collect biographical information immediately after Keats's death.

3 *P.M.Y.*
4 *The Poems.*
5 *Ibid.*
6 *P.M.Y.*
7 Letter from Lady Verney, 2.8.16, in possession of Mrs Phyllis Pritchard.
8 'The Preamble'.
9 *P.M.Y.*
10 *U.O.W.*
11 *Ibid.*

## 5  Festubert, Cuinchy, Richebourg, May – July 1916

1 *De Bello Germanico*, G. A. Blunden, 1930. Reissued with *U.O.W.* by the Folio Society, 1989.
2 *U.O.W.*
3 *The Middle Parts of Fortune*, Granada, 1977. An unexpurgated edition of *Her Privates We* by Private 19022, published by Plaza Press, 1929, and then by Peter Davies in 1964 – with an introduction by Edmund (B.K. B255)
4 I am grateful to Jones's biographer, Professor Thomas Dilworth of Toronto, for information concerning Jones's trench career.
5 *U.O.W.*
6 *Ibid.*
7 'Minnies' – short for *Minenwerfers*, German trench-mortars; 'ack-ack' – signallers' slang for 'anti-aircraft'.
8 *De Bello Germanico*. See note 1.
9 *P.M.Y.*
10 *De Bello Germanico*. See note 1.
11 *P.M.Y.*
12 Letter to his mother, 19.5.16, H.R.C.
13 *P.M.Y.* and *U.O.W.*
14 *U.O.W.*

15 *De Bello Germanico*. See note 1.
16 Marginal annotation in A.H's copy of *U.O.W.* in possession of C.M.B.
17 Letter to his mother, 25.9.16, H.R.C.
18 *U.O.W.*
19 Autobiographical reminiscence among papers at H.R.C.
20 *De Bello Germanico*. See note 1.
21 *Ibid.*
22 Diary, 1916.
23 Letter to his father, 26.6.16, H.R.C.
24 Letter to his father, 1.7.16, H.R.C.
25 *U.O.W.*
26 *Ibid.*
27 *Ibid.*

## 6  The Somme July – December 1916

1 'Two Voices' (originally 'The Survivors'), *U.O.W.* and *P.M.Y.*
2 Letter to his mother, 31.3.16, H.R.C.
3 Letter to his mother, 26.8.16, H.R.C.
4 *U.O.W.*
5 *Ibid* and *P.M.Y.*
6 *U.O.W.*
7 Edited version of long letters to his mother, 10.9.16, H.R.C.
8 Letter to his mother, 27.10.16, H.R.C.
9 See note 7.
10 *U.O.W.*
11 *Ibid.*
12 'At Senlis Once', *U.O.W.* and *P.M.Y.*
13 Letter to his mother, 27.10.16, H.R.C.
14 *U.O.W.*
15 *Ibid.*
16 Letter to his mother, 6.12.16, H.R.C.

## 7  Ypres and Passchendaele December 1916–December 1917

1 Letter to his mother, 26.12.16, H.R.C.

2   Letter to his sister Anne, 10.3.17, H.R.C.
3   *U.O.W.*
4   Letter to his mother, 10.9.16, H.R.C.
5   *U.OW.*
6   *Ibid.*
7   Letter to his mother, 22.4.17, H.R.C.
8   *U.O.W.*
9   Letter to his father, 28.5.17, H.R.C.
10  Letter to Hector Buck, 30.1.17.
11  Letter to Hector Buck, headed 'In de Oude Nachtingarl (Special Bier for Troupes)', 23.10.17.
12  Letter to his mother, 10.9.16, H.R.C.
13  Letter to Hector Buck, 22.6.17.
14  Sydney Dobell (1824 – 74) was the author of *Balder*, an unfinished lengthy dramatic poem which includes lines which simply repeat the exclamation 'Ah!' thirteen times.
15  Letter to his mother (headed 'Nightmare Abbey, Utopia'), 10.10.17, H.R.C.
16  William Ellis (?1700 - 1758), farmer and writer on agriculture and rural life and crafts.
17  Thomas Markwit: presumably Edmund meant White's friend *William* Markwit of Catsfield, Sussex, whose naturalist's calendar forms an appendix to the 1802 edition of *The Natural History of Selborne*. Perhaps Edmund can be forgiven this rare lapse of accuracy, being aged twenty and facing the horrors of Passchendaele.
18  William Cowper (1731 – 1800), poet; George Morland (1763 – 1804), painter of rustic scenes; Sir Joshua Reynolds (1723 – 92), celebrated portrait painter; George Crabbe (1754 – 1832), poet.
19  Letter to his mother (headed 'Nirvana'), 20.9.17, H.R.C.
20  Thomas Campbell (1777 – 1844), Scottish poet and writer of popular war-songs.

21  Letter to his mother, 23.6.17, H.R.C.
22  'Clare's Ghost' (originally 'Phantasies'), *P.M Y.*
23  'Vlamertinghe: Passing the Château, July 1917', *ibid* and *P.M.Y.* Cf. Keats's 'Ode on a Grecian Urn':
*Who are these coming to the sacrifice? . . .*
*And all her silken flanks with*
*garlands drest.*
24  Diary, 29.7.17.
25  Diary, 30.7.17.
26  Diary, 31.7.17.
27  *U.O.W.*
28  Diary, 1.8.17.
29  Diary, 2.8.17.
30  *P.M.Y.*
31  *U.O.W.*
32  *Ibid.*
33  'Transport Up at Ypres', *P.M.Y.*
34  A strong country beer.
35  Letter to Hector Buck (headed 'Feast of All Furies, Witches and Whatnots'), envelope stamped 5.10.17.
36  Letter to Hector Buck, 23.10.17.
37  *U.O.W.*
38  Letter to his sister Phyllis, 7.10.17, H.R.C.
39  *U.O.W.*
40  *Ibid.*

## 8   The Somme and Demobilisation

### January 1918 – February 1919

1   Letter to his mother, 1918. H.R.C.
2   *U.O.W.*
3   *Ibid.*
4   'Gouzeaucourt: The Deceitful Calm', *U.O.W.*
5   *The Poems.*
6   'Aftertones' from *The Mind's Eye*, Jonathan Cape, 1934 (B.K. A50).
7   Autobiographical ms. in possession of C.M.B.
8   Originally 'Winter Piece', *P.M.Y.*
9   George Borrow (1803 – 81), travelled widely through Europe, settled in Suffolk near Oulton

Broad; John Crome (1768-1821), artist, particularly watercolours, of the 'Norwich School'; Robert Bloomfield (1766-1823), Suffolk farm labourer and poet.

10  i.e. 'Shepherd' (1922).

11  See note 7.

12  *P.M.Y.*

13  See note 7.

14  *A Hong Kong House*, Collins, 1962 (B.K. A156).

15  Entitled 'In Love, to Mary', 1918, H.R.C.

16  Letter to Mary, 23.12.18, H.R.C.

17  Letter to his mother, 28.11.18, H.R.C.

18  *Ibid.*

19  Letter to his mother, 9.2.19, H.R.C.

20  Draft, 7.2.19, H.R.C.

21  See note 6.

22  *The Poems.*

## 9   Undertones of War

1  *Orwell: The War Broadcasts*, ed. W. j. West, Duckworth/BBC, 1985.

2  J. B. Priestley, *Evening News*, 1928.

3  *Poems dating from 1916*: 'Uneasy Peace' (Festubert, May), 'The Yellowhammer' (Hinges – Essars canal), 'The Festubert Shrine' (May), 'Festubert: The Old German Line' (May), 'In Festubert', 'Sheepbells' (Richebourg), 'The New Moon' (Auchy), 'Thiepval Wood' (September). *Poems relating to events of 1916 but probably written after 1918*: 'A House in Festubert', 'The Sentry's Mistake', 'Illusions' (a patrol with fellow soldiers Unsted, May and Bodle at Richebourg, June 1916), 'Two Voices' (the 'he' was Captain Wallace), 'Premature Rejoicing' (recalling August 1916), 'Escape' (recalling Mesnil 1-3 September 1916. Edmund noted, 'Poor Caldwell I think had this job. Barrow and Johns were probably two of the dead'),

'Preparations for Victory' (recalling Hamel, September 1916). 'Zero' (Hamel again), 'At Senlis Once' (recalling October 1916), 'An Infantryman', 'La Quinque Rue'. *Poems dating from 1917*: 'Transport up at Ypres' (January), 'January Full Moon, Ypres' (January), 'Les Halles d'Ypres' (January), 'Clear Weather' (early 1917), 'Zillebeke Brook' (on the road to St Omer, April), 'Trees on the Calais Road' (June), 'Bleue Maison' (at Maison Bleue, west of St Omer, June), 'The Pagoda' (a mined château on the Menin Road), 'Mont de Cassel' (Zuytpeene, September), 'Clare's Ghost'. *Poems recalling 1917 but probably written later*: 'The Zonnebeke Road', 'Trench Raid Near Hooge', 'Concert Party: Busseboom' (recalling actual event in a large hut near Vlamertinghe, in early spring), 'Rural Economy (1917)', 'Battalion at Rest' (recalling Houlle and Moulle; the 'Serjeant' was Ashford, 'Another' was H. C. Naylor), 'E.W.T.: On the Death of His Betty' (i.e. Ernest Tice), 'Vlamertinghe: Passing the Château, July 1917', 'Third Ypres', 'The Welcome' (recalling the Menin Road, September 1917), 'Pillbox' (recalling the Menin Road), 'Gouzeaucourt: The Deceitful Calm', 'The Prophet', 'A Farm Near Zillebeke' (near 'Vince Street'), 'Recognition' (recalling autumn 1917).

All other recollections and descriptions of war scenes are almost certainly later than 1918.

It is possible that a notebook of this date, presented to Christ's Hospital by George Rheam, may be this manuscript.

5  The phrase became the title of a poem in 1925: *P.M.Y.*

6  See letter to Philip Tomlinson, 1.1.23, in possession of R.H.D.

7  *U.O.W.* and *P.M.Y.*

8 *Ibid.*
9 Originally 'Old Battlefields', *Ibid.*
10 *U.O.W.*
11 'Preliminary' to *U.O.W.*
12 Letter to S.N., 12.7.44.
13 *U.O.W.*
14 *Ibid.*
15 'Values', *P.M.Y.*
16 Letter to his sister Lottie, 6.10.16, in possession of R.H.-D.
17 Diary, 18.7.17.
18 *U.O.W.*
19 Letter to his father, 26.6.16, H.R.C.
20 Letter, 16.6.32, H.R.C.
21 *The Poems of Wilfred Owen*, Chatto & Windus, 1931 (B.K. B47).
22 Letter to Mr Ara, undated (1947?) from Japan(?), H.R.C.
23 Letter in possession of C.M.B.
24 H. M. Tomlinson, 'War Books', *Criterion*, April 1930.
25 'A Tribute from the Field', *The Blue*, October 1917.
26 *Ibid.*
27 'The Feast of Five', *The Blue*, July 1917.
28 See note 25.
29 *U.O.W.* and *P.M.Y.*
30 *The Poems.*
31 *U.O.W.*
32 'Frank Worley D.C.M.', *P.M.Y.*
33 *U.O.W.*
34 Extract from a letter from Edward Gibbon to the future Lord Sheffield, 29.4.1767. Harrison quotes it in *Edmund Blunden, Sixty-Five*, ed. Chau Wah Ching, Lo King Man and Yung Kai Kin, Hong Kong, 1961.
35 *Ibid.*
36 *U.O.W.* and *P.M.Y.*
37 *U.O.W.*
38 *Ibid.*

### 10 Aftertones of War

1 Quoted on the title-page of *U.O.W.*
2 *Let the Poet Choose*, ed. James Gibson, Harrap, 1973.
3 Letter to S.S., 4.6.32.
4 Letter to S.S., 21.6.30.

5 Letter in possession of Laurence Whistler, dated 30.12.64.
6 'On Reading That the Rebuilding of Ypres Approached Completion', *U.O.W.* and *P.M.Y.*
7 'Fall in, Ghosts', reprinted in *Contemporary Essays*, ed. Sylva Norman, published Elkin Matthews & Marrot, 1933 (B.K. B60), and in *Edmund Blunden: A Selection of His Poetry and Prose*, ed. Kenneth Hopkins, Rupert Hart-Davis, 1950 (B.K. A108).
8 Letter to S.S., 30.1.28.
9 Letter to R.H.-D., March 1948.
10 Letter in the possession of R.H.-D.
11 *U.O.W.* and *P.M.Y.*
12 *P.M.Y.*
13 *The Bonadventure*, Cobden-Sanderson, 1922 (B.K. A12).
14 Letter dated August 1931, H.R.C.
15 *U.O.W.* and *P.M.Y.*
16 *Daily Express*, 8.11.68.
17 Shakespeare wrote in *Hamlet*: 'Hic et ubique? then we'll *shift* our ground.' A rare misquotation by Edmund and strange that he did not correct it in later editions – particularly since he entitled his account of his French trip in 1933 *We'll Shift Our Ground.*
18 i.e. Ernest Tice, W. J. Collyer and Arnold Vidler.

## Part Three 1919–1924
### 11 Suffolk
#### February – October 1919

1 *The Poems.*
2 Letter to Hector Buck, 22.8.19.
3 'War's People', *The Poems.*
4 'The Estrangement', *The Poems.*
5 'The Ancre at Hamel: Afterwards', *U.O.W.*
6 Letter to his mother, 7.1.19, H.R.C.
7 H.R.C.
8 *Ibid.*
9 Part of an undated draft of autobiography, written on the

reverse of a large brown envelope, in the possession of C.M.B.

10 *P.M.Y.*

11 *Siegfried's Journey*, Faber & Faber, 1945.

12 Extract from undated memorandum. See note 9.

13 *Ibid.*

14 *P.M.Y.*

15 The 'Joy' poems are discussed by Michael Thorpe in *The Poetry of Edmund Blunden*, Bridge Books, 1971.

16 'To Joy' and 'Harvest' became part of the song cycle *Oh Fair to See*, Boosey & Hawkes, 1965. It was recorded by Ian Partridge and Clifford Benson by Hyperion (1981).

17 Letter to the author from Mrs Joy Finzi.

18 *P.M.Y.*

## 12  Oxford
## October 1919 – May 1920

1 Ms. entitled 'Literary Oxford, the Group of 1919–20' H.R.C.

2 Drafted autobiographical notes in the possession of C.M.B.

3 Porter's collection of poetry was *The Signature of Pain*, Cobden-Sanderson, 1930, which includes a dedicatory poem by Edmund.

4 W. H. Davies (1871–1940), author of *Autobiography of a Super-Tramp* (1908) and poems reflecting the natural world.

5 See note 2.

6 Other members of the circle included the novelist Anthony Bertram (author of *The Pool*), Edward Liveing (author of the war autobiography *Attack*), the poets Bertram Higgins and F. V. Follett, the writer and sculptor E. W. Jacot, the Milton editor Bernard Wright, Henry Chapin the editor of Herman Melville, and the Shelley scholar Walter Peck.

7 All quotations concerning Robert Nichols are from the ms. referred to in note 2.

8 Beverley Nichols (1899–1959), Journalist, writer on gardens and the countryside as well as of several volumes of autobiography.

9 Alfred Noyes (1880–1959), poet, playwright, novelist and compiler of anthologies of a markedly traditional nature.

10 A line from Robert Nichols's poem 'Farewell to Place of Comfort'. Edmund repeats it in his 'In Memory of Robert Nichols', *P.M.Y.*

11 See note 1.

12 *In Broken Images, Selected Letters of Robert Graves 1914–46*, ed. Paul Ó'Prey, Hutchinson, 1982.

13 Marsh was literary executor of Rupert Brooke's estate.

14 Letter to his mother, 17.12.24, in possession of R.H.-D.

15 Copy of ms. in possession of C.M.B.

16 *P.M.Y.*

17 *The Letters of John Middleton Murry to Katherine Mansfield*, ed. C. A. Hankin, Constable, 1983.

18 All references to the Clare discoveries and Northampton visit are from the ms. referred to in note 2.

19 *The Poems.*

20 Mary Joyce was John Clare's first love, to whom he thought himself married even after his marriage to Martha Turner. He escaped from Epping asylum in 1841 in an attempt to join her.

21 See note 12.

22 See note 2.

23 'The Case for the Archdeacon', *Nation and Athenaeum*, 30.4.21. For further contributions to the press, see B.K. C261.

24 See note 23. The whole Wakeford case has been reviewed by John Treherne in *Dangerous Precincts*, Jonathan Cape, 1987. The book

comes to much the same
conclusion as Edmund.

25 Letter in possession of R.H.-D.

### 13 London and Suffolk June 1920 – April 1924

1 All extracts from Sassoon's diary
are from Siegfried Sassoon, *Diaries
1923–1925*, ed. Rupert
Hart-Davis, Faber & Faber, 1985.
2 Drafted autobiographical notes in
possession of C.M.B.
3 Autobiographical notes, H.R.C.
4 Letter to his mother, 9.3.55, in
possession of Mrs Phyllis Pritchard.
5 Letter to S.N., 7.3.22.
6 *Ibid.*
7 *The Dialectal Words in Blunden's
Poems*, Oxford, 1921. Tract No. V
of the Society for Pure English.
8 *P.M.Y.*
9 *Ibid.*
10 Letter to his mother, 10.4.24, in
possession of R.H.-D.
11 Letter to Hector Buck, 11.[?]4.21.
12 *In Broken Images, Selected Letters of
Robert Graves 1914– 46*, ed. Paul
O'Prey, Hutchinson, 1982.
13 *Ibid.*
14 *Ibid.*
15 *The Poems.*
16 *Ibid.*
17 *Ibid.*
18 *P.M.Y.*
19 *The Poems.*
20 *Ibid.*
21 *Ibid.*
22 *P.M.Y.*
23 *The Poems.*
24 *P.M.Y.*
25 Letter, 5.2.23, H.R.C.
26 *P.M.Y.*
27 *The Poems.*
28 *Ibid.*
29 *P.M.Y.*
30 *Ibid.*
31 *Ibid.*
32 H. M. Tomlinson, Introduction to
*The Bonadventure*, G. P. Putnam
New York, 1923.

33 *The Bonadventure,*
Cobden-Sanderson, 1922
(B.K. A12).
34 *Ibid.*
35 Letter to his parents, 17.12.21, in
possession of Mrs Phyllis Pritchard.
36 S.S. diary. See note 1.
37 Letter to s.s., 1.7.22.
38 S.S. diary. See note 1.
39 Letter to his parents, 8.7.22, in
possession of R.H.-D.
40 Poetic drama by Swinburne (1865).
41 S.S. diary. See note 1.
42 Letter to his father, 18.7.22, in
possession of R.H.-D.
43 From notes on the visit to Max
Gate, published at the conclusion
of Sylva Norman's essay on
Thomas Hardy for *The Great
Victorians*, ed. H. J. and Hugh
Massingham, Ivor Nicholson and
Watson, 1932.
44 Conversation repeated to the
author between Edmund and
Michael Meyer.
45 Letter to Philip Tomlinson, 30.7.23.
46 See note 43.
47 From Preface to Edmund's *Thomas
Hardy*, Macmillan, 1941.
48 'The English Poets', *The Poems.*
49 Lady Butterworth inherited the
papers from her aunt Alice Bird,
whose brother George was Leigh
Hunt's doctor.
50 From Address to Edmund's edition
of *A Song to David*,
Cobden-Sanderson, 1924.
51 Notes in possession of C.M.B.
52 Letter to Cobden-Sanderson,
31.3.27.
53 S.S. diary. See note 1.
54 'To Clare', *The Poems.*
55 Letter to Philip Tomlinson, 7.9.23.
56 *The Poems.*
57 *Ibid.*
58 Letter in possession of R.H.-D.
59 Letter from Mary Blunden to
Philip Tomlinson, 16.2.24, in
possession of R.H.-D.
60 Letters to Edmund during this
period from Cyril Beaumont and

Cobden-Sanderson are at Iowa University. See Miriam J. Benkovitz, 'Edmund Blunden and the Incitements of Japan', in *Books at Iowa*, (a magazine of the University of Iowa).

61 Letter to Cyril Beaumont, 2.3.24.

62 S.S. diaries. See note 1.

63 See n.4, p. 329.

## PART FOUR 1924 – 1931
## 14 Japan
## April 1924 – July 1927

1 H.R.C.

2 *Edmund Blunden: A Tribute from Japan*, ed. Masao Hirai and Peter Milward, Kenkyusha, 1974.

3 See Desmond Graham, *The Truth of War: Owen, Blunden and Rosenberg*, Carcanet, 1984.

4 From 'Shakespeare's Significances', read to the Shakespeare Association, 25.1.29, reprinted in *The Mind's Eye*, Jonathan Cape, 1934 (B.K. A50).

5 Letter to Takeshi Saito, 5.4.24.

6 A First Impression, (Tokyo), *P.M.Y.*

7 Quoted in letter from Edmund to Takeshi Saito, 25.1.53.

8 Letter to his father, 24.6.24, in possession of R.H.-D.

9 Letter to his father, 21.6.25, in possession of R.H.-D.

10 *The Poems.*

11 Letter to Philip Tomlinson, 18.12.25.

12 *P.M.Y.*

13 *Ibid.*

14 From 'Japanese Moments' in *The Mind's Eye*. See note 4.

15 Inscribed by Edmund in Lewis Bush's copy of *Cricket Country*. See *Edmund Blunden: A Tribute from Japan* (note 2).

16 *The Autobiography of William Plomer*, Jonathan Cape, 1975.

17 *Ibid.*

18 Letter to Hector Buck, 29.12.26

19 *In Broken Images, Selected Letters of Robert Graves 1914– 46*, ed. Paul O'Prey, Hutchinson, 1982.

20 *The Poems.*

21 See 'Imaginative Sympathy, A Remembrance by Tomoji Abe', *Edmund Blunden: A Tribute from Japan* (note 2).

22 Letter to A.H., 23.10.25.

23 *Edmund Blunden, Sixty-Five*, ed. Chau Wah Ching, Lo King Man and Yung Kai Kin, Hong Kong, 1961.

24 Edmund's review appeared in the *Times Literary Supplement* on 15.11.25.

25 From 'The Author's Last Words to His Students', *P.M.Y.*

26 *Edmund Blunden: A Tribute from Japan.* See note 2.

27 Letter to A.H., 9.10.23[?25].

28 Letter to Cyril Beaumont, 17.11.24.

29 'Inland Sea' (originally 'Japanese Nightpiece'), *The Poems.*

30 *The Poems.* Also in *Selected Poems*, ed. Marsack, Carcanet, 1982.

31 Anecdote supplied by Professor Yoshitaka Sakai.

32 From introduction to Robert Lloyd, *The Actor*, C.W. Beaumont, 1926 (B.K. B21).

33 From 'The Deeps', *The Poems.*

34 *Edmund Blunden, Sixty-five.* See note 23.

35 Letter to A.H., 1.8.25.

36 Letter to A.H., 29.8.25.

37 Letter to A.H., 3.9.25.

38 Letter to A.H., 18.9.25.

39 Letter to A.H., 1.10.25.

40 Letter to A.H., 1.8.25.

41 Letter to A.H., 1.9.25.

42 Letter to A.H., 3.12.25.

43 From John Clare's 'Love Lives Beyond the Tomb'.

44 Letter to A.H., 3.9.25.

45 Letter to A.H., 31.8.25.

46 'To A Spirit' (originally 'To . . .'), *The Poems.*

47 Letter to A.H., 8.9.25.

48 Letter to A.H., 21.9.25.

49  Letter to his father, 1.3.26, in possession of R.H.-D.
50  Letter to Cobden-Sanderson 8.3.27
51  Letter to his father, 13.7.26, in possession of R.H.-D.
52  Letter to A.H., 4.3.26.
53  Letter to A.H., 28.9.26.
54  Letter to A.H., 5.5.26.
55  Letter to S.S., 10.2.27.
56  *P.M.Y.*

### 15  London and Suffolk August 1927 – February 1931

1  Letter to Takeshi Saito, 15.8.28.
2  Letter to A.H., 3.4.28.
3  Letter to S.S., 3?.9.27.
4  Letter to Philip Tomlinson, 25.9.27.
5  Letter to Philip Tomlinson, 14.10.27.
6  Letter to Philip Tomlinson, 5.11.27.
7  *P.M.Y.*
8  From 'Edmund Blunden in Suffolk', East Anglian Press (1975?). Exact source and date untraced.
9  Quoted in a letter to Christopher Hassall, 9.4.53, H.R.C.
10  Letter from S.S., 10.10.31, in possession of C.M.B.
11  *Ibid.*
12  *Ibid.*
13  Letter to A.H., 26.8.29.
14  Letter to A.H., 12.9.29.
15  S.S. diary, 30.11.27, quoted by permission of R.H.-D.
16  A copy of this letter is in the possession of R.H.-D.
17  Letter, 17.6.28. .
18  The sonnet and note were enclosed in the same envelope as the letter above.
19  See letters to Takeshi Saito, 15.8.28, 24.9.28.
20  Letter to S.N., 15.2.32.
21  From Dr Johnson's *Lives of the English Poets.*
22  *P.M.Y.*
23  *The Poems.*
24  *P.M.Y.*

25  *Ibid.*
26  *The Poems.*
27  *P.M.Y.*
28  *Ibid.*
29  *The Poems.*
30  *Ibid.*
31  *Ibid.*
32  Letter from S.S., ?.5.28
33  *P.M.Y.*
34  *Ibid.*
35  ? Letter to S.N.
36  Letter to Takeshi Saito, 13.2.28.
37  Letter to Takeshi Saito, 15.8.28.
38  Letter from S.S., 20.12.[28], in possession of C.M.B.
39  See Michael Turner's 'Blunden – Revisions to *Undertones of War*', in *The Warden's Meeting: A Tribute to John Sparrow*, Oxford University Society of Bibliophiles, 1977.
40  Letter to Edmund, H.R.C.
41  Personal memorandum, H.R.C.
42  Letter to Takeshi Saito, 4.1.30.
43  Now in the New York Public Library.
44  ? Letter to S.S., 1930.
45  Letter from Adrian Bell to Kenneth Hopkins, 9.2.?? Copy in possession of R.H.-D.
46  *Ibid.*
47  Described by Adrian Bell. See note 45.
48  Quoted by Major the Rev. Philip Wright in a local East Anglian newspaper, 21.1.74.
49  Letter to his mother, 2.3.54, in possession of Mrs Phyllis Pritchard.
50  Diary, 1930.
51  Diary, 1930.
52  See note 45.
53  Letter to his brother Geoffrey, 18.11.24, in possession of R.H.-D.
54  Letter to his father, 9.10.30, in possession of Mrs Phyllis Pritchard.
55  Letter to Takeshi Saito, 12.2.30
56  B.K. B39.
57  *Sunday Times*, 21.12.30.
58  Letter from S.S., December 1930.

### 16  Yalding March – October 1931

1 Letter to Hector Buck, 9.10.29.
2 Letter to his father, 29.8.26, in possession of R.H.-D.
3 *P.M.Y.*
4 *Ibid.*
5 From the first line of Keat's 'Ode on a Grecian Urn'.

## PART FIVE 1931 – 1945

### 17 Oxford: Merton October 1931–October 1933

1 Letter to his mother, 8.3.32, H.R.C.
2 Letter to E.L Griggs, 16.1.33, H.R.C.
3 'Lascelles Abercrombie', P.M.Y.
4 Diary.
5 Letter to C.M.B. ?1945
6 Quoted in *Edmund Blunden, Sixty-Five*, ed. Chau Wah Ching, Lo King Man and Yung Kai Kin, Hong Kong, 1961.
7 Letter to S.N., 11.7.38.
8 Letter to C.M.B., 30.3.40.
9 See note 6.
10 *Ibid.*
11 Letter to his mother, 31.10.31, in possession of R.H.- D.
12 Letter to A.H., 23.10.31.
13 Letter to S.N., 26.3.32.
14 Quoted from letter of Joan Appleton in Desmond Graham's *Keith Douglas 1920–44*, Oxford University Press, 1974.
15 Letter to S.N., 1.5.33.
16 Letter to S.S., 22.9.32.
17 *Edmund Blunden, Sixty-Five*. See note 6.
18 ? Letter to Takeshi Saito.
19 Letter to Takeshi Saito, 31.1.39.
20 Letter to S.N.
21 Autobiographical notes, H.R.C.
22 Letter to Takeshi, Saito, 24.10.33.
23 Diary.
24 From 'Values', *P.M.Y.*
25 *P.M.Y.*
26 H.R.C.
27 'To Ethelbert White' (B.K. B45). Edmund wrote another poem of the same title for White's London exhibition of 1946 (B.K. B116).
28 All quotations of following characters from letters to C.M.B.
29 Typescript in possession of C.M.B.
30 Letter to S.S., 1.6.32.
31 Sassoon and Hart-Davis did not in fact meet until the 1950s, though they had engaged in considerable correspondence about Edmund's poems.
32 Letter to S.S., 17.11.31.
33 Letter to A.H., 18.11.31.
34 Letter to S.N., 10.2.32.
35 Letter to A.H., 7.2.32
36 Letters to A.H., 14.2.82 and 3.2.32.
37 Letter to S.N., 31.3.33.
38 Letter to S.N., 10.2.32.
39 Letter to A.H., 21.2.32.
40 Letter to S.N., 11.2.32.
41 Letter to S.N., 25.2.32.
42 Preface to *Halfway House*, Cobden-Sanderson, 1932 (B.K. A45).
43 *Ibid.*
44 *P.M.Y.*
45 Letter to S.N., 6.3.32.
46 Quoted in letter to S.N., 8.2.32.
47 *Ibid.*
48 Letter to S.N., 6.2.32.
49 Letter to S.N., 8.2.32.
50 Letter to S.N., 15.2.32.
51 *Ibid.*
52 e.g. letter of 9.2.32: 'You are severely reprimanded for not coming forward in 1918, or at all events before 1928.'
53 Letter to S.N., 14.2.32.
54 Ms. poem 'May 1916' in letter to S.N., 7.3.32.
55 Letter to S.N., 8.3.32.
56 Quoted in letter to S.N., 16.2.32.
57 In a letter to Takeshi Saito, 23.9.29, Edmund suggests writing a memoir of Brown ('It will lead . . . to Italy and New Zealand.... I have some useful references').
58 Among A.H.'s letters.
59 Letter to S.N., 18.1.33.
60 Letter to S.N., 12.6.33.

61 All descriptions of characters are taken from letters to S.N. over this period.
62 Dinner described in letter to S.N., 17.5.32.
63 Letter to S.N., 18.2.33.
64 *Poems 1930 – 40* Cobden-Sanderson, 1940 (B.K. A68)
65 Letter to S.N., 1.5.32.
66 Letter to S.N., 24.11.32.
67 Letter to A.H., 4.8.32.
68 Letter to S.N., 6.3.32. From Marvell's 'The Garden'.
69 Letter to S.N., 12.3.32.
70 Letter to S.N. 10.3.32.
71 Letter to C.M.B., 28.9.42.
72 Letter to S.N., 20.5.32.
73 Letter to S.N., 1932.
74 Letter to S.N., 21.3.32.
75 Letter to S.N., 16.6.33.
76 Letter to S.N., 21.3.33.
77 Letter to S.N., 25.4.32.
78 Letter to S.N., 3.10.32.
79 Noted by Philip Tomlinson in a letter to S.N., 7.3.32.
80 *Choice or Chance*, Cobden-Sanderson, 1934 (B.K. A52).
81 *P.M.Y.*
82 *Ibid.*
83 See note 80.
84 *Poems on Japan*, ed. Takeshi Saito, privately printed, 1967 (B.K. A171).
85 Letter in possession of C.M.B., dated 18.1.33.
86 Described in *Edmund Blunden, Sixty-Five*. See note 6.
87 Letter to S.N., 26.9.33.

## 18   Oxford and Germany
### October 1933–September 1939

1 *P.M.Y.*
2 Letter to R.H.-D., 14.8.39.
3 Letter to A.H., 24.8.39.
4 ? Letter to C.M.B.
5 Letter to S.N., 10.6.32.
6 Letter to S.N., 25.11.37.
7 See letter to R.H.-D., 23.11.38.

8 Letter to R.H.-D., 28.10.37. See also letters of 27.11.37 and 4.12.37.
9 Letter to Takeshi Saito, 28.1.37.
10 *Edmund Blunden: A Selection of His Poetry and Prose*, ed. Kenneth Hopkins, Rupert Hart-Davis, 1950.
11 Sunday Pictorial, 28.5.36.
12 *An Elegy and Other Poems*, Cobden-Sanderson, 1937.
13 'Cabaret Tune', *Ibid.*
14 *Ibid.*
15 *Ibid.*
16 *P.M.Y.*
17 Letter to Takeshi Saito, 21.9.37.
18 Diary.
19 Letter to S.N., 11.7.39.
20 Diary.
21 *Ibid.*
22 From 'The Author's Last Words to His Students', *P.M.Y.*
23 Diary in the possession of Merton College, Oxford.
24 Letter to S.N., 11.3.32.
25 Diary.
26 *The Times*, 1.5.37.
27 Letter, H.R.C.
28 *P.M.Y.*
29 *Ibid.*
30 *Ibid.*
31 *Poems 1930 – 40*, Macmillan, 1941 (B.K. A68).
32 *Ibid.*
33 *Ibid.*
34 Diary.
35 *Edmund Blunden, Sixty-Five*, ed. Chau Wah Ching, Lo King Man and Yung Kai Kin, Hong Kong, 1961.
36 Letter to his mother, 3.9.39, in possession of Mrs Phyllis Pritchard.
37 Letter, addressed to 'Sir O.' H.R.C.
38 Letter to his mother, 31.10.39, in possession of R.H.- D.
39 *P.M.Y.*

## 19   Oxford:War
### September 1939 – May 1945

1 Letter to S.S., ?.11.40.
2 Letter to C.M.B., 3.2.43.
3 Letter to C.M.B., 21.12.39.

4  Letter to C.M.B., 3.11.42.
5  Letter to C.M.B., 26.1.44.
6  Letter to S.N., 7.3.40.
7  Diary.
8  Letter to C.M.B., 28/29.6.40.
9  Letter to C.M.B., 19.4.43.
10  Letter to C.M.B., 6.3.44.
11  Diary.
12  *Ibid.*
13  *The Times*, 16.4.40.
14  Letter to C.M.B., 8.7.40.
15  Letter to C.M.B., 10.7.40.
16  Diary.
17  Letter to C.M.B., 8.11.42.
18  Diary.
19  *Ibid.*
20  Letter to C.M.B., 17.6.43.
21  Diary.
22  *Ibid.*
23  Letter to C.M.B., 28.4.43.
24  Letter to C.M.B., 9.7.41.
25  Diary.
26  Letter to C.M.B., 16.1.44.
27  Letter to C.M.B., 17.10.44.
28  Letter to C.M.B., 15.7.40.
29  Diary.
30  *Ibid.*
31  *Ibid.*
32  Letter to C.M.B., 27.1.43.
33  Diary.
34  See Clare's 'Love lives beyond the tomb'.
35  Diary.
36  *Ibid.*
37  *Ibid.*
38  Typescript of reminiscence, in possession of C.M.B.
39  *Ibid.*
40  Letter to S.S., 28.7.44.
41  Diary.
42  Letter to C.M.B., 26.7.41.
43  Letter to C.M.B., 2.4.41
44  Diary.
45  *Poems 1930–40*, Macmillan 1941 (B.K. A68).
46  *Ibid.*
47  *P.M.Y.*
48  *Poems 1930-40*, see note 45.
49  Quotation in letter to C.M.B., 2.3.40.
50  Diary.
51  *Ibid.*
52  *Ibid.*
53  Letter to C.M.B., 15.7.40.
54  Quotations from letters from Betjeman, in possession of C.M.B.
55  Letter to C.M.B., 7.1.43.
56  Letter to S.S., 15.3.43.
57  Letter to C.M.B., 15.4.43.
58  *Poems 1930–40*. See note 45.
59  Letter to C.M.B., 15.4.43.
60  Letter to C.M.B., 22.11.44.
61  *Ibid.*
62  Letter to C.M.B., 21.12.39.
63  Letter to C.M.B., 20.7.41.
64  Diary.
65  Letter to C.M.B., 19.7.40.
66  Letter to C.M.B., 15.12.42.
67  Anecdote supplied by C.M.B.
68  Undated draft in possession of C.M.B.
69  Letter, 4.3.44, in possession of C.M.B.
70  Letter, 8.2.44, in possession of C.M.B.
71  Letter to C.M.B.
72  Diary.

## PART SIX  An Interlude: Preoccupations
### 20  Book Collecting

1  'Bringing Them Home' from *The Mind's Eye*, Jonathan Cape, 1934 (B.K. A50).
2  Described in 'The British School' in *The Face of England*, Longmans, 1932 (B.K. A43).
3  See note 1.
4  *Ibid.*
5  *Ibid.*
6  Biographical notes typescript in possession of C.M.B.
7  *Edmund Blunden, Sixty-Five*, ed. Chau Wah Ching, Lo King Man and Yung Kai Kin, Hong Kong, 1961.
8  *The thoughtful man the city's inns explores*
    *With diverse monsters swinging at their doors;*

*Here the Red Lion lifts his curious
    back,*
*There the Blue Boar still meditates
    attack,*
*And over there the Pig stands topt with
    spars*
*And towards the stars the winged
    Dragon steers;*
*There in his rich black plumage sails the
    Swan,*
*A rara avis! earth now knows of none.*
*Not Africa herself brought forth this
    train,*
*These monsters all sprung from the
    artist's brain.*

9   Edmund corresponded at length
    about Charlotte Smith with
    Edward Finneron. See letters dated
    29.5.49, 21.8.50, 3.11.50, H.R.C.
10  *P.M.Y.*
11  *Ibid.*

## 21   Cricket

1   Quoted in letter, 7.6.47: H.R.C.
2   *Edmund Blunden, Sixty-Five*, ed.
    Chau Wah Ching, Lo King Man
    and Yung Kai Kin, Hong Kong,
    1961.
3   'Bowler's Turn', I.A.R. Peebles,
    Souvenir, 1960.
4   Letter to Edward Finneron,
    12.3.65, H.R.C.
5   Letter to C.M.B., 28.6.40.
6   From *Macbeth.*
7   *P.M.Y.*
8   *Cricket Country*, Collins, 1944
    (B.K. A76).
9   'Hammond of England', *P.M.Y.*
10  The original replacement of the
    book is humorously described by
    Sassoon in 'An Adjustment'. Ms. in
    possession of Dennis Silk.
11  Quoted in Preface to *Cricket
    Country*. See note 8.
12  Letter to C.M.B.
13  *Cricket Country*. See note 8.
14  *Ibid.*
15  H.R.C.

## PART SEVEN 1945–1950

### 22   The *Times Literary
Supplement*
May 1945 – December 1947

1   *P.M.Y.*
2   Letter in possession of Michael
    Meyer.
3   'Joy and Margaret', *P.M.Y.*
4   *Ibid.*
5   *P.M.Y.*
6   'High Elms, Bracknell', *P.M.Y.*
    The incident is described by
    C.M.B. in *Edmund Blunden,
    Sixty-Five*, ed. Chau Wah-Ching,
    Lo King-Man and Yung Kai-Kin,
    Hong Kong, 1961.
7   'Homes and Haunts', *P.M.Y.*
8   From a description of the evening
    given to Sassoon in a letter from
    R.H.-D., in possession of Edward
    Herrmann.
9   All three poems were published as
    a pamphlet by Rupert Hart-Davis
    for the occasion. Fifteen copies
    were printed and some were signed
    by all the diners – one in
    possession of R.H.-D., one in
    possession of Edward Herrmann, a
    third at H.R.C.
10  Letter, 2.11.46.
11  Letter to S.S., 29.7.47.
12  Letter from S.S., 7.8.47.
13  Letter to R.H.D., July 1948.
14  *Edmund Blunden, Sixty-Five*, See
    note 6.
15  Letter, 31.8.45, in possession of
    Lance Blunden.
16  The library remains intact as the
    Finzi Book Room at Reading
    University Library. A catalogue
    was produced by Pauline Dingley,
    University of Reading, 1981.
17  See *In That Place*, drawings by Joy
    Finzi, Libanus Press, 1987.
18  Diary.

### 23 Japan
### December 1947 – May 1950

1 *A Hong Kong House*, Collins, 1962 (B.K. A156).
2 Letter to R.H.-D., 17.5.49.
3 Letter to C.M.B., 13.4.40.
4 Letter to Philip Tomlinson, 3.8.49.
5 Letter, 5.4.48, in possession of Lance Blunden.
6 Letter, December 1948, in possession of Lance Blunden.
7 Letter, 30.10.48, in possession of Lance Blunden.
8 Diary.
9 Letter to R.H.-D., 8.8.49.
10 *Impressions of Japan*, ed. Mikio Hiramatsu, Shimbunsha, 1952.

## PART EIGHT 1950–1964

### 24 The *Times Literary Supplement*
### May 1950 – September 1953

1 H.R.C.
2 H.R.C.
3 Letter, 11.2.52, in possession of Laurence Whistler.
4 *The Christ's Hospital Book 1553 – 1953*, ed. Edmund Blunden, Eric Bennet, Philip Youngman Carter and J. E. Morpurgo, Hamish Hamilton, 1953.
5 *A Garland for the Queen*, Stainer & Bell, 1953 (B.K. B157).
6 *Poems by Ivor Gurney*, Hutchinson, 1954 (B.K. B167).
7 Copy in possession of C.M.B.
8 Letter, 8.9.52, in possession of Lance Blunden.

### 25 Hong Kong
### September 1953 – May 1964

1 Quoted in *The Lyttelton – Hart-Davis Letters*, John Murray, 1978.
2 *A Hong Kong House*, Collins, 1962 (B.K. A156).
3 See note 2.
4 'The Home of Poetry', *P.M.Y.*

5 *Eleven Poems*, Golden Head Press, 1965 (B.K. A168).
6 See note 1.
7 Volume of Crabbe in possession of C.M.B.
8 Letter to R.H.-D., 1961.
9 See note 2.
10 Letter to S.N., 1957.
11 See note 2.
12 Letter to A.H., March 1955.
13 In possession of C.M.B.
14 Diary.
15 See note 2.
16 *Poems of Sir Francis Hubert*, Hong Kong University Press/Oxford University Press, 1961 (B.K. B236).
17 At H.R.C. Edmund lists twelve grievances against the university and the English Department.

## PART NINE 1964–1974

### 26 Long Melford and Oxford
### May 1964 – February 1969

1 In possession of C.M.B.
2 Now in possession of Francis Warner.
3 Tubby Clayton (Rev. Philip Clayton 1885–1972). He was a chaplain at Ypres and co-founded (with the senior chaplain Neville Talbot) a rest-home for soldiers, at the bottle-neck leading to the salient. It was called Talbot House (T.H.) in memory of Talbot's brother, who was killed in action. Toc H is signaller's language for T.H.
4 Inserted in *Christ Church Meadow*, Oxford University Press 1965, as a holograph facsimile.
5 Anecdote supplied by Robert Levens.
6 Letter to S.S., 9.2.66.
7 H.R.C.
8 Anecdote supplied by Francis Warner.
9 *A Proper Gentleman*, Robson Books, 1977.

10 Printed privately by Martin Booth, 1966.
11 *London Magazine*, April 1966.
12 The portrait was never completed and its whereabouts is unknown.
13 *Eleven Poems*, Golden Head Press, 1965 (B.K. A168).

## 27 · Long Melford
## February 1969 –January 1974

1 Letter, 9.5.71, in possession of R.H.-D.
2 *A Proper Gentleman*, Robson Books, 1977.

3 *A Hong Kong House*, Collins, 1962 (B.K. A156).

### EPILOGUE

1 *The Gates of Memory*, Oxford University Press, 1981.
2 Letter to C.M.B., 3.2.41.
3 *P.M.Y.*
4 The window unfortunately gives Edmund's date of death as 1975.
5 In possession of R.H.-D.
6 *P.M.Y.*

# INDEX

E.B.= Edmund Blunden

# Index

# Index

# Index

# Index

# Index

# Index

and E.B.'s relationship with Mary, 138, 159; with E.B. at *T.L.S.* offices, 267-8; E.B.'s 50th birthday, 270; illness, 287, 290; death, effect on E.B., 303; also 108, 145, 161, 164, 167, 192, 273, 278

Tomlinson, H.M., 94, 107, 124, 131, 139, 164, 302

Tonbridge School, 241

Trapnell, Charlotte, (E.B.'s grandmother), 5

Turner, W.J., 107, 114

Tyler, Georgina Margaret, *née* Rogers, (E.B.'s grandmother), 6

Tyler, Henry, (E.B.'s grandfather), 6-8, 330 (n.19)

Upcott, Dr. A.W., 24, 31-2, 40

Uyeda, Torao, 276

Vansittart, Lord, *Black Record*, 217

Vaughan, Henry, 151, 206, 321

Verlaine, 35-36, 86

Verney, Sir Edmund, 6-7, 8

Verney, Margaret, Lady Verney, 6-7, 40, 48

Vidler, Arnold, 95, 101

Vines, Sherard, 147, 167

Visick, Mary, (née Oswin), 185, 231, 295

Voltaire, 244

Wagner, F.W., 236

Wakeford, Archdeacon John, 120-1

Waldman, Milton, 263

Walker, Ted, 323

Walmsley, Leo, 240

Walpole, Sir Hugh, 192-3

Walton, Izaac, 248-9

War, *see* E.B., *war*

Ware, Sir Fabian, 43-4

Warner, Francis, 252-3, 312, 313, 315, 326, 331 (n.50), 325 (ns. 2, 8)

Warner, Sir Pelham, 257, 259

Warrender, Alice, 132

Watling, E.F., 31

Waugh, Alec, 298

Way, Peter and Elizabeth, 300

Webling, Rev. A.J., 137, 155-6, 161, 249

Wells, Charles, 250-51

Wheare, Sir Kenneth, 204, 219

Whistler, Laurence, 98, 165, 194, 288, 326

Whistler, Rex, 165, 194, 233

White, Ethelbert, 191-2

White, Henry Kirke, 74, 250, 251

White, Jim, 312, 313, 320, 322

White, Rev. L.H., 35

Wilde, Oscar, 8

Wilkinson, Colonel C.H., 177, 227, 230, 253, 258, 302

Williams, Sir Edgar, 258

Williams, Margaret Maria, *see* Verney, Margaret

Williams, Samuel, 22, 33

Williams, Rev. Stephen, 184, 258

Williamson, Henry, 4

Wilmot, Chester, 257

Wimbolt, S.E., 36, 37

Woodhams, Geoffrey, 40

Woods, Margaret, 229

Woolf, Leonard, 139, 166, 173, 212

Woolf, Virginia, 3, 139, 212, 234

Woozley, Tony, 258

Wordsworth, William, 10, 48, 90, 109, 115, 248, 253, 313-14

Worley, Frank W., 95-96, 302

Wright, Harold, 174

Wyld, H.C.K., 183, 228

Yalding, 10-25, 28, 68, 78, 129, 130, 138, 167, 176-9, 210, 263-4 326

Yeats, W.B., 189, 190

Yeung, Ngai Hin, 296

Young, Andrew, 241

Young, Edward, 248, 300; 'Night Thoughts', 55-6, 131

Ypres and Ypres salient, 31, 66, 67-81, 89, 92, 100, 101, 197

Yu, Margaret, 295

Yuan, Sheila, 297

Yung, Kai Kin, 296, 312, 313, 318, 320